Dobson's *Encyclopaedia*

Dobson's *Encyclopaedia*

The Publisher, Text, and Publication of America's First *Britannica*, 1789–1803

Robert D. Arner

upp

University of Pennsylvania Press

Philadelphia

Permission is gratefully acknowledged to reprint materials from manuscript collections and repositories:

Morse Family Papers, Manuscripts and Archives, Yale University Library

Special Collections Department, Van Pelt Library, University of Pennsylvania

Boston Public Library, Rare Books & Manuscripts, used by courtesy of the Trustees of the Boston Public Library

Quaker Collection, Haverford College Library

John H. Hobart Manuscripts in the Francis L. Hawks and General Convention Collection of Early Episcopal Church Manuscripts (Record Group 117), Archives of the Episcopal Church, Austin, Texas.

Pennsylvania Academy of the Fine Arts

Library Company of Philadelphia

Thomas Dobson Miscellaneous Papers, Rare Books and Manuscripts Division, The New York Public Library, Astor, Lenox and Tilden Foundations

American Philosophical Society Library

Massachusetts Historical Society

Historical Society of Pennsylvania

Library of Congress Cataloging-in-Publication Data
Arner, Robert D.
    Dobson's Encyclopaedia : the publisher, text, and publication of America's first Britannica, 1789–1803 / Robert D. Arner.
       p.   cm.
    Includes bibliographical references and index.
    ISBN 0-8122-3092-2
    1. Dobson, Thomas, 1751–1823.   2. Encyclopaedia Britannica—Publishing—History.   3. Encyclopedias and dictionaries—Publishing—Pennsylvania—Philadelphia—History—18th century.   4. Book industries and trade—Pennsylvania—Philadelphia—History—18th century.   5. Philadelphia (Pa.)—Imprints—History.   I. Title
Z473.D6A75   1991
381'.45002'0974811—dc20   91-17624
                                                                              CIP

This book is dedicated with
the deepest love and affection
to my sons, Justin and James,
and to my wife, Connie,
whose presence makes all things possible.

Contents

Preface and Acknowledgments

Thomas Dobson was for a time the most prominent printer, publisher, and bookseller in the United States. Eventually he was overshadowed by his fellow Philadelphian Mathew Carey and Isaiah Thomas of Worcester, and he has been all but forgotten by succeeding generations of Americans. His name is not included, for example, in any standard biographical dictionary except Francis Drake's *Dictionary of American Biography* and *Supplement* (1879), which describes him as the author of a treatise on religion rather than as a publisher or printer. Only a handful of specialists and historians have kept his memory alive, and even they have never attempted to tell his story in detail. Moreover, their accounts often contain incorrect or contradictory information that perpetuates old errors or introduces new confusion into the historical and bibliographical record.[1] This book corrects those mistakes and brings Dobson to the attention of the American reading public once again as an important figure in the history of American publishing and printing, one of the men who helped to shape the cultural consciousness of the nation during the early years of the republic.

Dobson occupies a special position in the history of American printing. When he came to Philadelphia just after the revolutionary war, Robert Aitken and Francis Bailey, both craftsmen of considerable ability, were among the leading printers in the city. Their work, however, and that of most other printers who were active when Dobson arrived belongs primarily to the colonial phase of American printing, to an era characterized by small press runs and the careful craftsmanship of a cottage industry operating on the borders of traditional folk aesthetics. Dobson represents an intermediate phase of development, preserving some of the elements of fine printing through an emphasis on high quality workmanship and materials while at the same time exhibiting an energetic spirit of enterprise that looks forward to the age of mass production and mass marketing. Not Dobson but his former apprentices George and David Bruce in New York[2] or, in Philadelphia, the firm of Carey & Lea exemplifies this later phase of the publishing and printing business, when improved methods of distribution, new print technologies such as stereotyping and electrotyping, the mass production of paper, and the rise of the professional writing combined to make possible margins of profit undreamed of twenty years before. These developments all but brought to an end the age of the individual entrepreneur and printing establishments maintained within a single family.

Dobson's career spanned the years 1785 to 1822, when he retired from the bookselling business because of age and ill health. His dates thus coincide almost exactly with one of the great periods in American publishing, when printers in the United States, animated by a new spirit of independence and compelled by a desire to wrest the American market from the control of British books and bookmakers, transformed colonial print shops into printing offices capable of matching the English in quantity and quality and undercutting them in price. In some circles, the establishment of an autonomous printing industry, including all the allied crafts and trades, took on the character of a national crusade. Printers advertised their wares with patriotic appeals to support American manufacturing and heralded each new title that issued from their presses as the latest bit of evidence that arts, letters and the sciences were advancing in America more rapidly than any envious European nation could have imagined possible. Striving to disseminate the ideals of democracy and complete the liberation of American minds from the influence of foreign ideas, American printers moved gradually away from the concept of local and regional markets and began to think in terms of national audiences. Gradually, too, they fostered a national style of publication and the standardization of papermaking, bookbinding, typefounding, and typographical design. Their success opened opportunities for American authors and, beginning in the 1830s, eventually helped to inspire the first great outpouring of American writing in the literature of the period later known as the American Renaissance.

Dobson's major contribution to this great nationalistic enterprise, an eighteen-volume reprint of the third edition of the *Encyclopaedia Britannica* with American additions and emendations, forms the principal focus of this study. Begun in early December 1789 and completed in April of 1798, Dobson's *Encyclopaedia,* as it quickly came to be called, eventually included a *Supplement* (1800–1803) that extended the work to twenty-one volumes, one more than the British original from which it descended—by Dobson's own count, 16,650 letterpress pages in a quarto edition of 2000 sets, closely printed in double columns with 595 engraved copperplates. Published in spite of chronic economic and political instability, annual visitations of yellow fever, primitive transportation and delivery systems, and a sparse supply of cultivated readers to underwrite expenses, the *Encyclopaedia* was successfully marketed in direct competition with the British third edition and stands as a landmark in the history of American publishing and book illustration. It symbolizes not only Dobson's determination to complete the monumental task he had set for himself but also an entire era in the American past when printing was viewed not only as a profession but also as a public calling.

Except for the *Encyclopaedia* and, in 1814, the first American edition of the Hebrew Bible, Dobson's achievements might seem at first to be quite modest. He has been credited with publishing the first secular music written by an American and published in America, Francis Hopkinson's *Seven Songs for the Harpsichord* (Bristol 6718), although that claim has occasioned some dispute,[3] and he was the first American printer to include in the endpapers of some of his own publications a list of other titles "printed for and sold by" himself (Shera 269)—a small distinction, perhaps, but nonetheless indicative of the strategies he employed to sell the *Encyclopaedia* and to conduct his business on a daily basis. In the last analysis, moreover, that small distinction proves to be a major one, for there is nothing merely modest about maintaining an establishment for thirty-seven years, most of the time at a single address, in the highly competitive and economically risky world of early American publishing, where bankruptcy might lurk in the next unsuccessful edition. Though he appears at times to have approached the brink of financial disaster himself, especially when he was publishing the *Encyclopaedia,* Dobson succeeded where many others failed, and that fact alone would make his career worthy of study even in the absence of a major publication such as the *Encyclopaedia*.

In his professional capacities as printer, publisher, and bookseller, as well as in his role as an author, Dobson played an important but hitherto unacknowledged role in the development of American Unitarianism and the American Universalist movement, both before and after the locus of that activity shifted from Philadelphia to New England in the early 1790s. As a bookseller, for example, he stocked and advertised the works of Charles Chauncy, Elhanan Winchester, and other American and English ministers associated with liberal Christianity and with Arminian positions generally. As a printer, he was responsible for both the first collection of songs and music employed in the services of the First Universalist Church of Philadelphia (*Evangelical Psalms, Hymns and Spiritual Songs,* 1792; Evans 24951) and the seminal *Articles of Faith, and Plan of Church Government* (Evans 23009) that resulted from the Philadelphia Convention of 1790, the first national organizational meeting of Universalists in the United States (Robinson 58). Between 1794 and 1798, he served as the principal American publisher for the Universalist Joseph Priestley, who had fled to America to escape mobs incensed by his pro-French sympathies and who continued to preach in Philadelphia. Finally, as the author of several books about his own religious beliefs, Dobson rejected Trinitarianism and the notion of Christ's divinity independent of God, examined and dismissed as out of keeping with the character of God the Calvinistic doctrines of total depravity and eternal damnation, and argued against the Deistic position that reason unassisted by scriptural revelation was sufficient to lead to the discovery of religious truth. Though unoriginal in theology—a charge that might be laid at the door of Unitarianism in general in the eighteenth century—these writings are more closely related to his career as a publisher and printer than might at first appear, especially through his friendship with men like Priestley and Dr. Benjamin Rush. In conjunction with his work as a printer and publisher, his writings entitle Dobson to respectful consideration in any future account of the origins of Unitarianism in America.

Little has previously been known about Dobson's career apart from his work on the *Encyclopaedia*. The first and final chapters of this study provide brief accounts of his activities as a publisher and printer and an overview of his life. The biographical part of the story, however, must be told from the outside, for Dobson's writings reveal little about him except for his religious convictions. Unlike Benjamin Franklin and some other early American printers, he left no memoirs or diaries or vast cache of letters on which to base a detailed biography. A few letters have survived, however, and these, together with his writings, occasional anecdotes preserved by contemporaries who knew him or with whom he did business, and the many advertisements he placed in Philadelphia's newspapers, provide the material for an outline of his life. His emigration to America and the beginning of his career in Philadelphia, his rapid rise to prominence as one of the leading printers and booksellers in the city, and his emergence as a publisher of national reputation are the subjects of Chapter 1. Chapter 8 discusses the publications of the last twenty years of his career and notes in particular his attempt to expand his business from bookselling into copper manufacturing. This move, probably unsuccessful because of the times, resulted in his playing a small but previously unnoticed role in the early history of the copper industry in America.

The second through seventh chapters deal with the *Encyclopaedia* and are, in a sense, parts of Dobson's biography as well. Often using his own language, these chapters relate the story of the central event of Dobson's life, the publication of the *Encyclopaedia*. Chapter 2 discusses the proposals and shows the evolution of Dobson's ideas about the *Encyclopaedia,* which were undoubtedly influenced by many conversations with prominent Philadelphians. It also examines Dobson's use of patriotic themes as the key ingredients in the most extensive promotional campaign to that time in America, one that finally netted enough subscribers to begin work on the *Encyclopaedia* and, eventually, to see it through to completion.

The third and fourth chapters trace the progress of the *Encyclopaedia* through the press. The first nine volumes are discussed in the third chapter, the second nine in the fourth. This division reflects more than numerical neatness, for a devastating fire, unreliable subscribers, and local controversies about content caused Dobson significantly greater difficulty with the final half of the *Encyclopaedia* than he experienced with the first nine volumes. Though the chapters focus on different themes, both rely upon advertisements, receipts, and Dobson's correspondence to establish a timetable for the appearance of individual volumes of the *Encyclopaedia* and to speculate on the actual as opposed to the publicly announced date of completion of each volume. Several of these dates differ from those provided in Charles Evans's *American Bibliography* and subsequently accepted by previous commentators on Dobson.

Chapter 5 compares the texts of the first American and the third British editions and makes several important corrections to claims that have been made in other scholarship. This book is not intended as a bibliographical or textual study, so the two editions have been compared selectively rather than exhaustively, concentrating on subjects and themes most likely to yield important and informative differences. Minor alterations in spelling or vocabulary, what Dobson referred to in one of his advertisements as "minute improvements . . . on almost every page," are too often indistinguishable from compositors' corrections or mistakes and, without external corroborating evidence, cannot be taken as indications of the publisher's larger editorial purposes and policies. Numerous as they are, moreover, such small changes from one edition to the other do not significantly alter or affect general conclusions about the nature and extent of Dobson's "Americanization" of the British text.

The sixth chapter concerns the artists and craftsmen who contributed to the *Encyclopaedia:* engravers, papermakers, and typefounders. Many of the engravers are obscure, and merely enumerating their contributions to

Dobson's publication adds significantly to what has previously been known about them. Often, for example, the dates of their activity can be extended forward or backward by several years or more. The information provided in this chapter augments details available in the standard historical and biographical sources: David McNeely Stauffer's *American Engravers upon Copper and Steel* (2 vols.; 1907); Alfred Coxe Prime's two-volume *Arts and Crafts in Philadelphia, Maryland, and South Carolina, 1721–1785* (1929, 1932); Mantle Fielding's *Dictionary of American Painters, Sculptors, and Engravers* (enlarged ed. 1974); William Dunlap's *History of the Rise and Progress of the Arts of Design in the United States* (2 vols.; 1834), and George C. Groce and David H. Wallace's *New-York Historical Society's Dictionary of Artists in America, 1564–1860* (1957). The chapter adds no new names to the list of engravers known to have been at work during the early years of the republic.

Chapter 6 also identifies and briefly discusses some of the early American papermakers who might have provided the paper for the *Encyclopaedia* and offers brief accounts of the firms of John Baine & Grandson and Binny & Ronaldson, who brought the Scottish tradition of typefounding to America and cast the type that Dobson used for all but a few of his volumes. Papermaking was a well established industry in America by the time of the *Encyclopaedia,* but Dobson's project provided a decisive boost for typefounding that helped to establish it permanently in the United States.

The seventh chapter in this study discusses Dobson's *Supplement,* Volumes XIX, XX, and XXI. Most of the new material added to the *Encyclopaedia* appears in these last volumes, enough to swell the size of the American edition by one additional volume as compared with the British original. Next to these additions, perhaps the most intriguing aspect of the final volumes is the difficulty that Dobson experienced in getting one of his major new articles written and in bringing the *Supplement* to its long-delayed completion. Surviving correspondence makes it possible to tell this story in some detail and to add to the historical record information that illuminates the professional relationship between author and publisher in the early republic.

This book concludes with several appendixes that offer an overview of the publication history of the *Encyclopaedia* (Appendix A) and a list of all the engravings it contains, identified by number, short title, and engraver (Appendix B). Included are the names or initials of apprentices who executed plates to which a particular firm such as Scot & Allardice affixed its corporate signature. Attribution of unsigned work is difficult, but context, style, subject matter, or a combination of these three often provided a basis for speculation. Finally, Appendix C presents a list of titles printed by or or Thomas Dobson each year between 1785 and 1822, including many items not attributed to him in Evans, Bristol, Shipton, Shaw and Shoemaker, or their successors. This checklist presents in summary fashion the details of Dobson's career and makes it possible for the reader to evaluate at a glance Dobson's contributions to the early book trade in America and his impact on American publishing and printing.

The *National Union Catalogue Pre-1956 Imprints* lists copies of Dobson's *Encyclopaedia* held in libraries as widely separated as Maine and Idaho. Many of these listings, however, are out of date or were erroneous to begin with; approximately half of the libraries on the list report that they no longer own or never did own a copy of the *Encyclopaedia*. Nor does the Mansell listing indicate all surviving copies of the publication; it omits, for example, the copy now housed in the library of the H. F. du Pont Winterthur Museum in Winterthur, Delaware, as well as the one recently purchased for the rare books room of the Walter Langsam Library of the University of Cincinnati, which was originally purchased by the Baltimore millionaire Alexander Brown. For this book I used the editions at the Denison University Libraries, Granville, Ohio; the Margaret I. King Library of the University of Kentucky, Lexington; and the William C. Clements Library of the University of Michigan, Ann Arbor. A signature collation for the first eighteen volumes may be found in G. Thomas Tanselle's "Press Figures in America: Some Preliminary Observations," *Studies in Bibliography* 19 (1966): 123–60; the copy I used most frequently, that at Denison University, agreed exactly with Tanselle's collation. At the end of Appendix A, I have provided a collation for the supplemental volumes (XIX through XXI) based on the copy of the *Supplement* at the University of Kentucky.

Dobson's *Encyclopaedia* forms an important chapter in the cultural history of the United States, touching on literature and the arts and sciences as well as the history of printing, book publishing, book illustration, commerce and business, and American manufacturing. It also raises questions concerning the politics and gender of readership, the differences between an anticipated or virtual audience and an actual one, and the complex process by which ideas are transmitted to and absorbed by a national culture. Except in a general way, these questions are beyond the scope of the present study. So, too, is a detailed consideration of the encyclopedic form, which in any century both reinforces and reflects the prevailing taxonomic model of the universe, imposing its own system of categories on the disorderly world of perception and experience. In particular, the alphabetical arrangement and unified structure of the third edition of the *Encyclopaedia Britannica* which Dobson adopted and in one instance defended as though they had been his own ideas operated as a metaphor of order in an age of political and social turmoil, promoting the illusion that all knowledge could be quantified and internalized for eventual mastery. What part this and other ideas might have played in determining Dobson's decision to publish the *Encyclopaedia* or in influencing the reception of the book in America are large questions that can be touched on in these pages but that must await an account of other early American encyclopedias to establish the appropriate historical, political, and social context to aid understanding.

This book began as a favor to a friend and colleague in the history department of the University of Cincinnati, Frank Kafker, an expert on eighteenth-century encyclopedias. Knowing of my interest in the literature of early Philadelphia, he asked me to write a short piece for a collection of essays he proposed to edit on notable eighteenth-century encyclopedias. Neither he nor I guessed that this exercise would eventually lead to a book-length study.

Many libraries and librarians have lent assistance to make this project possible by providing advice and granting permission to quote from material in their collections. It is a pleasant duty to record my obligations to Barbara Tirppel Simmons, formerly manuscripts librarian of the American Antiquarian Society; Beth Carroll-Horrocks, manuscripts librarian of the American Philosophical Society; V. Nelle Bellamy, archivist of the Archives of the Episcopal Church; Laura V. Monti, keeper of rare books and manuscripts of the Boston Public Library; the librarian of Dr. William's Library, London; Diana Alten, manuscripts cataloger of the Haverford College Library; Carolyn Park, collections manager of the Historical Society of Pennsylvania; Phil Lapsansky, research librarian of the Library Company of Philadelphia; the Library of Congress; Louis L. Tucker, director of the Massachusetts Historical Society; Donald Anderle, associate director for special collections of the New York Public Library; John Catanzariti, editor of *The Papers of Thomas Jefferson* at the Princeton University Library; Daniel Traister, assistant director of libraries for special collections of the Van Pelt Library, University of Pennsylvania; and Judith Ann Schiff, chief research archivist, manuscripts and archives, Yale University Library. These libraries are acknowledged again in appropriate footnotes.

Special thanks are also in order to Dan Gottlieb, Carole Moser, Kathy Scardine, and Diana Schmidt, the staff of the Interlibrary Loan Department of the Walter Langsam Library, University of Cincinnati, for making it possible for me to conduct research at long distance from the necessary resources. To Charles Mauer and Florence Hoffman at Denison University, Granville, Ohio, where I frequently visited to consult copies of both the third British and first American editions of the *Encyclopaedia,* I offer my sincere thanks for advice, assistance, and generous hospitality.

I owe special debts of gratitude to several scholars of early American publishing history. Thomas Gravell provided invaluable information about papermaking and watermarks available nowhere else and examined on his own hundreds of pages of the *Encyclopaedia* trying to help identify Dobson's papermakers. John Bidwell of the William Andrews Clark Library at the University of California at Los Angeles generously answered my questions about paper and papermaking and undertook research I was unable to perform myself. Finally, James Green of the Library Company of Philadelphia read a short version of this study, corrected some errors and oversights, and asked questions that led to additional discoveries. I deeply appreciate the interest each of them has shown in the project.

The Department of English at the University of Cincinnati provided financial assistance and released time for a quarter, and the Charles Phelps Taft Memorial Fund supplied funds to help offset the cost of manuscript preparation. This book was also published with the aid of a grant from the Charles Phelps Taft Memorial Fund. Joseph Caruso, Dean of the McMicken College of Arts and Sciences, provided additional financial assistance to cover the costs of the illustrations found in this volume. To him, to the Department of English, to the members of the Taft Committee, and to the University I express my gratitude.

The writer of any book accrues a great many personal obligations along the way. Mine are most particularly owed to my wife, Connie, who supported me in ways beyond repayment, and to my children, Justin and James, for their sense of wonder. If there is merit in this work, it is largely the result of their presence and patience.

Notes

1. Perhaps the most baffling of all errors, as well as one of the most recent, appears in John Tebbel's *History of Book Publishing in the United States,* 4 vols.; volume 1: *The Creation of an Industry, 1630–1865* (New York: R. R. Bowker, 1972). After describing the *Encyclopaedia* more or less accurately—an ambiguous statement that the work consisted of "twenty-one volumes, with a supplementary

three volumes, in 1803" (116) is perhaps the main though not the only problem with this part of the discussion—Tebbel goes on to say that, although publishing the *Britannica* was "a formidable achievement, some scholars consider Dobson's edition of Rees' *Encyclopaedia* more important" (174). The attribution of the American edition of Abraham Rees's *Cyclopaedia* to Dobson is a mistake made by other commentators, but it is here compounded by Tebbel's claim that Dobson was responsible for both works (Samuel F. Bradford, who initiated the printing of Rees's *Cyclopaedia,* is discussed briefly in Chapter 8 of this study as one of Dobson's competitors). Tebbel compounds his error by offering a description of Rees's *Cyclopaedia* which closely matches one he has already given of Dobson's *Encyclopaedia* without seeming to realize that it is the *Encyclopaedia* rather than Rees's book he is actually describing.

2. For Dobson's former apprentices, see Robert R. Rowe, "Bruce, George," *DAB,* ed. Allen Johnson (New York: Scribner's, 1929), 3:181.

3. Tebbel, *History of Book Publishing* (1: 168), makes the claim for Hopkinson's *Seven Songs.* Oscar Sonneck discusses Hopkinson as the first native-born American composer (*A Bibliography of Early Secular American Music* [18th Century], *rev. and enlarged by William Trent Upton* [New York: DaCapo, 1964], 403–04) and includes *Seven Songs* in his bibliography but names no publisher. Harold Donaldson Eberlein and Cortlandt Van Dyke Hubbard briefly mention Dobson's role as a music publisher in "Music in the Early Federal Era," *Pennsylvania Magazine of History and Biography* 69 (1945): 110–11. Richard Crawford and D. W. Krummel also briefly treat Dobson's contributions to American music publication ("Early American Music Printing and Publishing," *Printing and Society in Early America,* ed. William L. Joyce, et al. [Worcester, Mass.: American Antiquarian Society, 1983], 201–02), giving Dobson high marks for the quality of his workmanship. Another scholar, however, Richard J. Wolfe, feels that Dobson's role as an early music publisher has been overstated and that John Aitken, who engraved the music Dobson is supposed to have published, deserves the lion's share of the credit (*Early American Music Engraving and Printing* [Urbana: University of Illinois Press, 1980], 120).

1. Bookseller, Printer, and Publisher: Thomas Dobson and the Philadelphia Trade, 1785–1800

The man responsible for America's first comprehensive encyclopedia was born in Scotland, probably in Midlothian or East Lothian County near Edinburgh, in 1751.[1] Thomas Dobson's family background, early life, and education are unknown, but he appears to have been the first member of his family to make a career of bookselling, publishing, and printing.[2] In later years, he was reputed to be the only printer in Philadelphia who could read Greek and Hebrew critically, but this is probably a rumor based on books he published in those languages.[3] There is no reliable evidence that he had a formal education beyond the customary instruction in reading, writing, science, and mathematics provided by the parish schools of Scotland.

On October 5, 1777, Dobson was married in New Grayfriars Parish in Edinburgh to Jean Paton of New North Parish; her father, the farmer James Paton, was already deceased when the marriage took place.[4] Even this early, Dobson listed his occupation in the church records as "bookseller," so that, by the time he came to America, he had already accumulated years of invaluable experience in that highly competitive profession. Three daughters were born to the marriage in Scotland: Margaret (February 15, 1779); Alison (October 6, 1780); and Catharine (November 15, 1782).[5] A son, Judah, who later joined his father in the bookselling business, was born in Philadelphia around 1792 and died there in September 1850.[6]

The Dobsons' youngest daughter, Catharine, was baptized on July 11, 1783, after the family had moved from Grayfriars to New North Kirk Parish. This is the last reference to the future publisher of the *Encyclopaedia* in official Scottish records. Shortly thereafter, scarcely waiting for ratification and final approval of the treaty granting independence to the thirteen former British colonies, Dobson brought his family to the United States and prepared to go into business for himself. Such a move so soon after hostilities had ceased suggests that he had been interested in prospects in America for some time and may, indeed, have been among the minority of Scotsmen who favored the cause of the rebellion from the beginning; certainly he was later to count among his closest acquaintances in Philadelphia many of those who had been most active and ardent in support of American independence. Since his interest in Universalist teachings appears to have antedated his emigration, it is also possible that restrictions on free worship in Scotland played a part in his decision to leave his native land.

The key figure linking Dobson to the Universalist church in Scotland is a minister named James Purves, who printed many of his own early tracts and treatises and even cast the Hebrew type he used in printing his etymological arguments for the proper interpretation of scriptural passages. Purves served as pastor of a small congregation of Universalists at Broughton just south of Edinburgh, officially accepting the pastorate on November 15, 1776. Intolerance was so pronounced in Presbyterian Scotland, however, that the group did not deem it prudent to declare itself publicly as a church of Universalist Dissenters until 1792, nearly a decade after Dobson had departed.[7] Whether he belonged to the gathering at Broughton cannot be determined, but he was aware of Purves's writings and thought well enough of them to offer three different titles for sale in the first list of religious books he advertised in America (*Pennsylvania Mercury*, June 10, 1785). Purves's *A Humble Attempt to Investigate and Defend the Scripture Doctrine Concerning the Father, the Son, and the Holy Spirit* (Edinburgh, 1784) and two other titles by him that are apparently unknown in any English edition, *A Representation of Events That Relate to the Church and the World, by Emblematical Figures* and *The Everlasting Gospel Commanded to Be Preached by Jesus Christ,* joined works by Charles Chauncy and Elhanan Winchester as the only selections on a list that left little doubt as to the bookseller's personal inclination toward liberal Christianity.[8]

The first proof of Dobson's presence in the United States is a brief, friendly letter written from New York on March 23, 1784, to the prominent Quaker merchant James Pemberton in Philadelphia. Dobson thanked Pemberton for the gift of a book on religion and religious seeking that had just been delivered by a third party and for concealing Dobson's name in some unspecified circumstances when revealing it might have proved embarrassing—a tantalizing remark that unfortunately cannot be clarified in the absence of information about Dobson's activities in Scotland. Dobson closed by offering best wishes to Pemberton's family from his own wife and children, a conventional conclusion that nonetheless reveals that the two families had previously met and that Dobson's family was with him in New York. He had already been in America long enough to form an acquaintance with an important Philadelphian who was to prove helpful later in his career.[9]

By December of 1784, Dobson had found his own way to Philadelphia, where he performed a small service for another prominent citizen, Dr. Benjamin Rush, that may provide a clue to his activities in the meantime. On December 22, Rush wrote to his friend and former mentor Dr. William Cullen in Edinburgh thanking him for the "very friendly letter" that had just been delivered by "Mr. Dobson."[10] This reference may mean that Dobson returned to Edinburgh briefly after visiting America and received Cullen's letter, dated October 16, from Cullen directly. It seems more likely, however, that the letter was included in other communications addressed to Dobson in Philadelphia by Cullen himself or, more probably, by some bookseller in Edinburgh with whom Dobson maintained a regular correspondence. If so, he was probably already assembling the inventory, including Cullen's *First Lines of the Practice of Physick,* that would enable him to open his first bookselling establishment in the city. The association with Rush and Cullen later resulted in the publication of numerous titles, among them Rush's eulogy on Dr. Cullen in 1790 (Evans 22862).[11]

When Dobson arrived in Philadelphia, he brought with him many titles that were in demand there, clearly hoping to take advantage of the disruption of intellectual commerce between England and America during the revolutionary war. This large collection of books suggested to some Philadelphians, Francis Hopkinson among them, that Dobson may have been acting initially as an American agent for an established firm in Scotland. Some years after Dobson's arrival, at any rate, Hopkinson wrote to Thomas Jefferson repeating this rumor, and not coincidentally, testifying to the impact that Dobson had already begun to have on the book trade of Philadelphia. "There is a Scotchman here," Hopkinson wrote in 1788, "who carries on publishing and Bookselling in a large way, a Mr. Dobson. He has reprinted several English books, and I believe is connected with some House in Scotland[,] for he seems to have substantial Capital, and a large Stock" (Jefferson, *Papers,* 14: 33). Hopkinson's conjecture cannot be confirmed, but his remarks make it clear that even before the *Encyclopaedia,* Dobson had attracted attention as one of the leading booksellers in the city. His sense of the market and the experience he had gained in Edinburgh had evidently given him an early advantage over most of his competitors.

In selecting Philadelphia as his place of residence and business, Dobson had chosen the only city in the young United States in which the *Encyclopaedia* could have been conceived, much less carried to completion. It was the most populous city in the nation, providing a concentration of cultivated readers and a cosmopolitan clientele unmatched by any other city in America. Lawyers, merchants, doctors, statesmen, politicians, educators, liberal clergymen, and aspiring workingmen who cast themselves in the mold of Benjamin Franklin, convinced that hard work and assiduous study were the ways to wealth and self-improvement, encouraged Dobson's initial enterprises and eventually provided a core of subscribers for the *Encyclopaedia*. The leading commercial city with the busiest port in the new nation, Philadelphia was soon to become the seat of the federal government and was already home to artists, novelists, and poets whose names are still remembered; it would shortly boast an opera and a legitimate theater as well. The University of Pennsylvania, the American Philosophical Society, the College of Physicians, and other organizations made it the leading American city in the pursuit of scientific and medical knowledge and imprinted a strongly utilitarian bias upon learning that helped to create a favorable climate for the reception of books that promised, as the *Encyclopaedia* did, to disseminate practical information. Dobson's edition of the *Encyclopaedia Britannica,* though largely pirated from an Edinburgh edition, bears indelibly the imprint of the city in which it was published, symbolizing just as surely as Independence Hall and the famous High Street Market the affluence, the inherent sense of order, and the spirit of intellectual endeavor that prevailed in Philadelphia at the close of the eighteenth century.[12]

In February 1785, Dobson opened his first book store in Philadelphia, located "in Front-street, between Market and Chesnut streets, two Doors South of Black-Horse-Alley" (*Pennsylvania Gazette,* February 15, 1785). "T. DOBSON has just imported a very large and valuable Collection of BOOKS," his initial announcement informed Philadelphians, "In Various Branches of Literature, consisting of many thousand Volumes." Shakespeare, Swift, Pope, Sterne, Smollet, Hume, and others were available in "good Editions, and the most elegant Bindings." The new bookstore boasted a "large Collection of Books in the different Branches of Medicine," as well as Bibles and "Books of Entertainment for Children." As a stationer, Dobson also carried the customary supply of "Writing-Paper, Quills, Ink-Powder, Pencils, Sealing-Wax" and the like, together with "Music," an item that was briefly to become a specialty for him, and, somewhat oddly, men's and women's boots and shoes and a few dozen bottles of fine old porter.

From his shop on Front Street, Dobson issued the first of a great many lists of books for sale, offering such titles as *Evelina, or the History of a Young Lady's Entrance into the World* and *Cecelia; or Memoirs of an Heiress (Pennsylvania Gazette,* March 2, 1785). Also advertised were *The Theatre of Education* from the French of the Countess de Genlis and *A Short Collection of the Most Esteemed Farces.* Complete catalogs would be available free, the advertisement promised, to anyone who stopped in to browse. For most of his career, Dobson would stock a preponderance of scientific, religious, and medical titles, but, except for the mention of "a large Collection of Books in the different Branches of Medicine" in his opening announcement, that emphasis is not apparent in his first few advertisements.

In his first shop, Dobson prospered. Soon, in fact, he was seeking new accommodations with more space and the prestige of an address not directly on the waterfront. On June 1, 1785, he announced his removal "from Front-street to Second-street, two doors north of Chesnut-street" (*Pennsylvania Mercury,* June 3, 1785; *Pennsylvania Gazette,* June 7, 1785) to Number 60 Second Street. In his notice to the public, he emphasized again his very large inventory of "excellent editions . . . in the freshest and most elegant bindings" and promised "regular supplies . . . of all new publications of merit" from Europe. He assured the newspaper readers of Philadelphia that anyone who patronized his shop could depend on "the utmost attention and the genteelest usage," and he hoped for "a continuance of that favor of the generous public which he has already experienced." In this impersonal, formulaic, and generic prose of eighteenth-century newspaper advertising, Dobson would continue to address his clients, including subscribers to the *Encyclopaedia,* for the next thirty-seven years.

Once established in his second place of business, Dobson immediately resumed the advertising campaign that had thus far brought such excellent results. Indeed, the day the business moved, he drew up several advertisements for new books "Just Published, and to be Sold by T. Dobson." One of these, featuring such medical works as Benjamin Bell's *System of Surgery* and Cullen's *Practice of Physick,* appeared in the *Pennsylvania Mercury* on June 3. A week later, over an internal date of June 1, the same newspaper carried Dobson's advertisement for Charles Chauncy's *Salvation of All Men* (1782) and *Benevolence of the Deity* (1784), Elhanan Winchester's *Choice Collection of Hymns,* and three works by James Purves mentioned earlier in this chapter. A more secular and less controversial collection of titles appeared as "Just Published" and "Sold by T. Dobson" in the *Pennsylvania Mercury* on August 5, 1785 (over an internal date of July 29): *The Works of Jonathan Swift, The Sorrows of Werter, Commodore Anson's Voyage Round the*

World, Captain Cook's Voyage Round the World, and five works by Tobias Smollett: *Travels Through France and Italy, Roderick Random, Peregrine Pickle, Humphrey Clinker,* and *The Adventures of Launcelot Greaves.* Together these advertisements address a diverse audience ranging from ministers and medical men to general readers.

On October 2, 1785, again in the pages of the *Pennsylvania Mercury* (and over a date of August 31, 1785), Dobson added five more titles to his expanding list, including *Pilgrim's Progress.* Another list was drafted on October 27 and printed the next day in the *Pennsylvania Mercury.* On November 11 (over a date of November 7), Dobson offered eighteen titles under the general heading of "Medical Books" (*Pennsylvania Mercury*). Eighteen additional titles appeared in an advertisement in the *Pennsylvania Gazette* on January 11, 1786, seven more on February 1, and still another seven on March 8; this last list included the second edition of the *Encyclopaedia Britannica* in ten volumes. Dobson added two more titles in an advertisement in the same newspaper (April 19), including Benjamin Rush's *Plan for the Establishment of Public Schools* (Evans 19974). Other lists appeared with regularity, among them a miniature catalog of twenty-three assorted titles on July 26, 1786 (*Pennsylvania Gazette*). These advertisements and many others like them dominate the Philadelphia newspapers in the years after Dobson began his business, indicating some of his own interests as a fledgling publisher and establishing him as an energetic entrepreneur and an influential presence in the local bookselling community.

Advertising books for sale is not the same as printing or publishing them, of course. As John McAllister cautioned the friend to whom he addressed a letter about Dobson, "We are not to understand . . . all the books advertised as 'Just Published and to be sold by T. Dobson' as having been printed and published *by himself*—the Booksellers exchanged each other's publications then as they do now."[13] Probable examples are item fifteen on Dobson's list of July 27, 1786, William Billings's (?) *Massachusetts Harmony,* published in Boston by John Norman in 1784 (Evans 18366) and the several works by Charles Chauncy. The ten-volume second edition of the *Encyclopaedia Britannica* advertised in the *Pennsylvania Gazette* on March 8, 1786 was certainly an import, and, judging from their prices, so were Benjamin Bell's *System of Surgery* and William Buchan's *Domestic Medicine.*[14] These last two titles would become steady sellers for Dobson and he would print his own editions of them, but they cannot be credited to him at this early point in his career.

At the same time, a reasonable case can be made for assigning some of these early titles to Dobson, including works not known in any earlier American edition and ones for which the advertisements seem to indicate that the bookseller was also the publisher. John Churchman's *Map of the Peninsula Between Delaware and Chesapeake Bays,* for example, appears as item twenty-two on Dobson's list of July 26, 1786, a year before the earliest date recorded by Charles Evans, who assigns the map to Eleazar Oswald. The first American edition of Jonathan Edwards's *History of the Work of Redemption,* advertised in the *Pennsylvania Mercury* on October 3, 1786, as an "AMERICAN EDITION . . . correctly printed with a good type and paper, and neatly bound, at a very easy price," may have been done by Dobson, or he may simply have been selling it for Shepard Kollock of nearby Elizabethtown, New Jersey. Thomas Newton's *Dissertations on the Prophecies Which Have Been Remarkably Fulfilled, or Are at This Time Fulfilling in the World,* advertised by Dobson in the *Pennsylvania Mercury* on June 22, 1787, is more problematical. Although this may be another of Kollock's titles (Evans 20589), Dobson describes it the same way that he does his own editions of, for example, William Paley's *Moral Philosophy* or Hannah More's *Sacred Dramas* (*Pennsylvania Mercury,* October 7, 1787, and October 22, 1788), as an American edition at half the London price. When advertisements or supporting letters and receipts provide evidence, titles such as the one by Newton have been assigned to Dobson in Appendix C of this study, but no claim is made for complete accuracy.

In 1786, Dobson collaborated briefly with several other booksellers and printers in Philadelphia—Francis Bailey, Joseph Crukshank (or Cruikshank), and the firm of Young, Stewart, and McCulloch—to bring out what the poet Joseph Hopkinson was later to describe as a "small school edition" of the *New Testament of Our Lord and Saviour Jesus Christ* (Evans 19511). This edition, Hopkinson recalled on the occasion of his delivering the first *Annual Discourse* before the assembled members of the Pennsylvania Academy of the Fine Arts in 1810, was risked only after long deliberation, careful estimates of expenses, and projections of probable sales. Hopkinson considered this collaborative effort a landmark of sorts in the history of Philadelphia printing and used it as a symbol of how far the printing industry had advanced since the timid, tentative early days just after the war. In Hopkinson's view, moreover, it was Dobson's pioneering *Encyclopaedia* that had encouraged the expansion of the American printing industry in the decades following the war to its present flourishing state (16–17).

While still at 60 Second Street, Dobson assured himself of at least a
small place of distinction in the history of American printing by bringing
out Alexander Reinagle's *Select Collection of the Most Favourite Scots Tunes*
(1787; Evans 20674), perhaps the earliest such collection of folk and non-
religious music published in America. That same year also saw the publication of the *Compilation of the Litanies and Vespers, Hymns and Anthems . . .*
Sung in the Catholic Church, engraved by John Aitken and accompanied by
a "New Introduction to the Grounds of Music" (Evans 20186). In 1788,
Dobson published Francis Hopkinson's *Seven Songs for the Harpsichord or*
Forte Piano (Bristol 6718) and *Set of Eight Songs* (Evans 21152). These
titles, together with William Shield's *Overture to the New Opera Marian*
(Evans 22142) and three songs by Alexander Reinagle in 1789 (Evans
22096–098), as well as Dobson's collaboration with William Young and
others in Reinagle's *Collection of Favorite Songs* in 1788 (Evans 21420),
establish him as an active and important publisher of early American music
(Sonneck 575).[15] According to Richard Crawford and D. W. Krummel, he
was the first American publisher to provide American musicians with folio
editions comparable to those available in Europe, printed on heavy paper
with a rolling press and using soft punched pewter plates. Although he
published almost no other music, with these editions, which are also among
the first to be printed *by* him rather than *for* him as he added printing to his
bookselling and publishing business, Dobson "introduced into America
the technology of a continuous music publishing industry" (Crawford and
Krummel 202).

On January 5, 1788, Dobson made his third and final move, vacating
the store at No. 60 Second Street in favor of one he built for himself
(according to McAllister again), the "large, elegant store in the New-Stone
House, in Second-street, between Market and Chesnut-streets, the seventh
door above Chesnut-street" (*Pennsylvania Mercury,* January 12, 1788).
Better known on the title pages of hundreds of imprints as "the Stone
House, No. 41, South Second-street," this address would become famous
in Philadelphia during the years in which the *Encyclopaedia* was steadily
emerging from the press—"the most public place of resort for literary
people in our city," Benjamin Rush called it in a letter to Jeremy Belknap on
June 6, 1791 (1: 583). Subscription papers for a new volume posted in
Dobson's store, Rush told Belknap on another occasion (May 1, 1791),
would "invite more encouragement than in the hands of any [other] individual in our city" (1: 573). In William Birch's engraving *Second and*
Market Streets, Philadelphia (1799), the locale of Dobson's bookstore may

still be glimpsed today much as it must have appeared looking north from Dobson's front door.

Dobson began his long tenure at No. 41 South Second Street in his usual fashion, by announcing the move to clients and customers in an advertisement for "a very large and elegant Collection of the best MODERN BOOKS . . . in the best and newest bindings, at the most reasonable prices" and a large assortment of writing paper, rulers, mahogany pencil boxes, penknives, and blotting paper. "Those who are pleased to honor him with their commands," the first announcement from his new address concludes, "may depend upon the best usage, as he hopes, by the most diligent attention and industry, to merit a continuance of the public favor" (*Pennsylvania Mercury,* January 12, 1788).

Shortly after he moved to No. 41 South Second Street, Dobson formed a brief partnership with another printer and bookseller, Thomas Lang of No. 21 Church Alley. Together Dobson and Lang printed about a dozen titles, six of them for Thomas Sarjeant, former master of mathematics in the Academy of the Protestant Episcopal Church in Philadelphia (Evans 21445–48 and 22127–28). They also printed *Judgements in the Admiralty of Pennsylvania in Four Suits,* the Honorable Francis Hopkinson presiding (Evans 22053), perhaps a political plum extended to Dobson as a favor by Hopkinson. No formal announcement of the dissolution of this partnership appears in any Philadelphia newspaper, but the name of Dobson and Lang cannot be found in volumes printed after 1789, the year Dobson began to advertise and print the *Encyclopaedia.*

While still in partnership with Thomas Lang, Dobson issued a prospectus for printing by subscription "in eight large octavo volumes" Edward Gibbon's *Decline and Fall of the Roman Empire* (*Pennsylvania Mercury,* June 18, 1788, over an internal date of June 12). Although he had printed a few handsome editions of major British writers such as William Cowper's *The Task* in 1787 (Evans 20304), this was his first effort at selling by subscription, and it was not successful. The *Decline and Fall* was to have been a deluxe edition not available in boards but "handsomely bound, gilt and lettered," with an "elegant [engraved] head of the Author, and all the Maps in the course of the Work." The price was "two Spanish milled dollars" per volume, with one dollar paid in advance "to enable the publisher to go forward with the undertaking." For those who might already own the three quarto volumes thus far completed in the London edition, Dobson offered a special subscription for the remaining volumes, "(being the continuation)," at "two French crowns per volume." Payment in ad-

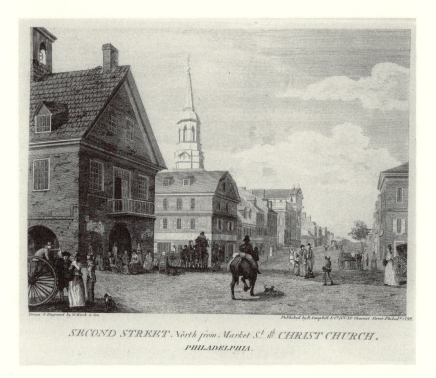

Figure 1. "Second Street, North from Market St., with Christ Church, Philadelphia." Engraved by William Birch and published in his *Views of Philadelphia* (1800), this street scene is one that Thomas Dobson must have enjoyed innumerable times from the front door of his shop at "No. 41 S. Second street." Were the rider heading south instead of north, Dobson's printing offices and bookstore would appear at the second shop below Market Street on the viewer's right. Photo courtesy of the Library Company of Philadelphia.

vance would be fully refunded if too few subscribers were forthcoming to make the edition economically feasible.

There is no record of any edition of the *Decline and Fall* published by Thomas Dobson. Perhaps Americans who might ordinarily have wanted a copy of the book had already purchased the earlier three volumes in the British edition and were reluctant to complete a set in which they had invested a good deal of money with a book printed in America. The same lack of success, moreover, was soon to greet Dobson's second attempt to publish by subscription. This time the book that became a victim of American disinterest was the first volume of Sir Edward Coke's *Institutes of the*

Laws of England or *Coke upon Littleton,* as the work is commonly known. Dobson issued his proposals on June 28, 1788 in the *Pennsylvania Mercury* at the urging of "several eminent lawyers," who had convinced him that an American edition of the book was badly needed and that it would sell not only because of its intrinsic merits and its reputation in the history of jurisprudence but also "on account of the very high price which the London edition bears and the frequent difficulty of obtaining it" even at that exorbitant cost.

Dobson's edition, the proposals declared, would be based on the thirteenth English edition, the most correct thus far, and would be further improved by the correction of lingering errors (presumably to be done with the help of American lawyers). It would be "elegantly printed, on superfine paper," matching the London edition page for page so there would be "no difficulty in references," and "handsomely bound in calf, lettered, so as to be at least equal in elegance to the London edition." At a cost of "Sixteen Spanish Milled Dollars," one-half of which was payable upon subscription, it would be put to press as soon as 500 copies were subscribed for—a date that never arrived. Like the edition of the *Decline and Fall,* it was probably too expensive for the average American purse, even for the purse of the average American lawyer, and was aimed, moreover, at a limited audience. One may doubt whether there were five hundred lawyers in Philadelphia, New York, and Baltimore combined at the end of the eighteenth century, let alone five hundred lawyers who did not already own *Coke upon Littleton.* In addition, Dobson's stress on the excellence of the London edition left his advertisements lacking the sense of patriotic urgency that he would summon so successfully to sell the *Encyclopaedia.*

From the failure of his first two attempts at publishing by subscription, Dobson probably learned that to sell an expensive book in Philadelphia required a far more extensive campaign of advertising than would have been necessary in Edinburgh or elsewhere in the British Isles. He put this new knowledge about the American market to use in numerous advertisements for reprints of popular British and Continental works, which appeared under the heading of "Books, American Editions" in a variety of Philadelphia newspapers. He also began to use the theme of American manufacturing extensively, promoting both patriotism and the popular image of the artisan printer as a public servant essential to the success of the American experiment in democracy. The first of these "American Editions" was William Nicholson's *Natural Philosophy* (*Pennsylvania Mercury,* July 24, 1788), offered to the public in the hope that sales would soon "furnish . . . proof of the preference with which America encourages *American Manufacture*." In advertising another major imprint, the first American edition of Adam Smith's *Wealth of Nations* (1789; Evans 221488), Dobson emphasized that he was making available to Americans at a critical, formative moment in the nation's history the most important economic treatise of its time. He implied that it might serve the nation as a source of ideas for deliberation and perhaps as a model for new social policies. Indeed, in demonstrating how personal gain could be combined with the common good and how a competitive society could also be a society of consensus which supported common causes, Dobson's advertisement seems something of a model for the conduct of American business. "The publisher flattered himself," Dobson began,

[that] he should perform an acceptable service to the generous and discerning Public, by presenting to them an elegant *American* Edition of this Work at this important period—Printed on a superfine paper and good type, handsomely bound and lettered, at not more than *one half the price* for which the London Edition can be imported and sold—He hopes in this instance for a continuance of that liberal encouragement which he has frequently received, and which it is his great ambition to merit. (*Pennsylvania Mercury,* January 13, 1790)

The most extensive list of Dobson's "American Editions," containing more than thirty titles, appeared in the *Pennsylvania Mercury* on February 17, 1789, about a month and a half before the first proposals for the *Encyclopaedia* were printed in the same newspaper (and in Andrew Brown's *Federal Gazette* and John Dunlap and David Claypoole's *Pennsylvania Packet*). None of these books or *The Wealth of Nations,* which was not published until later in 1789, was printed by Thomas Dobson, who had thus far acted almost exclusively as publisher and bookseller. Yet the "American Editions" are an important step toward the *Encyclopaedia,* for their financial success undoubtedly underwrote the later venture, at least in the early stages of production, and helped convince Dobson that the *Encyclopaedia* could find a market in America. More than that, as Hopkinson's letter to Jefferson suggests, they kept Dobson's name before the public and created his reputation as a publisher capable of completing large projects and producing work of high quality. Such considerations no doubt played an important role in making his campaign for subscribers to the *Encyclopaedia* a successful one, for perhaps he alone of all American printers of the period could have secured enough signatures to support a project that seemed to have so little chance of success.

By the time he started work on the *Encyclopaedia,* Dobson's business had expanded dramatically. In the first five years of the decade, he published or printed on his own more than one hundred twenty-five titles in addition to the first fourteen volumes of the *Encyclopaedia.* Besides continuing to reprint selected British and other European books, he brought out a number of works by American writers and several collections that had been compiled under the sponsorship of American learned societies. With the publication of Morgan Edwards's *Materials toward a History of the Baptists in Jersey* (1792; Evans 24292), for example, he became responsible for the second volume of an important projected history of American Baptists (the first, an account of Baptists in Pennsylvania, had been published by Isaac Collins and Joseph Cruikshank in 1770 [Hixson 19]). He also published Ebenezer Hazard's *Historical Collections* (2 vols., 1792 and 1794; Evans 24407 and 27105), the first volume of Benjamin Rush's *Medical Inquiries and Observations* (1793; Evans 26111), and, in 1793, volume 1, part 1 of the *Transactions* of the College of Physicians of Philadelphia (Bell 8–24; Evans 25992). Well into the nineteenth century, he continued to publish reports, transactions, and medical journals sponsored at least informally and often officially by the College of Physicians.

Dobson's connection with the American Philosophical Society was important to his career both early and late. Indeed, it may be taken as a paradigm of the interdependence among audience, author, and publisher that sustained his bookselling business at the local level. Although his customers included members of the society almost from the first—the Reverend Robert Blackwell, who was also a trustee of the University of Pennsylvania, made purchases as early as 1785[16]—his relationship with the society as an institution seems to have begun with his donation of the first five volumes of the *Encyclopaedia* in February 1792 (*Early Proceedings* 202). This gesture initiated a cordial business relationship from which Dobson gained prestige, patronage, access to local authors, and an occasional publishing assignment. The society, in turn, benefited by receiving additional donations through the years, including a gift of the *Supplement.* As late as 1817–18, the minutes of the society record thanks to Thomas Dobson for unspecified gifts, one of which was almost certainly the stone from Munich used for the first lithographic illustration created and published in America in the *Analectic Magazine* in July 1819 (*Early Proceedings* 472, 478–79; Oberholtzer 224).[17]

Like other American printers of the period, Dobson benefited from the passage of the first federal copyright act on May 30, 1790. Indeed, it is

probable that without such legislation in the offing to protect his investment in the *Encyclopaedia,* he would not have begun to publish it at all.
Designed to promote progress in the sciences and useful arts, the statute
protected only citizens of the United States and allowed printers to claim
economic ownership of works written and published in England or on the
Continent. Dobson was an energetic proponent of the legislation, copy-
righting in the roles of author, publisher, and proprietor during the first
decade of the law's existence more titles than almost any other American
printer (Goff, "First Decade," 113–28). His motive was not always personal profit. On March 31, 1796, for example, he tried to persuade John
Dickinson to file for copyright of *A Fragment* (Evans 30438) by pointing
out that it would not diminish the size of Dickinson's audience and would
protect the integrity of his language. "Unless Something of this kind is
done," Dobson importuned Dickinson, "most likely it will be reprinted in
such a manner as you would not wish to see it."[18] Dickinson remained
unpersuaded, however, and Dobson eventually printed *A Fragment* without either copyright protection or identification of its author.

Dobson's concern for what he considered to be John Dickinson's best
interests is one indication of his integrity and may be one reason why he
became successful so quickly in Philadelphia. Authors and customers felt
they could take him at his word. Both his integrity and the sincerity of his
patriotism are well illustrated by an anecdote from the middle 1790s
attributed to John Neagle, a former student of Gilbert Stuart's, involving
the always impecunious Stuart, who frequented Dobson's bookstore although he was not known to Dobson personally. Shortly after Heath,
Boydell, and Thompson had obtained a British copyright for their engraving of Stuart's portrait of George Washington without paying Stuart for
the painting or reserving any royalties for him, Dobson showed the artist
one of the engravings and asked his opinion of it. When Stuart denounced
the engraving, Dobson accused him of lacking the feelings of an American
and demanded to know why he did not respect either Washington or "'the
talents of the American painter who executed the original picture.'" After
hearing Stuart's story, he put all the prints back in the box, nailed it shut,
and, according to Neagle, "was never known to sell, or offer for sale, one of
those engravings" (Dunlap 1: 240–41).

In April 1794, Joseph Priestley emigrated to the United States to
escape the wrath of Englishmen angered by his public reply to Edmund
Burke's *Reflections on the French Revolution* and his sympathy for France.
Thanks in part to his association with Benjamin Rush, whose politics and

religion were agreeable to Priestley's (and, apparently, to Dobson's), Dobson became Priestley's principal American publisher, issuing fifteen different titles between 1794 and 1797. Priestley's *Appeal to the Serious and Candid Professors of Christianity* (Evans 27552), *A Familiar Illustration of Certain Passages of Scripture Relating to the Power of Man to Do the Will of God* (Evans 27553), and *General View of the Arguments for the Unity of God* (Evans 27554), all published in 1794, were consonant with many, though by no means all, of Dobson's convictions as a believer in Universalist teachings. Historically, however, the most important of Priestley's titles for which Dobson was responsible are *Discourses Relating to the Evidences of Revealed Religion* and *Unitarianism Explained and Defended* (1796; Evans 31050 and 31055), two sermons preached in the Universalist church in Philadelphia, which collectively symbolize the founding of the first permanent Unitarian church in America to adopt the use of that name (Robinson 22). The copyrights on both of these and on the first part of Priestley's *Considerations on the Doctrine of Phlogiston* (1796; Evans 31049) were issued to Thomas Dobson, which probably signifies that he printed or published them at his own risk in exchange for the exclusive right to all profits. Years after Priestley's death in 1804, Dobson printed *A Catalogue of Books in the Library of Joseph Priestley* (1816), which suggests that, despite differences on the issue of Christ's divinity, the two had become and had remained good friends.[19]

In 1797, Dobson himself became an author for the first but not the final time, writing and publishing several books for children: the two-volume *First Lessons for Children* (Evans 32054), *The Holiday, or Children's Social Amusement* (Evans 32055), and *Pleasing Instructions for Young Minds* (Evans 32056). Only the first of these survives, although all were deposited for copyright (March 6, March 23, and May 20, 1797). The last title is known only through an advertisement included in Dobson's edition of John Aikin's *Evenings at Home, or the Juvenile Budget Opened* (Evans 31698); the second is also advertised there and in *Porcupine's Gazette* on March 27, 1797, described as a book "intended to combine instruction with entertainment." Dobson advertised *First Lessons for Children, in Two Volumes* in the same newspaper on March 8, informing the public that "the design of these little books is to render the knowledge of the letters, and of spelling and reading easy and delightful to children." *First Lessons* seems to have been the most popular of the three; copies of it are still listed by Judah Dobson in the final catalog of *Books . . . of the Stock of the Late Firm of Thomas Dobson & Son* in 1823 (17), indicating that it had been reprinted several times. It is a simple primer, offering a one-line description and illustration of every letter of the alphabet ("The Rook feeds and guards her young"; "The Unicorn is said to be a fabulous animal") and moralistic tales that teach the golden rules of social conduct. Perhaps Dobson's son Judah, who would have been five years old at the time, inspired his father's first efforts as a writer.

The year following the appearance of Dobson's books for children was a tumultuous one in American politics, highlighted by the disclosure of the XYZ Affair, the passage of the Alien and Sedition Act, the Virginia and Kentucky Resolutions, and the arrests of democratic-republican printers such as Benjamin Franklin Bache, who dared to criticize the Adams administration in his newspaper, the *Aurora*. Americans of conservative inclination viewed the schisms in society with alarm and blamed the French government, Jacobin sympathizers in America, and international conspiracies for attempting to subvert the peace, prosperity, and domestic tranquility of the United States. Many publications decried the triumph of atheism and infidelity in America and around the world, but none was more notorious than John Robison's impassioned denunciation of the Society of the Illuminati, *Proof of a Conspiracy Against All the Religions and Governments of Europe* (Evans 34477). Dobson was the American publisher of this book, probably at the instigation of his friend Jedidiah Morse. Unlike Dobson, Morse was a staunch Presbyterian with little use for the theology of Unitarianism, but both were political conservatives who interpreted social disorder as a symbol of divine displeasure and a symptom of the impending death of the republic. Morse continued to believe in Robison's conspiratorial theories long after they had been disproved (Phillips 73–101), but for most Americans, presumably including Dobson, the furor over the Illuminati quickly faded. William Dunlap, for example, "looked into" Robison's book in Dobson's bookstore when he was visiting in Philadelphia in April 1798, and pronounced it merely a "curious work" (2: 241); he seems to have put no faith in it from the first. The Illuminati are remembered today chiefly because of Charles Brockden Brown's "Memoirs of Carwin" (begun in 1798 but not completed until 1805) and *Ormond* (1799), both of which reflect Brown's reading of Dobson's edition of Robison.

Closer ties between Brown and Dobson can be established. In 1799, Dobson became one of a group of booksellers who supported the publication of *Arthur Mervyn,* joining Asbury Dickins, Henry and Patrick Rice, Hugh Maxwell, and Robert Campbell in an investment as cautious and calculated as his earlier decision to help publish a small school edition of the New Testament had been. Maxwell was the printer, publisher, and promoter of the enterprise; the others agreed to subscribe for as many copies as they thought they could dispose of at a profit. With a few notable exceptions such as Susannah Haswell Rowson's *Charlotte,* American fiction did not sell well in the United States; Americans preferred to invest their money in established authors such as Fielding, Goldsmith, and Sterne. But there was apparently enough profit in this particular speculation to encourage Dobson and the others to maintain the "marketing congerie" (Parker 472) they had established and underwrite the first volume of Brown's next novel, *Edgar Huntley* (1799). This time the results were apparently not as promising, and Dobson, who over the years carried few novels in his inventory, did not again support a work of fiction by an American writer.

Dobson turned author once again in 1799, producing a work far more important than his earlier excursions into children's literature. *Letters on the Existence and Character of the Deity; and on the Moral State of Man* (Evans 35413) is to his spiritual autobiography what the *Encyclopaedia* is to his career as a publisher and bookseller, the seminal and indispensable book. Over a span of five years, it appeared in several different editions and at several stages of development, each representing the refinement of a thought or theme. The ideas expressed in it spawned Dobson's last two books, *Thoughts on the Scripture Account of Faith in Jesus* (1807; Shaw and Shoemaker 12442, and 1808; ND 0302504) and *Thoughts on Mankind* (1811; ND 0302502). The coexistence in a single personality of a fervent religious faith and a deep belief in scientific progress as exemplified by the *Encyclopaedia* and other books that Dobson published may seem odd from a modern perspective, but the more familiar examples of Benjamin Rush and Joseph Priestley serve as reminders that it was not uncommon in eighteenth-century Philadelphia.

Dobson makes no claim for originality in the *Letters.* "Most of the thoughts are such as the author has met with in the course of reading or conversation," he says on the first page of the Preface (iii). The purpose of the book is to draw "the attention of young persons to the study of those subjects which are universally important" (iv), a declaration that links the work to his earlier primers for children. The first subject, explored in Letter I, is the insufficiency of the senses to furnish evidence of the Deity or establish the truth that the visible universe "is not an end in itself but bespeaks God behind it" (13). Scripture, not nature, is the only reliable source of revelation. Religious faith is also required, Letter I goes on to assert, to provide a foundation for a system of morality and to insure social order (17–18). These sentiments represent Dobson's redaction of some of the fundamental tenets of Scottish common sense philosophy and a restatement of certain basic principles of the theology and social philosophy of liberal Christianity, particularly in the attack on the deistical idea of the self-sufficiency of reason.[20]

After providing an overview of scriptural history and a brief consideration of the Creation in relation to the Creator (Letter II, 23–38), Dobson moves on to a discussion of Christ as the promised Messiah, a historical and yet mystical identity testified to by "that wonderful assemblage of predictions, which . . . found their fulfillment in Jesus Christ" (Letter III, 59). Read in conjunction with Letter VI, in which Dobson expresses his belief that Christ is not only "the instrument by whom the love of God was manifested to man, but also . . . an active voluntary agent" in the great work of redemption (106), this part of Dobson's book reveals his Arianism, that is, his belief that Christ is more than merely a mortal man though less than the equal of God; he is "the only begotten of the Father, the first being whom God brought into existence (at what time is impossible to be known) and the Agent by whom he created all things" (Letter VI, 100–101). This view distinguishes Dobson's Unitarianism from Priestley's, which is founded on the Socinian interpretation of Christ as a human being whose resurrection typifies but is not instrumental in attaining the resurrection of all men.[21]

The final major idea urged by Dobson in this first version of *Letters* is the Arminian notion, embraced also by the Unitarians and the Universalists, that God's design for mankind is ultimately "to recover all mankind to holiness and consequent happiness. This appears to be the uniform object of all the Divine dispensation in every age and state," Dobson declares, "and will continue to be the object of all dispensations of God toward men in every future state, till the whole shall be saved, and not one lost" (139–40). The book then closes with a promise to resume the subject of universal salvation at a later date (144), a promise that Dobson eventually kept.

Letters was reviewed by Charles Brockden Brown in the *Monthly Magazine and American Review* in September 1800. "Though the author of this work has not thought proper to prefix his name to it," Brown's review begins, "yet we have good authority for ascribing it to Mr. THOMAS DOBSON, printer and bookseller of Philadelphia." Before turning to the work itself, Brown praises Dobson as a "public-spirited and useful citizen" (196) who, "with a zeal which . . . has not been exceeded by any other individual of his profession in America, . . . disseminates the fruits of the genius and learning of others" (196–97). Then he summarizes the main points of *Letters,* noting in particular Dobson's Arianism and his belief in a pre-existent state of being and quoting extensively from the third and seventh letters. "We do not perceive that he has advanced anything which can be pronounced *new,*" Brown concludes, "but he writes like a serious, well-informed and sensible man" (198). Brown's remarks are favorable throughout, perhaps in partial repayment for Dobson's role in publishing *Arthur Mervyn* and *Edgar Huntley,* the fruits of Brown's own genius, as well as in acknowledgment of his importance as a publisher who promoted arts, letters, and learning in America.

The last important book that Dobson published in the eighteenth century was "an Elegant Edition of the NEW TESTAMENT" (ND 0302496), as his proposals termed it—the same title that, in Joseph Hopkinson's view, had launched both him and Philadelphia on their grand careers in printing in 1786. Beginning on December 6, 1800, proposals appeared in *Poulson's American Daily Advertiser,* describing the work as an easy-to-read edition especially printed in "*large plain Type*" cut on purpose for the work and designed for "*persons whose eyesight is weak, or otherwise impaired.*" The book comprised one large quarto volume of approximately eight hundred pages with complete marginal references and accurate translations. It was advertised as a bargain at four dollars and was scheduled to be put to press as soon as four hundred subscribers had been signed. Once that number had been attained, the advertisement went on to say, the price would rise to five dollars in boards for volumes not previously subscribed.

No copies of this edition are known to have survived. That it was eventually completed, however, seems clear from Joseph Dennie's *Port Folio* for Saturday, February 14, 1801, which reported that the edition was "in the press, and in a state of great forwardness." The editor of the *Port Folio* had no doubt that it would sell out rapidly once it was issued. "We have a pledge in the professional knowledge and correctness of the publisher for the accuracy of his collations," Dennie averred, testifying to Dobson's reputation for work of high quality. Moreover, said Dennie, "The specimen of a large and well defined type, attached to his proposals, promises that this edition will be perspicuous to the eyes of every aged, and of every midnight student" (1: 51).

Dobson's life away from the press and the print shop is difficult to trace. Unlike his great Philadelphia predecessor in the printing trade, for example, he was interested in science only as a publisher, not as a scientist, and he was not in any sense a prominent public figure. Although it has been asserted that he was a member of the American Philosophical Society (Kruse 85), no evidence supports this contention. Apart from the world of business, his only interest in societies seems to have been confined to charitable and benevolent organizations. "The industrious man," he wrote in the 1799 edition of *Letters*, "is generally enabled to assist the poor and distressed . . . and his own heart is softened and ennobled while he sympathizes with and relieves their affliction" (167–68). Acting in concert with this sentiment, he was a subscribing supporter of the Philadelphia Dispensary for the Medical Relief of the Poor, an organization founded on April 12, 1786 (*Freeman's Journal*, August 5, 1789). He belonged as well to the St. Andrews Society, perhaps the most important of the charitable organizations that flourished in Philadelphia in the last decade of the eighteenth century (Stephens pt. 2, 50), and served for a time as president of the Caledonian Society (Hardie 208), described in the *Philadelphia Directory* of 1793 as a mutual benefit society designed for the relief of widows and orphans of deceased members (205). Dobson was listed as president again in 1796 (Stephens pt. 2, 55) and probably served in that capacity in other years as well. This cannot be determined, however, because not all city directories published during this period included the names of officers and members of Philadelphia's benevolent organizations.[22]

On August 5, 1789, the same day that Francis Bailey's *Freeman's Journal* printed the list of contributors to the Philadelphia Dispensary, Dobson also signed his name to a petition addressed to the Supreme Executive Council of the State of Pennsylvania on behalf of a prisoner named James Large—an unwitting victim, the petition affirmed, of gross imposition upon a foreigner—for release from "the Gaol of the city of Philadelphia."[23] Other signators were James Pemberton, Benjamin Rush, John Swanwick, and Jacob Barge, among other Philadelphia notables, and nearly every other established printer and bookseller in Philadelphia. Such petitions were common in late eighteenth-century Philadelphia as a form of poor relief supplementing the alms house and the workhouse.[24] The presence of Dobson's name on this document is entirely in keeping with his quiet involvement in other charitable activities.

By the end of the eighteenth century, Dobson had built a substantial reputation for unostentatious benevolence and probity in the conduct of his business. He was well established in Philadelphia's professional and commercial community by ties of friendship, mutual economic interest, and, for want of a better name, political loyalties. He had become one of the most successful publishers and printers in the city, with many important titles to his credit, including the first American editions of half a dozen major and many important minor works. He was also esteemed as a publisher of American scientific and medical works and, occasionally, creative fiction as well. The publication of the *Encyclopaedia* had in the meantime solidified his reputation and made him one of the principal printers in the United States as well (Wroth and Silver 125). The story of that publication begins with Dobson's efforts to create an American audience and convince subscribers that an undertaking of such size and scope could be accomplished in the United States, despite what many feared was a prohibitive shortage of native manufactories and skilled workmen in virtually every craft and trade required for book production. His proposals constitute the first phase of an undertaking that eventually came to symbolize for a generation of Americans the maturation and independence of the American book industry.

Notes

1. Cemetery records and Dobson's death certificate (Department of Records of the City of Philadelphia) both give his age as seventy-two at the time of his death on March 9, 1823, establishing 1751 as the year of his birth.

2. For booksellers in Scotland before 1775, see George Bushnell's chapter (277–378) in Henry R. Plomer, *A Dictionary of the Printers and Booksellers Who Were at Work in England, Scotland and Ireland from 1726 to 1775* (London: Oxford University Press, 1932 [for 1930]); and Ian Maxted, *The British Book Trades, 1710–1777: An Index of Masters and Apprentices Recorded in the Inland Revenue Registers at the Public Record Office, Kew* (Exeter: Published by the Author, 1983). No Dobson is listed in either Maxted's or Plomer's compilation.

A T. or Thomas Dobson was included in the Edinburgh directory from 1783 through at least 1790, after Dobson moved to America, so he could not be the man who is the subject of this study. James Dobson, successor to Robert Clark as stationer, engraver, and lithographer, appeared in the city directories at 1 and 2 St. James Square between 1776 and 1780; thereafter the firm of Dobson, Molle and Company ("Wholesale Stationers, Lithographers and Printers") occupied the same address, then moved nearby to 56 Nicolson Street in 1784. This firm or possibly a bookbinder named Samuel Campbell (not to be confused with the American printer of the same name, already established in New York in the 1760s), who was present at the christening of Dobson's second and third daughters, may have been the source of the weekly numbers of the *Encyclopaedia Britannica* as they emerged from the press in Edinburgh.

3. Wesley Washington Pasko, *American Dictionary of Printing and Bookmaking, Containing a History of These Arts in Europe and America, with Definitions of Technical Terms and Biographical Sketches* (New York, 1894; repr. Detroit: Gale Research,

1967), 146, reports that Dobson could read Greek and Hebrew with facility. Dobson's advertisements for the Hebrew Bible (1814), however, make it clear that he had contracted with expert linguists to oversee the publication of these volumes, and his use of Greek and Hebrew to mount an etymological argument against the divinity of Jesus in the second version of *Letters on the Existence and Character of the Deity* (1802) relies decisively on James Purves's *Humble Attempt to Investigate and Defend the Scripture Doctrine Concerning the Father, the Son, and the Holy Spirit,* which he had printed in 1788 (see the discussion of both these books in Chapter 8).

4. The date of Dobson's marriage is given in the pre-1800 marriage indexes of Canongate and Edinburgh.

5. The birth dates of Dobson's daughters are entered in Edinburgh's Old Parish Register 685, 1/36 and 1/37, respectively. Attending the baptism of the second two daughters as witnesses were Dobson's brother (or, possibly, his father) William, a baker by trade, and "Samuel Campbell, Bookbinder, Edinburgh." This information was supplied by Gwen MacLeod of the Association of Scottish Gene-alogists and Record Agents and the Scottish Genealogy Society (letter of February 2, 1989), to whom I am indebted for her careful research.

6. For Judah Dobson's probable dates of birth and death, see John McAllister, Jr. to Charles A. Poulsen, October 24, 1855, Box A.L.S. (McAllister), HSP. McAllister identifies himself as the son-in-law of the printer, papermaker, and bookseller William Young, perhaps Dobson's best friend in Philadelphia. He pro-vides the following glimpse of Dobson's domestic life:

> Judah Dobson, William W. Young, and a daughter of John Smith . . . were infants at the same time—the parents all resided in the same neighborhood (about Chesnut and 2nd Sts)—the mothers were all Scotch Ladies, and were on such intimate terms with each other, that when one of them would go out in the afternoon to make a visit, she would leave her baby with one of the others to be nourished and taken care of during her absence. . . . William W. Young was born in July 1792. Judah Dobson died in Sept 1850—so that he was perhaps 58 or 59.

(Quoted by permission of the Historical Society of Pennsylvania.)

For McAllister, see Charles M. Morris, "Memorial Notice of John McAllister, Jr." [June 29, 1786 to December 17, 1877], *Pennsylvania Magazine of History and Biography* 2 (1878): 92–95. For Charles A. Poulsen, translator of Constantine S. Rafinesque's *Monograph on the Fluviatile Bivalve Shells of the River Ohio* (1832), see Samuel Austin Allibone's *A Critical Dictionary of English Literature and British and American Authors* . . .; 2 vols. and supplement (Philadelphia: J. B. Lippincott, 1899) 2: 1664 and 1724.

Jean Paton Dobson's death on March 7, 1818 is reported in the entry on Thomas Dobson in the card catalog of the American Antiquarian Society, Worces-ter, Mass.

7. Unlike Chauncy and Winchester, Purves was unknown to most Americans, but in 1788 Dobson nonetheless issued the first and only American edition of Purves's *Humble Attempt* (Evans 21413), as well as his *Observations on Doctor*

Priestley's Doctrine of Philosophical Necessity and Materialism in 1797 (Evans 32732). For a brief biographical sketch and bibliography of Purves's writings, see *DNB* 16: 493–94.

Most of the central doctrines of Purves's brand of Universalism may be found in his critique of Joseph Priestley, of whose Socinian position that Christ was merely a human child born to Mary and Joseph he strongly disapproved; this set Purves apart from the Unitarian movement, as Earl Morse Wilbur has observed (*History of Unitarianism in Transylvania, England, and America* [Cambridge, Mass.: Harvard University Press, 1952], 320). As outlined in the *Observations* and as summarized in the *DNB,* Purves's beliefs included the pre-existence of the human soul of Christ; the duty of free enquiry in matters of religion; the universal salvation of mankind; and the doctrine that Christ, though inferior to God the Father, is more than mere man. His theology was "high Arian," writes the author of the entry in the *DNB,* and his most distinctive position stressed the duty of free inquiry into the meaning of the Scripture without sectarian bias. Dobson's writings on religion contain these major doctrines, together with an underlying Christology and a strategy of argumentation involving the presentation of historical and etymological evidence identical to that employed by Purves in the *Observations.* Indeed, Purves's attack on Priestley may have inspired Dobson's own re-examination and rejection of Priestley's Socinianism in *Letters on the Existence and Character of the Deity, and on the Moral State of Man* (Evans 35413) and other writings. For although Dobson's name does not appear even as an apprentice in the extensive public records maintained at Kew, he may have learned printing from Purves.

8. Brief accounts of Winchester's and Chauncy's roles in the development of American Unitarianism may be found in David Robinson, *The Unitarians and the Universalists* (Westport, Conn.: Greenwood Press, 1985), 339–40 and 233.

9. The letter from Dobson to James Pemberton (March 23, 1784) is quoted by permission of the Historical Society of Pennsylvania from the Pemberton Papers, vol. 40, p. 134; it corrects the information about Dobson's arrival in the United States provided to Charles A. Poulsen in the correspondence from John McAllister cited in note 6, above. McAllister had written that "my Father in Law, Mr. Young, arrived here, with his family, from Scotland June 27, 1784—I have always understood that he was here before Mr Dobson came—but it would seem that Mr D. was not long after him." McAllister's remark in the same letter that "Mr Dobson had been in the employ of a bookseller in Glasgow or Edinburgh" suggests a period of apprenticeship, as does also the designation of "Clerk" that Dobson gave on the occasion of the baptism of his first daughter, Margaret, on February 15, 1779. For James Pemberton (August 26, 1723–February 9, 1809), see *DAB* 14: 413.

10. Benjamin Rush, *Letters of Benjamin Rush,* ed. Lyman H. Butterfield, 2 vols. (Princeton, N.J.: Princeton University Press, 1951) 1: 346 and 348, n. 1. Butterfield does not identity the "Mr. Dobson" referred to in Rush's letter to Cullen as the man who would become his principal bookseller and printer, but the connection with Edinburgh makes it seem likely that Rush's visitor and the subject of this study are one and the same.

11. Among the first titles Dobson offered for sale was Cullen's *First Lines of the*

Practice of Physic, including the recently completed fourth part. The advertisement in the *Pennsylvania Mercury* (June 7, 1785) made the unusual claim that the work had been "published and corrected by the Doctor himself," which Dobson changed to "printed under the author's own inspection" for a later advertisement in the same paper (November 11). Even though the book was imported, these claims seem to indicate a close collaboration between Cullen and the American bookseller which may have dated back to Dobson's days in Edinburgh.

12. This brief portrait of eighteenth-century Philadelphia derives in part from Russell B. Nye's *Cultural Life of the New Nation, 1776–1830* (New York: Harper & Row, 1960), 111–13 and 125–28, and Henry F. May's *The Enlightenment in America* (New York: Oxford University Press, 1976), 197–222. Travel narratives of Brissot de Warville, Moreau de St. Mery, and Charles Janson were also useful.

13. McAllister to Poulsen, October 24, 1855, Box A.L.S. (McAllister), HSP.

14. A survey of book prices in England and America based on random newspaper advertisements suggests that English editions often brought two and a half to three times more in America than in London. In his advertisement in the *Pennsylvania Mercury* on November 11, 1785, for example, Dobson listed Benjamin Bell's *System of Surgery* at 15 shillings per volume; the price per volume in the *London Chronicle* (January 25, 1785) was 6 shillings.

This ratio continued for some time. In his proposals for the Hebrew Bible (eventually published by Dobson), Jonathan Horowitz pointed out that an American edition of that work would cost the purchasers only about half the price ($15; $14 for subscribers) that it sold for in England (4 guineas). This proposal is item NH 0534148 in the *National Union Catalog, Pre-1956 Imprints,* 754 vols. (Chicago: American Library Association; London: Mansell Information, 1968–1981), 255 (1973): 467. The copy of the proposal used by Oscar Wegelin to write his article on Mills Day's proposed Hebrew Bible (see Chapter 8) is in the rare book collection of the Klau Library, Hebrew Union College, Cincinnati. I wish to thank the staff and administrators of this institution for the opportunity to examine both Horowitz's and Mills Day's proposals. For the identity of "J. Horwitz" (not "H.," as in the *National Union Catalog,* see Harry Simonhoff, *Jewish Notables in America, 1776–1865: Links in an Endless Chain* (New York: Greenberg, 1956), 159–61.

15. Sonneck, *Bibliography of Early American Secular Music,* 575. Upton does not include Dobson in his list of "General publishers in Philadelphia associated with musical interests" (579) in his revision of Sonneck's *Bibliography,* 579, but on page 575 mentions him and Henry and Patrick Rice as "among the more important printers and general publishers more or less associated with musical interests" during the period covered by his bibliography.

16. The Reverend Robert Blackwell's early purchases from Dobson's bookstore and stationer's shop (June 27 and August 11, 1785) are recorded in the Wallace Papers, vol. 4, pp. 46 and 52, HSP. For a sketch of Blackwell, see Rush's *Letters* 1: 439, n. 2. Blackwell's name appears frequently in city directories and newspapers of the period as a member of the Board of Trustees of the University of Pennsylvania, the Abolition Society, and the American Philosophical Society, among others.

17. Dobson published volumes 4 (Evans 35106) and 5 (Shaw and Shoemaker 1755) of the *Transactions* of the American Philosophical Society. The fourth volume

appeared in 1799 after some unpleasantness about missing plates and questions about who was responsible for restoring the plates and paying for the proper publication of the volume. Dobson eventually capitulated (see *Early Proceedings* 284–86). This incident appears to have been the only difficult one in the relationship between the printer and the society, and it could not have been taken very seriously by either side; on December 27, 1799, the society authorized Dobson to print Volume 5 as well (ibid. 302). The terms for both volumes were identical: in exchange for the copyright, Dobson would give the society one hundred copies in boards and would "open a subscription where as many as please shall have copies in boards at the price of two Dollars each provided the copies Subscribed for are taken & paid for within Six months from the time of Publication." Unsubscribed copies would cost three dollars in boards (ibid. 237). Again there was a delay with some of the plates, but work was reported moving forward in April 1802 (ibid. 322) and was completed later that year. See also Thomas Dobson to John Vaughan, February 5, 1796, American Philosophical Society, which repeats and clarifies terms also published in the *Early Proceedings*, 302.

18. Dickinson explicitly instructed Benjamin Rush, to whom he had entrusted the manuscript of *A Fragment,* "that no Steps might be taken to secure a Copyright." Rush disagreed but informed Dobson of Dickinson's wishes when he gave the manuscript to the printer. In a letter to Dickinson on February 16, 1796, Rush tried without success to talk his friend out of his decision to publish without copyright. (*Letters* 2: 770–71). Dobson's letter to Dickinson is in the Logan Papers, vol. 12, p. 65, HSP, and is quoted here by permission.

19. The First Society of Unitarian Christians in Philadelphia was founded by John Vaughan, the treasurer of the American Philosophical Society who was known to Dobson both personally and professionally; Ralph Eddowes, a former pupil of Priestley's, who would later edit several Unitarian collections for Dobson; and James Taylor.

According to Priestley, the first part of *Observations on the Doctrine of Phlogiston* was printed by "Mr. Dobson . . . at his own risk," with five hundred copies earmarked for the radical republican printer Joseph Johnson (Priestley's British publisher) in England. See Priestley's letter of July 28, 1796, to Theophilus Lindsey in *Original Letters from Dr. Joseph Priestley, F. R. S., to the Rev. Theophilus Lindsey, 1766–1803, and to the Rev. Thomas Belsham, 1789–1803,* Film No. 4988, British Records Relating to America, quoted by permission of the librarian, Dr. William's Library, 14 Gordon Square, London.

A copy of the catalog of Priestley's books is in the holdings of the American Antiquarian Society, Worcester, Massachusetts; another is located at the Historical Society of the Presbyterian Church of America, Valley Forge, Pennsylvania.

20. The best account of the origins of American Unitarianism may be found in Robinson, *Unitarians and the Universalists.* Also useful are Conrad Wright, *The Beginnings of Unitarianism in America* (Boston: Starr King, 1955) and Daniel Walker Howe, *The Unitarian Conscience: Harvard Moral Philosophy, 1805–1861* (Cambridge, Mass.: Harvard University Press, 1970).

21. See note 7.

22. A brief discussion of the St. Andrews Society as a relief agency for the poor may be found in John K. Alexander, *Render Them Submissive: Responses to Poverty in*

Philadelphia, 1760–1800 (Amherst: University of Massachusetts Press, 1980), 129–30. The constitution and rules of the society, restructured and reformulated after the revolutionary war, may be conveniently consulted in Evans 23698. Information about the Caledonian Society may be found in various city directories, as indicated above.

23. "To His Excellency the President and Honourable Members of the Supreme Executive Council of the State of Pennsylvania," August 5, 1789, Gratz Collection, Pennsylvania Series, "Provincial Conference," Case 1, Box 16, "Barge," HSP; quoted by permission.

24. For similar petitions, see Alexander's brief discussion of the Philadelphia Society for Alleviating the Miseries of Public Prisons, founded in 1787 (130).

2. Building a National Audience: From Prospectus to Publication

When the English traveler Charles William Janson visited the United States between 1793 and 1806, one of the differences he detected in the ways Americans and Englishmen conducted their affairs was that American publishers relied on subscription sales far more than did their counterparts in the British Isles. In Scotland and England, Janson said, printers normally assumed the cost of book production in advance, often investing large sums in a project before a single volume could be put to press and trusting to the ordinary course of trade to turn a profit. In America, however, where printers' purses were proverbially thin and the bookbuying public was widely scattered, a different strategy was required. "If works of great extent, such as the Encyclopaedia Britannica . . . are attempted there to be copied," Janson wrote in obvious allusion to Dobson's recently completed magnum opus, "many months are passed in procuring subscriptions, and for this purpose riders are sent out to every large town, by which means almost every inhabitant is solicited to lend a hand" (425).

At first glance, Janson's comments seem to offer an invaluable eyewitness account of how Dobson's *Encyclopaedia* was marketed and distributed, invoking an image of circuit-riding salesmen travelling from door to door or setting up local agents to act in their behalf. Indeed, that is exactly how the fabled Parson Weems sold Mathew Carey's editions of William Guthrie's *New System of Modern Geography* (1794–95) and Oliver Goldsmith's *History of the Earth and Animated Nature* (1795), among other titles (Green 27; Gilreath 1981, 31–32). But the *Encyclopaedia* was too expensive and its publication schedule was too protracted for it to be marketed in this manner. Outside the major cities, with their large professional classes, few Americans could have afforded the investment that Dobson's book required, nor would the wary folk who lived in small towns and settlements or on the edge of the frontier be likely to part with ready money for the mere promise of a publication whose completion lay an unpredictable number of years in the future. Moreover, Dobson himself disapproved of door-to-door solicitation, writing to Jedidiah Morse on May 20, 1802, that he had "never followed" the practice and strongly advising Morse against it. Although it might at first appear to benefit an author, Dobson warned, it ultimately "sinks the book in the public estimation and never fails to take the trade out of the booksellers [sic] hands, who of course is no longer interested in it."[1] Perhaps Janson's story accorded with his own impressions of how democracy and the book trade worked together in America, but Dobson's testimony makes it clear that the *Encyclopaedia* was not sold in the way that Janson describes.

On one point, however, Janson is correct. Many months did indeed elapse between Dobson's first published proposals on March 31, 1789 (over a date of March 30 in the *Pennsylvania Mercury* and several other newspapers), and the announcement on December 15 that printing had begun; the first full volume would not be ready for customer approval until the spring of 1790, more than a year after the first call for subscribers. Dobson employed the intervening months to conduct the most extensive promotional campaign that had yet been seen in British North America, dwarfing by comparison James Rivington's aggressive and well-coordinated effort to sell his edition of John Hawkesworth's *New Voyage Round the World* in 1773 and 1774 (Farren 97–99). Distrusting colportage, Dobson relied on traditional bookselling practices familiar to him since his days in Edinburgh and well established in America by the early decades of the eighteenth century (Farren 42–92).[2] He appealed for subscribers through newspaper advertisements and, occasionally, advertisements printed on the spare leaves of books or the wrappers of magazines, and he distributed broadsides and four-page pamphlets for display in the shops of selected booksellers throughout the United States, many of whom supplemented his campaign with their own advertising. Situated as he was in the national capital, he could reasonably expect that the audience for the proposals in Philadelphia's newspapers would include, in addition to local readers, the statesmen, politicians, and other professional people who frequently visited the city on business, but proposals separately printed and distributed to other booksellers could reach an even broader national readership. They also offered an opportunity to describe his project in greater detail than was possible in the newspaper notices. In whatever form or print medium they appeared, the proposals consistently stressed the quality and unprecedented size of the American *Encyclopaedia*, promised that only American craftsmen and American manufactures would be used to publish the book, and called upon the patrons of the arts and sciences in America to rally in support of an arduous and difficult project whose success, if achieved, would redound almost as much to the honor of the subscribers as to the profit of the publisher. Gradually, too, the proposals expressed Dobson's growing sense of the possibilities of producing an American edition that would be something more than a reprint of a British publication, if not yet truly an American encyclopedia in every respect and detail.

The date of Dobson's first set of proposals, late March of 1789, seems significant for understanding the larger purposes of the *Encyclopaedia* and for comprehending at least part of its appeal to Americans at the time. The announcement that an American encyclopedia was in the planning stages was timed to coincide as closely as possible with the news that George Washington had been selected as the country's first President under the newly ratified Constitution and with Washington's inauguration on April 30, 1789. The expectation of these events undoubtedly helped inspire the *Encyclopaedia,* not only by holding out the promise in Article I, Section 8, of the Constitution of the first national copyright act (a promise that was subsequently fulfilled by the enactment of federal legislation on May 30, 1790), but also by appearing to herald (prematurely as matters turned out) the restoration of social, political, and economic stability to a country long rent by inflation, rebellion, and apparently irreconcilable ideological differences. The *Encyclopaedia* may thus be regarded as both a celebration of the new order of things in America, a testament to the faith of one American printer that the President and the Constitution would bring about a coherent society in which business and commercial enterprise could flourish, and as an attempt to foster that stability. In the world of history as experienced, politics, human affairs, and even science may be messy, chaotic, and unpredictable. An encyclopedia, and especially the encyclopedia that Dobson chose to reprint,[3] speaks with the voice of unchallenged authority and offers its taxonomy and its version of scientific objectivity as a reassuring metaphor of the underlying order of the universe, the way things really are despite disturbing appearances to the contrary. Dobson's *Encyclopaedia* brought Old World order and authority as well as the examples of the past to bear on unruly New World experience, offering a rebuke to democratic excesses that imperiled culture and learning. Intended for the libraries of gentlemen of leisure, it dramatized and insisted upon the primacy of the historical perspective, re-establishing knowledge in its proper position in the hegemony of power in America. It was perhaps as much a social and political project as it was an economic one for its publisher.

Selling the *Encyclopaedia* was made easier for Dobson by the utilitarian nature of the third edition of the *Encyclopaedia Britannica*[4] and by the emergence in America of "new democratic beliefs that all citizens should have the opportunity to partake equally of available knowledge, that all citizens were equally capable of mastering profitable knowledge, and that knowledge was power." These "deepest of American vanities," as Rollo Silver has aptly called them (1967, 114), complemented the prevailing utilitarian ideology of the second half of the eighteenth century and served to nationalize the widespread faith in science and progress that Americans shared with most other citizens of the Western world. Purchase of the *Encyclopaedia* could thus be rationalized as both a step toward self-improvement and as an altruistic gesture benefiting the country as a whole. Even so, Dobson faced an uphill battle, for until the appearance of the first completed volume, many Americans remained skeptical that the printer could actually perform what his proposals promised and that an American edition of any book, however pragmatic or patriotic its purposes, was worth the investment that the *Encyclopaedia* required. Money was scarce during the closing decade of the eighteenth century, and those who were able to purchase luxuries such as books were not accustomed to buying American editions.

Dobson's first set of "Proposals . . . for Printing by Subscription Encyclopaedia Britannica" appeared simultaneously in the *Pennsylvania Mercury,* the *Pennsylvania Packet,* and the *Federal Gazette* on March 31, 1789. The conditions of subscription were modeled closely on proposals originally prepared in Edinburgh by Andrew Bell and Colin Macfarquhar, with only a few changes to suit local circumstances.[5] The most significant of such changes was a brief paragraph addressed to "all the lovers of science and literature in the United States of America," whom Dobson called on to provide both "patronage and encouragement . . . towards an American edition of a work every way worthy of their notice." Although he termed the work "A New Edition, Corrected, Improved, and Greatly Enlarged," he was following the wording of the original proposals for the British *Britannica,* which used this language to differentiate the third from the second editions. The possibility of making American corrections and improvements had not yet occurred to him, for he still referred to the work as the "Encyclopaedia Britannica." At this point, it was only another American edition, albeit an unusually large one, of a British book.

Dobson's other alterations in Bell and Macfarquhar's proposals were comparatively minor. He changed the price and the projected date of publication for the first weekly number, and he added some information about the quality of the type and the paper. Otherwise he followed the guidelines laid down for the British *Britannica*. He would eventually modify some of these rules in order to attract purchasers and subscribers who could not afford the substantial cash outlays he demanded, but by and large they governed the printing, sale, and distribution of the *Encyclopaedia* for more than a decade.

I. The work will be printed on a superfine paper, and new types (cast for the purpose by Baine & Co., Philadelphia) which will be occasionally renewed before they contract a worn appearance.

II. It will be published in weekly numbers, at One Quarter of a Dollar each; and the publication will be continued with all possible regularity. No book will be delivered, on any consideration, unless the money be paid at the same time. The first number will be published some time in the month of August.

III. Each number will contain forty pages of letterpress, closely printed; and from a view of the material as now arranged, it is supposed the whole may extend to three hundred numbers, or fifteen volumes in quarto; but whether, or how far, these limits may eventually be exceeded, must depend upon the number and value of the literary productions and scientific discoveries that shall occur, or the hints and communications that may be received, during the progress of the publication.

IV. Those who do not choose to take the work in numbers, may have it in *volumes*, or in *half* volumes, as published, it being proposed to deliver the volumes in parts at Twenty Shillings (Pennsylvania currency) each in boards, or £ 1.17.6 for the *volume* complete. Of those who take the work in volumes or half-volumes, no money will be required until the first volume is finished, when the payments of the first and second volumes are to be made; and the payment of each succeeding volume to be made on the delivery of the volume preceding it.

V. In the course of publication will be delivered nearly four hundred Copper-plates, elegantly engraved; which by far exceed in number those given in any other Scientific Dictionary.

VI. At the close of publication will be delivered an elegant Frontispiece, the Dedication, Preface, and proper Title pages for the different volumes.

Because neither Dobson nor Bell and Macfarquhar knew how large the *Encyclopaedia* would be, the estimated number of copperplates and total volumes proved to be inaccurate. This also explains why the wording of the third condition is vague and tentative. Dobson was not being purposely evasive so as to leave room for any specifically American "hints and communications" he expected or even hoped to receive. He was, rather, confronting with Bell and Macfarquhar the paradoxical nature of the encyclopedic form, which promises totality of coverage on the one hand while on the other assuring subscribers that volumes published late in the alphabetical series would include the most recently discovered information. The emphasis on product—the quality of the paper, the number of engravings, and so on—offsets the emphasis on process, which otherwise would undercut the function and importance of encyclopedias as sources of information and emphasize the importance of yearbooks, manuals, gazeteers, and even newspapers.

Dobson did not make his projected date of publication for the first weekly number, "some time in the month of August," or even come close to it. Not until December 15 was he able to say that "the Work is now in the Press" (*Pennsylvania Mercury*) and to provide a new date of publication, January 2, 1790, for the expected first installment. The long interval between the predicted August and the actual January dates may mean that subscriptions under the weekly plan (or subscriptions in general) were slow in coming, or it may reflect a problem in finding pressmen, compositors, and engravers. At any rate, Dobson met his second deadline, and the initial weekly number of the *Encyclopaedia* appeared according to his revised schedule on the first Saturday in January, 1790.

The price of Dobson's American *Encyclopaedia* was the same as the price in Edinburgh, $2.66 Pennsylvania currency per half volume in boards or $5.00 for a whole volume[6] (the advertisement for the *Britannica* in the *Edinburgh Gazette* on September 27, 1788, quotes the British price at one guinea, the equivalent of $5.00). Dobson beat the Philadelphia price of $5.75 for the first volume of the Edinburgh edition given in an advertisement placed by another bookseller, Robert Campbell, in the *Pennsylvania Packet* on April 6, 1789, but not by the customary two-to-one margin. He also was compelled to advertise far more heavily than the publishers of the Edinburgh edition, who placed few notices in newspapers in the British Isles. Despite the small price differential and the increased costs of advertising, however, Dobson's campaign seems to have kept sales of the third edition of the *Britannica* to a minimum. Campbell, who also received subscriptions for Dobson's *Encyclopaedia,* was apparently the only local bookseller who offered the competing British edition, and perhaps only a few early volumes.

Dobson's prices remained remarkably stable over the first few years of publication but began to rise around the middle of the decade in response to high inflation brought on by French immigration to Philadelphia in the aftermath of the French Revolution and increases in wages and the overall cost of production. Eventually, Dobson also felt compelled to tack on surcharges and penalty payments for subscribers who, having put forward little money, took their obligations to the printer cavalierly (some original subscribers probably never did honor their contracts) and left him to devise whatever strategies he could to offset losses in anticipated revenue. Their tardiness compounded the problem of undercapitalization which forced American publishers like Dobson to favor subscription sales in the first place as a way of underwriting large publications and may have threatened the continuation of the *Encyclopaedia*.

For several months, Dobson's proposals ran as originally printed in the *Federal Gazette,* the *Packet,* and the *Mercury.* They did not appear in any other newspapers until June 24, 1789, when a proposal was printed in the *Pennsylvania Gazette.* By that time, Dobson had made major changes in his text, although these revisions are not reflected in the *Pennsylvania Gazette,* perhaps because proposals appeared only twice more in that newspaper, on July 29 and August 5, and were not worth the bother of correcting. The revised proposals that appeared in the *Mercury* and the *Federal Gazette* on June 6 and in the *Packet* on June 26 represent a major turning point in Dobson's conception of the *Encyclopaedia,* for they are the first to drop the word "Britannica" from the title. Henceforward, Dobson would trade the prestige of England's empire of learning for the increased promotional value of an *Encyclopaedia* that, in name at least, had divorced itself from its reliance on European resources.

To underscore this change, Dobson announced for the first time that the "superfine paper" he had been touting for months would be made in Pennsylvania (unfortunately, he did not identify the mills) and that local paper would be used for the entire edition. He also declared, again for the first time, that "every part of the Work will be executed by American artists" and added the name of the Philadelphia engraver Robert Scot to his own and John Baine's as the American craftsmen who were primarily responsible for the project. Proof copies of some of Scot's first plates, he reported, "may be seen at T. Dobson's Store," an announcement that must have given an important boost to his advertising campaign. At last there was something tangible to show potential subscribers.

The change in title from the *Encyclopaedia Britannica* to the *Encyclopaedia* was more than merely a strategy designed to make it easier for Dobson to sell his book to American audiences. It was also a first step toward meeting "the demands of authority and authenticity" that one student of the encyclopedic form, Warren Preece, has identified as a critical factor in determining the public's reception of any encyclopedia as a true book of knowledge (800). At the time it appeared, the *Encyclopaedia* had little chance to be more than a cultural curiosity, a testament to the condition of cultural liminality that existed in America at the moment. Though no longer a political dependent of England, the United States was still very much a cultural colony of the mother country, and the appeal of the *Encyclopaedia* lay mainly in its promise of reuniting the American intellectual community with vital and sustaining European traditions and learning. Dobson's revised title, however, at least created the illusion that intellectual authority resided in the text itself and not in English authors; for recently emancipated Americans, an American *Britannica* would have been an intolerable contradiction. The change in name was thus both a psychological necessity and a strategy that, in relation to the actual "American" content of the book, poignantly expressed the anomalous cultural identity of Americans in the closing decades of the eighteenth century.

The third and last version of Dobson's proposal appearing in Philadelphia's newspapers was first published in the *Pennsylvania Mercury* and other papers on December 15, 1789. It carried the important information that the actual printing of the *Encyclopaedia* had begun and that proof sheets of the first few pages and illustrations could be seen at Dobson's shop. It also announced that the first weekly number would be ready for subscribers on January 2. This close to actual publication, Dobson sounded cautiously optimistic, begging "leave to return his grateful Acknowledgments for the very liberal Encouragement he has met with in this important Undertaking, from the generous public." Even so, he solicited "a Continuance and increase of patronage," assuring "the Encouragers of this Work, that in its Progress no endeavors shall be wanting on his part, to give universal Satisfaction." With the publication of the first weekly number only a few weeks away, Dobson would shortly be able to provide concrete evidence of the quality of his workmanship and to shift his attention from writing proposals to composing advertisements. The preliminary phase of his enterprise was nearly completed.

Even as he filled Philadelphia's newspapers with appeals for subscribers, Dobson was drafting and distributing broadside proposals, more elaborate than the newspaper versions, to booksellers and other merchants in a dozen American communities. Although many and perhaps most of these proposals were posted in shops in Philadelphia, they also enabled Dobson to address a national body of potential subscribers and thus added an important dimension to his advertising. One such proposal, tentatively dated 1789 by Charles Evans (Evans 45466), advertises the "Encyclopaedia Britannica" instead of the *Encyclopaedia*. Ignoring an apparent aberration on Dobson's part regarding the text of the proposal he published in the *Pennsylvania Gazette* (see the discussion on page 33), this title would mean that Evans's dating is correct and that Dobson printed this version of his proposals before he changed his title to the *Encyclopaedia* in June 1789. Unfortunately, there are no subscribers' signatures affixed to this set of proposals, so nothing can be learned about the identities of Dobson's earliest customers. Nevertheless, the broadside proposal is valuable because it reprints in full the two-page "Address of the Compilers" originally prepared by Bell and Macfarquhar to "Shew the Nature and Plan of the Publication" and because it lists the names of all the persons authorized by Dobson to act as agents for selling the *Encyclopaedia*. In Philadelphia, subscriptions were handled by Dobson himself and "by Messrs. Young, Campbell, Bailey, Cruikshank, Hall and Sellers, Rice, Prichard [sic], Seddon, Aitken, Woodhouse, and Spotswood—"

In *New York* by Messrs. Campbell, Allen, Hodge, Gaine, M'Clean, and Berry & Rogers—In *Boston* by Messrs. Guild and B. Larkin—In *Worcester* by Isaiah Thomas—In *Wilmington, Delaware,* by J. Adams—In *Baltimore* by Rice and Co. and J. Price—In *Annapolis,* by S. Clark—In *Fredericksburg,* by Callender and Henderson—In *Norfolk* by J. M'Lean—In *Richmond,* by T. Brand—In *Wilmington, North Carolina,* by J. Campbell—In *Charleston* by J. McComb, jun.

Although some of those whom Dobson selected to handle out-of-town subscriptions have eluded all efforts to identify them, others figure prominently in the history of early American printing. No information could be found about Dobson's agents in Annapolis, Fredericksburg, and Richmond, and no history of printing in North Carolina mentions J. Campbell in Wilmington;[7] he was probably exclusively a bookseller or merchant, as were some of Dobson's other agents. Nearly as elusive are "J. McComb, jun." of Charleston, South Carolina, described in John Milligan's *Charleston Directory* for 1790 (Evans 22670) as an auctioneer "behind the exchange" (25), and James Price, who is listed as a merchant on page 77 of the city directory of Baltimore for 1800 (Evans 380409). All the rest have left other records of their existence, beginning with Isaiah Thomas, the leading printer of the period and founder of the American Antiquarian Society. Despite his association with the *Encyclopaedia,* however, Thomas had apparently all but forgotten about the book two decades later when he compiled his *History of Printing in America* (1810), for nearly everything he said about it was wrong: the number of volumes (he counted twenty instead of twenty-one); the rate of publication (two half volumes annually); and even the title, which he gave as *The British Encyclopaedia* (an encyclopedia of this title, also known as Nicholson's *British Encyclopaedia,* was printed in Philadelphia by Samuel A. Mitchell and Horace Ames in 1816–17).[8] Oddly, too, this mention of the *Encyclopaedia* is the only notice of Thomas Dobson's work in the entire history, although Dobson was still an active and prominent printer in Philadelphia at the time Thomas wrote.

Because Dobson had a connection with Isaiah Thomas, it seems strange that the firm of Thomas and Andrews is not listed as Dobson's subscription agent in Boston. Instead, Dobson relied on Benjamin Guild (1749–1792), the proprietor of the Boston Book Store and circulating library, and Benjamin Larkin (1754–1803). Guild's name adorns the imprints of only eight known titles, three of which are his own catalogs. Compared with Thomas, both Guild and Larkin were obscure printers and booksellers. Larkin's shop at No. 46 Cornhill issued approximately fifty titles over the years (Franklin 264; 332–33). (Across the street at No. 47 Cornhill was the shop of Ebenezer Larkin, Jr., where, according to an advertisement placed in Benjamin Russell's *Columbian Centinel* by the bookbinder Henry Bilson Legge, prospective clients could examine a complete set of the *Encyclopaedia,* one of many such sets bound by Legge and a partner identified only as Mirick.) Since any printer would naturally wish to post subscription lists in the most prominent shops,[9] it may be that Thomas and Andrews were not interested in the *Encyclopaedia* on the terms Dobson proposed (according to Mathew Carey's Account Books, Dobson's standard discount to booksellers at this time was one-seventh of the advertised price, but he may have offered a larger discount to authorized subscription agents).[10] It would be interesting to know how many sets of the *Encyclopaedia* Guild and Larkin sold in Boston and the surrounding area, but no signed subscription lists appear to have survived in any city.

In Delaware, Dobson turned to James Adams of Wilmington to handle subscriptions to the *Encyclopaedia*. Adams, the first printer in that state, was born in England and worked as a journeyman printer for Franklin and Hall until 1761, when he left Philadelphia for Wilmington. That same year he issued the first titles printed in Delaware, *The Child's New Spelling-Book* and *Advice of Evan Ellis to his Daughter when at Sea* (Hawkins 34–47; Wroth 37–38). Dobson's agent in nearby Baltimore, Rice and Company, was also closely connected with the Philadelphia printing establishment and functioned as a branch operation of the Philadelphia firm of James Rice and Company; it was one of the important bookstores in Baltimore (Minick 83).

Although Dobson made an effort to sell the *Encyclopaedia* all along the eastern seacoast and in several important inland communities, he looked for the greatest number of sales in the large cities of New York and Philadelphia and authorized the greatest number of agents there. Of the six designated agents in New York, the last one, Berry and Rogers, is alone in not being listed in any of the standard studies or bibliographies of printers and printing in that city during the federal period. However, Edward Berry and John Rogers of No. 35 Hanover Square appear frequently in Evans' *Bibliography*. Among their publications Evans lists Susannah Carter's *Frugal Housewife* (24180) and Mrs. Pinchard's *The Blind Child; or Anecdotes of the Windham Family; Written for the Use of Young People* (24693), both published in 1792.

The name of Hugh Gaine (1726–1800) is the most readily recognizable among Dobson's New York agents. Gaine, a sometimes Tory printer, was pilloried by Philip Freneau in his rollicking satire "Hugh Gaine's Life" and was notorious as a man of wavering political persuasions who in his newspapers alternately supported both sides during the revolutionary war. Notwithstanding a temporary taint of treason, Gaine re-established himself after the war as one of the most prominent printers in the city and became for a time president of the Typographical Society of New-York. His *New-York Gazette; and the Weekly Mercury,* his almanacs, and his diaries of the revolutionary period continue to be regarded as major contributions to American literary history.[11]

Samuel Campbell, who maintained a bookseller's and stationer's shop at 124 Pearl Street and who printed *The Death of Abel* (1764), among other titles, owns the small distinction of being the first American bookseller to include in his catalogs the dates of publication of the books listed for sale (Shera 269). He also defrauded Noah Webster of regional royalties for the *Grammatical Institutes* by flooding the Hartford market and printing fifty thousand unauthorized copies at the last minute before his contract with Webster was due to expire. He was thus instrumental, in a negative way, in inspiring Webster's campaign for a federal copyright statute (Silver 1967, 107–09). In 1788, Campbell, Hugh Gaine, and Thomas Allen, another of Dobson's agents, became partners in a printing office and bookstore, although each man also "maintained a separate place of business in his individual name" (Hildeburn 148–50).

Archibald M'Lean, another of Dobson's New York representatives, was a highly respected printer in the city, according to the brief eulogy printed after his death on September 22, 1798, during the yellow fever epidemic of that year. "One of the editors and proprietors of the New-York Gazette and General Advertiser," he left to lament his passing, said that obituary (*Philadelphia Gazette,* September 25), "a disconsolate widow, and a numerous train of connections."

Archibald's brother John M'Lean began in business as a partner of Charles Webster, who moved to Albany and formed the firm of Webster and Skinner (Howell and Tenney 371–72) in 1783. For three years (1784–1787) M'Lean worked on his own, then, in 1788, entered into partnership with his brother. He left New York to supervise the *Norfolk and Portsmouth Journal* in Norfolk, Virginia, where he also served briefly as one of Dobson's subscription agents; he died in 1789 (Evans 22032; *One Hundred and Fifty Years of Printing* 61, item 178).

Dobson's final associate in New York, Robert Hodge, was also for a time one of Samuel Campbell's partners. Together they produced the patriotic *Self-Interpreting Bible* (1790–92), the allegorical frontispiece of which was designed by William Dunlap (Silver 1967, 155). Hodge also maintained a separate establishment at No. 11 Water-Street.

Among the eleven printers and booksellers "entrusted with Subscriptions" (as Dobson later put it) in Philadelphia, the closest to him personally was William Young. Young came to Philadelphia in 1784[12] and entered into a partnership with Peter Stewart and John McCulloch the next year. This association lasted until 1788, when each opened a separate printing office. Young's shop was located at "No. 52 Second Street, the corner of Chesnut-street" (*General Advertiser,* January 4, 1792). He published the *Universal Asylum and Columbian Magazine,* an important early literary journal founded in part by two of Dobson's other Philadelphia agents, Thomas Seddon and William Spotswood, and by one of Dobson's engravers, James Trenchard. He also owned and operated several paper mills in Delaware County, as well as the Delaware County Paper Warehouse on Bond Street in Philadelphia, for which one of his price lists for the year 1790 survives (Evans 48762). He sold the stock of his bookstore to William Woodhouse on October 8, 1801 (*Philadelphia Gazette,* October 19, 1801) in order to concentrate exclusively on the sale and manufacture of paper. On February 14, 1805, Young announced in the *United States Gazette* the transfer of ownership of both the Delaware Paper Mill Warehouse and the Whitehall Printing Office to William Bonnell and George Fulton of "No. 24 Chesnut Street, between Front and Second Streets."

Another of Dobson's subscription agents, Joseph Crukshank (spelled

"Cruikshank" in Dobson's proposals) is mentioned briefly in Isaiah Thomas's *History*. A Quaker printer who formed a brief partnership with Isaac Collins (Hixson 18–22), he printed on his own from 1770 to 1824. He was a partner with Morris Truman in a paper mill erected on Darby Creek in 1778 but sold out to Truman in 1785 (Gravell 1979, 207, item 178). His continued involvement in papermaking is evident from a letter written by Mathew Carey to the president of the Bank of Pennsylvania in 1794, in which Carey speaks of having bought $1500 worth of paper "from Crukshank within the last 15 months" (quoted in Green 30). Between 1791 and 1798, the years during which most of the volumes of the *Encyclopaedia* were being published, his shop was located at 87 Market Street (Brown and Brown 53: 387). He and his brother James were partners for a brief time and maintained a shop at 87 High Street (*Porcupine's Gazette*, September 4, 1797).

The partnership of Hall and Sellers, who are also listed as subscription agents in Philadelphia, is one of the most famous in the annals of printing in that city, largely because David Hall, the father of Dobson's agent (also named David), had been a partner of Benjamin Franklin. Extensive surviving records of this firm have enabled historians to learn a great deal about the business of early American printing. From their shop located at 149 Chestnut Street between 1791 and 1794 issued, among other titles, the *Pennsylvania Gazette*, a newspaper begun by Franklin in 1729 and continued without interruption until 1815. For unknown reasons, Dobson advertised sparingly in the pages of this familiar and established newspaper during his protracted campaign to sell the *Encyclopaedia*.

Both Francis Bailey and Robert Aitken, two more of Dobson's agents, were excellent craftsmen who ranked among the most respected of Philadelphia's printers, booksellers, and bookbinders. Bailey came to Philadelphia from Lancaster, Pennsylvania, and opened a shop on Market Street in 1778. The following year, he started the short-lived *United States Magazine* and, in 1781, the more successful *Freeman's Journal, or North American Intelligencer*, to which Philip Freneau was a regular contributor. In 1786, Bailey published Freneau's first volume of poems. He is generally credited with having coined the phrase "the Father of His Country" to describe George Washington. He returned to Lancaster in 1800 but came back to Philadelphia with his son Robert a few years later and set up shop on Crown Street (*One Hundred and Fifty Years of Printing*, 56, item 165; Brown and Brown 53: 223; Jackson 11–12).

Robert Aitken also turned out work of superior quality, though as a bookbinder rather than as a printer. Born in Paisley, Scotland, Aitken came to Philadelphia in 1769; he went back to Scotland to learn the craft of bookbinding before returning to Philadelphia to stay around 1774. Between 1775 and 1776, Aitken published the *Pennsylvania Magazine, or American Monthly Magazine* with Thomas Paine as editor and chief contributor. He was, according to Hannah Dustin French, "the only one of the Scottish binders known to have cast his lot with the Patriots" (3). In his shop on Front Street he published "the first complete English-language Bible . . . in the New World" (Hudak 548), which was officially endorsed by the Congress of the United States in 1782 (the so-called "Bible Congress" [Wroth 1951, 37]). An "excellent binder," according to Isaiah Thomas (2: 239), a "workman who added the grace of an artistic nature to a sure and learned craftsmanship" (Wroth 1938, 211–12), Aitken retired from the profession in 1801 and died July 15, 1802 (Silver 1967, 28–29). An advertisement for the sale of his shop on the corner of Laetitia Court and Black Horse Alley, listing thirty-four fonts of type (including one each of Greek and Hebrew) and "two excellent mahogany presses" (*Aurora*, January 21, 1801), provides valuable information about the contents of a typical American print shop at the end of the eighteenth century.

Much less information survives about several of Dobson's other Philadelphia agents. Robert Campbell, who in 1789 had a shop at No. 40 South Second Street, "Five Doors above Chesnut, opposite the [Thomas Dobson's] stone house," later moved to 53 Second Street, then to 54 South Second, and finally, in 1795, back to No. 40 South Second (Brown and Brown 53: 339). In 1797, Campbell printed Susannah Haswell Rowson's *Mentoria* (Evans 12345), and his advertisements for other titles appear with some regularity in Philadelphia newspapers. He has already been mentioned as perhaps the only bookseller in the city who sold both Dobson's *Encyclopaedia* and the third edition of the *Encyclopaedia Britannica,* announcing the arrival of the first volume of the British publication on April 6, 1789 (*Pennsylvania Packet*), less than a week after Dobson had issued his first proposals but more than six months after the volume was advertised for sale in the *Edinburgh Gazette.*

Another Philadelphian, Thomas Seddon, advertised as a "Bookseller and Stationer, in Market Street, near Front Street" (*Pennsylvania Packet,* April 8, 1790) and was one of four local printers and engravers who published the *Columbian Magazine* before it was bought out and renamed by William Young. William Spotswood, who was also part of the quartet of publishers and engravers behind the same magazine, once bid unsuccessfully to publish Jeremy Belknap's *Foresters* (Silver 1967, 98–99). His numerous advertisements indicate that he specialized in literature for children, although other titles are of course listed among his wares. In 1789–90, his shop was located on Front Street, between Market and Chestnut (Brown and Brown 54: 129).

For William Woodhouse, who also kept a shop on "Front-Street, near Chesnut-street" and, later, "near Market street, at the Bible and Crown," Isaiah Thomas had high praise (2: 238). Woodhouse died soon after the *Encyclopaedia* commenced publication, but his son of the same name carried on the family trade and eventually bought out William Young's bookselling establishment. William Pritchard, "Bookseller and Auctioneer," published Peter Markoe's tragedy *The Patriot Chief* in 1784 and teamed briefly with Peleg Hall to operate a shop "between Front and Second-Streets" about the time his name appeared on Dobson's list (Jackson 227). In 1797, he printed James Purves's *Observations on Doctor Priestley's Doctrine of Philosophical Necessity and Materialism* (Evans 32732) for sale exclusively at Dobson's bookstore.

The name Rice on Dobson's list probably refers to Henry and Patrick Rice, who shared with Dobson an interest in music publishing (which continued longer than his) and with whom Dobson collaborated on editions of Charles Brockden Brown's *Arthur Mervyn* and the first volume of *Edgar Huntley* (Parker 472). Their shop was on "south side Market Street, next door but one to Second Street" (*Pennsylvania Packet,* June 16, 1790). However, the name may also refer to James Rice and Company, whose satellite establishment in Baltimore was Dobson's agent in that city and whose bookstore was one of the most flourishing in Philadelphia.

Dobson's creation of a network of publishers, printers, booksellers, and other merchants to serve as subscription agents and distributors for the *Encyclopaedia* was not unprecedented in American publishing. In 1774, James Rivington had also used a farflung system of booksellers to market John Hawkesworth's account of Captain Cook's first voyage (Farren 97–98). Other printers, too, including publishers of magazines, established agents in cities distant from their own in attempts to address the broadest possible readership and minimize the problems of distribution, although they operated on a smaller scale than Rivington or Dobson. Dobson himself served as an agent for the *Medical Repository* (Smith 436–37) and subscribed for an additional fifty copies (Mitchill 14) which he sold to physicians in Philadelphia. In this system lay the promise of reaching a national audience on a regular basis and the roots of a national style of book production, but the fulfillment of that promise would have to await improvements in communication and methods of transportation.

The efforts of Dobson's agents, combined with responses to advertisements and proposals that Dobson placed in Philadelphia newspapers, resulted in 246 names on the subscription list with which he began to print the *Encyclopaedia* (Hopkinson 16)—hardly enough, it would appear, to begin a major project.[13] Yet this figure is misleading, for it is known that some subscribers ordered more than a single copy. George Washington, for example, ordered two sets because he wished to encourage the enterprise,[14] and there must also have been booksellers among the number who ordered multiple copies at a discount, perhaps as many as ten or twelve, for resale at their own shops. Isaac Beers of New Haven, whose name does not appear on any list of Dobson's designated agents but who assisted Dobson's sales campaign at a distance with advertisements designed to stimulate local sales of the *Encyclopaedia* (*Connecticut Journal,* April 13, 1791), may have been one of them. Dobson must also have been encouraged to number among his patrons not only the President of the United States but also the secretary of state, Thomas Jefferson,[15] and America's revered elder statesman Benjamin Franklin, who, with only a few months to live, subscribed on a weekly basis and sent the first numbers to Ezra Stiles with the famous statement of his religious creed in a letter dated March 9, 1790.[16] Such men were the principal audience at whom Dobson's advertisements had been aimed, the political *raison d'être* of the *Encyclopaedia*. Their signatures must have helped greatly to convince him that his project was possible, though success still only glimmered on the distant horizon. Events would justify his decision to begin publication, for he would soon be able to announce plans for an edition twice the size he had originally intended.

Notes

1. Thomas Dobson to Jedidiah Morse, May 20, 1802. Case 6, Box 2, American Prose, HSP; quoted by permission.

2. Arnand C. Chitnis, *The Scottish Enlightenment: A Social History* (London: Croom Helm, 1976), 38–39, briefly describes the subscription method of publication in Edinburgh.

3. The first sentence of the preface to the third edition of the *Britannica* leaves little doubt as to the political assumptions of its chief editor, the Rev. Dr. George Gleig, that literacy and learning are the province of those who maintain control over society. "The utility of science, and the delight which it affords the human mind, are acknowledged by every man who is not immersed in the grossest ignorance" [i]. The implications of Gleig's language and the root contradictions in which he becomes involved make his preface as intellectually challenging as the preface to the

Encyclopédie which Robert Darnton has so brilliantly analyzed in "Philosophers Trim the Tree of Knowledge: The Epistemological Strategy of the *Encyclopedia*," *The Great Cat Massacre and Other Episodes in French Cultural History* (New York: Basic Books, 1984), 191–211. With its alternate acceptance and rejection of Newtonian principles and Lockean psychology, Gleig's preface struggles to resist the implications of what Lewis P. Simpson, writing of the relationship between politics and knowledge in the eighteenth century, has described as "the radical displacement of a transcendent reference for either natural or social order . . . by the subjectification or internalization of nature and history" ("The Ideology of Revolution," *The History of Southern Literature*, ed. Louis D. Rubin, Jr., et al. [Baton Rouge: Louisiana State University Press, 1985], 57).

4. "Utility ought to be the principal intention of every publication," the editors of the first edition of the *Encyclopaedia Britannica* declared in the first line of the Preface. "Wherever this intention does not plainly appear, neither the books nor the authors have the smallest claim to the approbation of mankind" (I, [i]). The editors of the second and third editions remained true to that vision.

5. For terms of the *Britannica,* see Paul Kruse, "The Story of the Encyclopaedia Britannica, 1768–1943," PhD diss., University of Chicago, 1958, 67–81.

6. City directories of Philadelphia for 1796 (Evans 31235), 1797 (Evans 32868), and 1800 (Evans 38549) contain tables showing the rate of exchange of Pennsylvania dollars into pounds sterling and into the currency of other states. These rates remained consistent through the middle and late years of the *Encyclopaedia.*

7. Among studies of North Carolina printing consulted for J. Campbell were George W. Paschal's *History of Printing in North Carolina, 1749–1946* (Raleigh, N.C.: Edwards & Broughton, 1946); Douglas C. McMurtrie, *Eighteenth-Century North Carolina Imprints, 1749–1800* (Chapel Hill: University of North Carolina Press, 1938); and Stephen B. Weeks, *The Press of North Carolina in the Eighteenth Century, with Biographical Sketches of Printers . . . and a Bibliography of Issues* (Brooklyn, N.Y.: Historical Printing Club, 1891).

8. Isaiah Thomas, *The History of Printing in America, with a Biography of Printers and an Account of Newspapers,* 2 vols. (Albany, N.Y.: Joel Munsell, 1874), 2: 7.

9. Dobson's shop seems proof enough of this preference. In January 1791, Benjamin Rush advised Jeremy Belknap that Dobson's was the best place in Philadelphia to display subscription papers (*Letters* 1: 573). He seems to have given the same advice to Elihu Hubbard Smith, who placed with Dobson twenty copies of the *Medical Repository* that Smith, Dr. Edward Miller, and Dr. Samuel Latham Mitchill were publishing. Dobson sold all twenty and ordered twenty more. See *The Diary of Elihu Hubbard Smith (1771–1798),* ed. James E. Cronin (Philadelphia: American Philosophical Society, 1973), *Memoirs of the American Philosophical Society,* vol. 95, 436–37.

10. See, for example, item 175, dated January 4, 1793, in the Account Books: "Encyclopaedia 1 Sett 8 Vol £18.15/Deduct 1/7 2.13. 6 1/2." Other entries indicate that this rate reflects a consistent discount, at least to Carey (Mathew Carey Papers, 1785–1859, Misc. Mss. Boxes C and Folio Volumes C, American Antiquarian Society, Worcester, Mass.; quoted by permission.

11. Alfred Lawrence Lorenz, *Hugh Gaine: A Colonial Printer-Editor's Odyssey to Loyalism* (Carbondale: Southern Illinois University Press, 1972); Hugh Gaine, *The Journals of Hugh Gaine, Printer,* ed. Paul Leicester Ford, 2 vols. (New York: Dodd, Mead, 1902). For "Hugh Gaine's Life" see *The Poems of Philip Freneau,* ed. Fred Lewis Pattee, 3 vols. (Princeton, N.J.: The University Library, 1903) 2: 201–14.

12. In his letter to Charles Poulsen (October 24, 1855), John McAllister dates Young's arrival in Philadelphia and, incidentally, helps to corroborate the date of Dobson's arrival as well. "My Father in Law, Mr. Young, arrived here, with his family, from Scotland June 27. 1784—I have always understood that he was here before Mr. Dobson came—but it would seem that Mr. D. was not long after him" (Box A.L.S. [McAllister], HSP.

13. For example, in the advertisement for *The Four Gospels* in the endpapers of his edition of Jedidiah Morse's *America* (1790), Dobson specified that "The work will be put to press as soon as 600 copies are subscribed for." *The Four Gospels* was not printed until 1796. For *Coke upon Littleton,* Dobson sought 500 subscriptions, which he did not get. It seems reasonable to infer from these instances that the 246 names subscribed for the *Encyclopaedia* amounted to considerably more than the same number of subscriptions.

14. For Washington's subscriptions, see David Edwin's testimony in William Dunlap, *History of the Rise and Progress of the Arts of Design in the United States,* 2 vols. (New York: George P. Scott, 1834) 2: 199, and George Washington, *The Writings of George Washington, from the Original Manuscript Sources, 1745–1799,* ed. John C. Fitzpatrick, The Bicentennial Edition, 39 vols., vol. 36: August 4, 1797–October 28, 1798 (Washington, D.C.: U.S. Government Printing Office, 1941), 11.

15. Thomas Jefferson, *The Papers of Thomas Jefferson,* ed. Julian P. Boyd et al., 24 vols. (Princeton, N.J.: Princeton University Press, 1950–), 14: 32–33.

16. "Letter to Ezra Stiles, March 9, 1790," in *Benjamin Franklin: Writings,* ed. J. A. Leo Lemay (New York: Library of America, 1984), 1178–80. Franklin told Stiles that he had arranged for numbers of the *Encyclopaedia* published after his death to be sent to Stiles for the library at Yale. However, the copy presently owned by the Beinecke Rare Book Room and Manuscript Library bears the signature of "Ja. [James] Hunter June 9 1797" (Paul C. Allen, Assistant to the Curator of Modern Books and Manuscripts, letter to the author, January 7, 1991).

3. A Progress Through the Press: The *Encyclopaedia*, Volumes I–IX

The first weekly number of Dobson's *Encyclopaedia* was issued on schedule on January 2, 1790, the second on January 9. No announcement of either of these installments appeared in the Philadelphia newspapers, but the third number was advertised in both the *Federal Gazette* and the *Pennsylvania Mercury* on January 16 and in the *Pennsylvania Packet* on January 20. Thereafter, notices of new weekly numbers appeared regularly in the *Federal Gazette* until May 11, when installment Number 20 was advertised with the promise that weekly numbers would continue to be published in the future. Only weekly Number 15 was advertised out of sequence, announced on April 19, 1790, after Numbers 16 (April 12) and 17 (April 17) had already been announced. Number 15 contains the second part of the article on America as edited and amended by Jedidiah Morse, and Morse's manuscript was probably overdue. Because each installment numbered exactly forty pages, however, and because several weeks remained before the first half volume would be completed and ready for the binder, Dobson could probably continue with the printing of weekly numbers subsequent to Number 15 without worrying about the sequence of pagination. If that is indeed what happened, the event proved unhappily prophetic, for Morse's tardiness later delayed the publication of the twentieth volume of the *Encyclopaedia* for nearly eighteen months.

Only the first ten weekly numbers of the *Encyclopaedia* were advertised in the *Pennsylvania Mercury* (January 16–March 4) and the *Pennsylvania Packet* (January 20–March 3), which led Charles Evans to conclude that after issuing the first four hundred pages (the first half volume) in weekly numbers, Dobson abandoned this costly and complicated method of publication (8: 128).[1] The additional ten announcements in the *Federal Gazette,* however, contradict Evans's conclusion and suggest that Dobson did indeed continue to publish weekly numbers until the first eighteen volumes had been completed, as he would have been obliged to do to keep faith with his subscribers on the installment plan. The disappearance of advertisements for weekly numbers is part of a pattern of promotion that includes the discontinuation of announcements for half volumes after the appearance of the second full volume. It signifies that Dobson wished to enroll no new subscribers on the weekly installment plan, not that he was no longer publishing weekly numbers.

Weekly numbers were advertised in the *Federal Gazette* as follows:

Number 3—January 16 and 20, 1790
Number 4—January 23
Number 5—January 30
Number 6—February 6 and 10
Number 7—February 13 and 17
Number 8—February 20 and 24
Number 9—February 27, March 3
Number 10—March 6 and 10
Number 11—March 13 and 17
Number 12—March 20
Number 13—March 27, April 3 and 5
Number 14—April 6, 7, 8, and 11
Number 15—April 19
Number 16—April 12 and 14
Number 17—April 17
Number 18—April 24
Number 19—April 28
Number 20—May 11

In both the *Pennsylvania Mercury* and the *Pennsylvania Packet,* the advertisement for weekly Number 10 did not announce the latest installment as such but instead as "Volume I, Part I," with "Ten Elegant *Copperplates.*" The advertisement in the *Federal Gazette* referred to the same installment simply as weekly Number 10 and did not mention copperplates. Moreover, even when Dobson advertised his last weekly number in the *Federal Gazette,* he did not follow the pattern he had established in the other two newspapers by announcing Volume II, Part II, or Volume I complete but identified the newest forty pages only as "No. XX." This small difference in advertising strategy suggests that Dobson intended all along to use different newspapers for different public notices—the *Mercury* and the *Packet* for weekly numbers until half volumes appeared, and the *Federal*

Gazette for weekly information until the first volume had been completed. The evidence of the advertisements suggests that the *Encyclopaedia* was presented to the American public following a coherent and comprehensive plan Dobson had worked out in advance.

Although weekly Number 20 was advertised on May 11, no official announcement of the completion of Volume I appeared in any Philadelphia newspaper until June 18 (*Pennsylvania Mercury*). Clearly, however, Dobson was ready to distribute copies of Volume I even before this date. On May 1, 1790, he presented a copy of the first volume and his promise of all the others in the set "in succession as they are published" to the Senate of the United States, seeking the senators' "patronage and encouragement in an undertaking of such magnitude and utility." Senator Robert Morris of Pennsylvania, at Dobson's request, read Dobson's brief letter on the floor of the Senate on May 5, placing "a volume of the work therein mentioned . . . on the table." (*U.S. Congress* 1: 1007) and thus leaving no doubt that the first volume was completed and available well before Dobson announced it to the general public.[2] Surviving receipts and other evidence establish that Dobson regularly allowed several weeks (in some cases, months) to elapse between the publication date of a given volume and the day he chose to notify the public.[3] Some of this time undoubtedly was allowed for pages to dry and for the binder to complete his work on sets subscribed for as half or full volumes, especially those (like Isaiah Thomas's)[4] that were to be gilt and bound in expensive Russian or Moroccan leather. Dobson may also have wished to insure that subscribers of long standing had every opportunity to receive their copies before he opened sales to new customers.

Dobson's weekly advertisements served much the same purpose as his earlier proposals, allowing him to modify and refine his marketing campaign and to provide progress reports on the *Encyclopaedia*. When he announced weekly Number 3 in the *Pennsylvania Mercury* on January 16, for example, he informed the public that work was proceeding as promised— surely a good sign for American industry—and emphasized the quality of the American craftsmanship that went into the production. "One number is published every week," he reported, "elegantly printed on superfine paper manufactured in Pennsylvania with a beautiful new type cast on purpose by Baine and Co., Philadelphia, and the copperplates engraved by Mr. Scott [sic] . . . in a stile [sic] which it is hoped will do no dishonour to the country." Perhaps he felt that he had praised Scot too faintheartedly on this occasion, for in an advertisement for weekly Number 10 (Volume I, Part I), he took pains to underscore the "Ten Elegant *Copperplates*, engraved by *Scott*" as equally important as John Baine's "beautiful Type" and the "Superfine Paper Manufactured in Pennsylvania" as focal points for American pride (*Pennsylvania Packet*, April 8, 1790; *Pennsylvania Mercury*, April 13, 1790). Since early American engravers had a reputation (often well deserved) for executing crude work (Weitenkampf 48–50), Dobson's use of the word "Elegant" in this advertisement, together with the availability in his shop of proof sheets of Scot's first illustrations, were important reassurances to prospective purchasers that their money would not be wasted on inferior workmanship.

In the advertisement for Volume I, Part I, Dobson also disclosed that the *Encyclopaedia* was now going forward "under the patronage of such a liberal Subscription, as makes it necessary to print double the Number originally intended"; the press run would be two thousand rather than one thousand copies. This was not a decision he could have made lightly, for paper was the single most expensive item involved in book production, and unnecessary copies would seriously cut into his margin of profit. In addition, he informed readers that the *Encyclopaedia* was now an American edition in fact as well as name, "enriched with various Improvements, by Gentlemen eminent in the respective Sciences in this Country." These "Improvements" add to the importance of the *Encyclopaedia* and internalize the patriotic themes upon which Dobson's proposals and advertisements also depend.

No firm evidence exists to show how many subscribers Dobson had secured by March 1790. His decision to double the impression this early in the publication process supports the inference that the 246 names on his original subscription list represented a considerably larger number of subscribed copies than the figures seem to indicate. The regular appearance of weekly numbers probably helped increase public confidence in the project, possibly resulting in a brief flurry of subscriptions between January and March. Most of those who have previously written about Dobson's *Encyclopaedia*, however, believe that Dobson did not reach even his first one thousand subscribers until after Volume VIII appeared in early 1793.[5] This belief apparently rests on Joseph Hopkinson's statement in the *Annual Discourse* (1810) that Dobson "printed two thousand copies" of the second and subsequent volumes but did not reprint Volume I until "after he had completed the eighth [volume]" (17), which has been taken to mean that Dobson had no *need* to print additional copies of Volume I before that time.

Hopkinson's remarks, however, may be interpreted differently. Dobson may have had no *time* to reprint the first volume until the pace of new subscriptions slowed and he was able to return to backlogged work. This conjecture gains some support from a letter Dobson wrote to Isaac Wayne, the son of General Anthony Wayne, in 1802, outlining the background of the late general's subscription and requesting payment for volumes delivered to the estate. Wayne originally subscribed, Dobson said, in April of 1792, at which time he received the second, third, fourth, and fifth volumes in exchange for a payment of $25.00—according to the "Conditions of Subscription," payment for four volumes and one volume in advance. Dobson did not forward the first volume until April of 1796, when he included it in a shipment with ten other volumes (VI–XV) printed since the date of Wayne's subscription.[6] Apparently in April 1792, Dobson did not have any spare copies of Volume I; otherwise, he would have delivered that volume to General Wayne at the time, along with Volumes II–V. Together with Hopkinson's statement and Dobson's declaration in the advertisement for Volume I, Part I, this evidence suggests that Dobson was close to having attained one thousand subscribers as early as March 1790 and that he surpassed that number before April 1792.

After deciding to double the number of impressions, Dobson picked up the pace of advertising. In addition to newspaper advertisements, subscription sheets, and a volume of the *Encyclopaedia* to display, he now employed another medium of advertisement. Sometime before he finished the second part of Volume I and probably almost immediately upon completing the first part, he printed as a separate title the long article on America, now subdivided into two books of twelve brief chapters each. This publication enabled those who still had doubts about the quality and content of the American edition to purchase a sample of the *Encyclopaedia* without the commitment of a subscription. Dobson would shortly do the same with articles on anatomy, astronomy, chemistry, and others.

Reprinting articles from the *Encyclopaedia* not only helped promote the larger publication but also offered additional income with minimal effort, since little work or expense was required to transform long articles into books. In the case of *America* in particular, Dobson's planning paid off handsomely, for the book went through three more editions (1795, 1798, and 1808) and apparently sold well in all three.[7] In the endpapers of the first edition of *America,* moreover, Dobson included a version of the original conditions of subscription and a progress report on the *Encyclopaedia*. The announcement that the first volume of the *Encyclopaedia* would be ready for subscribers sometime in May establishes the publication date of *America* as the early spring of 1790. "Subscriptions are still received by Thomas Dobson," this inserted advertisement ended, "and by all others entrusted with proposals."

Dobson's advertisement that the first whole volume of the *Encyclopaedia* had been completed (*Pennsylvania Packet,* June 18, 1790) also noted that the second volume was "considerably advanced" but told little else of consequence. Dobson advertised Part I of Volume II in the *Pennsylvania Mercury* (over a date of October 7, 1790) in the issue dated October 9. The second part of Volume II followed shortly thereafter, announced in the same newspaper (over a date of February 16, 1791) on February 19. Dobson had also finished the text of Volume III, the notice said, but publication was being held up because the copperplates were not completed. The fourth volume was "going forward."

Although some of the nineteen copperplates in Volume III contain more than one illustration and are correlated with more than one article, the plates themselves provide no clues to the engravers' delay. Perhaps the reason was that Volume II, which contained fifty-nine plates (the title page says sixty, but plate 85, "The Northern Hemisphere with the Figures of the Constellations," is missing from the article on "Astronomy"), was so time-consuming. Executing a large number of plates could easily have resulted in a backlog of work for Scot and his apprentice Samuel Allardice, who along with James Thackara and John Vallance had by now joined Scot in engraving for the *Encyclopaedia*. Production would soon reach such a pace that Ebenezer Hazard, who in 1791 tried to find someone in Philadelphia to engrave a map for Jeremy Belknap, admitted defeat and reported to Belknap with more than a trace of exasperation that he could not find any "good engraver who is disengaged. Dobson keeps them hard at work, and I cannot get them to say what they *suppose* such a plate will cost" (quoted in Silver 1967, 153).

"The third volume is now delivered to the public," Dobson declared in an advertisement in the *Pennsylvania Mercury* on May 3, 1791 (internally dated May 2), "and above half the fourth volume is printed off, and the copperplates in great forwardness." Just as he had recently discontinued announcing weekly numbers of the *Encyclopaedia,* he now stopped advertising half volumes and did not do so again until the final volume. In the meantime, he reported that the *Encyclopaedia* was going forward as projected. "The subscription is now nearly filled up," he said, and he thanked the "generous public for its unexampled liberality." Such strong support for so important a project, he declared, not only "encourages useful enterprises" in general but also reflects "the highest honor on the patrons of science and American manufactures." Patron and printer were equally to be congratulated for a project so useful and in every way worthy of the youthful, exuberant spirit of the new nation.

Although Dobson no longer announced half volumes, it is possible to speculate on some dates of publication on the basis of surviving receipts. Thus, for example, Volume IV was not announced in the *Pennsylvania Mercury* until September 17, 1791 (over a date of September 16),[8] but as early as July 4, Jasper Yeates had received his copy of the seventh half volume and paid in advance for the eighth;[9] this information establishes at least an outside date for Part I of Volume IV. The advertisement for the whole of Volume IV advised would-be subscribers that time was rapidly running out. "Such Gentlemen as wish to possess this valuable work," Dobson says for the second but certainly not the last time during the publication of the *Encyclopaedia*, "will please apply without delay, to prevent their being disappointed, as the subscription is now nearly filled up." He enjoined present subscribers, again not for the final time, to pick up and pay for the volumes they had ordered. The failure of some subscribers to keep faith with the terms of their subscription was on the verge of becoming a major problem for Dobson and the *Encyclopaedia*, though it did not yet threaten the project or the publisher.

In March 1792, one of Dobson's main outlets, the *Pennsylvania Mercury*, ceased publication, forcing him to seek another newspaper for his advertisements, for Volume V was very near its completion. Indeed, if Dobson was holding to his schedule, as there is every reason to believe he was, the fifth volume may have been completed as early as February or even January, and Daniel Humphreys, the printer of the *Mercury*, might already have had final copy of Dobson's advertisement in his hands when he decided to stop publication on March 1. That seems the most plausible explanation of why Dobson's advertisement for Volume V, which appeared in *Dunlap's Daily Advertiser* on Saturday, March 10, 1792, was both the briefest and the least circulated advertisement that Dobson issued during the entire run of the *Encyclopaedia*, almost as though it were an afterthought. It appeared only one more time in Dunlap's newspaper (March 14) and nowhere else in any other Philadelphia publication. It is easy to miss this advertisement in Dunlap's cramped and crowded pages, especially after becoming accustomed to Dobson's usual quarter-column or half-column spreads. Besides the obligatory information about the contents of the volume, alphabetically arranged from the British prospectus, this brief advertisement only repeated the price of each volume, which had not increased since the original proposals, and reminded would-be purchasers that sets would not be broken. The *Encyclopaedia* could be "Furnished to Subscribers only."

With the *Pennsylvania Mercury* out of business, Dobson turned most frequently to Andrew Brown's *Federal Gazette* and John Ward Fenno's *Gazette of the United States* to advertise the publication of volumes after Volume V. However, the news that Volume VI had been completed first appeared in Benjamin Franklin Bache's *General Advertiser* (July 20, 1792), one day before Brown's and Fenno's newspapers ran the advertisement. Thereafter, it appeared regularly in both *Gazette*s for several months, but not again in Bache's paper. In this advertisement, Dobson predicted that subscriptions would be "closed by Christmas," and he announced the first increase in prices, an additional ten dollars for subscribers who enrolled after September 1, 1792. He again addressed those troublesome patrons who had not yet picked up or paid for their volumes. "The very great expense attending the undertaking," he said, made it necessary to return to a strict adherence to the original policy of requiring payment on delivery. After September 1, anyone who had not picked up the volumes that had been ordered would be subject to the new ten-dollar surcharge. The informal coalition of printer and patron was beginning to show signs of strain.

In the notice for Volume VII, published in the *Federal Gazette* on January 17 and in the *Gazette of the United States* six days later (over a date of January 13), Dobson mentioned for the first time that the *Encyclopaedia* would run to eighteen volumes instead of the fifteen that he had been predicting since 1789. For those who had adhered to the conditions of subscription, the price would remain the same, two and two-thirds dollars per half volume and five dollars for a whole volume in boards. Dobson slightly altered the wording of his warning that the subscription was about to close, but otherwise there was nothing noteworthy in this advertisement.

The same cannot be said, however, of the advertisement for Volume VIII, which was first published in the *Federal Gazette* on April 5, 1793. Dobson's problems with unclaimed volumes had continued to mount, and he felt compelled to abandon momentarily his public identity as a selfless, patriotic printer and to appeal directly to his recalcitrant subscribers, describing his financial situation with some urgency. He had a good deal of money at stake in the enterprise and had experienced some financial inconveniences, so much so that the *Encyclopaedia* may have been in danger of foundering:

As several gentlemen who have honored this undertaking with early subscriptions, have only received a small part of the work, they are earnestly requested to complete their sets, as soon as published, immediately, while the publisher still has it in his power to supply them with the parts which have not been furnished. As the subscription will very possibly be closed by the first of July, next, the publisher cannot undertake to complete sets after that period, and those who wish to become possessors of this truly valuable and important work, will please apply before the expiration of that time, that they may not be disappointed.

The very heavy expense necessarily incurred in carrying on this work, makes it indispensably requisite for the publisher to adhere more strictly than he has to the original conditions, of delivering the volumes only on being paid for them.

Dobson had reached the lowest point in the history of the first nine volumes of the *Encyclopaedia*. The characteristic reticence of his public style makes it difficult to decipher his language so as to learn how precarious the situation was, but the concatenation of modifiers that admit of no alternatives—"earnestly," "immediately," "necessarily," "indispensably," and "strictly," among others—in conjunction with a host of adjectives, nouns, and verbs which bear a similar emotional burden conveys the message that the publication, and perhaps the publisher himself, was genuinely in jeopardy. Even so, Dobson was able to look forward to filling his subscriptions in July, and he had not entirely lost faith in the "several gentlemen" who had not yet honored their commitments. Perhaps he comforted himself with the belief that only one such notice would be required to correct the situation.

If so, he proved to be mistaken, for monetary concerns continued to plague him. They surfaced again in his advertisement for Volume IX, initially in the form of a broad hint that the cost of subscribing was likely to increase after "the first day of September next." The advertisement appeared in the *Pennsylvania Gazette* on June 15, 1793, so potential subscribers had more than two months to take advantage of the original cost per volume and half volume, plus the ten-dollar surcharge tacked on as of September 1, 1792. Again Dobson felt the need to admonish tardy customers:

Those who have subscribed, and got only a small part of the work, are requested to complete their setts, as far as published, as soon as possible, as after the first of next September, by which time the Tenth Volume is expected to be ready, the Publisher will not consider himself bound to make up those setts which are not completed up to that period.

To this he added only a brief reminder of a policy he was trying desperately to reinstate and enforce: "No part of the work will be delivered unless paid for."

More about the publication of Volume IX, the halfway point in Dobson's enterprise, may be found in a letter from Dobson to Jasper Yeates in Lancaster, Pennsylvania on April 12, 1793. "In the Encyclopaedia," Dobson explained, "I am now come to the article *Lancaster*."[10] He wondered whether Yeates knew someone who might write a brief article about the town to counterbalance the British entry (he finally received such an article, late, and inserted it out of alphabetical order at the end of the volume). The article on the English Lancaster appears in Part 2 of Volume IX, so that Dobson had certainly completed the printing of Part 1 before April 12. Moreover, since the entry on Lancaster comes near the end of the second part, he must have been much closer to finishing the volume than the official June date would indicate.

Despite deepening financial problems, publication of the *Encyclopaedia* was proceeding ahead of schedule. In two and a half years Dobson had produced nine volumes of the work, an average of one every three and a half months—far better than the five months per volume he projected in his proposals. But a dramatic change was about to occur, and the tenth volume he confidently predicted would be ready by September 1 was not officially announced until December 11. The completion of Volume IX of the *Encyclopaedia* marks a change in fortune for the publisher from which, there is reason to believe, he took a long time to recover.

Notes

1. One commentator who has followed Evans in making this mistake is Lawrence C. Wroth in *The Colonial Printer* (Portland, Me.: Southworth-Anthoensen, 1938), 294.

2. Dobson also presented editions of the *Encyclopaedia* to the American Philosophical Society and, on December 16, 1790, to the Senate of Pennsylvania; see Thomas Dobson, Petition for Permission to Present to the Senate of Pennsylvania the *Encyclopaedia*, Library Company Collection, HSP.

3. A receipt made out to the Whig Society, for example, records payment for "the Seventeenth, Eighteenth & Nineteenth half volumes" on April 15, 1793, although Volume IX (the eighteenth half volume) was not officially announced until June 12, 1793 (*Pennsylvania Gazette*). Another receipt to the Reverend Mr. Robert Blackwell for the "19.20.21.22.23.24.25th half volumes" means that Blackwell received the second half volume of Volume XII and paid for one half volume in advance (as required by the terms of subscription) on August 27, 1794, although the earliest advertisement for Volume XII did not appear until November 5. Sometime late in 1797, Dobson also received payment from the Reverend Mr. Blackwell for "the 35 & 36th half volumes"—that is, for the final volume of the first eighteen—even though no public notice for the first half volume of Volume XVIII appeared before January 9, 1798; indeed, Dobson did not file for copyright of that

half volume until January 4 (*Porcupine's Gazette*). Another receipt establishes that the jurist Jasper Yeates received the same final two half volumes on December 12, 1797. Finally, Dobson declared unequivocally in his letter to Isaac Wayne that the first eighteen volumes of the *Encyclopaedia* were completed "in April 1798" as opposed to the first official notice of May 19 in *Porcupine's Gazette*. These receipts may be supplemented by Mathew Carey's Account Books, which regularly show him receiving and paying for volumes of the *Encyclopaedia* in advance of their official publication. The evidence seems conclusive that the advertised dates for volumes of the *Encyclopaedia* are approximate rather than actual and that Dobson did not notify the general public of the arrival of each volume until a time convenient for him. See Thomas Dobson, receipt to the Whig Society, Hobart Papers of the Archives of the Episcopal Church, Austin, Texas; receipt to Robert Blackwell, Wallace Papers, vol. 4, pp. 57 and 63, HSP; receipt to Jasper Yeates, Society Collection, HSP; Dobson to Isaac Wayne, Esq., February 16, 1802, Special Collections, Van Pelt Library, University of Pennsylvania.

The Account Books of Mathew Carey at the American Antiquarian Society reveal that on January 4, 1793, Carey paid Dobson £18.15 for the first eight volumes of the *Encyclopaedia*, although Volume VIII was not officially available until April 5; Carey received a set of seven volumes on December 6, 1792, although Volume VII did not officially appear until January 17, 1793 (Carey Account Books, vol. 1, items 175, 178). These are only a few of the many entries in Carey's ledgers that help establish a regular and consistent pattern of subscription and trade distribution of new volumes of the *Encyclopaedia* in advance of notification of the general public.

4. Isaiah Thomas's expensive copy of the *Encyclopaedia* is at the American Antiquarian Society, Worcester, Mass.

5. This is the opinion of Tebbel, *History of Book Publishing*, 1: 116; Judy L. Larson, "Dobson's *Encyclopaedia*: A Precedent in American Engraving," in *The American Illustrated Book in the Nineteenth Century*, ed. Gerald W. R. Ward (Winterthur, Del.: Henry Francis duPont Winterthur Museum, 1987), 24; and Ellis Paxton Oberholtzer, *The Literary History of Philadelphia* (Philadelphia: George W. Jacobs, 1907), 224.

6. Thomas Dobson to Isaac Wayne, Esq., February 16, 1802, Special Collections, Van Pelt Library, University of Pennsylvania. General Wayne was in Philadelphia in April 1792, having just lost his seat in the House of Representatives (March 16) as the representative from Georgia's First District to a challenge from his former friend and the former representative General James Jackson. On April 12, 1792, Wayne received word from secretary of war Henry Knox that he had been appointed to command the American army in the Northwest Territory. See Paul David Nelson, *Anthony Wayne: Soldier of the Early Republic* (Bloomington: Indiana University Press, 1985), 219–23.

7. The three subsequent editions of Morse's *History of America*, all published by Dobson, are identified in Evans (29111 and 34147) and Ralph R. Shaw and Richard H. Shoemaker's *American Imprints* (New York: Scarecrow Press, 1958–[65]), item 15654.

8. A belated advertisement for this volume appeared as well in Benjamin

Franklin Bache's *General Advertiser* on December 12, 1791 (over a date of September 24), one of the few advertisements Dobson placed in Bache's newspaper.

9. Thomas Dobson, receipt to Jasper Yeates, July 4, 1791, Society Collection, HSP.

10. Thomas Dobson to Jasper Yeates, April 12, 1793, Stauffer Collection, vol. 31, p. 2478, HSP.

4. Losses, Crosses, and Vexations: The *Encyclopaedia*, Volumes X–XVIII

Fire was a fact of life in every early American city. Philadelphia was better prepared than most to deal with such disasters but still suffered its share of major conflagrations, while minor fires erupted almost every night.[1] The blaze that broke out early Sunday morning, September 8, 1793, soon grew into a major fire, consuming several outbuildings belonging to the tallow chandler Andrew Kennedy before spreading to the shop of Thomas Dobson. Detected around 3:30, the flames left devastation in their wake despite the best efforts of local citizens to bring them under control. The next day, the *General Advertiser* provided all the known details:

Two buildings, the property of Mr. Kennedy, together with the works & improvements, which he has of late been at very great expense in erecting, were entirely consumed. The fire proceeded from thence (consuming in its way two small frames, the property of Mr. Flickwir) to the printing offices of Mr. THOMAS DOBSON, which were nearly destroyed, with printing materials to a large amount. We cannot form a just calculation of the whole loss, but, by the best information we can at present collect, suppose that Mr. Dobson and Mr. Kennedy, together, are sufferers to the amount of at least £2,000.

The *General Advertiser* went on to report the deaths of two people killed when a brick wall collapsed during the blaze, a young man named William Cooper and the nine-year-old daughter of William Richardson. Another girl, the daughter of Roger Flahavan, was seriously injured as well, but "hopes are entertained of her recovery." Apparently Benjamin Franklin Bache, the republican editor of the *General Advertiser,* had not heard another part of the story, for he failed to mention the heroic role played by French sailors and officers from the frigate *Le Preciouse* and the India ship *La Ville de Orient* then anchored in Philadelphia's harbor. John Dunlap first reported that story in his *Daily Advertiser* (September 9, 1793), but it was left to John Ward Fenno, somewhat oddly given his federalist sympathies, to tell it in detail.

Like Bache and Dunlap, Fenno praised the spirited efforts of the citizens of Philadelphia to fight the fire on their own. Owing to the "confined situation" of the conflagration, however, their efforts would have been in vain. "All the back buildings of Mr. Kennedy, and several others and their contents . . . [were] entirely consumed," wrote Fenno. "Mr. Dobson's office [was] nearly in the same situation" (*Gazette of the United States,* September 11, 1793). Then the French sailors arrived:

They brought their engine with them, and by means of the hose, conveyed the water through the smoke and flames to the very spot where the fire raged. Mr. Dobson is particularly indebted to these intrepid sons of Neptune for the preservation of his dwelling house—as it was extremely difficult and entirely impossible in some directions to bring a large city engine in immediate contact with the fire. . . . The loss of Mr. Dobson is heavy, as he had a very large amount of types, *& c.* exposed and destroyed.

Already on Monday, September 9, Thomas Dobson had expressed his gratitude to all who fought the fire. The "friendly zeal" of his neighbors, he said in the *Philadelphia Gazette,* had "forcibly impressed his heart with sentiments of gratitude," which he trusted would never be eradicated. As for the French seamen, he would long remember, he assured them, their "indefatigable activity in the cause of humanity." Still, his losses had been great. Two thousand pounds—more than $5,300—was a substantial sum, and the greater portion of it, as Fenno's comments appear to indicate, probably fell to Dobson. Subscribers must have expected that work on the *Encyclopaedia* would be suspended for a long time, if not, indeed, entirely given up.

But Dobson was back in business before the month was out. The key figure in his quick recovery, according to Dobson himself, was Mathew Carey. On September 18, Dobson explained the situation in a special advertisement in the *Gazette of the United States,* which he addressed "To the Subscribers for the *Encyclopaedia*":

Thomas Dobson begs leave to return his grateful acknowledgments for the liberal support and encouragement he has received. He takes the earliest opportunity of informing them [the subscribers], that notwithstanding the loss he has sustained, by having his Printing-Office burnt down in the dreadful fire last Sunday morning, so much of his property has been preserved, that with the assistance of a New fount of Type he has, purchased which Mr. [Mathew] Carey had just imported for his own use, and with a spirit which does honor to his benevolence, consented to part with, the printing of the Encyclopaedia will be re-commenced in about one week; and he hopes to show his Sense of the Public Favor, by the continued Regularity of Publication.

If Dobson was close to meeting his prediction in the advertisement for Volume IX that the next volume of the *Encyclopaedia* would be ready for general distribution around the first of September, the fire of September 8 may well have destroyed more than types and printing equipment. It may have burned almost an entire impression, two thousand copies, of Volume X, although there is no way of knowing the layout of the printing office in relation to the bookstore or the number of copies that were printed and stored in Dobson's shop. If the copies were not destroyed, however, it is hard to understand why Volume X did not appear until December 11, 1793 (*Gazette of the United States*), for even supposing that Dobson could not resume printing until early October, based on past performances he should have been so close to completing Volume X when the fire struck that little time would have been required to finish it. Nor is there any evidence that Volume X was completed six or eight weeks before the general announcement, as was Dobson's custom with other volumes. The minutes of the American Philosophical Society, for example, record the receipt of only "Vols. VI, VII, VIII, and IX" on December 6, 1793 (*Early Proceedings* 216), indicating that Dobson had not completed Volume X even then or perhaps that the ink was still drying. Otherwise, the volume would have been included in his donation.

The advertisement for Volume X is of interest for several reasons. First, it contains an allusion to yet another natural catastrophe, the yellow fever epidemic of 1793, which undoubtedly played a part in slowing the production schedule of the *Encyclopaedia* and contributed to the rapid spread of the fire in September. Many citizens who might ordinarily have manned pumps and filled buckets in the early autumn of 1793 had sought safety in the country or the suburbs. Dobson acknowledged their continuing absence in a separate paragraph appended to his advertisement, noting that "a number of families are still in the country" and enjoining those who had returned to "call or send for their volumes." Because he did not know who had returned, this seemed the best way to insure that the new volume was distributed to all subscribers.

The advertisement for Volume X also contains a reference to the fire of the previous autumn, for Dobson found it necessary to explain that certain items were missing from the volume. The book "makes its appearance in an imperfect state," he wrote, because the fire of September 8 had destroyed "a great quantity of his printing materials," among them "the Figures, with which he was printing the Tables of Logarithms." These "were melted down by the violence of the fire" and, unlike the commonly stocked Long Primer oldstyle he had been able to buy from Mathew Carey, had to be reordered and recast, a tedious and time-consuming process. To maintain any semblance of a schedule, therefore, he had been forced to bring out Volume X without the tables, but he promised to include them as a separate insert in Volume XI, "which is now in considerable forwardness."

Historically intriguing though they are, the allusions to the epidemic and the fire of September 8 are not the principal sources of interest in the advertisement for Volume X. They are surpassed by Dobson's emphasis on money, which would henceforward be one of the major themes—indeed, *the* major theme—of advertisements for the *Encyclopaedia*. Trying to be both firm and diplomatic, Dobson found himself forced by circumstances to "take . . . the liberty" (as he put it),

of representing to such subscribers as are in arrears, the indispensable necessity of punctuality, both in picking up the volumes as soon as possible after publication, and of paying for them when taken. Many of his subscribers having got only one, two, three, *&c.* volumes, and several volumes remain UNPAID. That the work hangs in all its different stages of commencement and though the importance of a few dollars may be but a trifle to the individuals, yet the accumulation of these trifles UNPAID lays the publisher under very serious embarrassments, and deprives him of the use of some Thousands of Dollars which at this time would be of very essential service. For these reasons the Publisher finds himself under the necessity of recurring to the original terms of publication, and in future no volumes will be delivered but only to those who take and pay to [sic] the time of publication.

The statement that the "work hangs in all its different stages of commencement" is Dobson's most complete description of the *Encyclopaedia* while it was still in the process of publication. Many volumes and half volumes had undoubtedly been bound; others lay in sheets about the shop, and the printer was understandably unwilling to incur further expenses of preparation and publication for an unreliable clientele. Storage alone must have been a major problem, and every volume still uncalled for represented a dead loss to the publisher. Dobson's awkward, stilted, and syntactically convoluted language seems an apt metaphor for his own embarrassed situation, avoiding a full disclosure of how badly off he may really have been at the moment and attempting to preserve a respectful tone and to remind subscribers of the importance to the nation's pride of the project upon which both the printer and the purchaser had embarked. The emphasis on "very essential service" seems to suggest that the *Encyclopaedia* itself may have been at risk, for by their tardiness some of his subscribers were depriving him of cash to reinvest to keep the publication moving. Dobson would be compelled to repeat this plea in many advertisements still to come, though he never again elaborated on his own financial condition at such length.

The announcement that the eleventh volume of the *Encyclopaedia* was completed appeared in the *Gazette of the United States and Evening Advertiser* on April 26, 1794 (over a date of April 22). Dobson's first order of business in that advertisement was to assure subscribers that the volume contained the logarithmic tables missing from Volume X. Then he reminded anyone who might still be thinking about subscribing that an increase of ten dollars had taken effect on September 1, 1793—he had forgotten to include this information in the advertisement for Volume X— and emphasized that the new price applied also to subscribers who were in arrears as of the effective date of the increase. The price would again go up by ten dollars on July 1, he reported, although this increase would not be tacked on as a surcharge to current subscribers who had failed to keep their accounts in good standing. But for the sake of the entire undertaking, he earnestly entreated dilatory patrons to appear and claim their volumes, for as time passed and new subscribers entered orders that included volumes already printed, he was finding it increasingly difficult to withhold books from sale. "The publisher," he stated emphatically for the third or fourth time, "does not hold himself bound to make up any setts after the first of July next."

As was his custom, Dobson also provided a progress report on the volume then in production. Volume XII, he said, was "in some forwardness," which according to his formula seems to indicate that it was not very far along. Although a receipt made out to Robert Blackwell indicates that Volume XII was finished as early as August 27, Dobson did not announce completion until November 3 (*Gazette of the United States*), making this the first volume since the fire to be so long in officially arriving. From then on, such six-month intervals would become the rule rather than the exception. The only volume after Volume XII to be completed in the same time that Dobson regularly required for each of the first nine volumes would be Volume XIV (four months between announcements); the public would have to wait nearly nine months between Volumes XIV and XV and longer still for the final volume of the *Encyclopaedia*. Whether a scarcity of funds, pressing new projects, or other reasons were to blame, Dobson, who had announced four volumes in a single year (1793), would barely manage two a year from this point until the end.

The advertisement for Volume XII set a new condition for subscribers, the payment of a $20 surcharge plus the price of one volume in advance.

Evidently Dobson was still trying to recoup his losses from the fire and re-establish the *Encyclopaedia* on a firm financial footing. Although nominally the cost of an individual volume remained the same, $2.66 per half volume and $5 for a whole volume, the surcharge in effect amounted to an increase of $1.11 per volume for previously unenrolled subscribers. The advertisement for Volume XII was the briefest since the announcement of Volume V and contained little besides the news of the surcharge and the familiar refrain that subscribers should pick up and pay for their sets "as expeditiously as possible, or otherwise it will be impossible to complete them at all." There was no information about Volume XIII, but Dobson announced that he would close subscriptions on the first of January 1795.

This time he kept his word. When the thirteenth volume of the *Encyclopaedia* was advertised in the *Gazette of the United States* on April 10, 1795, Dobson confirmed that "the subscriptions for this valuable work" had been closed "sometime ago." Nevertheless, although it was no longer possible to subscribe to the *Encyclopaedia,* for anyone with enough ready money who wanted to buy the book, this posed no real problem. "The Publisher has still a few sets on hand on sale at 110 dollars the set," Dobson reported. The increase to $110 since the proposals had established the cost per volume at $5 reflected the $20 surcharge and represented an overall increase of better than 20 percent in five years.

To take advantage of Dobson's offer on the few remaining sets, a purchaser was required to put down the entire $110, which would have bought the thirteen volumes already completed "and the remaining five volumes . . . when published." Thus any additional sales would have generated an immediate cash flow, which Dobson appears sorely to have needed to compensate for the shortfall caused by defaulting subscribers. Predictably, the advertisement for Volume XIII ended with the usual plea to those subscribers to pick up and pay for volumes they had not yet received and a repetition of the familiar warning that any who failed to do so soon would be subject to additional charges. Both refrains gained added urgency from Dobson's admission that "the lying out of so much money is a serious injury to the publisher," an uncharacteristic disclosure of personal finances that must have been painful to make.

The advertisement for Volume XIII concluded with the information that the next volume was "in considerable forwardness"—that is, well advanced. Thus it would be only four instead of six months before the *Gazette of the United States* carried the announcement of Volume XIV (August 8, 1795, over a date of August 4). This advertisement, as usual, "very particularly" requested subscribers to "take away and pay for the volumes now ready" and offered interested but unsubscribed readers the entire set on terms identical to those presented in the advertisement for Volume XIII. The wording was slightly changed, perhaps to clarify the intent of the earlier advertisement. The cost remained $110 per set of eighteen volumes, but now Dobson was explicit in requiring "the whole money to be paid on delivery of the volumes now ready, and the remainder of the work to be furnished to the order of the purchaser when ready, without further charge." He added that the price of $110 would hold for three more months, after which another increase of $10 would take effect.

The advertisement for Volume XIV began with a declaration that the fifteenth volume was "in the press, and considerably advanced," Dobson's formulaic way of saying that it was nearly finished. Subscribers who remembered his announcement must have wondered, therefore, as the months rolled by and Volume XV did not appear, whether financial problems had at last become unmanageable and overwhelmed the publisher of the *Encyclopaedia* in unpaid obligations. A full nine months elapsed before Dobson officially announced the arrival of a new volume in David Claypoole's *American Daily Advertiser* on April 30, 1796 (over a date of April 26), and the advertisement offered neither explanation nor any acknowledgment of the long delay.

There was, however, much other business to report, including the new provision that subscribers of long standing who had not yet completed their sets would be subject to an additional charge of one dollar per volume on the first fifteen volumes if they did not appear on or before "the first day of September 1796" and pay for all the volumes they had ordered. Dobson had also kept his promise to increase the total price to any heretofore unsubscribed purchasers, so that now all eighteen volumes would cost $120, cash on the line. These terms would continue "until the first day of September next, unless the copies are all disposed of before that time." That final afterthought, surely a permissible ploy for a printer under considerable financial pressure, reflected wishful thinking rather than the actual state of sales and subscriptions, for Dobson was not close to selling all copies of the *Encyclopaedia* and indeed never would do so.

Why was the fifteenth volume so long in coming? Since none of the major articles in the volume was rewritten, it was not because Dobson had been held up by a missing manuscript, as he had most probably been with weekly Number 15 and would be again with the second volume of the *Supplement*. Perhaps other projects claimed a greater share of his attention.

He had good reason to feel disenchanted with the supporters of the *Encyclopaedia* and must have needed money to continue the enterprise. In 1795 he undertook a major ten-volume series of Andrew Duncan's *Medical Commentaries* from 1780 to 1794 (Evans 29057–62), as well as a second edition of Jedidiah Morse's *History of America* (Evans 29111), to all appearances a money-making book.[2] The next year he brought out a new edition of *The Wealth of Nations* (Evans 31196) and the fourth volume of Benjamin Rush's *Medical Inquiries and Observations* (Evans 31144), two titles he probably counted on to earn a reasonable profit. Besides indispensable revenue, these books offered at least temporary respite from the *Encyclopaedia* and its attendant woes.[3]

Whatever the causes for the delay, the fifteenth volume was to prove the most problematical in the *Encyclopaedia;* only the second volume of the *Supplement* would rival it, for entirely different reasons. The nature of the difficulty is indicated by a brief, separately paged essay appended to the volume "by the *particular desire,*" Dobson tells us in a headnote, "of the Society called Quakers." Entitled "A Vindication of the Character of George Fox," the appendix was inspired by a sketch of Fox included as part of the article "Quaker" in "the Encyclopaedia, Vol. XV. page 734." It was addressed to "*the Editor of the American Edition of the Encyclopaedia*" and took Dobson to task without naming him explicitly for reviving "*a stale, and, heretofore, fully refuted Calumny traducing the religious character of George Fox.*" The "Vindication" was written not only to clear Fox's character of base and baseless charges and to give readers a chance to judge the truth for themselves but also to provide the publisher of the *Encyclopaedia* an opportunity to recant and, by printing and inserting the essay at the end of the appropriate volume, "*disclaim any injurious Partiality [sic] having influenced him in the Republication of said Extract.*" The essay was signed "John Drinker, Clerk" of the Philadelphia Meeting for Sufferings and dated "15th 12 month 1796."[4]

The minutes of that December meeting of the Society of Friends and of several subsequent meetings at which Dobson and the entry under "Quaker" were items on the agenda tell the story behind the "Vindication." They begin *in medias res,* as it were, after a version of the Quakers' rebuttal had already been written:

An Essay being prepared as proper to be offered to the Editor of a new Edition of the Encyclopaedia lately published, reviving under letter Q a stale Abuse of the Character of George Fox, the same on being deliberately attended to is concurred with, directed to be signed on Behalf of this meeting by the Clerk, and a correct copy handed to said Editor; an account of his reception of it to be reported in course, to the care whereof the following Friends are appointed—Jas. Pemberton—Thos. Morris—Thos. Stewardson—with the Clerk.[5]

Clearly, this was not a minor matter. Many of the wealthy merchants of Philadelphia on whom Dobson depended for subscriptions belonged to the Society of Friends, as did many prominent politicians and even some scientists and physicians. Their goodwill was essential to the continuation of the *Encyclopaedia*. As was his custom, however, Dobson had simply reprinted the entry on "Quaker" as published by the editors of the Edinburgh edition without considering the different audience the American edition would have; very likely neither he nor his compositors read the essay with a critical eye, but only as a letter-by-letter project. Written by the opinionated and thoroughly Presbyterian Reverend Dr. George Gleig, who had taken over the editorship of the *Encyclopaedia Britannica* after the death of Colin Macfarquhar, the article describes Fox as "one of the most extravagant and absurd enthusiasts that ever lived," an unwitting and witless dupe "employed by certain deists to pave the way for their system of natural religion . . . (734)." The Quakers themselves were referred to as modern Druids fortunately rescued from their foolish worship of nature by the sound common sense of men such as George Keith, William Penn, and Robert Barclay. Although the article covered five full pages (733–738) and had some favorable things to say about Quakers, particularly in regard to their stand against slavery, Dobson's inattention to editorial detail might still have sunk the *Encyclopaedia* even at this late date had it occasioned a major loss of subscribers.

That it did not do so and that the damage was contained as effectively as it appears to have been were probably owing to the intercession of James Pemberton, who had already performed at least one favor for Thomas Dobson at the outset of the printer's career (see Chapter 1). Pemberton, one of the founders of the Philadelphia Meeting for the Sufferings in 1756, continued as an influential member until 1808 (DAB 16: 157). Despite John Drinker's signature on the document, it may have been Pemberton who actually authored the "Vindication," for polemical writing in defense of his religion was part of his background. (Could it have been his own *Apology for the People Called Quakers* [1756] that he had sent to Thomas Dobson in 1784?) If so, preparing the essay in advance of the actual meeting may be viewed as an ingenious tactic, for it gave the members a focus for their anger and an action to pursue, possibly forestalling more dramatic action such as boycotting the *Encyclopaedia* or canceling subscriptions. This is speculation, to be sure, but it is at least possible and perhaps even probable that James Pemberton deserves some credit for saving the *Encyclopaedia*.

The membership was not finished with the issue, however. At the January meeting on "19th 1 mo 1797," the Friends took up the matter once again. The committee charged with visiting Dobson and explaining the Quakers' point of view reported that Dobson had taken the matter under consideration and that a further interview had been scheduled. That interview took place, and on "16 2 mo" the committee reported that the publisher had agreed to print the society's essay in the next volume of the *Encyclopaedia*, although he would not bear the expense himself. The members of the Meeting then proposed some alterations and amendments to the essay (Cadbury Papers 311). Finally, on "15 6 mo 1797," a last and rather testy comment was entered in the minutes:

The Printer of the Work called the Encyclopaedia having inserted in his last Volume the Essay relative to the Attack on the religious Character of Geo. Fox, his demand therefore being £10.10. 7 1/2, the Treasurer is desired to pay if said printer persists in his demand. (Cadbury Papers 317)

The matter did not end there, though the June entry contains the last words directly concerned with Dobson. How deeply his unintentional affront had stung the Quaker community may be judged from a letter by the Philadelphia Meeting for Sufferings to the Friends in London on "19th of 1st mo 1798." Apparently motivated by news of the proposed British *Supplement* (which they mistakenly referred to as a second edition), they wrote to alert the London Yearly Meeting to the forthcoming publication and to call attention to the offensive remarks about George Fox that had already appeared in Volume XV. Their letter summarized the minutes of the January meeting and outlined their own course of action with Dobson, recommending a similar strategy if the London Yearly Meeting deemed it appropriate. "Some time ago a Book called the Encyclopaedia was published in this City," the letter began,

which being likely to have an extensive circulation, and in which was given a very false character of George Fox, Friends here thought it right to apply to the Editor and to point out the gross misrepresentation, upon which he agreed to insert such refutation for the calumnies as we should draw up, in consequence of which an Essay for the purpose was prepared and was printed and bound up in one of the Volumes . . . and as we are informed that the false account was taken from a Scotch

Edition of a similar Book of which a 2d Edition is said to be contemplated we submit to your consideration the propriety of your endeavouring to have the error confuted in the like way. (Cadbury Papers 326)[6]

Even as the Quaker controversy moved towards its conclusion, work continued on the *Encyclopaedia*. The first advertisement for Volume XVI appeared in Andrew Brown's *Philadelphia Gazette* on November 24, 1796 (over a date of November 23), some seven months after the initial announcement of the troubled fifteenth volume. It was a small advertisement consisting of only two brief paragraphs, the first outlining the contents of the volume as Dobson customarily did in his advertisements, the second restating the familiar terms of purchase. "Those who have got part of the work and not completed it up to the present volume," Dobson wrote for perhaps the eighth or ninth time, "are earnestly solicited to take the volumes and pay for them before the . . . end of the year."

Dobson did not specify why the end of the year was important, but when the advertisement for Volume XVII appeared in *Porcupine's Gazette* on June 1, 1797, it stated that the price of an eighteen volume set in boards was now $125 instead of the recent $120. "The price will soon be raised" again, the advertisement concluded.

As if to make amends for the brevity of his previous announcement, Dobson added several paragraphs to the advertisement for Volume XVII. Nearing the end of his enterprise, he grew positively garrulous (for him, at least), combining a bit of almost nostalgic reminiscence with some reflections on his own disappointment upon discovering that not all of the "gentlemen" on whose "patronage and encouragement" he had depended were equally honorable or trustworthy. He reserved some of the blame for himself for being too trusting and naive, expensive habits that no successful businessman could afford to cultivate. His thoughts on the events that had occurred and the lessons he had learned while bringing out the *Encyclopaedia* amount to a summary *postmortem* on one of the most important projects in early American publishing history. "By the original conditions of publication," Dobson recollected,

no part of the work was to be delivered without being paid on delivery; and the price of one volume was always to be paid in advance, that the publisher might be enabled to carry forward a work of such extent and expense.

A confidence, however, in many of those who patronized the undertaking has occasionally led to remissness in that particular. Several volumes have been delivered to subscribers without payment having been regularly made, and of many sets a number remain in the hands of the publisher; and though the amount of a few volumes, unpaid, may seem, and really is, but a small matter to the individual, yet a thousand such amounts form an aggregate of very important and serious inconvenience to the publisher, who is therefore under the necessity of recurring to the original terms of publication. No volume, therefore, will be furnished, on any account, unless the price is paid.

After so long a preamble, Dobson's conclusion sounds a trifle weak, especially since he had said the same thing as long ago as the advertisement for Volume VIII in April 1793. Moreover, even after announcing his disillusionment in this manner, he still did not follow his own provisions to the letter, for in April 1798, he forwarded the final three volumes of the *Encyclopaedia* to General Anthony Wayne's estate even though the general had been dead for several years and the general's son had evidently not requested the books. Dobson admitted that the *Encyclopaedia* was a special project for him, involving an unusual bond of trust between publisher and subscriber, and that, taken in by his own patriotic propaganda, he had allowed his feelings to interfere with his judgment. Mistakes generate a momentum of their own, of course. Once he had suspended the rules to please one or another important patron, he found that he would have to keep on suspending them despite accumulating evidence that such leniency put the *Encyclopaedia* in jeopardy. It may well be, however, that only such flexibility could have kept the necessary number of subscribers on the rolls, holding out the promise of payment sometime in the future and thus enabling Dobson to continue the project until its completion.

That Dobson's payment policies, inconsistently applied, could create confusion becomes evident in the correspondence of his most famous customer, George Washington. On August 14, 1797, only recently retired to Mount Vernon, Washington requested his agent Clement Biddle in Philadelphia to find out from Dobson whether any volumes of the *Encyclopaedia* had been published since the fall of 1796. "The 16th is the last I received," he told Biddle. He had given away one of the two sets for which he had subscribed, and he now asked Biddle to pass on his instructions for binding the other set (36: 11).

Washington had cause to be concerned, for Volume XVII had been available to the general public for two and a half months and to subscribers for even longer. Yet Dobson had not sent on the general's copies, and the reason could only be that he had at last decided to enforce his policy of payment in advance for each successive volume. Washington seems to have been operating on different assumptions, which Dobson's practices if not his stated policies encouraged, and thus had not, apparently, sent payment for Volume XVII when he received the sixteenth volume. "Request Mr. Dobson to have all that are published, neatly bound and sent to me, except the *last Vole,* which may be retained as a sample to bind the remainder by," Washington wrote to Biddle on September 6, 1797. "I do not recollect, but suppose the receipts will show, whether he has been paid for *both* sets I subscribed for, or only one; be that as it may, he shall be satisfied on the delivery" (36: 27). Money had clearly been one of the topics of discussion between Dobson and Biddle, but Washington continued to expect shipment of at least one copy of Volume XVII before making payment.

This stalemate continued for several months. On January 29, 1798 (after the first part of Volume XVIII had been printed and copyrighted), Washington wrote again to Biddle about the missing final volumes of the *Encyclopaedia.* "As Mr. Dobson's bill is not exhibited," he explained, "I am unapprised of what is charged in it, or of what is coming from him." He repeated his earlier instructions about retaining the final volume as a model for binding all the others, but he still seemed to misunderstand Dobson's terms. As soon as all the published volumes but the last were sent to him, he said, Dobson would receive the cost "without delay" (36: 146).

In fairness to Dobson, it must be admitted that Washington's directions to Biddle, passed on always at second hand, it would appear, were sometimes contradictory and confusing. Washington was always careful about money, moreover, and may have been playing his own game on this occasion. Thus on March 3, 1798, he communicated again with Biddle, this time directing that his own set of the *Encyclopaedia* should be "bound in gilt calf" (36: 178) and reiterating his intention not to pay Dobson until the book had been put into Biddle's hands and the account forwarded in appropriate fashion. Given Washington's status, this was an impossible situation for the publisher, and he seems to have capitulated at last. On March 19, 1798, too early for the second part of Volume XVIII to have been completed, Washington briefly notified Biddle that he now approved of all arrangements and expected to receive the final volumes of the *Encyclopaedia* "accompanied by Mr. Dobson's account of cost" on the next packet from Philadelphia (36: 188). By July 29, he still had not received them (36: 373). This one delinquent delivery had stretched into a saga, but the story at last concluded, somewhat anticlimactically, on August 13, approximately five months after the first eighteen volumes were completed, with Washington's note to Biddle that the books had finally arrived and were "in good order" (36: 411).

With the end of the *Encyclopaedia* at last on the horizon, Dobson returned to a technique of advertising he had not employed since the completion of the second volume, announcing each part of Volume XVIII instead of waiting until the entire book was finished. His advertisement for Volume XVIII, Part 1 (*Porcupine's Gazette,* January 9, 1798, over a date of January 6) contained the information, as required by law, that on January 4 he had filed a claim of copyright with Samuel Caldwell, clerk of the District of Pennsylvania.[7] The second part, the advertisement said, was "in great forwardness" and would "speedily be finished." For sets that were still on hand, Dobson had dropped his price back to $120, but he advised any interested purchasers that "if any copies remain unsold, when the work is completed, the price will be one hundred and thirty-five dollars per set, in boards." And there was further elaboration of the familiar problem with subscribers, with Dobson complaining that many sets of "from two to ten or twelve volumes remain in the publisher's hands, unpaid for." Such customers were counseled that, "unless these volumes are taken and paid for, they [the subscribers] cannot have their sets completed without paying, in all, one hundred and twenty dollars for the set" regardless of what the price had been at the time of enrollment. Books, it seems, even useful ones like the *Encyclopaedia,* were a luxury a subscriber could still deny himself when money became a problem. Unfortunately, it is not known how many of those who subscribed in 1789 did not fulfill their part of the contractual bargain.

Although Dobson had promised that the second part of Volume XVIII would be finished speedily, subscribers had to wait longer between the seventeenth and eighteenth volumes than for any other volume in the entire *Encyclopaedia,* Volume X included. More than eleven months elapsed between the appearance of Volume XVII (June 1, 1797) and the official completion of Volume XVIII on May 19, 1798 (*Porcupine's Gazette;* according to Dobson's letter to Isaac Wayne, Volume XVIII had actually been completed sometime in April). Nor was any explanation offered for the inordinate delay in closing out this part of the project. The final advertisement appeared without flourish or fanfare, as if the *Encyclopaedia* were just another publication and not the result of nine years of dedicated labor. "The Edition is nearly sold out," Dobson commented almost laconically, offering remaining sets of "18 *volumes, complete*" for a variety of prices: "$135 in boards; $162 in sheep; $180 in calf; $189 in calf, gilt; and $207 for either red Russia or Morocco, gilt." Perhaps he was too preoccupied with planning for the *Supplement* to do much celebrating. At any rate, it was not until he published his proposals for a continuation of the *Encyclopaedia* that he admitted to any sense of accomplishment upon having finished the first eighteen volumes, identifying himself in the prospectus for the *Supplement* as the same printer who had just "happily completed the *American Edition* of the *Encyclopaedia*" (*Porcupine's Gazette,* December 15, 1798). Were it not for the adverb, no one would ever have suspected how he felt.

But Dobson's work was not entirely over. He had still to enter the entire eighteen volumes for copyright protection, for example. This he did on June 22, 1798 (Goff, "First Decade," 102–03). Also, according to the original terms of subscription, he was obligated to provide subscribers with a frontispiece, a title page for each volume, and a dedication. With this last item the *Britannica* could be of no use as a model, for it was dedicated to King George III and spoke of knowledge as though it were an imperial prerogative, dependent on the King's support and the fate of British armies in the raging war with France. Dobson wrote a different dedication, setting aside for the moment his own disappointments and forgetting the disillusioning breaches of faith that had made the publication of the *Encyclopaedia* a greater trial than it had to be. In a final display of the faith in which the enterprise had been founded, Dobson inscribed the eighteen volumes of the American *Encyclopaedia* with an understated eloquence unmatched by any of his other public utterances.

TO THE Patrons of the Arts and Sciences; the promoters of useful and ornamental Literature in the United States of America, whose communications have enriched this extensive and important work; and by whose generous encouragement this arduous enterprise has been brought to its completion; *The American Edition of the Encyclopaedia* is Dedicated, with the most grateful respect, by their much obliged servant, *THOMAS DOBSON.*

The first eighteen volumes of the *Encyclopaedia* were reviewed in Charles Brockden Brown's *Monthly Magazine, and American Review* in 1799 (1: 134–35), probably by Brown himself. The reviewer took note of Dobson's intention to "lay before the public an account of recent improvements . . . in a supplementary volume" (135) and congratulated the publisher for what he had already accomplished. "The magnitude of the work far exceeds any thing ever before issued from the press in the United States," he declared, and the public was deeply in Dobson's debt for the "great labour, expense, and hazard" (135) which he had incurred to bring it to conclusion. "We sincerely hope that the circulation of it, while it affords a liberal compensation to the publisher, and encourages similar attempts in the future, may be the means of diffusing a taste for scientific and literary pursuits among the people of America" (135). Then Brown presented his prose version of the elaborate emblematic frontispiece of the *Encyclopaedia*. He cast Dobson in the role of the Archangel Michael and the reader of the *Encyclopaedia* as Adam in a scene adapted from Book XI of *Paradise Lost* that provides some indication of how deeply the *Encyclopaedia* was embedded in the popular ideology of American progress and how entirely science had displaced religion in the eighteenth century as the locus of faith in the restoration of the original condition of paradise:

The Encyclopaedist conducts his reader to a lofty eminence, from which he is enabled to descry the boundless prospect that stretches before him; he points out to his view the accumulated labours, experience, and wisdom of ages; he assists him to survey the history of the human mind in its progress from rudeness to refinement, and to teach him to anticipate the glorious destiny which awaits the full developement [sic] and exertion of intellectual energy in a more enlightened age. (135)

Brown conceded that many mistakes, unnecessary repetitions, "and even culpable omissions" (135) plague the *Encyclopaedia,* but he attributed these to the great number of writers and the diversity of talents necessarily employed in so compendious a work. He especially praised the plan of organization, which provides the reader with a clear picture of the "relation which the various objects of knowledge bear to one another" in mutual "dependency and subserviency" (135)—metaphors that stress the political implications of the encyclopedic form. Those who live at great distances from large libraries will have special reason to thank Dobson, Brown's review concluded, for even if no encyclopedia can possibly treat topics with sufficient minuteness to satisfy the specialist or talented amateur, Dobson's edition nevertheless provides enough information to "serve as an index" (135) to other, more specific sources.

Despite Dobson's claim in the advertisement for the eighteenth volume that the *Encyclopaedia* was "nearly sold out," this was far from being true. The firm of Thomas and Judah Dobson listed encyclopedias for sale when it went out of business (*Catalogue* 1822, 8) and Judah Dobson still advertised copies the year of his father's death (*Catalogue* 1823, 14). But the main reason for discounting Dobson's statement is that he continued to conduct vigorous postpublication sales campaigns even before the *Supplement,* which gave him a different reason for resuming advertisements, had been added to the other volumes. Between 1798 and 1800, when Volumes XIX, XX, and XXI became part of the package, three such campaigns were undertaken. The first commenced in mid-December 1798, the second in

March 1799, and the third in December 1800 (extending into January 1801). In each campaign, advertisements ran for at least a month in selected Philadelphia newspapers, and each campaign offered potential purchasers different financial arrangements.

The first advertisement of the first campaign appeared in the *Gazette of the United States* on December 15, 1798. It simply offered for sale a "work . . . now completed in eighteen large quarto volumes" for the same amounts up front as had appeared in the announcement for the second part of the eighteenth volume: $135 in boards, $162 neatly bound in sheep leather, and so on up to Russian or Moroccan leather at $207. This advertisement was accompanied by the first notice of Dobson's intention to publish a *Supplement*.

Apparently, Dobson did not have many takers for his offer, perhaps because few people could afford to put down the total price at once. At any rate, he seems to have felt that this was a problem, and in March 1799 he tried another approach, offering the *Encyclopaedia* on installments through a modified plan of subscription. This time there were only two conditions:

I. A Volume in boards will be delivered to each subscriber in the first week of every month, till the whole be delivered, which will take a period of 18 months.
II. Every subscriber on receiving the first Volume, to pay

	20 *dollars*
On receiving the second	15
the third	12
the fourth	10
the fifth	10
the sixth	8

and five Dollars for each of the succeeding Volumes till the whole be delivered, which will amount in the whole to One Hundred and Thirty-Five Dollars, being the present price for complete setts.

Any subscriber who may choose to have the whole in a shorter time than eighteen months, may have any number of Volumes that may be agreeable at the same time at the above prices.

To prevent any misunderstanding it is proper to express that no Volume will be delivered to any person without the money; and as the Setts on hand are few in number, it will be requisite that such as choose to become Subscribers should apply as early as possible to prevent disappointment.

The Complete Setts may be had as above, or bound in various manners. (*Gazette of the United States,* March 7, 1799)

Although much of the content of this advertisement is familiar, including the usual line about the small number of remaining sets, the pricing strategy seems original with Dobson, and quite ingenious. Whether or how well it worked is, of course, impossible to determine without access to sales records, but the fact that Dobson later tried a modification of it for his third promotional campaign suggests that he was satisfied with the results. The third time, however, he tailored his arrangements to make it even easier for would-be subscribers to find the necessary money at their own convenience. By the time he initiated the third campaign in December 1800, he was well into work on the *Supplement,* and he knew that any new subscriber now was one more potential purchaser for the additional three volumes. Moreover, every day that passed dated the information in the original eighteen volumes, which must soon force him to reduce prices, especially in the case of competition. Thus any accommodation he could make now and still receive full price would be worth the additional wait for his money. Accordingly, his new conditions allowed subscribers to receive one new volume every three months, paying "Seven Dollars and a Half for every Volume in boards, payable on delivery" (*Gazette of the United States,* December 6, 1800). The total price would still be $135; as before, subscribers had the option of paying in advance for as many volumes as they could afford. This plan, Dobson said, would remain open until January 15, 1801, but on January 19 he reinserted the same advertisement and ran it for an additional week (January 24). He still had many copies of the *Encyclopaedia* to sell.

The road from Volume IX to Volume XVIII of the *Encyclopaedia* had been long and difficult for Dobson, requiring two years more than were needed to bring out the first nine volumes. The period had begun with a devastating fire and witnessed an increasing number of defaulting subscribers and a controversy with the local Quaker community that undoubtedly damaged sales despite its eventual resolution. Moreover, according to Dobson's former apprentices George and David Bruce, another fire may have ended the second half of the enterprise in the same unfortunate fashion in which it had begun. Although Philadelphia's newspapers fail to report any such occurrence, an omission difficult to explain considering that stories about fires in Boston, Charleston, and Salem, among other places, appeared in the same papers during the same period of time, the brothers Bruce recalled that they left Philadelphia in favor of New York in 1798 because of an outbreak of yellow fever and "the destruction of the Dobson plant by fire" (*DAB* 3: 181). If this is true, it would have driven Dobson toward an increasing dependence upon other printers in the city, dictating a turn to publishing instead of printing at least until he had had an opportunity to rebuild. With or without the fire, however, he had probably already made the decision to turn to Henry Budd and Archibald Bartram as printers of the final three volumes of the *Encyclopaedia*.

Notes

1. For fires in Philadelphia during the late eighteenth century, see *Moreau de St. Mery's American Journey [1793–1798]*, trans. and ed. Anna M. Roberts and Kenneth Roberts (Garden City, N.Y.: Doubleday, 1947), 330–31; see also Russell Blaine Nye, *The Cultural Life of the New Nation, 1776–1830* (New York: Harper & Row, 1960), 125.

2. Dobson's issuing four editions of *America* attests to the popularity of the book. Mathew Carey's Account Books (American Antiquarian Society) include many orders for multiple copies of the work: eight copies on May 27, 1805 (vol. 19, item 8465); twenty copies on May 7, 1807 (vol. 21, items 883–884); six copies in January, 1808; eighteen copies on May 4, 1808; twelve copies on August 2, 1808 (vol. 23, item 1601); six copies on February 27, 1810 (vol. 23, item 1442); and twenty-four copies on November 22, 1810 (vol. 24, item 1965).

3. Dobson may also have been slowed by a problem with the engravings. The total of forty-one plates puts Volume XV third among the individual volumes of the *Encyclopaedia*, behind Volumes II and XVIII (each with fifty-nine illustrations), and both of those volumes were delayed because of the illustrations. Nine engravers worked on plates for Volume XV in an erratic pattern that suggests a good deal of subcontracting; one engraver, Joseph Bowes, was entirely new to the enterprise. His contribution of a single engraving, together with several other small and scattered assignments in the same volume, suggests that not only Ebenezer Hazard but also Dobson was finding it difficult to locate engravers who could be counted on to meet a deadline.

4. George C. Groce and David H. Wallace, *The New-York Historical Society's Dictionary of Artists in America, 1564–1860* (New Haven, Conn.: Yale University Press, 1957), lists John Drinker as a miniaturist, portrait painter, and drawing master active in Philadelphia in the late 1780s and through the early 1800s.

5. Quaker Collection, Cadbury Papers, MS 950, Haverford College Library, Haverford, Pennsylvania; quoted by permission.

In the *Federal Gazette* on January 24, 1792, one Thomas Morris advertised his services as a house carpenter. Two men of that name, a brewer ("86 North Second Street") and a wood sawyer ("south, between fifth and sixth street"), are listed in the *Philadelphia Directory* for 1797.

The name of Thomas Stewardson, merchant, may be found in many newspaper advertisements. His residence is listed in the *Philadelphia Directory* for 1797 as "35, north second street" (174).

6. The dismay caused by Dobson's reprinting of a long discredited version of George Fox's life had yet another consequence. Not content with refuting calumnies after the fact, the Meeting for Sufferings voted at the same session during which the membership drafted its letter to London to approve proposals by the Quaker printer Isaac Collins to issue "a Journal or historical account of the life [of] . . . George Fox" (Bristol 10267). Collins's biographer, Richard F. Hixson, attributes

this publication largely to the commercial success of Collins's publication of Job Scott's *Journal* (165–66), and that may well have been the economic motive. But it seems unlikely that Collins would have obtained or even tried to obtain his required one thousand subscribers to begin printing had it not been for the recent and highly publicized problem with the representation of George Fox in the *Encyclopaedia*. As evidence of the notoriety Dobson's mistake had attained, consider the entry in William Dunlap's *Diary* on August 27, 1798: "Read several articles in ye Enc: particularly Quaker" (2: 333). Dunlap often reports reading in the *Encyclopaedia*, but this is the only occasion on which his remarks indicate a special motive other than a personal or professional interest in what the article may contain (for example, on August 24, 1797, he read the article on "Grafting" to help him with his own fruit trees [2: 138]).

Before Collins's edition of Fox's journal could appear, the local Quaker community found itself on the defensive once again, this time because of an American edition of Johann Lorenz von Mosheim's *Ecclesiatical History,* which again was highly unfavorable to the Quaker religion and which had been cited in the offensive article that Dobson reprinted. Once more, John Drinker (if it truly was he) picked up his pen, drawing on his earlier "Vindication" to produce *A Vindication of the Religious Society Called Quakers: Addressed to the Editors of the American Edition of Mosheim's 'Ecclesiastical History'* in 1799 (Evans 37475).

7. One provision of the first federal copyright act required the claimant "to exhibit his certificate of copyright by advertising it in one or more newspapers for four weeks within two months of registration." Another required that "within six months of publication he should deposit a copy of the work with the Secretary of State." See Martin A. Roberts, "Records in the Copyright Office of the Library of Congress Deposited by the United States District Courts, 1790–1870," *Papers of the Bibliographical Society of America* 31 (1937): 84. These provisions mean that Dobson took no risk in distributing copies of Volume XVIII, Part 1, before he announced it officially in the newspapers or served notice of his filing for copyright, for he had undoubtedly already registered the book (see discussion of actual publication versus official announcement date in Chapter 3). Moreover, since the second part of Volume XVIII was to be officially announced as completed on May 19, 1798, Dobson knew that he would not miss the six-month deadline between his deposit of the title as completely published and his actual completion of the entire eighteen volumes. The book may have been finished and deposited in early April, even though copyright was not technically secured until June 22.

5. The Text of the American Edition: Jedidiah Morse and Other Contributors

The American *Encyclopaedia* differs in small but sometimes significant ways from the third edition of the *Encyclopaedia Britannica*. Although Dobson apparently did not plan for American additions at the outset of the enterprise, new material became a selling point of the publication in the advertisement for Volume I, Part 1, on April 8, 1790 (*Pennsylvania Packet*). This important advertisement announced not only that the size of the edition had been doubled but also that the *Encyclopaedia* had been and would continue to be "enriched by various Improvements, by Gentlemen eminent in the respective Sciences in this Country." Unfortunately, Dobson never specified who these authors were or what they had contributed (only one contributor, Jedidiah Morse, is known for certain).[1] He also left the reader to speculate on the nature and purposes of such improvements. His final statement on the subject in the Preface to the first eighteen volumes is as vague as his first, saying only that "some articles have been inserted, and many have been revised and important improvements made in them. . . . Through every volume," he continues, "useful though minute improvements have been introduced which contributed to the excellence of the work" ("Preface," xviii). Except for a general tendency to praise all things American whenever opportunity arises, there appears to be no clearly defined ideology governing these improvements and no policy determining which articles were to be changed. What was added or omitted often seems to be a matter of editorial prejudice or the almost accidental availability of new material.

Among the "minute improvements" that distinguish the American *Encyclopaedia* from the third edition of the *Encyclopaedia Britannica* Dobson undoubtedly counted such items as the brief addition to the entry under "President," which expanded the British text slightly to include a reference to the chief executive of the United States (14: 499). Several items were also added to the article entitled "Chronology," including the year 1787, when the General Convention met in Philadelphia "for the purpose of forming a new Constitution" (4: 775). Another new date, 1789, was memorable both because it marked the first meeting of the American Congress under the newly ratified Constitution and because it brought the storming of the Bastille and the first French constitution (4: 775), events still viewed by most Americans as encouraging to the cause of democracy when Volume IV was published in 1791. It is likely that Jedidiah Morse, who provided much other material for the *Encyclopaedia,* was the source of these and other similar emendations in the entry "Chronology."[2]

Although such items may have added to the timeliness and general appeal of the American *Encyclopaedia* in the short term, in the long run they expose the lack of a coherent editorial plan from entry to entry or volume to volume. After paying this attention to the new American government, for example, the *Encyclopaedia* fails to add anything to the *Britannica*'s brief and unsatisfactory entries under "Amendment," "Congress," "Constitution," or "Delegate." These terms had acquired new meanings as a result of recent events in American history and thus afforded Dobson a legitimate opportunity to make new contributions to knowledge and ideas while still serving the broadly nationalistic purposes of the American *Encyclopaedia.* But he did not seize the opportunity. With the *Federalist* at his disposal and, indeed, with all the Founding Fathers still alive, he passed up the chance not only to enhance his American offerings for contemporary readers but also to secure an audience among later generations of Americans, who, in the absence of some such special source of interest, would have little reason to consult his book once it had been superseded by a new encyclopedia. An article on the new American government by James Madison or Alexander Hamilton or even by a contemporary closely associated with them and familiar with their writings would have ensured the lasting value of the *Encyclopaedia.*

The partisan politics of the period may account for Dobson's failure to create a new entry for the Declaration of Independence, a document still too intimately identified with the controversial politics of Thomas Jefferson to be comfortably included. It had not yet become part of the political mythology of American ethnogenesis, one of the revered texts of the secular religion of democracy that Americans were to fashion out of filiopiety and sheer cultural necessity as the nineteenth century advanced and the Founding Fathers died off. Still, its absence creates an ideological void within the *Encyclopaedia* in which the British definition of "rebellion," for example, is allowed to stand unchallenged: "Subjects of the King, either in open war, or rebellion, are not the King's enemies, but traitors" (16: 28). This definition is technically correct, of course, but left without even an implicit rebuttal in the form of some account of the political instrument designed to legitimize the revolutionary struggle, it must have made disquieting reading for those who had pledged their lives, their fortunes, and their sacred honor to the cause of independence. Such an entry might also have provided the missing ideological focus for the *Encyclopaedia* as a whole.

The absence of American biography from the first eighteen volumes of the *Encyclopaedia* is another omission that seems especially blameworthy and is a further reflection of the culturally anomalous status of the United States during the Federal period. It illustrates continuing American diffidence in the face of and deference to both the supposed primacy of British history and the permanence of the encyclopedia as a privileged literary form to whose pages only exceptional characters may gain admittance, unlike the magazine or the newspaper. Such articles might have helped define an ideological center for the *Encyclopaedia* by celebrating American achievement instead of reflecting the values and reporting the accomplishments of the mother country. This is especially true because most if not all Americans deserving of an entry in the American *Encyclopaedia* would at this time have been associated with the revolutionary war. If, as S. H. Steinberg has written, "the history of encyclopaedias is an informative guide to . . . the development of political ideas and social conditions" in a nation (3), then the absence of men such as General Nathaniel Greene from Dobson's *Encyclopaedia* is a large part of its meaning, as well as an indication of how unplanned the American additions were. Greene, who died June 19, 1786, was almost immediately memorialized by an article in James Trenchard's *Columbian Magazine* (September–October, 1786), from which Dobson could have taken material for an entry. Even Benjamin Franklin, America's foremost citizen of the world, would have to await the *Supplement* for coverage.

According to Charles Evans's *American Bibliography,* one of the major differences between the texts of the British and the American editions of the *Encyclopaedia* is that two important articles in the natural sciences, "Anatomy" and "Chemistry," were entirely rewritten by American authorities (8: 28). When the essays in question in each edition are compared, however, this distinction vanishes. Except for a few inconsequential discrepancies in pagination between the two versions of the article, the texts are identical.[3] Perhaps Evans was misled by Dobson's having printed these articles separately (Evans 24206, *Anatomy,* and Evans 23817, *Chemistry*) as part of the promotional effort for the larger publication, as an attempt to make additional money on the edition by reprinting major articles as separate books, and as a way of making the latest scientific information conveniently available to those who might not wish to buy or be able to afford the entire *Encyclopaedia*. Evans's claim that Americans had achieved "a high standard of scholarship" (8: 28) even as early as the 1790s is flattering to national vanity, but it cannot be substantiated by the evidence of the *Encyclopaedia*.

Evans's belief in the American authorship of these and several other scientific articles also implies a close working relationship between Dobson and Philadelphia's scholars and scientists, as though they waited around Dobson's shop for the next installment of the *Encyclopaedia* to arrive from Edinburgh so they could read and correct it if necessary. Although they undoubtedly supported Dobson's venture with subscriptions and occasional suggestions, there is little evidence that any other relationship existed. As the Quaker controversy shows, Dobson was capable of reprinting damaging articles from the European edition, apparently in all innocence, that close, consistent, and professional editorial supervision would have caught.

Even scientific oddities slipped by. In the article on "Motion," for example, George Gleig expresses his opinion that the element of fire is responsible for the natural force of gravity. Gleig derived the idea from William Jones's *Essay on the First Principles of Natural Philosophy* (1762), who in turn derived it from John Hutchinson's *Moses Principia* (1724). It was rejected by Oxford University as Jones's M.A. thesis (Hughes 365–68) and was so entirely at variance with received opinion that any American scholar looking over the *Britannica* would certainly have caught it. That it appears intact in the *Encyclopaedia* constitutes negative evidence regarding the direct involvement of American men of science in Dobson's enterprise.

In one respect, however, the American *Encyclopaedia* did improve upon the scientific coverage of the third edition of the *Encyclopaedia Britannica,* and American scientists—most likely the mathematician and astronomer David Rittenhouse, a regular customer in Dobson's shop—would seem to be deserving of the credit, at least in a roundabout way.[4] Inserted into the article on astronomy on signature pages *dddd* through *nnnn* between $4C^2$ and 4D are forty pages of solar and lunar tables taken from Charles Mason, entitled *Mayer's Lunar Tables Improved by Charles Mason* (London, 1787).[5] Mason's *Tables* had been further *"revised and corrected,"* Dobson informed the public in a broadside advertisement designed especially to highlight this addition, *"by Gentlemen in this City eminent for their*

Abilities" (Evans 56169). Mason might lay some claim to at least symbolic American citizenship, for it was he and Jeremiah Dixon who surveyed the famous Mason-Dixon line between Maryland and Pennsylvania in the 1760s. After a stay of some years in England, he returned to the United States and died in Philadelphia in February 1787.[6] He was certainly known personally to Rittenhouse and other members of the American Philosophical Society and perhaps even to Dobson. The broadside advertisement for Volume III of the *Encyclopaedia* announcing the inclusion of Mayer and Mason's *Tables,* a coup of sorts in the cut-and-paste school of encyclopedia compilation, provides one of the few surviving pieces of evidence that some American scientists did indeed have a hand, although perhaps only indirectly, in determining the content of the American edition.

By far the most important contributor to the revised American *Encyclopaedia* was Jedidiah Morse, minister of the First Congregational Church in Charlestown, Massachusetts, and father of American geography. A staunch, even reactionary Federalist with a tendency to engage in public controversies, Morse shared with the Universalist Dobson a conservative social philosophy and, eventually, an unconcealed dread of foreign conspiracies against American democracy.[7] His *Geography Made Easy* (1784) had made him a celebrity when he passed through Philadelphia in November 1786, pausing on his way to assume temporary pastoral responsibilities in Midway, Georgia, to preach a sermon in the Reverend John Ewing's First Presbyterian Church and to outline to Benjamin Franklin his plans for a comprehensive American geography. Later, on his trip further south, Morse would dine with General Washington, an experience that left a permanent impression on him personally and politically. Dobson may have met Morse on this first visit to Philadelphia or perhaps not until Morse returned to that city on his way back to Connecticut in August 1787. Since the third edition had not yet been advertised in Scotland, this would have been too early for the publisher to approach Morse about a contribution for the *Encyclopaedia*. Nevertheless, geography was much on Morse's mind at the time, for he published an advertisement in Daniel Humphreys's *Pennsylvania Mercury* ("To the Friends of Science," August 7, 1787) soliciting assistance in assembling materials for a new geographical volume about America. That book, *American Geography* (Evans 21978), confirmed Morse's reputation as the foremost American geographer when it appeared in 1789, its publication planned to coincide with the inauguration of George Washington and Morse's own installation as pastor at Charlestown. On the strength of *American Geography,* Dobson invited Morse to look over and rewrite where necessary the all-important article on America for the new *Encyclopaedia* (Phillips 33).

Like "Anatomy" and "Chemistry," Morse's article was later subdivided into chapters and sold as a separate volume. Although Charles Evans has asserted that the piece was "entirely rewritten" (8: 28), Morse in fact contributed only about ten original pages (approximately thirteen thousand words), expanding the essay from nearly eighty pages in the British edition (538–617) to nearly ninety in the American version (538–626). The total number of new pages, however, tells only part of the story, for Morse also occasionally reduced the British coverage of a topic or event in the process of rewriting it from an American point of view. Although revised material accounts for only ten percent of the article, raising some questions about the appropriateness of crediting Morse with having written the entry or the book which grew out of it, many of his changes are substantial and contribute greatly to the American flavor of the *Encyclopaedia,* even if they are not sufficient to establish it unequivocally as an American book. If the first eighteen volumes of the *Encyclopaedia* may be said to reflect a coherent ideology, it is to be found in this essay.

The article on America is divided into two parts. The first concerns the natural history of America, with material on the American Indians, and the second highlights the main events of the American Revolution. The first part contains few revisions, one of which appears at the beginning of the article. From the first sentence in the British edition, Morse deleted a parenthetical reference to "*Americus Vesputius,* falsely said to be the first discoverer of the continent," an excision that looks forward to a later brief addition praising "Christopher Columbus, and . . . the illustrious navigators who inherited the spirit of enthusiasm of that great man" (541). Foregrounding the role of Columbus in this manner, slight as it is in this instance, is in keeping with the general sentiment of Americans of the period, who honored Columbus by naming settlements and cities after him and who, in such contemporary poems as Joel Barlow's *Vision of Columbus* (1787), idealized him as the mythic father of a race of explorers, pioneers, and empire builders. There were still many who felt that his name and not Amerigo Vespucci's should have been given to the new world.

After this emended preamble, "America" continues with several paragraphs about the nation's lakes, mountains, and rivers. This at first appears to be an original contribution by Morse, but the same information in the same words appears in the thirteenth paragraph of the British article. The only alteration Morse makes in this part of the text is to substitute for the British explanation his own rationale for the "excessive moisture" (539) of the American climate, citing the influence of the two great oceans that border the continent and dropping British references to the "luxuriance of [American] vegetation" and comparisons between European and Asian rivers and those in North and South America. Otherwise, Morse simply moves information in the British text to the beginning of his essay, subdivides a single paragraph into several briefer ones, and reorganizes the order of presentation. He also alters a few words and phrases along the way, exchanging "particularity" for "peculiarity" in the thirteenth paragraph, for instance (a compositor's error ?), but on the whole the natural history of America is the same in both the British and American texts.

Though Morse's most recent biographer cites "America" as evidence of Morse's early interest in American Indians (Phillips 199), that part of the essay, too, consists almost entirely of the words of the British author, who was probably James Tytler.[8] In all, Morse added to the discussion in the third edition only a few brief phrases disagreeing with Don Antonio Ulloa's opinion that the skins and skulls of the Indians are "thicker than the skins and skulls of many other nations of mankind" (543), a theory the author of the article in the *Britannica* accepted without question. Except for a few transpositions of phrasing and the substitution of words like although for though, however, the next six and a half pages are identical in the American edition and the *Britannica*.

Not until Morse reached the subject of the status of women among the American Indians did he offer a major interpolation into the British text. He agreed with the English author that the condition of Indian women in their own societies was "far from being so slavish as it appears" (548), but he went into far greater detail on the topic, explicitly taking issue with the geographer Dr. William Robertson and several other writers. "We do not mean," he wrote apologetically,

in this place, to engage in an inquiry concerning the comparative respectability and importance of the female character in the various stages of society and improvement; an inquiry . . . which has employed the pens of some of the most learned and eloquent writers of the present age, and concerning which there are still various, and very opposite, opinions. This, however, we think we may, confidently and safely, assert, that the condition of the women among many of the American tribes is as respectable and important as it was among the Germans, in the day of Tacitus, or as it is among many other nations, with whom we are acquainted, in a similar stage of improvement. (549)

For evidence to support this generalization, Morse drew upon the reflections of "the ingenious Mr. William Bartram" (549), appropriating and editorially altering several paragraphs from Bartram's "Observations on the Creek and Cherokee Indians, 1789." This work was not published until 1853; it was previously believed that only Benjamin Smith Barton, who referred to it briefly on page 46 of his *New Views of the Origin of the Tribes and Nations of America* in 1797 (Evans 31777), had seen it during Bartram's lifetime.[9] It is now clear that Bartram also sent a copy of the manuscript to Morse, probably in delayed response to Morse's request for information concerning the "Indians [of America], their tribes, language, numbers, characters, and disposition towards the United States" in the advertisement in the *Pennsylvania Mercury* in August 1787.[10] Morse profited from Bartram's generosity by making one of the few new contributions in "America" to knowledge about American Indians.

Morse took greater liberties with Bartram's "Observations" than he had thus far with the text of the British article. Without entirely misrepresenting Bartram's reflections, he inserted, altered, and deleted words to bring the naturalist into closer conformity with points he himself wished to make about the Indians' manners and customs. In the text below, omissions from Bartram have been italicized and Morse's interpolations into Bartram's prose are enclosed in brackets.

"Their business, or employment," says the ingenious Mr. William Bartram, "is chiefly in their houses *the house, as it is with other women,* except at [those seasons] *the season* when their crops [of maize, & c.] are growing, at which times they generally turn out with their husbands or parents; *,* but they are by no means compelled to do [this,] *such labor. There are not one-third* and one seldom sees a third as many females as males at work[,] in their plantations." "You may depend upon my assertion," (says the same gentleman, who had ample opportunities of studying the customs and manners of the southern Indians, of whom he is speaking, in this place) "that there are *is* no people[,] any where[,] who love their women more than these Indians do, or men of better understanding in distinguishing the merits of the opposite sex[,—] or [men] more faithful in rendering suitable compensation. They are courteous and polite to their women,—[and] gentle, tender, and fondling, even to an appearance of effeminacy[.], *to their offspring.* An Indian *never* [man seldom] attempts*, nay, he cannot* [to] use *towards* a woman, *amongst them any* [of any description, with] indelicacy *or indecency,* either of *in* action or of language."

"In the hunting season, that is, in Autumn *autumn and winter,* and in winter, [when] the men are generally out in the forests, *when* the whole care of the house or family devolves *falls* on the women; *, who are then* [at these times they are] obliged to undergo a great *good* deal of labour *labor* [and fatigue] such as cutting wood, [& c.] *cutting and bringing home the winter's wood, which they toat* [sic] *on their back and head a great distance, especially those of the ancient large towns, where the commons and old fields extend some miles to the woodland.* But this labour *labor* is in part alleviated by the assistance of the old men, who are past their hunting days, or who are no longer capable of serving in war *and no longer participate in the wars, who remain in the* *towns.*" But nothing more clearly shows the importance and respectability of these women among the Indians than this circumstance, that, among some of the tribes, they are permitted to preside in the council of their country: to this we may add, that several of the Florida nations have, at different times, been governed by the wisdom, and the prudence of female caciques. (549)

After these borrowings from Bartram, Morse inserted another new paragraph on the subject of the Indians' supposed practice of polygamy, then picked up and followed the British text again word for word for many pages. Not until he reached the British reference to "the ingenious Mr Jefferson" (556), which he altered to "our countryman Mr Jefferson," did he make even an adjustment in point of view.[11] The next dozen or so pages appear verbatim in both texts; indeed, Morse did not depart from his model again until he incorporated into his essay some details about Indian tumuli (570–71) from Benjamin Smith Barton's *Observations on Some Parts of Natural History* (1787). From there until the beginning of the second part of the article (five and a half pages), the history of the United States of America, Morse made only infrequent and minor changes in the text. What he added throughout the section is of far greater interest to textual critics and bibliographers than to ethnologists, naturalists, or cultural anthropologists.

The second part of the essay on America concerns the revolutionary war. In this section, as might be expected, Morse made more revisions and inserted more new material than he did in the first part. The changes began almost immediately, in the second paragraph under the British subheading "*AMERICA, (United States of)*." After asserting that "the beginning of every political establishment is contemptible" and citing as proof the handful of "banditti" who were responsible for laying the foundations of Rome, the British edition claimed that the United States had come into being in a similar way, as the result of "the turbulence of some North Americans, and the blunders of some British statesmen" (574). Morse retained the British author's suggestion that American civilization might one day "surpass even the splendour of Rome" (574 in the British edition), but he naturally altered the genealogical emphasis, thereby retaining for Americans the grandeur of Roman aspiration to world empire without the imputation of a guilty origin. "The beginnings, even of the most celebrated political institutions of the Old World," he wrote,

are generally involved in fable and obscurity. The barbarous manners of savage tribes in the early and uncultivated state of society, renders [sic] the research of the historian painful and unsatisfactory. Very different were the circumstances which gave birth to this new republic. (575)

Morse next took issue with the British account of the causes of the revolutionary conflict. In the British edition, the outbreak of the war was ascribed to "secret emissaries" sent from France, "for many ages . . . the profest [sic] and natural enemy of Britain," who after the conclusion of the final French and Indian War began to spread "dissatisfaction among the British colonists" and who eventually succeeded in diminishing and ultimately destroying "that warmth of attachment to the mother-country" which had heretofore so peculiarly characterized Anglo-American relations. Thanks to French machinations, concludes the British interpretation, the colonists "began to view . . . [England] rather in the light of a sovereign than of a parent; and to examine, with a scrupulous nicety, the nature of those ties that rendered them parts of her empire" (575).

In responding to these allegations and in defending Americans against the charge of filial ingratitude, Morse often used the words of the original British indictment (this is not the only passage in the article that seems to have been dictated by a British allegation rather than by the intrinsic importance of the subject). He explained the disaffection of Americans as a consequence of the clash between Britain's "desire for power" and America's innate "abhorrence of oppression,. . . . love of liberty, and . . . quick sense of injury" (576). English writers, he asserted, have sought the origin of the revolutionary conflict "in any source rather than their own misconduct" (576). In particular, they have used the Revolution as an occasion to "gratify the cravings of their national animosity" and to indulge in "wild conjectures" and "declamatory expletives against the Gallic faith and honor" (576). The fact was, Morse went on, that absolutely no evidence of secret French emissaries ever existed "which the purity of historical truth can admit." He would have done well to recall this sentiment a few years later when, on the flimsiest evidence (hearsay testimony), he accused freemasonry and the French example of seeking to subvert world order and overthrow all established religions and governments.

After this disagreement with the British editor, Morse followed the British writer's argument without changing a word for seven and a half pages (approximately ten thousand words). His next interpolation into the British text, moreover, is only a brief, inconsequential sentence of transition following the account of the engagements at Lexington and Concord (583 in the British edition, 584 in the American). He did not make a substantive alteration for another half page. Then, discussing the battle of Breed's or Bunker's Hill, he changed the British claim that American losses "did not exceed 500" (583) to the more precise (and patriotic) "139 killed and 314 wounded" (584). This small emendation led to a larger one. Morse deleted the phrase "with justice" after the British claim of victory in this battle, as well as all references in the British edition to the fact that Americans were entrenched on high ground and that, therefore, "the greatest [sic] display of valour was on the side of their enemies" (583). Instead, Morse pointed out the vast differences between the experience of the British and American troops. "Although this was the first time the Provincials had been in actual service," he wrote, "they behaved themselves with the spirit of veterans, and by no means merited the appellation of *cowards*, with which they were so often branded in Britain" (584). The part of this sentence after "and" is identical in the British and American editions and offers one explanation of why Morse made so few changes, comparatively speaking, in the British account of the War for Independence. Though obviously the product of a British writer, the article on "America," particularly in the section devoted to the American Revolution, strives for a balanced view of recent and still painfully controversial events.[12]

Following the battle of Breed's or Bunker's Hill, the two texts proceed identically for the next three and a quarter pages. Like the earlier block of identical pages, these pages largely concern diplomatic and political overtures on both the British and the American sides, a topic about which Morse does not appear to have been well informed. The next change of any consequence deletes the British reference to the defeat of Generals Richard Montgomery and Philip Schuyler at Crown Point and St. John's (587), replacing it in the American text with an account of the American "council of war at Ile aux Noix" and General Schuyler's illness (588); both texts resume with General Montgomery's successful efforts to win over Britain's Indian allies to the American cause. Then the texts go on the same for nearly five and a half additional pages, reaching the narrative of the first British attempt to take the port city of Charleston in 1776 before they diverge again.

This time the divergence is of significant length. Morse's version provides considerably more detail than the British editor supplied (although he employs only six hundred words to twice that many in the British edition). Morse's source is David Ramsay's *History of the American Revolution* (1789), and his main purpose in appropriating this account of the battle of Sullivan's Island is to celebrate the heroism of Colonel William Moultrie and his men in their victory over vastly greater numbers of British soldiers and superior firepower. Against the British claim that American losses in this engagement must have been very great because "reinforcements had poured into the fort during the whole time of the action" (592), Morse introduces Ramsay's figures: the garrison of Fort Moultrie (as it was renamed after the battle) consisted of 275 regulars and a few militia, and the Americans sustained a total loss of only ten men killed and 22 wounded (592). Morse's account of the battle responds to British praise of the bravery of Captain Morris of the *Bristol* and Sir Peter Parker among the attacking forces by emphasizing the size of the cannonade which the British ships could bring to bear on the tiny, hastily constructed fort (270 cannons against 26), the excellent marksmanship of the American gunners, and the coolheaded valor of William Moultrie. Morse used the same counterbalancing rhetorical strategy elsewhere in the article to underscore the sharp difference between British and American points of view.

The three and a half pages following the battle of Sullivan's Island are once again identical in both the British and American editions. By now the war had reached the decisive phase in the middle colonies, beginning with the British investment of Philadelphia and General Washington's surprise success against the Hessians at Trenton. To this exploit as recorded in the *Britannica* (595) Morse added only a sentence: "After this gallant exploit, General Washington again returned into Pennsylvania" (596).

Like Washington, however, Morse saved his best for another battle, the decisive encounter at Princeton. The success of Washington's surprise of the Hessians at Trenton, wrote the British editor, had brought in a sufficient number of recruits to enable the general to "leave Philadelphia" (595); Morse's version, carefully avoiding any imputation of retreat, abandonment of the city, or even tactical withdrawal, put it that Washington was now able "to pass the Delaware" (596). The British edition then reported on Washington's plans to attack a division of British forces under Colonel Charles Mawhood at Maidenhead, midway between Princeton and Trenton, in which attack on January 3, 1777, they were repulsed by a determined bayonet charge by the valiant British soldiers. Nevertheless, for a variety of reasons, the British saw fit to pull back in the direction of Brunswick, leaving the surrounding countryside free for Washington's forces to reoccupy.

Except on the matter of reoccupation, Morse saw matters very differently. He commended Washington's boldness in maintaining his position in New Jersey "notwithstanding . . . accounts . . . of the enemy's rapid advance toward him" (596). In the late afternoon and evening of January 2, these British troops, including the full contingent under Lord Charles Cornwallis, occupied Trenton on the other side of a small, easily forded creek and awaited only the return of daylight to annihilate the outnumbered American army once and for all and put an end to the rebellion. "This was, indeed, the crisis of the American Revolution," Morse wrote, but "a night's delay turned the fate of the war, and produced an enterprise, the magnitude and glory of which, can only be equalled by its success" (596). Leaving behind a line of fires as a ruse to fool Cornwallis, Washington slipped away over roads turned suddenly and providentially from quagmire into frozen mud as "firm and smooth as pavement" (596), fell on Mawhood's astonished troops at Princeton, and, despite the loss of the valiant General Hugh Mercer, achieved a victory which left the British, defeated and discouraged, retreating to the security of Brunswick.

Morse also rewrote the battle of Brandywine, a "general engagement" dominated entirely by the British in the British edition and ending with "the approach of night" as the only circumstance that saved Washington's army from being "totally destroyed" (596). Even Morse could not deny the American defeat, evident in an unadorned account of casualties (600 British, 1200 Americans), but he insisted that Washington was on the verge of winning the battle when fate intervened in the form of an erroneous report about the disposition of Lord Cornwallis's forces. It was during this battle, Morse added with evident goodwill and admiration, that "the celebrated Marquis de la Fayette . . . first bled in the cause of liberty, which he had espoused with enthusiastic ardor. His wound was slight, but it endeared him to Americans" (597). At this point in his career, Morse was an admirer rather than an enemy of the French, but it is well to recall that his article was written and published, both in the *Encyclopaedia* and as a separate title, a few months after the storming of the Bastille.

Morse and the British editor agreed on the details of the loss of Philadelphia and the forced removal of the American capital to York, Pennsylvania. They disagreed again, however, on the defense of the Delaware by Fort Mifflin, to which Morse devoted approximately thirteen hundred words in comparison with four hundred words in the *Encyclopaedia Britannica*. As he had when describing the defense of Charleston, Morse used Ramsay's *History of the American Revolution* as his source, which provided not only facts but also a rationale for claiming Pyrrhic victory: "The long protracted defense of the Delaware, deranged the plans of the British, for the remainder of the campaign, and consequently saved the adjacent country" (598).

Both texts proceed identically for three full pages, covering General John Burgoyne's fateful attempt to invade the colonies from the north in pursuance of the British plan to sever New England from her middle and southern sources of support. Morse's account of the battle of Saratoga, however, departs significantly from the British version, omitting the British claim that the American forces vastly outnumbered Burgoyne's army (599; American edition 601). Morse also transposed the order but did not otherwise change several facts provided by the British edition, including the information that every part of Burgoyne's army was within range of American artillery. The principal difference between the two texts is that Morse included all thirteen articles of capitulation and a detailed enumeration of captured prisoners and supplies, thereby expanding his account by several hundred words over the British version.

For the next three and a half pages, the texts are again identical. Then Morse inserted a paragraph (605) castigating the British for the rape and pillage of Charleston after the fall of that city in 1780, asserting that "profligate conduct of the refugees, and the officers and soldiers of the British . . . was incredible. Negroes were seduced or forced from their masters; furniture and plate were seized without decency or authority; and the most infamous violations of every law of honor and honesty were openly perpetrated." British arms and honor, he declared, "incurred an everlasting stigma" (606).

Morse's next addition, though brief, was an important one, denying the British charge that after the death of Count Casimir Pulaski during the failed attempt of the combined French and American forces to take the city of Savannah, the two allies fell to quarreling bitterly (604). "So far from reproaches or animosity arising between them," Morse wrote in direct reply to the British text, "their common misfortunes seemed to increase their confidence and esteem for each other; a circumstance fairly to be ascribed to the conciliatory conduct of General [Benjamin] Lincoln on every occasion" (606). The text then resumed identically in both editions for another page.

One of the longest of Morse's additions follows the account in both editions of the Americans' disastrous failure to take either Paulus Hook in New York or the newly erected British post on the Penobscot River in Maine (605 in the British edition, 607 in the American). For nearly two pages, Morse detailed the massacre of the settlers of Wyoming, Pennsylvania, and the activities of "Col. [John] Butler and [Joseph] Brandt, a half blooded Indian, of desperate courage, ferocious and cruel beyond example" (607). Butler, "a Connecticut Tory" (608), deceived and defeated his cousin Colonel Zebulon Butler and also massacred a garrison of American troops and settlers near "Wilkesborough" (608) before slipping away into the fastnesses of the Pennsylvania forests. Though undoubtedly a bloody affair, this massacre had little effect on the progress or outcome of the Revolution and was probably included as a piece of anti-Tory propaganda and, perhaps, as an expression of Morse's outrage over the betrayal of the American Revolution by a citizen of his home state of Connecticut. Ever alert to the hidden enemy lurking beneath the shelter of respectability, Morse found a perfect villain in Colonel John Butler.

Morse also heavily edited another item having to do with warfare against the Indians on the frontier, this one unfavorable to the Americans. In the British account of General John Sullivan's operations against Britain's Indian allies in upstate New York, the American troops were blamed for executing "in the most ample manner the vengeance [against the Indians] they had projected," particularly for transforming the abundant gardens and orchards of the Indians into "a desert" (605–06). Morse attempted to exonerate the Americans, admitting that this lush countryside "would have been converted into a desert, had it not been for the humane forbearance of General [Edward] Hand and Colonel [Lewis] Dubin [sic: Dubois]" (609).[13] Even so, he confessed, "the desolation . . . was . . . only to be justified by the savage character and example of their enemy" (609).

For the next six pages, Morse made no changes or additions to the British text except to take note of the defeat of Lieutenant Colonel Banastre Tarleton at the hands of Lieutenant Colonel William Washington during skirmishes around the city of Charleston (610) and to point out that, when captured after the battle of Cowpens, Tarleton's men were not harmed in any way by their American captors although they had themselves been merciless plunderers (616). Morse also doubled the size of the account of the battle from approximately six hundred to nearly twelve hundred words.

Another major revision of the British edition occurs in Morse's account of Yorktown and events in and around Virginia leading up to Cornwallis's surrender. The British edition, quite naturally, relates these events from a British point of view, detailing the plans laid by Sir Henry Clinton and Sir Samuel Hood to effect a rescue of the bottled-up British army. Morse's version (619–24) narrates the gradual encirclement of Cornwallis's forces by the combined French and American army moving in from Williamsburg and by the French fleet under Admiral François de Grasse; Sir Samuel Hood disappears entirely from this account. It emphasizes especially Washington's cleverness in deceiving Sir Henry Clinton into believing that his real object was New York, a strategy that allowed "French and

American armies to pass [towards Virginia] without opposition" (619). Morse also added to his account of Cornwallis's surrender a paragraph reporting that "the honour of marching out with military colours" was refused to the British general "as it had been refused to General Lincoln [at Charleston]; who was now selected to receive the submission of the royal army at York-Town in the same manner his own submission had been received by the British about 18 months before at Charleston" (622). In addition, he was careful to mention the simple marble obelisk that the grateful Congress of the United States had already dedicated at Yorktown to honor not only Washington but also America's French allies in the persons of la Fayette, Rochambeau, and de Grasse.

After this final tribute to French valor and assistance, Morse brought the Revolution to a speedy conclusion, adding a brief account of the British evacuation of New York (celebrated as a holiday in that city for many years after the event), a sketch of General Washington's resignation as commander-in-chief of the Continental army ("perhaps the most singular and interesting [such ceremony] that ever occurred" [624–26]), and the entire text of the "Farewell Address." "Of the extent of territory, population, commerce, revenue and wealth of this growing empire," he promised in his final paragraph, "a particular account shall be given, under the article *United States*" (626). This promise indicates that Morse and Dobson were contemplating a major addition to the *Encyclopaedia,* but no such article appeared until the third volume of the *Supplement.*

In these contributions to the *Encyclopaedia,* Morse voiced the sense of communal pride and accomplishment shared by most of his countrymen and expressed the general feeling of gratitude and goodwill toward the French. Whatever the value or historical accuracy of his alterations and additions, they incorporated the nationalistic themes of Dobson's advertising into the text of the American edition, thereby giving the *Encyclopaedia* at least some claim to being a national rather than a regional or local publication. Despite his reputation as the father of American geography, however, Morse was not as successful with his geographical contributions, largely because his personal views about America and American society were localized, politically partisan, and often idiosyncratic. He made no attempt, for example, to represent fairly the vital political dialogue then taking place within the United States. Piously loyal to his home state of Connecticut, he firmly believed that Connecticut Congregationalism provided the only workable model for federal government and viewed all other regions of the nation with suspicion, even at times including the other states in New England. He especially distrusted what he saw as the lax morality of the South, combining his dislike of Southern idleness with an unrelenting attack on slavery as two of the major themes of his geographical writing. As the 1790s wore on, moreover, he reversed his position on the French Revolution and came to regard the southerner Thomas Jefferson as a godless revolutionary radical, the main symbol of the democratic excesses that were sweeping the nation. Such deeply held convictions were widely recognized even in Morse's own day as detrimental to his work as a geographer.[14] They introduced dissensus and disagreement into a book that had been planned as an expression of American consensus and a celebration of American achievement in the arts and sciences.

Because the third edition of the *Encyclopaedia Britannica* used Morse's *American Geography* as a principal source of information about the United States, the problems outlined above are not confined to Dobson's American edition. Many items about America are identical in the two editions, marking the British as well as the American text with Morse's indelible signature. Thus, for example, the article on "Connecticut," the single longest entry given to any state, is the same in both editions. Its purpose is to establish the honest, upright, God-fearing, literate, liberty-loving, and frugal farmer of Connecticut as the ideal American citizen and federal theology as God's gift to the United States. In both editions, moreover, the incorruptible yeoman of Connecticut is placed in stark contrast to the typical gentleman of leisure in Virginia, a portrait that provoked a written remonstrance from James Madison when it appeared originally in the *American Geography*.[15] "At almost every tavern or ordinary on the public road," Morse wrote of Virginia,

there is a billiard table, a backgammon table, cards, and other implements for various games. To these public houses the gambling gentry in the neighbourhood resort to kill time which hangs heavily upon them; and at this business they are extremely expert, having been accustomed to it from their earliest youth. The passion for cockfighting, a diversion not only inhumanly barbarous, but infinitely beneath the dignity of a man of sense, is so predominant, that they even advertise their matches in the public newspapers. (659)

As deeply as Morse's prejudices are embedded in both encyclopedias, however, they are, predictably, more deeply inscribed into the American than the British text. How closely Morse may have worked with Dobson on textual changes must remain a matter of conjecture, but some alterations seem the sort that only Morse would have recommended. Dobson, after all, did not usually concern himself with the content of the *Encyclopaedia,* as the Quaker controversy demonstrates. Thus it was probably Morse who restored to the article on Maryland in the American edition some sentiments that were first printed in his *American Geography* but not reprinted in the British encyclopedia. Both editions criticize the people of Maryland for leading "very retired and unsocial lives," the hallmark of those societies in which "negroes perform all the manual labour" and "their masters are left to saunter away life in sloth, and too often in ignorance." But the American *Encyclopaedia* adds several paragraphs, reprinting the text as Morse had originally published it in the *American Geography.* "That pride which grows on slavery," the American edition insisted, "and is habituated to those, who, from their infancy, are taught to believe and feel their superiority, is a visible characteristic of the inhabitants of Maryland" and of all the inhabitants of the "southern states" (10: 617). The British article appears in the tenth volume on pages 614–15, and the American article occupies pages 616–19, with pages 617, 618, and 619 marked with an asterisk to denote inserted material for the compositor and binder.

Other paragraphs restored from the *American Geography* in the American *Encyclopaedia* seem less ideologically focused, although they still appear to reflect the concerns and advice of Morse. The entry on Carolina, for example, includes coverage of the Coree and Tuscarora uprising of 1712, the extermination of the Yemassees, and the heroism of Governor Hugh Craven, which did not appear in the third edition of the *Britannica.* Morse's interest in the history of American Indians may explain the restoration of the material about early conflicts between them and the colonists, and in Governor Craven, who was both a frontier hero and a gentleman, he may well have seen a predecessor of the American leaders such as Washington.[16]

Another change in the American *Encyclopaedia* anticipates the editorial additions that would eventually fill an extra volume in the *Supplement.* The river "Patomack," a five-line entry in the British third edition, grew into an article of several paragraphs, almost certainly because its waters were soon to lave the shores of the new seat of American government and because it carried travelers past Georgetown and Alexandria to within sight of Washington's (and Morse's) beloved Mount Vernon. Such descriptive entries, at which Morse excelled, take on the qualities of topographical poetry, focusing and fusing in evocative rural symbols the recent history of America with a nationalistic sense of place and an intimation of the rising tide of American commerce, art, and industry. Mount Vernon broods benevolently above a scene of peace, prosperity, and plenty, a symbolic expression of

Washington's pastoral and presidential care of the destiny of the new American nation.

Morse's presence in the American *Encyclopaedia* may be detected in omissions as well as in restored or new material. The most important of such deletions resulted in the loss of the six-page entry on "New England" that appeared on pages 660–66 in Volume VI of the *Britannica* immediately following the lengthy entry on "England." It is easy to understand why an American editor might not wish to represent the most important commercial region in the new republic as but a mere afterthought of English history. The decision to omit the article entirely, however, rather than to move it to its appropriate place in the alphabetical arrangement represents an editorial judgment of an entirely different order. Although no reasons for this decision are given either in the text or in any surviving correspondence between Morse and Dobson, it is not difficult to discern why this drastic editorial step had to be taken.

The second half of the article was not the problem. It relied on Morse's *American Geography* for much of its content, including Morse's favorite metaphor of New England as "a nursery of men" for the rest of the United States (664) and his stinging rebuke of such "odious and inhuman" practices as "duelling, gouging, cock-fighting, and horse-racing" (666) in the American South. The first half, however, featured an overview of the history of Puritan New England that charged the original settlers with "blind fanaticism" and "intemperate religious zeal" (661). It focused especially upon the persecution of the Quakers, whom in evident disdain it identified as "these new enthusiasts" (662) even as it blamed the inhabitants of New England for not treating Quakers charitably and putting into practice the principles of religious toleration embodied in Charles II's proclamation of 1661 (662). The "spirit of persecution" (662), fed by "the melancholy which these persecuted [Puritan] enthusiasts had brought with them from their own country" (662), flared up once again in the witchcraft trials of 1692, during which, the article alleged, "young girls were stripped naked, and the marks of witchcraft searched for upon their bodies with the most indecent curiosity; and those signs of scurvy which age impresses upon the bodies of old men, were taken for evident signs of the infernal power" (662). Had the citizens of New England consulted "the constitution of the mother-country, where the people who have the legislative power in their own hands are at liberty to correct abuses" (662), they might have avoided the crimes against humanity that now stained their history. The article makes no distinction between Pilgrims and Puritans, lumping both together in its blanket indictment of American superstition and credulity and even reporting incorrectly that the "Puritans" came to America in "1621" after purchasing "the charter of the English North Virginia Company" in "1521." The article on "New England" is one of the lowest points of historiography in the third edition of the *Encyclopaedia Britannica,* and Morse was entirely right to reject it.

At the same time, the decision to omit the article left the American edition without adequate coverage of the region, which is surely one of the omissions about which Charles Brockden Brown was complaining in his review ("Encyclopaedia," 1: 135). The first eighteen volumes of the *Encyclopaedia* contain no entries on New Hampshire, Rhode Island, Vermont, or the province of Maine. "Providence" appears as a "plantation," not as a city, and merits only a few remarks. "Massachusetts" receives a mere five lines with directions to "see *New England*" (10: 633), which of course does not exist in the American edition. The entry on "Boston" is slightly expanded and updated from the British edition, but even with such changes it occupies only four short paragraphs. Although these deficiencies are carried over from the third edition of the *Britannica,* there is still some cause for surprise at Dobson's failure to expand his coverage of New England and give American readers the "greatly improved" edition he had promised. He was later to blame these omissions on a "want of proper material,"[17] but that is not the entire explanation; Morse's *American Geography* covers New England extensively and was a ready source of better information than the *Britannica* supplied. Either Morse was otherwise occupied when most of the entries about New England went to press, or he tacitly approved of the prominence the British edition gave to Connecticut and saw no reason to change the information. This would have been consistent with his distrust of the liberalization of religion in Massachusetts and his conviction that Rhode Island was a community always on the edge of anarchy. It is also possible, of course, that Morse and Dobson were already planning the article on New England that would be Morse's major contribution to the *Supplement* and that they decided to wait until this later date to correct the imbalance in coverage.

Not all geographical material about America in Dobson's *Encyclopaedia* may be credited to (or blamed on) Jedidiah Morse. The entry on Delaware, for instance, was expanded in Volume V of the American edition by five unnumbered pages (signatures 4X*–4X*$_2$) inserted between pages 718–21 and was almost certainly not Morse's work. Indeed, at the end of his article on "Delaware" in the *American Universal Geography* in 1793,

Morse praised the substantial and "well written sketch" of that state that had appeared in "the American edition of the Encyclopaedia" (509), which is an unlikely self-indulgence even for Morse if he had been the author. Internal evidence suggests that the writer was a native of the state, for the article refers to facts and details such as the recent election of deputies for the state constitutional convention of 1791–92 ($4X^*_2$) of which an outsider would probably not have been aware. The author also employs the formally correct appellation of "the *Delaware State*" when speaking of Delaware historically, but his use of italics on those occasions and his obvious preference for "the state of Delaware" ($4X^*$) throughout the article indicate that he looks forward to the change of name he knows the constitutional convention will be called on to approve.[18] He refrains from criticizing or even commenting on the fact that Delaware is a slaveholding state, which Morse would not have overlooked, praises the performance of Delaware's troops in the French and Indian and the recent revolutionary wars, and in general displays an intimate knowledge of and interest in the history, topography, geography, and current state of affairs in Delaware that a casual observer could not be expected to have acquired.

A brief comment in the opening paragraphs of James Freeman's *Remarks on the American Universal Geography* seems to indicate that the author of the revised and expanded article on Delaware was the Reverend Samuel Miller, who was born in Dover, Delaware, and received the degree of Doctor of Divinity from the College of New Jersey in 1792. At the time of the writing of the essay (judging from the reference to the imminent constitutional convention, this would have been early 1791), Miller was serving under Charles Nisbet as the first principal of the College of Carlisle (later Dickinson), Pennsylvania, and would soon be ordained and appointed as one of the pastors of the associated Presbyterian churches of New York (*DAB* 12: 636–37). Freeman refers to Ebenezer Hazard's *Historical Collections* (1792), Jeremy Belknap's two recent volumes of the *History of New-Hampshire* (1791, 1792), and "a description of the state of Delaware by Mr. Miller" (3) as among the works that "have enabled Mr. M[orse] to give more correct accounts [in the *American Universal Geography*] of the several countries they describe" than he had been able to offer in the *American Geography* (4). Since Miller is not known to have written any separately published account of Delaware, and since Morse was undoubtedly familiar with the article in the *Encyclopaedia,* it seems clear that the "description" to which Freeman is alluding is the entry on Delaware in Dobson's publication. Although Dobson did not disclose the identity of his contributor, the information must have been common knowledge among America's community of clergy.

Unlike Jedidiah Morse, who scrupulously credited his sources, Samuel Miller was not always so conscientious. Although the margins of his article on "Delaware" refer repeatedly to Samuel Smith's *History of the Colony of Nova-Caesaria, or New-Jersey* (1765), David Hume's *History of England* (1754–62), and other works he had consulted, he failed to acknowledge his indebtedness to Thomas Jefferson, from whose chapter on the mountains of Virginia (Query IV) in *Notes on the State of Virginia* (1782) he borrowed extensively in order to account for "the origin of the flat and low lands" ($4X^*_2$) of Delaware and the neighboring states. Because the *Notes* was widely read during the Federal period and was regarded as perhaps the most important scientific text written by an American, Miller probably felt that identifying his source would be unnecessary. The chapter from which he borrowed describes "the passage of the Patowmac [River] through the Blue ridge" mountains (Peterson 48). It begins with Jefferson's speculation that the rivers east of the Allegheny Mountains were once dammed up "by the Blue ridge of mountains" (48) and formed a tremendous lake that finally broke through the mountain barrier, inundating the plains below and leaving behind spectacular geologic evidence of the ancient "disrupture and avulsion" (48). In one of the most famous passages in the *Notes,* Jefferson called the huge piles of rock and the "terrible precipices" that overhang the Potomac River along much of its course "monuments of a war between rivers and mountains, which must have shaken the earth itself to its center" (49), a subconscious reflection, as William J. Scheick has conjectured, on the revolutionary conflict raging in Virginia even as Jefferson penned these lines.[19]

Miller had no such symbolic purposes in mind. Nevertheless, Jefferson's paragraphs are clearly the source of Miller's attempt to explain why "the whole Peninsula, lying between the bays of Delaware and Chesapeak, as well as large tracts of the adjacent country, has many appearances of *made ground*" ($4X^*_2$)—that is, solid ground that has been made by filling in a marsh or embanking a river. Miller appropriates not only Jefferson's general geological speculations but also, on occasion, even the very language of the *Notes*. "It has been conjectured," Miller writes, "that it may have been formed by earth, washed down from the high grounds and mountains lying westward," a hypothesis that, in his judgment, "receives much confirmation from the aspect of a large extent of the country eastward of the great range of the Alleghany mountains."

It is well known that several of the largest rivers in the middle states, viz, the Hudson, the Delaware, and the Patowmac . . . make their way through the ridges of high mountains. The clefts, through which these majestic currents roll, discover every appearance of violence and disrupture. The broken ragged faces of the mountains, on each side of the respective rivers; the tremendous rocks, which overhang the passage, and constantly seem ready to fall for want of support; the obstruction of the beds of the rivers, for several miles below, by rocks and loose stones; all these things, taken together, seem to be so many traces of a war of the elements, and the ravages of a power which nothing could oppose.

It has been supposed, that, in the extended plain behind these mountains, there was formerly collected a vast lake of water; that continuing from time to time to rise higher, it at length broke over, and tore the mountain down from its summit to its base. ($4X^*_2$–$4X_2^*$)

Like the article on "Delaware," the one on "Pennsylvania" was heavily revised, though not much expanded, again apparently without direct assistance from Morse. It grew from four pages in the *Britannica* to five in the American edition and was almost entirely rewritten, even though the British editors had used the *American Geography* as their primary source (14: 132). Only two lengthy paragraphs near the end of the entry describing the copper springs of Pennsylvania and the subterranean rivers near Reading (14: 133; American edition 133–34) and one brief paragraph about the Mason-Dixon line between Pennsylvania and Maryland (131; American edition 133) were retained from Morse as identical in the two accounts. Even then the American edition deleted a sizable passage on Pennsylvania's caves and grottoes that seems to have fascinated the British editors when they encountered it in Morse's geography. Most of the European history concerning William Penn's procurement of the proprietorship from Charles II was also excised from the American text. The space thus saved was used to enlarge the account of the Indians of Pennsylvania, to summarize the revolutionary and more recent history of the state, and to bring information about Pennsylvania's politics and productivity up-to-date. Where the British edition spoke about the state constitution of 1776 (132), for example, the American edition went into detail about the provisions of the constitution of 1790 "as at present existing in 1795" (132), thus establishing the year in which Volume XIV was published as the date of composition of the article as well.

Much of the new material in the entry for "Pennsylvania" concentrated on the Quakers and their enviable record in race relations. On several occasions, Penn's famous treaty with the Indians was referred to obliquely (but never named), accompanied by the questionable assertion that the condition of the American Indians was "much altered for the better" by the coming of these white men and that the Indians now lived "as well clothed and fed as the European peasantry in many places" (133). This statement, however, which is derived from the *American Geography,* explicitly contradicts the claim on the preceding page that few or no "*Aborigines* or *Indians*" still reside in the state because, "as the country improves and becomes more occupied, they remove further back into the wilderness." Such contradictions reveal that several sources were used for the revised article and little attempt was made to reconcile their opposing views.

The Quakers' attitude toward slavery and their treatment of black Africans in general were also singled out for praise. Pennsylvania acquires a certain symbolic stature in the American *Encyclopaedia* as a foil to Maryland and other slaveholding states, a theme transferred intact from the pages of the *American Geography.* "The Negroes, or black people," the revised text declares,

were never very numerous in the province; as the Quakers were always adverse to the detestable traffic in these people; and at present, the total abolition of holding them in bondage is fast advancing, among all sorts of people in the state; the importation of them, for sale, having long since ceased; so that there are but few, or no slaves, now in the country, except such as are introduced by strangers. (132)

Individual settlements in Pennsylvania also fared well in the "improved" *Encyclopaedia,* inspiring several examples of the entirely new material that Dobson had promised in his prefatory remarks. There were several paragraphs on the settlement of the United Brethren, "vulgarly called Moravians," at Bethlehem—its waterworks, its ferry on the river Lehigh, its "pleasant and healthy situation" (3: 202), which brought to it as frequent visitors such "Gentlemen and Ladies" of Philadelphia who liked to "travel for their health or pleasure" (202). At the last possible moment, Dobson received an article on "Lancaster" written by Jasper Yeates in response to Dobson's request of April 12, 1793 (see Chapter 3). Dobson gave it a full two columns on the final page of Volume IX, apologizing for the interruption of the alphabetical sequence. The article was as up-to-date as the Philadelphia-Lancaster Turnpike, approved by the Pennsylvania Assembly on April 10, 1792, and now "rapidly proceeding." Yeates mentioned, too, the steeple of the Lutheran church, designed by "[Abraham and William] Colliday of Philadelphia" and thought by all to be "the neatest, best proportioned, and most elegant piece of work of the kind in the United States." Such entries give the *Encyclopaedia* a decidedly local flavor, especially in the absence of articles on towns such as Hartford, Connecticut, and adequate coverage of New England in general.

Perhaps the most extensively revised article in the entire *Encyclopaedia* was the entry on "Philadelphia," a reflection both of local chauvinism and of the problematical content of the article as it appeared in the *Britannica*. Though Morse's text was obviously available to him, George Gleig, the editor of the *Britannica*, drew on it sparingly and selectively and instead chose to devote most of his article to information gleaned from Mathew Carey's *Short Account of the Malignant Fever* (1793; Evans 25255) and William Currie's *Description of the Malignant, Infectious Fever Prevailing at Present in Philadelphia* (1793; Evans 25366), the latter published by Dobson (see Appendix C). From Morse, Gleig extracted only a few paragraphs of information about the religious sect known as the Dumplers, "a very extraordinary people who live within 50 miles of Philadelphia . . . [at Ephrata]" (14: 459). With the exception of a few introductory paragraphs generally describing some of the features and institutions of the city and remarking on the role of the Quakers in its history, the rest of the nearly three-page article Gleig devoted to an account of the yellow fever epidemic of 1793, including a detailed description of the symptoms and the death agonies of a typical victim of the disease and a list of burials (taken from Carey) from August through November, the most dangerous months for the spread of the fever. Besides leaving the reader of the *Britannica* with an impression of the capital city of the United States as a cross between a charnel house and an asylum for religious enthusiasts, Gleig's article threatened to awake the barely slumbering controversy over the origins of yellow fever that had divided (and would again divide) the city's medical community into warring camps, one side believing that the epidemic was brought by foreign ships and the other (including Dr. Benjamin Rush) arguing that it arose as a result of unsanitary conditions in the city. Whether or not Gleig's article was politically motivated—it is hard to believe it was not—his picture of Philadelphia would obviously not do.

Dobson's revisions of the article on "Philadelphia" expanded Gleig's entry from three to four pages, but all the material was new. Except for a few details of latitude and longitude and distance from the Atlantic Ocean in the opening paragraphs, several of which Dobson also corrected, nothing in the piece remained the same. With civic and national pride at stake, to say nothing of the little information Gleig's article provided about the city, Dobson turned to two readily available sources to put together a new entry in which Philadelphians could find a familiar image of their city.

The first of these sources was James Hardie's *Philadelphia Directory and Register* (1793; Evans 25585), which, like Currie's pamphlet on the yellow fever, Dobson had published. From it he gathered information about the streets of the city, its form of government, its churches, and its institutions: the hospitals, the libraries, the "seminaries of learning," and the charitable and benevolent societies. Often Dobson lifted Hardie's text verbatim, as he was already practiced at doing with his "American Editions" and, of course, the text of the *Encyclopaedia*. Predictably, the revised article made no mention of the yellow fever epidemic, unless the prominence granted to the various hospitals of Philadelphia might be taken as an oblique reference to their compelling presence and importance in recent Philadelphia history. Dobson paid special attention to the University of Pennsylvania, the American Philosophical Society, and other organizations that enhanced the city's reputation as a leader in learning. It was an appropriate emphasis for an article in an encyclopedia published in that city.

Dobson's second source provided perhaps the single most remarkable paragraph in the *Encyclopaedia*, even though, as with the passages from Hardie's *Directory*, Dobson reprinted it word for word and so can claim only the credit of an editor and not an author. Nonetheless, the new context in which he placed it, very near to the end of the article on Philadelphia, and the material that preceded it give to the passage the power of metaphor and symbol, allowing it to be read as a synecdoche for the innocence, industry, orderliness, and prosperity of the community as a whole, as well as an emblem of the way that commerce is conducted, in an atmosphere of trust and friendship and mutual good faith, throughout the United States. That passage is a description of Philadelphia's High Street Market taken from page 24 of Benjamin Davies's *Some Account of the City of Philadelphia* (1794; Evans 26853). Dobson omitted Davies's criticism of the "too contracted" space allotted to each stall, the "numerous offals" that "give offence to the eye," the huge size of the throng—"too great an interruptive in the principal street of the city"—and the country girls who too often marketed themselves along with other wares sold at the same vendue (25–26). Instead, he took only the paragraph that focused on the theme of American abundance and the orderly conduct of business affairs:

> There is not a place in America, or, perhaps, in Europe, which can boast of a better market of fresh provisions, than Philadelphia. Nothing affords a more impressive image of the number of the inhabitants, and the plenty with which they are supplied, than a walk through High-street, on the morning of a market day. Here is the principal market-place, which abounds, twice every week, (on Wednesdays and

Saturdays) with the greatest plenty of butchers' meat, poultry, eggs, butter, flour, cheese, and vegetables. Butchers' meat, and vegetables, may be had at the same place, on any day of the seven, except Sunday. The clerks of the market, officers appointed by the corporation, attend on all the stated market-days, to detect frauds, prevent the sale of unwholesome provisions, discourage forestalling, and to preserve good order. (14: 460)

The value of the High Street Market as a symbol of Philadelphia, Pennsylvania, and the nation was first detected not by Davies but by a foreigner, Brissot de Warville, with a considerable assist from Benjamin Franklin. "If there exists," wrote Brissot, citing Franklin's observation,

an Atheist in the universe, he would be corrected on seeing Philadelphia—on contemplating a town where everything is so well arranged. If an idle man should move into existence here, on having constantly before his eyes the three amiable sisters, Wealth, Science, and Virtue, the children of Industry and Temperance, he would soon find himself in love with them, and endeavour to obtain them from their parents.

Such are the ideas offered to the mind on a marketday at Philadelphia. It is, without contradiction, one of the finest in the universe. Variety and abundance in the articles, order in the distribution, good faith and tranquility in the trade, are all here united. One of the essential beauties of a market, is cleanliness in the provisions, and in those who sell them. Cleanliness is conspicuous here in everything; even meat, whose aspect is more or less disgusting in other markets, here strikes our eyes agreeably. ("Letter XVI: On the Market of Philadelphia," 134)

Clearly a symbol of prosperity and social order, the High Street Market amazed Brissot not least of all because "to maintain order in such a market in France, would require four judges and a dozen soldiers" (134). Stylistically, it offers an analogue to the *Encyclopaedia* as a literary form, distributing God's plenty in an orderly fashion that bespeaks (if offal, urban crowds, and country prostitutes are kept out of sight, that is) the innate order underlying nature and society. In contrast, the marketplace of Paris was clearly a seedbed of social disorder and revolution, as events subsequent to Brissot's passage had shown. The High Street market was the imaginative center of Philadelphia, the single institution that, better even than Independence Hall or any other example of the city's architecture, organized and integrated a view of the life of the city and of the nation as a whole. Davies had read Brissot's passage, perhaps even memorized it, and relied on it in formulating his own praise of Philadelphia's and the nation's commerce. His description makes it clear that the wealth of the city depends on the produce of the country, the unobtrusive efficiency of the government, and the honesty and goodwill of America's citizens. In this roundabout way, through secondary resources, both the agrarian and the urban spirits of Benjamin Franklin descend into the pages of the *Encyclopaedia*.

In addition to major revisions in the article on "Philadelphia" and other entries on American geography, the *Encyclopaedia* diverges in innumerable small ways from the text of the *Encyclopaedia Britannica*. A comparison of the two discloses "minute improvements" (to use Dobson's words for them) on every fourth or fifth page at least: changes in spelling from the British "AMAK" to the American "AMAC" ("a small island in the Baltic Sea"), for example, or in point of view, from the British "in this country" to the American "in England" (both of these occur in Volume I on pages 512 and 461, respectively). Yet there is little sense of overriding purpose to these alterations, for in the same volumes and often on the same pages where Dobson editorially busied himself with such repairs, he allowed to stand typographical or even substantive errors in the British third edition. When the British editors supplied errata at the end of a given volume, Dobson dutifully corrected the mistakes they had identified. When they did not, or when they did not do so until a great while after a given volume had been issued, he did little except suppress the errata sheet. This was his tactic, for example, with the list of errors at the end of the British fourteenth volume, although he did correct some errors in Volumes XII and XIII.[20]

Had Dobson consistently revised other items in the *Britannica* as extensively as he did the ones pertaining to his home state, city, and locale, he would have produced a text of considerably greater interest than the one that now exists. All in all, his emendations (for as publisher and printer, he must ultimately be held responsible for them) are erratic, often lacking ideological justification or editorial method that would have given coherence to the *Encyclopaedia* and provided an integrating sense of national purpose. It is impossible for the modern reader and must have been nearly as difficult for the contemporary reader of the American edition to predict which items would be revised and which would not. There was much that only Americans knew about America that did not find its way into these eighteen volumes. There were American lives that deserved to be remembered. Perhaps sometime near the outset of the enterprise, as early as the death of Benjamin Franklin, Dobson became cognizant of these problems, but, bound by the alphabetical arrangement, he could not address them until the *Supplement*.

Before proceeding to the volumes in the *Supplement,* another aspect of the *Encyclopaedia,* one in which Dobson as printer and publisher took great pride, deserves consideration. As he repeatedly advertised, all the work involved in the production of the American edition was to be executed by American craftsmen, artisans, and artists. The fire of 1793 prevented him from fully making good on his promise, but he came close enough to make the *Encyclopaedia* a milestone in the history of American book illustration and a focal point for any account of papermaking, typefounding, and engraving in the early republic.

Notes

1. Only Morse was publicly identified by Dobson as an American contributor to the first eighteen volumes; Jasper Yeates and Samuel Miller were also almost certainly contributors, though not publicly acknowledged. The material used in revising the article on "Pennsylvania" was adapted from sources in print and not written specifically for the *Encyclopaedia.* Several other contributors, notably Drs. John Prince and David Hosack and the inventor Chester Gould, were acknowledged for their contributions to the *Supplement,* along with Jedidiah Morse once again.

2. Another possibility is the Philadelphian James Hardie, compiler of the *Philadelphia Directory* for 1793 (Evans 25585), which contained a "*Chronological Table of Remarkable Events, Which Have Happened from the First Discovery of America to the Present Period.*"

3. For some reason, the typesetting in the American edition got ahead of the pagination of the British text of "Chemistry" around 4: 446. Within a few pages, the problem had been magnified into a half page lead over the original text. To compensate, Dobson inserted a half-page "Explanation of the Plates" not found in the British edition over two columns as a title heading (4: 455), allowing the British text to catch up. From that point on, the two texts proceed with the same pagination. In the third British edition, the article on "Chemistry" occupies pages 374 to 635 of the fourth volume; in Dobson's edition, it commences on page 374 and concludes on page 637. Again, typesetting and not content accounts for this slight difference. I have also compared the separately printed texts of these two articles with the British originals and have discovered no differences.

4. For Rittenhouse, see *DAB* 15: 632. A receipt made out by Dobson to Rittenhouse for a set of Francis Hopkinson's *Works* on August 6, 1792, establishes that Rittenhouse was a customer of Dobson's about the time that Mayer and Mason's *Tables* were added to the *Encyclopaedia* (American Prose, 12941, p. 49a, HSP; quoted by permission).

5. For commentary on the work of Tobias Mayer (1732–62), see Robert Grant, *History of Physical Astronomy* (London, 1850), 488. More recent appraisals are Eric Gray Forbes, "Tobias Mayer (1732–1762): A Case of Forgotten Genius," *British Journal for the History of Science* 5, no. 77, pt. 1 (June 1970): 1–20; and Forbes, "Who Discovered Longitude at Sea?," *Sky and Telescope* 41 (January 1971): 4–6.

6. For Mason, see *DNB* 12: 1302 (1917).

7. Dobson's writings, particularly the second part of *Letters on the Existence and Character of the Deity* (1802; Shaw and Shoemaker 2149), reveal his own conservatism, as does his publication of John Robison's *Proof of a Conspiracy Against All the Religions and Governments of Europe* (1798; Evans 34477).

8. For Tytler's role as editor and compiler of the *Encyclopaedia Britannica,* see Kruse, 56–67.

9. Barton refers to Bartram's manuscript in *New Views of the Origin of the Tribes and Nations of America* (1797; Evans 31777), 46. Bartram's "Observations" was first published in the *Transactions of the American Ethnological Society,* 3, pt. 1 (New York: George P. Putnam, 1853), 11–81.

10. Morse's advertisement invites anyone possessing information on any of the subjects of interest to him to communicate with him directly in New Haven or through the Philadelphia booksellers Robert Aitken, William Spotswood, or Daniel Humphreys.

11. The late Julian Boyd, then editor of the *Papers of Thomas Jefferson,* attributes this change in text to Thomas Dobson, a natural enough mistake, and points out that Sowerby's item No. 4890 identifies Jefferson's copy of the *Encyclopaedia* (Jefferson's *Papers* 14: 412n.).

12. Perhaps the most remarkable example of the British editor's attempt to be fair to the American side of the revolutionary struggle is the following passage summing up the American attempt to take Quebec:

> In this action, it must be confessed that the valour of the provincial troops could not be exceeded. They had fought under as great disadvantages as those which attended the British at Bunker's Hill, and had behaved equally well. (588)

13. No officer named Colonel Dubin appears in Frederick Cook, "Roster of Officers in Major General John Sullivan's Expedition "(1779), *Journals of the Military Expedition of Major General John Sullivan Against the Six Nations of Indians in 1779, with Records of Centennial Celebrations* (Auburn, N.Y.: Knapp, Peck & Thomson, 1887), 316–29. Lewis Dubois was Colonel and commanding officer of the fifth New York Regiment (329).

14. The noted German geographer Christoph Ebeling, for example, thought that Morse indulged too freely "in general reflections on people and their characters" in his writings (quoted in Phillips 32). The Unitarian minister James Freeman, admittedly an unsympathetic reader, went further: he found Morse a gullible man too ready to believe his informants without questioning their authority or integrity. In his sixty-one-page *Remarks on the American Universal Geography* (Evans 25510), published in 1793 when the *Encyclopaedia* was not yet half completed, Freeman charged Morse with a catalog of crimes against good scholarship, citing chapter and verse to illustrate each indictment: "A want of uniformity in his method and his plan—Inconsistencies and contradictions—Inaccurate maps—Want of Judgment in selecting his materials and authorities—Local, professional, and religious preferences—Appearances of haste and carelessness—Mistakes and omissions" (5).

15. Madison's letter to Morse, dated May 1792, is reported in William B. Sprague's *Life of Jedidiah Morse, D. D.* (New York, 1874), 212. A better-known response is St. George Tucker, *A Letter to the Rev. Jedidiah Morse, A. M., Author of the American Universal Geography, by a Citizen of Williamsburg, Virginia* (1795; Evans 29662). As the title indicates, this was a reply to the same passage appearing in a later text by Morse, the *American Universal Geography* of 1793.

16. Somewhat ironically, Hugh Craven's popularity would again become apparent a few decades later when William Gilmore Simms idealized him as a southern slaveholding aristocrat in *The Yemassee* (1835).

17. Thomas Dobson to Jedidiah Morse, May 10, 1799, Morse Family Papers, Mss 358, Yale University Library; quoted by permission.

18. John A. Monroe, *History of Delaware,* 2d ed. (Newark: University of Delaware Press, 1987), 82.

19. William J. Scheick, "Chaos and Imaginative Order in Thomas Jefferson's *Notes of the State of Virginia*," in *Essays on Early Virginia Literature Honoring Richard Beale Davis,* ed. J. A. Leo Lemay (New York: Burt Franklin, 1977), 221–34.

20. The errata sheet supplied by the editors of the *Britannica* at the end of Volume XIV covers Volumes I–XIV and identifies errors not noted in earlier lists. Dobson corrects all errors in Volume XIV but none in any earlier volume until making a rather important addition to Corollary 6 in "Of Refraction by Spherical Surfaces" in "Optics." The addition reads, "This proposition is true in lenses and mirrors, but not in single refracting surfaces" (13: 289). Presumably urged by someone who knew the importance of the information, Dobson squeezed it into the margin in small type. He repaired four other typographical errors in Volume XIII after this one, but none before it or in any previous volumes.

6. Artists and Artisans:
The *Encyclopaedia* as American Artifact

When Thomas Dobson advertised in June 1789 that "every part" of the *Encyclopaedia* would be "executed by American artists," he was following a precedent established by other American publishers. Several printers had previously made a selling point of the fact that the paper they were using in a given edition had been manufactured in the United States, and a few had even boasted of American engravings (it was more usual, however, to market books on the strength of English illustrations). The magnitude of Dobson's project, however, gives it special value in the history of early American publishing and printing. The quantity of paper involved in the *Encyclopaedia,* for instance, called upon American papermakers to produce high-quality paper in amounts never before deemed possible (for eighteen volumes in an edition of 2000 copies, 7200 reams would have been required).[1] Similarly, Dobson's need for nearly 600 copperplates offered steady professional employment to engravers who until then had sustained themselves by engraving watches, calling cards, and dog collars. Dobson was also the first American printer who could claim that he would use only type cast by an American manufacturer for use on one particular publication.[2] The combination of size, paper, type, and copperplate engraving sets the *Encyclopaedia* apart from other early American publications and makes it, as Lawrence Wroth has written, the most significant achievement "of professional craftsmen working together for an enlightened publisher" (1938, 294) that had yet been seen in the United States.

Although the papermaking process was about to be revolutionized by new technologies, at the end of the eighteenth century techniques were not much different from those that had been used since the Middle Ages. Around 1690, the invention of the "Hollander" for cutting and tearing rags reduced the time required to turn fabric into fiber, but many steps still lay between the mortar and the finished sheet, and most of these processes had to be done by skilled workmen by hand. In the making of paper, the quality of the final product was determined not only by the quantity and quality of rags and the purity of the water but also by the ability of the vatman, the coucher, and the dry finisher (Shorter 22; Wroth 1938, 122–26). When Dobson commenced his *Encyclopaedia* in 1789, papermaking was as much a craft as it was an industry, although that status would begin to change in the opening decades of the nineteenth century.

The source or sources of Dobson's paper are not known for certain. In the absence of other evidence, the most reliable clues would seem to be the watermarks in the *Encyclopaedia*. However, since American papermakers were beginning to pursue product uniformity during this period, watermarks were waning in popularity, and only three recur in the entire publication. The initials "I B," identified in Thomas Gravell and George Miller's *Catalogue of American Watermarks, 1690–1835* as belonging to John Bicking (figures 330, 332, and 334), appear deep in the gutter of some of the early volumes. Bicking's mill was established on Beaver Creek in what is now East Brandywine Township, Chester County, Pennsylvania sometime before 1791; Bicking's use of the "I B" watermark is not documented before 1813, however, which leaves open the possibility that this watermark in the *Encyclopaedia* belongs to a paper manufacturer as yet unidentified (Gravell and Miller 1979, item 17).

A second occasional watermark, the initials "T D," is not identified in any of the standard catalogs of early American watermarks. Although it is possible that these initials stand for the papermaker Thomas Davis, co-owner of a paper mill on the east branch of the Brandywine in Chester County, Pennsylvania (Miller and Gravell 1979, item 75), it is more likely that they identify the publisher himself, impressing Dobson's identity indelibly upon the *Encyclopaedia* at the outset of the enterprise. That Dobson purchased a paper mould with these initials from Nathan Sellers on July 7, 1792 makes this supposition likely.[3]

The only other recognizable watermark besides "I B" and "T D" that shows up in the early volumes of the *Encyclopaedia* is the top part of the letters "S" and "R," or "Save Rags" (figure 419 in Gravell and Miller, 1979). This watermark, alas, also represents a dead end, for although it usually occurs in company with the initials "J/W," neither mark has been assigned to any papermaker. No watermarks appear after Volume VI.[4]

Circumstantial evidence links Dobson to at least one paper manufacturer of the period. Measurement of the pages of Isaiah Thomas's copy of the *Encyclopaedia,* which is in its original binding, suggests that the size of Dobson's sheet was somewhat smaller than the usual 18″ by 23″ medium sheet of the period. Several times during the 1790s, he ordered paper moulds from Nathan Sellers measuring 17 5/8" by 22 3/4". On September 9, 1797, the papermaker William Levis paid Sellers £6.4.9 for refurbishing a paper mould of the same unusual size, suggesting that one or both of Levis's mills, the one on Darby Creek that he had inherited from his father in 1793 or the one on Ridley Creek that he had bought from John Lungren in 1795 (Gravell and Miller 1979, items 119, 124), might have been among Dobson's regular sources.[5]

Another possible source of Dobson's "superfine paper manufactured in Pennsylvania" is Morris Truman's mill in "Upper Darby Township, Delaware County," offered for sale on November 27, 1794 (*Federal Gazette*). "The paper mill is 105 feet long by 30 feet wide," Truman's advertisement reads, "containing two vats, three engines, four presses, a fixing furnace and press, & c. and is in good order, having been lately thoroughly repaired." Originally erected by Truman and the printer Joseph Crukshank, this mill was operated by Truman alone between 1785 and 1788, when Evan Truman joined his brother in the enterprise. It was sold to John Matthews in April 1799 and continued in operation as a paper mill until 1859, when it was converted into a cotton mill (Gravell and Miller 1979, items 127, 178).

Truman's and Levis's mills were only two of many producing paper in Delaware County, where abundant supplies of clean water made possible the production of high-quality paper. Others include the Willcox mill in Concord Township, an established concern managed after 1767 by Mark Willcox (Gravell and Miller 1979, item 196) and still going strong in the late eighteenth century (Weeks 94). As late as 1801, Dobson is known to have bought paper from John Lungren, who must, therefore, have continued in business at another location after he sold his mill on Ridley Creek to William Levis. There were also the Aaron Matson mill on Chester Creek (Weeks 94); the Samuel Levis mill on Darby Creek (Gravell and Miller 1979, item 119); and Isaac Levis's mill on Ridley Creek (Weeks 94). Joseph Crukshank, with whom Dobson entered into more than one business dealing, was still in the paper business as late as 1795, when Mathew Carey purchased over $1500 worth of paper from him; Carey also purchased $4000 worth from William Lewis and $1900 worth from Mark Willcox. In 1793, too late to be in on the beginning of the *Encyclopaedia* but certainly not too late to serve as a source, Dobson's friend William Young established a paper mill on the Brandywine at the village of Rockland in Delaware, the Delaware Paper Mills—not in Pennsylvania, of course, but with a warehouse in Philadelphia close by Dobson's establishment (Gravell and Miller 1979, item 198; Wilkinson 30; *Philadelphia Gazette,* October 9, 1801). Because paper mills could not operate in freezing weather and because Dobson's project demanded large amounts of paper, it is certain that he required the production of more than one mill during the course of publication. Thus all of these mills as well as others not mentioned may have supplied paper for the *Encyclopaedia*.

Not all of Dobson's motives for buying paper manufactured in Pennsylvania appear to have been altruistic or chauvinistic. By using paper of local manufacture, he not only eliminated much of the cost of shipping and handling imported paper and was assured of ready replacements in case of unforeseen emergencies, but he also avoided what Alexander Hamilton was to term the "competent duty" (10: 334) already protecting the American paper industry from British imports even before Hamilton presented his celebrated "Report on the Subject of Manufactures" to Congress in 1791. In 1789, when work on the *Encyclopaedia* began, that duty stood at a hefty 10 percent of the total valuation of the consignment, 10.5 percent if the paper was shipped in foreign vessels.[6] With Dobson's goal of producing a high-quality publication at an affordable price, using local paper made economic sense even without the added benefit of the patriotic propaganda it provided.

Dobson's decision to use only American-made type produced by "John Baine and Grandson in Co." was also motivated by both practical and patriotic considerations. Baine's arrival in Philadelphia on August 18, 1787 (Silver 1965, 6) marks the beginning of typefounding as a large-scale industry in the United States (Wroth 1938, 111). It was obviously to Dobson's advantage to have a supplier of this important commodity close at hand. Indeed, Dobson's first proposal shows that he was counting on Baine's type from the outset of the enterprise, and it may be doubted whether, without that element in place, he would have attempted the *Encyclopaedia*. At the same time, because many American printers regarded Baine's type faces as inferior and "turned either to London or Glasgow" when time permitted (Conkwright 27), Dobson's patronage of the Philadelphia foundry must be regarded at least in part as a disinterested effort to support an industry essential to the independence of American printing. Perhaps he also felt that his large order gave him some leverage to control the quality of Baine's craftsmanship.

John Baine was over 70 when he brought his foundry tools and his grandson from Edinburgh to America on July 4, 1787 (Silver 1977, 188).

The Baines settled first in New York, advising the "fraternity of printers" in that city of their arrival in the *New-York Journal* on July 19 and in the *Daily Advertiser* the following day. "They intend here to establish their Type-foundery," the editors of both newspapers reported in advertisements undoubtedly prepared by Baine himself, "and will vend their types much cheaper than can be imported, should they be encouraged by the printers in this country, which it is believed they will be from patriotic as well as convenient motives." New York, however, could not vie with Philadelphia as a publishing center, and soon the Baines, possibly with encouragement from Dobson, established the first foundry in America not in New York as they had announced but on Pine Street near the printing and bookselling center of the city.

If there was indeed a problem with the quality of John Baine's type, most likely it did not become apparent until the first volume of the *Encyclopaedia* had been issued and the elder Baine had died at the age of 77 on August 18, 1790. He left the firm to his namesake and grandson, who lacked his grandfather's ability as an engraver. Unfortunately for the younger Baine, that skill is critical to typefounding, for the talent of the person who cuts the original punch determines not only the aesthetic design of the printing surface of the individual face—the ratio of stroke to substroke, for example, or the proportion of shaded to open area—but also the overall pattern of print on the page. In addition, some of Baine's faces were cast in softer metal than was desirable, leading to rapid and excessive wear, and he also seems not to have been deeply interested in the business to begin with. Nevertheless, for some years after his grandfather's death, he continued to supply type from several different addresses in Philadelphia—38 Pine Street (1791–1793); 145 Walnut and 18 Lombard (1794); and 71 Lombard (1795–96)—attempting at least twice to sell the foundry before finally disposing of most of his materials to the printer Francis Bailey and to Binny & Ronaldson in 1799 (Brown and Brown 54: 223; McCulloch 187; Silver 1965, 7–8).[7] His efforts to sell his property may be traced through advertisements in the *Federal Gazette* and *Dunlap's American Daily Advertiser* (January 16 and April 16, 1793):

John Baine, Letter-Founder, in Philadelphia, intending to decline the business he now follows, offers for sale the whole of the materials with which his foundery has been carried on for upwards of sixty years; consisting of between forty and fifty different fixed founts, elegantly cut, with suitable moulds for each; together with punches for the major part of them, which will enable any person who may become a purchaser to strike new setts of matrixes. The terms will be made known, by applying at No. 38, Pine street.

N. B. If a sale is not effected, he means to continue the business to the first of May, 1794. A person every way capable of conducting the business will be procured.[8]

In his second advertisement, dated March 17 but not published until April 16, Baine seemed less concerned with assuring printers of an uninterrupted supply of founts of type than with getting rid of the establishment, although he did provide plenty of forewarning and invite last-minute orders. His advertisement indicates that his sales were not confined to Philadelphia and offers some historically interesting particulars about the contents and selling price of a foundry in the early American republic:

> For Sale at the Foundery of John Baine, No. 72 Lombard Street—a few founts of *PRINTING TYPES,* of different sizes, made of superior metal. As also his FOUNDERY, consisting of every article necessary to carry on the business extensively.
> Those printers in the United States who have had founts of letters from him, and want sorts to perfect them, are requested to forward their orders by the latter end of May next, otherwise they cannot be executed. Any application for the purchase of the foundery after that period must be made to Mr. PETER LEO, at Messrs. H. & P. RICE's book-shop, No. 30, Market-street, who will give the necessary information and pay due attention to any letters (post parcel) sent him on the subject. If a sale is not effected by next fall, the FOUNDERY will be disposed of in lots so the Printers may be able to supply themselves with those founts they make most use of.
> N. B. To avoid unnecessary application, the lowest price that will be taken for the FOUNDERY, collectively, is FOUR THOUSAND FIVE HUNDRED DOLLARS.

"John Baine and Grandson in Co." provided type for the first nine volumes of the *Encyclopaedia.* Then the fire of September 8, 1793 compelled Dobson to renege on his promise to use only American type to print the *Encyclopaedia* and use a font of imported type for Volume X. It is likely that he continued to use this imported type through Volume XVI, which officially appeared on November 23, 1796. By that time, the firm of Conden and Harrison had attempted with no success to fill the void created by John Baine's retirement from the typefounding trade (McCulloch 187), and Archibald Binny and James Ronaldson had commenced the partnership that was to lead to the first successful typefoundry in the United States (Silver 1965, 20). Although this partnership began on November 1, 1796 (Conkwright 27), the first notice of their arrival in America seems not to have appeared until January 9, 1797 (*Philadelphia Gazette*), when the fledgling firm was still struggling for customers.

BINNY & RONALDSON, Letter Founders (from Edinburgh), inform the PRINTERS of the UNITED STATES, that they have erected a FOUNDERY, at the end of Eleventh and Cedar street, Philadelphia. where they carry on the business in all its branches. From their letter having given satisfaction in Britain and the attention that shall be paid to their business here, it is presumed that they will deserve the support of the trade.

LETTER FOUNDERS wanted, three or four Journeymen, and a few boys of decent parents, as APPRENTICES—who will meet with suitable encouragement—Apply as above.

N. B. Metal scabbards of all sizes and with the greatest exactness.

On December 13, 1796, less than a month before this advertisement was published, Thomas Dobson became one of the earliest customers of Binny & Ronaldson, appearing in their shop with 728 pounds of worn-out type. For this he received $58.17 1/2 credit, "which he left on deposit against future purchases" (Conkwright 28). He drew against that credit for a few small purchases before returning on March 3, 1797, to place an order for "a large font of new Binny & Ronaldson Long Primer" amounting to 527 pounds and totaling $235.42 1/2. "This," writes P. J. Conkwright, "was the foundry's first substantial sale" (28).

With this type Dobson printed Volumes XVII and XVIII of the *Encyclopaedia*. Evidence linking the *Encyclopaedia* to Binny & Ronaldson's type comes from James Watters, the ill-fated printer who published the *Weekly Magazine* in which Charles Brockden Brown's writing first appeared and who served as managing editor of the *Encyclopaedia* during the final two years of production. In announcing the terms of subscription to the *Weekly Magazine* (of which Dobson was one of many patrons), Watters informed readers that the type of his new journal would be "of the same size with that used for the Encyclopedia" (*Proposal* [1])—that is, Long Primer oldstyle, which Watters, like Dobson, had purchased from Binny & Ronaldson (Conkwright 29). Moreover, a comparison of the characteristics of Watters's type and the type of Volumes XVII and XVIII of the *Encyclopaedia* reveals the familiar distinguishing features of Binny & Ronaldson Long Prime oldstyle: a large upper bowl in the capital R, a unique curl in the tail of the same letter, and non-lining figures. One difference is that Dobson does not use a short *s* instead of a long *s* in italics as provided in Binny & Ronaldson type (Conkwright 31), but this is probably to be explained by his wish to keep the typography of the final two volumes consistent with that of the first sixteen. Binny & Ronaldson Long Primer oldstyle was also used by Henry Budd and Archibald Bartram to print Dobson's three-volume *Supplement*.

Binny & Ronaldson's typefaces eventually evolved away from the influence of John Baine, but in this early type, as John Alden has noted, the Baine tradition is clearly in evidence (274). Although Baine-style type may not have been beautiful, as Dobson himself was given to calling it, it does possess certain aesthetic qualities appropriate to a text like the *Encyclopaedia*. The simplicity of the typeface, as several commentators have noted, is well suited to a neat and dignified presentation of great amounts of information (Hyder 72; Silver 1967, 153), and the cleanness of the line helps to establish visually a sense of "the reticence, the discipline, and the quiet sureness" (Wroth 1938, 293) that mark neoclassical typography. These attributes assist the work in marshaling and deploying hosts of facts and details into austerely symmetrical double columns and function to create a consistent, quietly reassuring metaphor of man's ability to classify and control the complexity of empirical experience, reinforcing faith in the underlying taxonomy of knowledge that governs the divisions and subdivisions of the *Encyclopaedia*.

But typographic design is not the major visual attraction of Dobson's book. That honor goes without dispute to the "542 copperplate engravings" (actually there were fewer than that in Dobson's first eighteen volumes) which adorn and illustrate the articles in the text. Though some of these are stiff and crude in execution, the overall quality of the engraving represents a marked advance over American engraving of the preceding generation. "In these plates by such skilled craftsmen as Scot, Thackara, Vallance, Trenchard, Allardice, the Smithers, and Seymour," writes Lawrence Wroth, "one observes the coming of age of American book illustration" (1938, 294). That is at once a testimony to the importance of their work in the history of American book publishing and engraving and a critique of their limitations as artists, for illustration involves primarily the reproduction of other works of art instead of innovation.[9] With a few striking exceptions, the artists who worked on the *Encyclopaedia* were content to copy work originally engraved by Andrew Bell for the *Britannica* (as Bell, in turn, copied some of his from illustrations already published in British magazines [Larson, 36, 38] and earlier editions of the same encyclopedia). Most of the American engravers contributed little or nothing of their own to the *Encyclopaedia*.

Eleven names must be added to Wroth's list of Dobson's engravers: James Akin, William Barker, Joseph Bowes, Thomas Clarke, William Creed, John Draper, Benjamin Jones, Alexander Lawson, William Ralph, Francis Shallus, and Henry W. Weston. Some of them are all but unknown beyond the pages of the *Encyclopaedia*. William Creed, for example, created only one engraving for Dobson's publication, a map of Europe (number 188) in Volume VII—the sole surviving example of his work, it would appear. He also left a brief advertisement in Baltimore's *Maryland Journal* (January 3, 1792) that, in the absence of further information, must serve as both biography and epitaph. His prose provides a convenient catalog of items which required the services of an engraver and testifies to the low esteem in which engraving was held as an art form in America before the *Encyclopaedia* gave it some respectability.

> William Creed, Engraver, (who is just arrived, with his Family from London) Begs leave to inform the Inhabitants of this Town, that he engraves in the most elegant Style, Bankers' Drafts, Checks, Post-Bills, Bills of Exchange, Bills of Parcels, Direction-Cards, Visiting Tickets, Cards of Address, Maps, Plans, etc. etc. He also engraves Coats of Arms, Crests and Ciphers, on Plate, either plain or ornamental, likewise, sinks Ciphers on Silver Seals, etc. Those Ladies and Gentlemen who will please to favour him with their Commands, may depend upon their being executed in the neatest Manner, and on the most reasonable Terms.
>
> N. B. His Stay in Town is limited to Three Months, from whence he will proceed to Philadelphia, where he intends to settle. Applications may be made to Messrs. Goddard and Angell, who will show Specimens of the Advertiser's Performance. (Prime 2: 68)

William Creed's single contribution to the *Encyclopaedia* pales beside the work of Robert Scot. Scot's signature appears on 147 plates and, in company with his partner Samuel Allardice's (Scot & Allardice), on an additional 29; as many as two dozen unsigned engravings may also have been done by him. Although not all the plates that bear his signature were actually executed by him, his engravings far outnumber those of any other artist and appear in almost all the volumes of the *Encyclopaedia* and *Supplement*. Without his availability and assistance, the *Encyclopaedia* might well have proved to be the chimerical undertaking that many people at the time believed it would be.

Robert Scot was born in Edinburgh on October 2, 1745. He attended the University of Edinburgh but left to become a watchmaker. Later, he served as an apprentice to Sir Robert Strange, an eminent Edinburgh engraver, and from him learned the art of line engraving (Magee 27). By 1778, Scot had emigrated to America and settled in Fredericksburg, Virginia, where he was evidently engaged in engraving currency for the state. In a letter to George Webb, Treasurer of Virginia (September 15, 1778), he complained that he had not yet received the "Type Mettal" he had requested some two months earlier and that he could not continue without it. "I am now entirely at a Stand," he wrote, "nor can I proceed further in the Money Plates, until I am supplied as above" (Quenzel 99). Several years later, in 1780, Scot was paid the considerable sum of £2103.8 by the state of Virginia for his aid in detecting counterfeiters (Jefferson, *Papers* 4: 36n).

Scot's services to Virginia were not limited to engraving plates for currency. In 1780, Thomas Jefferson, who was then governor of the state, requested him to engrave and cast an Indian medal, for which Jefferson recommended that he receive £3206.14 "when the Treasurer is in a Situation to discharge it" (*Papers* 4: 35). Jefferson thought Scot's workmanship "extraordinary good" (4: 36) and on May 30, 1781, commissioned another medal "of the kind formerly made" and half a dozen additional pieces to have on hand as presents for other Indian leaders who might pay diplomatic visits to Charlottesville (*Papers* 6: 43). Twelve years later, Jefferson's familiarity with Scot's work probably influenced him to accept David Rittenhouse's recommendation of Scot as the first engraver of the United States Mint and to appoint Scot to that position on November 23, 1793 (Stewart 30–31).

On May 29, 1781, just one day before he received Jefferson's commission to strike seven Indian medals, "Robert Scot, late Engraver to the State of Virginia," had announced his arrival in Philadelphia (*Pennsylvania Packet*). He set up shop on the "west side of Front-Street, next door to the corner of Vine Street" and there advertised his first important work, a map showing the investment of Yorktown, Virginia, by Washington's forces (Stauffer 2: 274). Two years later, Scot married Eunice Beal of Philadelphia and joined the Quaker Meeting at Fifth and Arch streets. A Master Mason in the local lodge, he became a member of the St. Andrews Society in 1786, for which he later engraved a certificate of membership that is still used today. In 1787, the year it was established, he also engraved the certificate of membership for the College of Physicians (Magee 28). Of all the engravers then active in Philadelphia, he was the obvious choice for Dobson to approach with proposals for the *Encyclopaedia*.

Scot remained at his first business address in Philadelphia until April 1785, then moved to "No. 154, in Chesnut-street, N. E. corner of that and Second-street" (*Independent Gazetteer,* April 30, 1785). On March 26, 1787, his landlord, one John Shields, advertised "the house at present occupied by Mr. Robert Scott [sic]" for rent in the *Independent Gazetteer,* and Scot moved to "Chesnut street, No. 36" (*Pennsylvania Packet,* May 14,

1792). From there, he relocated at 2 Carters Alleys (1793), then at 4 Carters Alley (1795), and then at 115 Walnut Street (1799–1807). His final listed addresses were 7 N. Twelfth Street (1808), 13 N. Twelfth (1809–1811), 9 N. Twelfth (1813–1814), and 11 N. Twelfth (1816–1817; Brown and Brown 54: 123). While still employed by the Mint, Scot died on November 3, 1823 (Magee 32).

Only a few of Scot's engravings for the *Encyclopaedia* stand out from the rest, and not for aesthetic reasons. One of these, number 108 (Volume III), contains ten different figures, illustrating everything from "Balaena Mysticetus: The Whale" (Figure 1) to "Balistes Vetula or Old Wife" (Figure 10). Most of the plate, however, is devoted to illustrations of various views, parts, and functions of the "Flying Bridge" (Figures 2–8) used especially in warfare. Scot edited out of Bell's engraving all the ruins, cottages, and castles with which the Scottish engraver had crowded the background (one version of Bell's illustration also deleted the ruins, although it still included a long coastline in the background).[10] These subtractions not only greatly simplified Bell's illustration, preserving what was essential for an understanding of the mechanics of the flying bridge. They also adapted the engraving to an American locale, where there were no ruins, castles, or aristocratic and peasant classes associated with them. In addition, Scot's deletions brought his engraving into line with an emerging American aesthetic of simplicity and functionalism, thus Americanizing Bell's illustration in more than superficial ways.

Another specifically American alteration may be found in Scot's engraving of "Illumination" (number 179, under "Electricity") in Volume VI of the *Encyclopaedia*. In the third British edition, this plate is completely dark except for a large disk of light in the center and the scripted letters "G^{III}R" (George III Rex) beneath the disk. Scot reproduced most of the plate as found in the British edition but replaced "G^{III}R" with an interlocking scripted "USA." And in number 194, "Flags" (Volume VII), Scot added the flag of the United States to the British illustration, dropping the red flag of anarchy then associated in the American imagination with the French Revolution but, somewhat curiously, retaining all the flags of the English admiralty. Thus the dual identity of America, politically independent from England but influenced in almost every conceivable way by the example of English culture, finds graphic expression in the iconography of the *Encyclopaedia*.

Most of Scot's alterations of Andrew Bell's engravings, however, seem to have been intended to clear up spatial clutter rather than to plant political messages. Perhaps they arose from nothing more than Scot's unwillingness to attempt Bell's intricate and difficult background detail unless it was absolutely necessary to the purpose of the picture. Thus in another plate in the third volume, plate 101 ("Fig. 3 BOS 3 a. Musk Bull & Cow"), Scot removed Bell's landscape and brought the cow from behind the hill where Bell had hidden her and into clear view. Insofar as they reflect a preference for unadorned simplicity and common sense realism over unnecessary ornamentation, changes such as these convey implications that may be interpreted as political, but politics was probably not uppermost in Scot's mind when he made most of them.

Scot continued to contribute to the *Encyclopaedia* after his appointment to the Mint. Dobson also secured the services of a number of other engravers, including several of Scot's former apprentices and journeymen. On April 10, 1789, for example, less than two weeks after the first proposal for the *Encyclopaedia* had appeared, Scot had placed an advertisement in the *Maryland Journal* for a "Journeyman Engraver, who understands his Business," promising "long and constant Employment" for the proper applicant. Clearly, this advertisement reflects Scot's recent conversations with Dobson, and the promise of long and constant employment was offered in connection with Dobson's project. A youth of fourteen who had only recently emigrated from Scotland responded. Before his untimely death on August 24, 1798, during the yellow fever epidemic of that year, Samuel Allardice would sign or initial 62 engravings, together with another 19 that must be partly credited to him as a member of the firm of Scot & Allardice. Among the unsigned illustrations are another eight or nine plates that are almost certainly his handiwork. Both before and after becoming a business associate of Robert Scot, Allardice was nearly as important to the completion of the *Encyclopaedia* as Scot himself.

The first illustration Allardice created for the *Encyclopaedia,* number 32, is the first engraving in the second volume; the initials "SA" are clearly visible beneath the signature of Robert Scot. By the time he signed his first engraving, number 206 in the seventh volume (1793), Allardice had boyishly hidden his initials, or sometimes only the "A" for Allardice, in several dozen engravings. Perhaps the most interesting and amusing of these may be found in Plate 88, "Trajectorium Lunare," in which he inscribed "SA" like a secret coat of arms—an engraving within an engraving, as it were—in the center leg of a planetarium table in such a way as to comment intertextually on the gravity of astronomy and encyclopedias versus the playfulness of art. In other engravings, he camouflaged his initials beneath the bushy tail of a wolf (119) or tucked them away on the face of a fallen leaf in the foreground near the bottom of the plate (138).

Figure 2. The frontispiece of Dobson's *Encyclopaedia,* engraved by John Vallance. Copied from the third edition of the *Britannica,* the iconography foregrounds the arts and sciences against a background of Egyptian antiquity (the pyramids) and, in the middle distance, Adam and Eve in the Garden of Eden. The *Encyclopaedia* thus makes graphically vivid at the outset that its purpose is the reclamation of knowledge, especially knowledge of natural history, originally possessed by Adam in the Garden but lost to him and to all mankind as a consequence of the Fall. Photo courtesy of the Library Company of Philadelphia.

America.

AMERICA; one of the four quarters of the world, probably the largeſt of the whole, and, from its late diſcovery, frequently denominated the *New-World*, or *New-Hemiſphere*.

1
Boundaries.
This vaſt country extends from the 80th degree of north, to the 56th degree of ſouth, latitude; and, where its breadth is known, from the 35th to the 136th degree weſt longitude from London; ſtretching between 8000 and 9000 miles miles in length, and in its greateſt breadth 3690. It ſees both hemiſpheres, has two ſummers and a double winter, and enjoys almoſt all the variety of climates which the earth affords. It is waſhed by the two great oceans. To the eaſtward, it has the Atlantic, which divides it from Europe and Africa; to the weſt, it has the Pacific or Great South-Sea, by which it is ſeparated from Aſia. By theſe ſeas it may, and does, carry on a direct commerce with the other three parts of the world.

2
North and South continent.
America is not of equal breadth throughout its whole extent; but is divided into two great continents, called *North*, and *South*, *America*, by an iſthmus 1500 miles long, and which, at Darien, about Lat. 9° N. is only 60 miles over. This iſthmus forms, with the northern and ſouthern continents, a vaſt gulph, in which lie a great number of iſlands, called the *Weſt-Indies*, in contradiſtinction to the eaſtern parts of Aſia, which are called the *Eaſt-Indies*.

3
Grand objects which America preſents to view.
"Next to the extent of the New-World, the grandeur of the objects which it preſents to view, is moſt apt to ſtrike the eye of an obſerver. Nature ſeems here to have carried on her operations upon a larger ſcale and with a bolder hand, and to have diſtinguiſhed the features of this country by a peculiar magnificence. The mountains of America are much ſuperior in height

4
Its mountains.
to thoſe in the other diviſions of the globe. Even the plain of Quito, which may be conſidered as the baſe of the Andes, is elevated farther above the ſea than the top of the Pyrenees." The moſt elevated point of the Andes, according to Don Ulloa, is twenty thouſand, two hundred, and eighty feet, which is, at leaſt, ſeven thouſand, one hundred, and two feet above the Peak of Teneriffe, which is the higheſt known mountain in the ancient continent. (See the article ANDES.)

5
Its rivers.
From the lofty and extenſive mountains of America deſcend rivers with which the ſtreams of Europe, of Aſia, or of Africa, are not to be compared, either for length of courſe, or for the vaſt volumes of water which they pour into the oceans. The Danube, the Indus, the Ganges, or the Nile, in the Ancient Hemiſphere, are not of equal magnitude with the St. Laurence, the Miſſouri, or the Miſſiſlippi, in North-America; or with the Maragnon, the Orinoco, or the Plata, in South-America. The rivers in the latter of theſe American continents are like vaſt arms of the ſea. (See the articles ST. LAURENCE, MISSOURI, &c. &c.)

6
Its lakes.
"The lakes of the New-World are no leſs conſpicuous for grandeur than its mountains and rivers. There is nothing in other parts of the globe which reſembles the prodigious chain of lakes in North-America. They may be properly termed inland ſeas of freſh water; and even thoſe of the ſecond or third claſs of magnitude, are of larger circuit (the Caſpian ſea excepted) than the greateſt lake of the ancient continent." (See the articles SUPERIOR, HURON, ERIE, &c.)

The luxuriance of the vegetable creation in the New-World is extremely great. In the ſouthern provinces, where the moiſture of the climate is aided by the warmth of the ſun, the woods are almoſt impervious, and the ſurface of the ground is hid from the eye, under a thick covering of ſhrubs, of herbs, and weeds. In the northern provinces, although the foreſts are not then encumbered with the ſame wild luxuriance of vegetation, the trees of various ſpecies are generally more lofty, and often much larger, than are to be ſeen in any other parts of the world.

America.

7
Exceſſive luxuriance of vegetation.

8
Remarkable prevalence of cold in America.
One of the moſt remarkable circumſtances, or features, of the New-World, is the general predominance of cold, throughout the whole extent of this great continent. Though we cannot, in any country, determine the preciſe degree of heat merely by the diſtance of the equator, becauſe the elevation above the ſea, the nature of the ſoil, &c. all affect the climate; yet, in the Ancient Continent, the heat is much more in proportion to the vicinity to the equator than in any part of America. Here the rigour of the frigid zone extends over half that which ſhould be temperate by its poſition. Even in thoſe latitudes where the winter is ſcarcely felt in the Old-Continent, it reigns with great ſeverity in America, though during a ſhort period. Nor does this cold, prevalent in the New-World, confine itſelf to the temperate zones; but extends its influence to the torrid zone alſo, conſiderably mitigating the exceſs of its heat.—Along the eaſtern coaſt, the climate, tho' more ſimilar to that of the torrid zone in other parts of the earth, is neverthelefs conſiderably milder than in thoſe countries of Aſia and Africa which lie in the ſame latitude. From the ſouthern tropic to the extremity of the American continent, the cold is ſaid to be much greater than in parallel northern latitudes even of America itſelf.

9
Dr Robertſon's reaſons for this ſuperior degree of cold, *Hiſtory of America*, vol. II. p. 10, 11, 12, & 13.
For this ſo remarkable difference between the climate of the New-Continent and the Old, various cauſes have been aſſigned by different authors. The following is the opinion of the celebrated Dr Robertſon on this ſubject. "Though the utmoſt extent of America towards the north be not yet diſcovered, we know that it advances nearer to the pole than either Europe or cold, Aſia. The latter have large ſeas to the north, which are open during part of the year; and even when covered with ice, the wind that blows over them is leſs intenſely cold than that which blows over land in the ſame latitudes. But, in America, the land ſtretches from the river St Laurence towards the pole, and ſpreads out immenſely to the weſt. A chain of enormous mountains, covered with ſnow and ice, runs through all this dreary region. The wind paſſing over ſuch an extent of high and frozen land, becomes ſo impregnated with cold, that it acquires a piercing keeneſs, which it retains in its progreſs through warmer climates; and is not entirely mitigated until it reach the gulph of Mexico. Over all the continent of North-America, a north-weſterly wind and exceſſive cold are ſynonimous terms. Even in the moſt ſultry weather, the moment that the wind veers to that quarter, its penetrating influence is felt in a tranſition from heat to cold no leſs violent than ſudden. To this powerful cauſe we may aſcribe the extraordinary dominion of cold, and its violent inroads into the ſouthern provinces in that part of the globe.

"Other cauſes, no leſs remarkable, diminiſh the active

Figure 3. The first page of Jedidiah Morse's revised article on "America" from Volume I of Dobson's *Encyclopaedia*. The page is typical of the layout and design employed throughout the entire publication and shows John Baine's handsome Long Primer oldstyle typeface to advantage. Photo courtesy of the Library Company of Philadelphia.

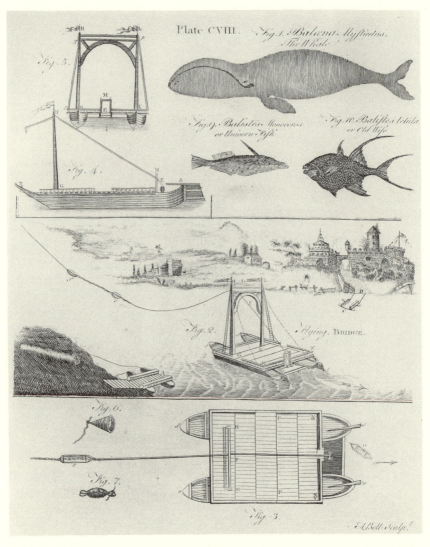

Figure 4. Andrew Bell's engraving of the "Flying Bridge," plate 108, from the third edition of the *Encyclopaedia Britannica*. Note the ruins, cottages, and castles in the background. Photo courtesy of the University of Cincinnati PhotoGraphic Services.

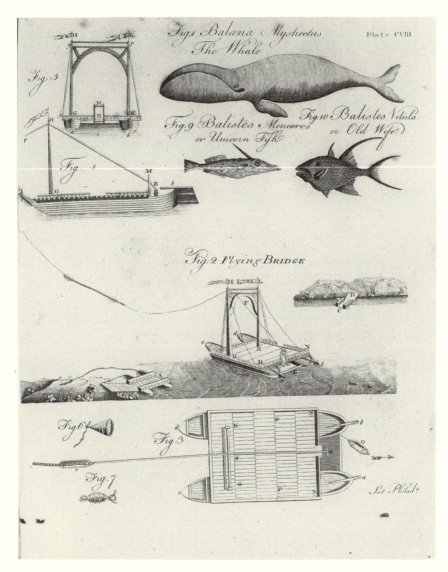

Figure 5. Robert Scot's engraving of the same "Flying Bridge" simplified and Americanized by the omission of the European architecture. Photo courtesy of the Library Company of Philadelphia.

Figure 6. Andrew Bell's engraving of the "White-Headed Eagle," plate 190 in the third edition of the *Britannica*. Photo courtesy of the University of Cincinnati PhotoGraphic Services.

Figure 7. James Trenchard's "White Headed Eagle," seen in all its stately magnificence as the emblem of the United States of America. Such changes provided a visual dimension to complement the Americanization of the text of the *Encyclopaedia*. Photo courtesy of the Library Company of Philadelphia.

Figure 8. James Akin's "Mustellae," plate 333—the only etched plate in the first eighteen volumes of the *Encyclopaedia*. Though all but forgotten by art historians, Akin appears to have been, next to Alexander Lawson, perhaps the most talented and versatile of the engravers who worked for Thomas Dobson. Photo courtesy of the Library Company of Philadelphia.

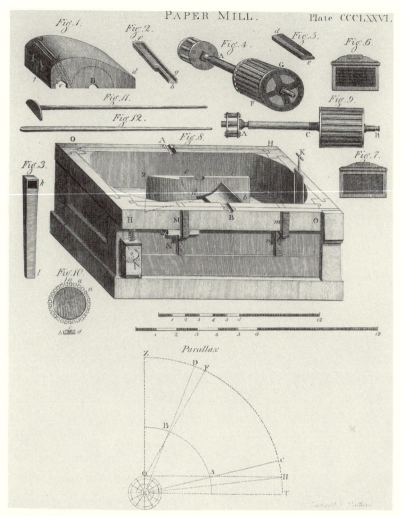

Figure 9. John Vallance's engraving of an eighteenth-century "Paper Mill," plate 376 (volume XIII) of the *Encyclopaedia*. Shown here in breakaway detail is the engine that, in the words of the *Encyclopaedia* itself, "performs the whole action of reducing the rags to paste, or, as it may be termed, of trituration" (13: 709): the chapiter (Figure 1), which covered the engine; the dalot, or hole-scupper (Figure 2) through which the finished paste was conveyed to repositories for further work by couchers and other craftsmen; the vat (Figure 3); the roller (Figures 4, 9, and 10: perspective, plane, and profile views) and trundle head (point A) with 7 spindles on one end and 27 teeth or blades on the other; a cutaway view of the indented faces of the roller teeth (Figure 10, *aaa*); the plates (Figure 5) and the levers to raise or lower the axis of the roller parallel to the plates (Figure 3, OAH and OBH); the wire cloth and hair cloth frames (Figures 6 and 7) that retained rag fibers; the sockets on the frame of the vat in which the roller points rested (Figure 3, points A and B): and cogged wheels for raising or lowering the levers that controlled the distance of the roller from the plates and iron bands and wedges for holding the levers in place (points H, MN, mn, and Nn, respectively). Figures 11 and 12 are tools used by the vatmen and other workers in a typical factory.

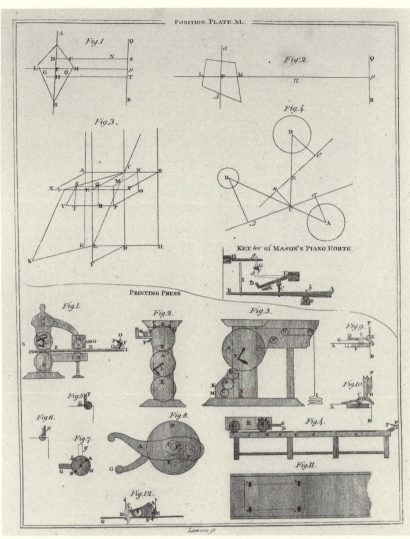

Figure 10. An illustration of Nicholson's steam-powered printing press engraved by Alexander Lawson for the *Supplement* to the *Encyclopaedia* (plate 40). Innovations in print and papermaking technology and the development of steam power in the early decades of the nineteenth century soon made it possible to produce much larger editions than the *Encyclopaedia,* while sacrificing, however, craftsmanship and quality. By the middle of the century, print factories that catered to as well as helped to change the taste of the reading public courted mass markets far beyond any that Dobson could have imagined only a generation earlier. Photo courtesy of the Library Company of Philadelphia.

Sometime in 1793, or perhaps a little earlier, Scot took Allardice into partnership, forming the firm of Scot & Allardice. In that year, the two engraved the well-known and often reprinted *Plan of the City and Suburbs of Philadelphia* (Barker and Haskell 67). No engravings over their joint signature appear in the *Encyclopaedia* before 1794 (Volume XII) or after 1796 (Volume XVI), indicating that their partnership may have been short-lived. On November 6, 1797, Allardice placed an advertisement in the *Aurora* for two apprentices to work in his shop "back of No. 210, Market-street," thus apparently confirming the end of the partnership and suggesting that even on his own he did not lack for customers.

In the several years that they remained together, Scot and Allardice affixed their signatures to 29 plates in the *Encyclopaedia,* none of them very striking either in execution or in subject matter. Following a practice begun by Scot when he operated on his own, the new partners had assigned as many as ten of these signed plates to apprentice workmen, including five executed by Francis Shallus. A native of Philadelphia, Shallus was born around 1773 and was the son of a revolutionary war officer. He was taken on by Scot in 1792, most likely in response to an advertisement Dobson placed in the *Pennsylvania Packet* in May for "a Youth about 14 years of age" who possessed "a Taste for Drawing and the advantage of a good Education."[11] Shallus apparently could lay claim to both.

Like Allardice before him, Shallus almost immediately began to initial engravings below the signature of Robert Scot. His first such plates, numbers 252 and 253 (both entitled "Jesuits Bark [Chincona officinales]"), number 258 ("Knighthood"), and number 264 ("Larius Cinnamonum"), appear over the initials "FS" in Volume IX of the *Encyclopaedia* in 1793; this is four years earlier than any work previously ascribed to him (Stauffer 1: 245). Shallus also engraved numbers 280, 281, 287, and 288 in Volume X (also 1793) and numbers 297 and 306 in Volume XI (1794), sometimes using a long, scripted "S" or "Shallus" to identify his work. When Scot and Allardice joined forces, he remained as an apprentice and engraved the first illustration attributed to firm, number 369 ("Mimosa") in Volume XII, as well as four additional plates (numbers 312–314 and 369) which bear his initials beneath their corporate signature. He signed "F. Shallus" to only two plates in the *Encyclopaedia,* number 404 in the series "Pneumatics" and number 415, an illustration of the "Printing Press," both in Volume XV. More interested in local politics than in engraving, Shallus served for a time as captain of the First Light Infantry of Philadelphia (1805) and eventually operated a circulating library (1813 onward). He is probably best remembered as the compiler of *The Chronological Tables for Every Day of the Year*

(1811), not as an engraver. He died November 12, 1821. The estimate of his abilities as a "poor workman" (Stauffer 1: 245) is not likely to change even though the plates in the *Encyclopaedia* which were not previously identified as his work more than double the number of known engravings by his hand.

Two other apprentices of Scot & Allardice made few contributions to the *Encyclopaedia*. John Draper was to sign two plates in Dobson's *Supplement*, numbers 25 and 29 (a gruesome illustration of the guillotine) and two more in the first eighteen volumes, "Phaens Copterus Ruben (Flamingo)" (number 392 in Volume XIV) and the second plate in a series on "Surgery" (number 484 in Volume XVIII). Both of these earlier contributions are identified only by the initials "JD" beneath the signatures of Scot (484) and Scot & Allardice (392).

Little is known of Draper or his work. In 1810 his name appears as one of the members of a firm whose main business lay in engraving banknotes, Murray, Draper, Fairman & Co., which took over the American edition of Rees's *Cyclopaedia* from Samuel F. Bradford in 1815 and became Fairman, Draper, Underwood & Co. upon the death of George Murray in 1823. Draper's name turns up in connection with a variety of other firms until 1860 or so, but the plates he engraved for the *Encyclopaedia* are the only surviving examples of his work (Larson 45–49; Stauffer 1: 69).

The third and last of Scot's apprentices, Benjamin Jones, initialed four engravings signed by Scot & Allardice, numbers 84, 85 and 93 in Volume XIV (the second and third plates in the "Perspective" series and "Machine for Boring Wooden Pipes," respectively) and number 401 in Volume XV, the third illustration in the series "Pneumatics." He also signed his own name to eight additional engravings in the *Encyclopaedia,* presumably after he was no longer an apprentice: numbers 491, "Surgery"; 493–495, "Naval Tactics"; 508, "Thrashing Machine"; 512, "Articulate Trumpet"; 519, "Defense and Passage of a River" in the series on warfare; and 540, "Winteria Aromatica," all in Volume XVII (1798). During the yellow fever epidemic of 1798, Jones was one of the fortunate few who was admitted to and then discharged from the city hospital (*Philadelphia Gazette,* September 13 and 25). Sometime later, he formed a partnership with the miniaturist Joseph Roberts, who in the late 1790s seems to have divided his time between Philadelphia and Charleston (Prime 2: 32). Roberts died in early December, 1802, and on the fourteenth of that month, the *Philadelphia Gazette* carried Jones's request that all debts owed to the former "partnership of Roberts and Jones" be promptly paid and all claims against it be

brought to his attention. Jones married Alice Howard Hill, also of Philadelphia, on June 28, 1804, and was apparently still alive as late as 1837
(Stauffer 1: 147; Groce and Wallace 357).

Beginning with Volume II, James Thackara and John Vallance joined
Robert Scot and his apprentices in engraving for the *Encyclopaedia*. Indeed,
only one other full signature appears through the first six volumes, that of
James Smither, Sr., in Volume V, Plate 157 ("Denmark, Norway, Sweden
& Finland"). Predictably, then, Thackara and Vallance are collectively and
individually responsible for more engravings than any other artist except
Scot, with 71 plates signed by the firm, another 46 signed by Vallance, and
an additional 28 by Thackara. A few unsigned plates may also be their
work.

John Vallance was born in Glasgow in 1770 and brought to America as
an infant in 1772. He was apprenticed to James Trenchard and married
Trenchard's niece Elizabeth in 1790. That year he also entered into part-
nership with another of Trenchard's former apprentices, James Thackara.
Their first business address, 72 Spruce Street, was a house belonging to
Thackara's father, William. The earliest known work to bear the signature
of "Thackara & Vallance" is an engraving entitled *View of the Falls of
Niagara,* which was published in the *Universal Asylum and Columbian
Magazine* in June 1790 (Lewis 1959, 19). About this time, they also began
contributing to Dobson's *Encyclopaedia*. In 1792, they executed *A Plan of
the City of Washington,* the earliest official map of the new capital and easily
their most famous and frequently reprinted work (Barker and Haskell 64).

In December of 1794, Vallance was one of thirty artists who helped to
found the short-lived "Columbianum, or American Academy of the Fine
Arts," an "Association of Artists of America for the Protection and Encouragement of the Fine Arts." The group held its first meeting on December 29 and declared itself formally organized as of January 1, 1795, though
it lacked a constitution and by-laws (Sellers 2: 67–68). The members of the
group pledged "to promote, to the utmost of our abilities, the Fine Arts—
now in their infancy in America" and "to use our utmost efforts to establish
a school or academy of Architecture, Sculpture, Painting, etc. within the
United States."[12] As the forerunner of the Pennsylvania Academy of the
Fine Arts, the Columbianum organized and conducted the first exhibition
of contemporary art in the United States, which opened in the Senate
Chamber of the State House (Independence Hall) on May 22, 1795. By
that time, however, eight British-born artists had withdrawn from membership over the issue of patronage and had attempted to establish a rival

organization, the "Columbianum, or National College of Painting, Sculpture, Architecture and Engraving" (Sellers 2: 68). Their act of secession led to the end of the first formal attempt to create a professional association of artists in the United States.

For reasons unknown, Thackara and Vallance dissolved their partnership around the time that the Columbianum was prematurely passing into history. The date customarily given is late 1796 or early 1797, but the last plate in the *Encyclopaedia* to bear the joint signature of the firm appears in Volume XII in 1794, indicating that the two engravers parted company some years earlier than is usually supposed.[13] Early in the nineteenth century, Vallance joined two other engravers in establishing a new firm, Tanner, Vallance, Kearny & Co., who specialized in banknotes. In 1810, he also served as treasurer of a new organization, the Columbian Society of Artists in Philadelphia. Vallance's wife died during the yellow fever epidemic on October 4, 1798, but he outlived her by many years and died at the age of 53 on June 14, 1823.[14]

Vallance began to contribute individually signed and executed copperplates to Dobson's *Encyclopaedia* with Volume XIII in 1795, eventually preparing 30 illustrations on his own in addition to the plates on which he collaborated with James Thackara and another two plates that may be tentatively attributed to him (numbers 484 and 485). According to Alexander Lawson, he was "certainly the best engraver at this time (1794) in the United States; and had he been placed in a more favorable situation, he would have been a fine artist" (Dunlap 2: 122). Perhaps this is why Dobson selected him to engrave the frontispiece of the *Encyclopaedia,* easily the most dramatic and important engraving that he contributed to the project. An emblematic and allegorical illustration depicting various figures in classical garb engaged in studying or explaining the various arts and sciences, the frontispiece places these images against a background suggestive of idealized antiquity and mythology, including classical architecture and Egyptian pyramids and obelisks. A scene apparently representative of the Garden of Eden occupies the center background, a graphic reminder that in a postlapsarian world, the universal knowledge of nature originally bestowed upon Adam but lost with the Fall of Man can be recovered only by the slow process of scientific discoveries which it is the business of encyclopedias to record and preserve. The balloon ascensionist rising to the left of center (the viewer's right), in contrast to the layered and allusive complexity of the rest of the imagery of the frontispiece, is probably intended as a reference to James "Balloon" Tytler, who contributed so much to both the second and third editions of the *Britannica* (Kruse 56–67). All details in the frontispiece are copied in reverse from the British edition.

James Thackara, Vallance's associate in business, was born in Philadelphia on March 12, 1767, three years after his father had emigrated from England to America.[15] Like Vallance, he studied under James Trenchard (and possibly also under Robert Scot). Also like Vallance, he married into the family of his master, wedding Trenchard's daughter Hannah on May 26, 1790. Thackara's earliest known engraving is the frontispiece for Robert Dodsley's *Selected Fables of Esop*, inscribed in 1786, the same year he began his apprenticeship with Trenchard (his indenture was cancelled in 1789, before his marriage to Trenchard's daughter). In 1787, he also engraved an illustration for George Fisher's *American Instructor*, followed by "A View of the New Market from the Corner of Shippen & Second Streets" in the *Columbian Magazine* in 1788. Between 1795 (Volume XIII) and 1797 (Volume XVII), he contributed 28 individually signed copperplate engravings to Dobson's *Encyclopaedia*, together with six more illustrations that may with some confidence be ascribed to him and one that may be tentatively attributed. The subject matter of his plates is largely scientific or technological in nature (e.g., "Optics," "Pneumatics," and "Ship-Building"), with few attempts at animals or other anatomical forms. His best known engraving, however, for which he received $168 in 1798, was executed not for Dobson but for the Carpenters' Company of Philadelphia and is still in use today.

During his long career, Thackara occupied many different business addresses, commencing with his shop at 122 Spruce Street. Other addresses included 23 George Street; 72 Spruce Street (the first address of Thackara & Vallance); 177 S. Second Street; 43. S. Second Street (near Dobson's print shop); 75 Spruce Street; and 35 Spruce Street (Brown and Brown 54: 134). Although Thackara was not among the original group of artists who established the Columbianum, he joined them shortly afterwards and was promptly appointed chairman of the committee to draft a constitution. Attempting to further the cause of art in the eyes of the average citizen, he published *The Young Ladies and Gentlemens* [sic] *Complete Drawing Book* sometime between 1796 and 1799, with 32 copperplates copied from English originals. Later, in 1813–1814, he and his son William Wood Thackara substantially revised and updated this volume as *Thackara's Drawing Book for the Instruction of Young Ladies and Gentlemen*. One of Philadelphia's more prominent artists, he was named curator of the Pennsylvania Academy of the Fine Arts from 1816 to 1826. Although he completed his last known engraving in 1834, he continued as an active promoter of the arts even after his retirement in 1837.

Nor were all of Thackara's energies devoted to the advancement of American art. Deeply involved in Pennsylvania politics in the early nineteenth century, he served as clerk of the Pennsylvania House of Representatives and as a member of the House itself. Between 1821 and 1833, he was also one of the commissioners who oversaw the building of Philadelphia's famous Eastern State Penitentiary, which attracted international attention. After a long career highlighted by his public service and by his special devotion to the arts, Thackara died on August 15, 1848, at the age of 81 and was buried in St. Peter's Episcopal Churchyard in Philadelphia.[16]

Thackara's efforts to establish art on a professional basis in the United States and to improve the quality of American art are his most important legacies to the cultural history of America. His energy is commendable, but his engravings, unfortunately, leave much to be desired. The always acerbic Alexander Lawson, even though (or perhaps because) he had been apprenticed to Thackara and Vallance during his early years in Philadelphia, portrayed both of them as would-be artists who were incapable of turning out work that was worthy of the name of art. "They thought themselves artists," Lawson wrote, apparently forgetting what he had said about Vallance as a talented artist victimized by the circumstances of American culture, "and [imagined] that they knew every part of the art; and yet their art consisted in copying, in a dry, stiff manner with the graver, the plates for the Encyclopaedia, all their attempts at etching having miscarried" (Dunlap 1: 423). Surely this assessment is too harsh, for some of Thackara's and Vallance's contributions to the *Encyclopaedia* possess great charm and can still be viewed with pleasure. On the whole, however, no plate except the frontispiece by either Thackara or Vallance, whether executed singly or together, is memorable. Their work represents a dead level of competence that publishers of encyclopedias offered in competition with Dobson's were quick to seize upon as an area of vulnerability in his publication.

Thackara's father-in-law, James Trenchard, also contributed a substantial number of plates to the *Encyclopaedia,* 25 signed engravings in all. The fourth son of George and Jane (Wood) Trenchard, James was born in Penns Neck, Salem County, New Jersey, in 1746 and may have come to Philadelphia as early as 1773 or 1774 (Cook 14–16; Crompton 1960, 381). After serving an apprenticeship with James Smither, Sr., who also engraved plates for the *Encyclopaedia,* Trenchard went into business for himself, advertising "all kinds of Engraving and Seal-cutting done in the newest and neatest fashions" in the *Pennsylvania Gazette* on June 11, 1777, and identifying the location of his shop as "Front Street five doors above Market-Street." Trenchard was a member of the "fourth class, Fourth Batallion" of militia captained by Charles Wilson Peale and called into active service during the Revolutionary War (Cook 17). After the war, he resumed the business of engraving and moved his shop to "the North side of Spruce-street, between Second and Third-streets" (*Pennsylvania Gazette,* September 22, 1784). By 1785, he had moved to the corner of Walnut and Second streets (Brown and Brown 54: 136). The next year he received £10 from the American Philosophical Society for designing and cutting the device on its certificate of membership, which is still in use today. Still, business must have been slow, for a few years later he paired with a man named Hallberg, who is otherwise unknown to historians of American art, to open a "Drawing School, For the Instruction of Ladies and Gentlemen . . . at the house of Capt. Emerson's North Side of Walnut street between Front and Second streets" (*Pennsylvania Herald,* January 5, 1788). Trenchard's later business addresses include 159 Mulberry (1791) and 72 North Fourth (1793; Brown and Brown 54: 136).

In 1786, Trenchard joined Mathew Carey, Charles Cist, Thomas Seddon, and William Spotswood (the latter two among the booksellers officially "entrusted with subscriptions" for Dobson's *Encyclopaedia*) in announcing plans to publish the *Columbian Magazine.* Highly praised by historians of American journalism as the finest literary periodical printed in the United States during the early years of the republic, the magazine was, like Dobson's *Encyclopaedia,* a patriotic venture designed to give voice to "the genuine spirit of liberty" which had already so graciously "extended its benign influence over these independent and highly favored republics" (*Pennsylvania Gazette,* September 9, 1786). Trenchard, the only engraver among the five partners, became responsible for nearly all of the art work in the journal, with an occasional assist from his pupils Thackara and Vallance. In January of 1789, after months of monetary losses for the magazine, he found himself sole owner of the enterprise. Within a year, however, increasing costs forced him to turn the publication over to William Young, who retitled it the *Universal Asylum and Columbian Magazine* and attempted to cut the costs of production by drastically reducing the number of illustrations. A variety of economic circumstances doomed Young's effort also, and in December of 1792 the magazine went out of business for good. Trenchard, meanwhile, had gone to England, where he visited with Benjamin West. He returned to America around 1797, was sued for divorce by his wife, and disappeared from the historical record. It is not known when he died.[17]

Some of Trenchard's engravings for the *Columbian Magazine* were taken from drawings by his friend Charles Wilson Peale; a few he appears to have drawn himself before turning them into illustrations. Most, however, he copied from other engravings already in print in a variety of sources, making patriotic innovations as he deemed necessary. In the *Columbian Magazine* for December, 1789, for example, he copied William Burgis's *View of the Ancient Buildings Belonging to Harvard-College,* originally published in 1726, but left out the royal cartouche. Wherever possible, he followed the same practice in the *Encyclopaedia.* He dramatically metamorphosed Andrew Bell's engraving of a diving white-headed eagle in plate 190 ("*Falco*") in Volume VII, for instance, into the stately symbol of America, vigilant and alert upon a naked branch. This illustration is perhaps the most striking visual representation in the *Encyclopaedia* of the nationalistic pride that inspired Dobson's project to begin with.

Yet Trenchard, like Thackara and Vallance, was not an exceptional engraver. The rest of the birds in the plate in which the newly re-interpreted white-headed eagle appears, for instance, are stiff, lifeless, and two-dimensional (to do Trenchard justice, the engraving by Bell which he used as a model exhibits many of the same defects). Their strong outlines suggest the lingering power of the limning tradition in the visual arts in America,[18] but the lines within the figures—the shadings and the crosshatchings—seem to have been weakly and tentatively incised. Between Volume VII in 1793 and Volume XV in 1796, Trenchard was responsible for 29 signed and two unsigned copperplates in Dobson's *Encyclopaedia,* all of which appear faded and washed out in comparison with most of the other engravings in the same publication. There seems more truth than envy or self-aggrandizement in Alexander Lawson's charge that Trenchard's efforts at engraving resulted in "poor scratchy things" at best (Dunlap 1: 382).

The most colorful and longest lived of the artists who engraved for the *Encyclopaedia* was James Smither, Sr., from whom Trenchard had learned his trade. Smither, who was born in England, probably in Surrey County, in 1740,[19] first set up shop in Philadelphia "in Third-street, from the Cross-Keys, corner of Chesnut Street" on April 21, 1768 (*Pennsylvania Journal*). There he advertised his proficiency at "all manner of Engraving in gold, silver, copper, steel, and all other metals," listing "coats of arms, and seals . . . stamps, brands and metal cuts for printers," as well as "ornamental tools for book-binders [and] . . . ornaments [for] guns and pistols" among his specialties. In pragmatic Philadelphia, however, even all these skills were not enough, and shortly after this advertisement appeared, Smither proposed a drawing school "at the Golden Head, in Strawberry-alley . . . where young gentlemen and ladies shall be carefully instructed in that useful art, at Twenty Shillings a quarter, and Ten Shillings entrance" (*Pennsylvania Gazette,* January 16, 1769). "This art has the greatest number of admirers," Smither asserted, taking care to emphasize utility and practicality and to avoid aesthetics altogether,

and no wonder, since in a kind of universal language, or living history, it represents to our view the forms of innumerable objects, which we should be otherwise deprived of, and helps us to a knowledge of many of the works of nature and art, by a silent communication.

With almost no alteration, this statement could serve as a rationale for the inclusion of so many illustrations in the *Encyclopaedia.*

On September 12, 1771, Smither married Rachel Betterton of Philadelphia.[20] When the British occupied the city during the revolutionary war, Smither, who had engraved a number of the plates for Pennsylvania currency, counterfeited them for the benefit of the enemy. Consequently, when the British evacuated and moved to New York, Smither felt compelled to accompany them, finding work with the Tory printer Hugh Gaine. A proclamation issued by the Supreme Executive Council of Pennsylvania on June 25, 1778 accused him of high treason, but, like Gaine, he must have offered a satisfactory explanation for his actions. Once the passions of war had cooled, he returned to Philadelphia and set about attempting to restore his trade (Stauffer 1: 254–55). Another advertisement for an "Evening Drawing School" similar to but shorter than the one of 1769 appeared in the *Independent Gazetteer* on October 23, 1790.

Smither began contributing to the *Encyclopaedia* with Volume V as the only other artist besides Scot, Thackara, and Vallance whose signature appeared in Dobson's publication in its earliest stages. He executed 29 illustrations, mostly plants and maps and views of cities; perhaps the best of his pieces is "Remains of the Great Temple of the Sun in Palmyra" (number 372 in Volume XIII). Engravings over his name are also to be found in the *American Magazine, or General Repository* in March of 1769, the *Pennsylvania Magazine, or American Monthly Museum* in January, February, and March 1775, and the *American Universal Magazine* on January 2, 1797 (Lewis 1959, 2, 16). Of his magazine illustrations, the outspoken Alexander Lawson commented: "He tried to make designs and engravings . . .

but they were poor scratchy things, as were all the rest of his work" (Dunlap 1: 382). Once when copper was scarce in Philadelphia, Lawson continued, he had purchased three plates on which Smither had engraved a large ground plan of the city and, without any misgivings about the quality of the work he was destroying, "cut them up for small plates" (Dunlap 1: 184).

Smither lived until January 10, 1829, attaining the age of 89. His son, James Smither, Jr., who engraved one plate for the *Encyclopaedia* (number 203, "Frangilia") in Volume VII in 1793, was not as fortunate, falling victim to yellow fever in September of that same year.[21] Strangely enough, although the elder Smither had engraved 10 plates for Volume VII and although he continued to be listed as an engraver until his death, his name does not again appear on any of the plates of the *Encyclopaedia* or in the supplemental volumes.[22]

Smither's total of 29 plates ranks him with Allardice, Scot, Trenchard, Thackara, and Vallance among the six major engravers of the *Encyclopaedia*. None of the remaining artists was individually responsible for even as many as ten signed illustrations. James Akin's official total, for example, stands at eight—numbers 315, 333, 337, 338, and 345 in Volume XII and numbers 486, 490, 492 in Volume XVIII—and includes the only plate in the first eighteen volumes of the *Encyclopaedia* to bear the label "*Aqua-forti Fecit,*" number 333 ("Mustellae"). The fact that he was able to master the essentials of etching when, according to Alexander Lawson at least, such other engravers as James Thackara and John Vallance were unable to do so, together with his competence at engraving woodcuts (Hamilton 47), testifies to his versatility and his technical mastery of the various arts of illustration.

Born in 1773 (Stauffer 1: 4), Akin was a native of South Carolina who never failed to announce that fact in the signatures to his engravings. An orphan, he was taken in by Bishop Smith (not the Bishop William Smyth of a later generation) of South Carolina and came to the attention of the prominent South Carolina patriot and politician John Rutledge (*DAB* 16: 258–60). Akin had apparently learned the art of engraving in South Carolina but was living in Philadelphia in 1795 when Rutledge, a staunch Federalist, recommended him for a clerkship to Timothy Pickering, newly created secretary of state under President Washington who also held that post for some years during the Adams administration. "I do not recollect how long he wrote in the office," Pickering later told the Newburyport lawyer Theophilus Parson, "but after some time he returned to his professional capacity of engraving," in which line and in drawing "he performed some services in relation to the state department" (*Papers* 14: 134).[23]

As an engraver, Akin was fond of historical subjects, especially those that glorified his South Carolina heritage. Among the engravings he advertised for sale at his shop on "Powell street, 4 doors from 5th st. between Spruce and Pine streets" were several depicting the battles of Eutaw Springs and the Cowpens, as well as the capture of Major Andre (Prime 2: 65). In 1800, he teamed with another engraver, William Harrison, Jr. to produce "an elegant design in remembrance of the late illustrious General Washington" (Bristol 10958a; Evans 49001). Several of his engravings appear in the *Juvenile Magazine, or Miscellaneous Repository of Useful Information,* published in Philadelphia in 1802–03 (Lewis 1959, 8). During those years, his address is listed as 37 Pewter Platter Alley (1801–03) and, later, as 143 Walnut Street (1803–05; Brown and Brown 53: 220).

This last address poses a problem for anyone attempting to ascertain Akin's whereabouts after his work on the *Encyclopaedia,* for on February 3, 1803, he signed an agreement with author and sea captain Edmund March Blunt (*DAB* 2: 397–98) to move to Newburyport, Massachusetts, and work as an engraver for Blunt under a surety of $5000.[24] He was probably easily induced to leave Philadelphia because of the "distress of annual pestilence," as he later put it in a letter to Pickering (Pickering, *Papers* 43: 69). At some point, probably early in the nineteenth century before he met Blunt and accepted Blunt's offer, Akin studied engraving in London "under an eminent master," or at least so he claimed in an advertisement in the *Newburyport Herald* on January 8, 1805.[25]

In Newburyport, Blunt soon reneged on his agreement with Akin and refused to pay him for work that Blunt deemed substandard and overpriced. On November 3, 1804, he publicly accused Akin of being a thief, alleging that he had stolen two pieces of a copperplate and "one ream and nine" of Blunt's paper. In December 1804, Akin sued Blunt in the Supreme Judicial Court of Massachusetts for libel and defamation of character (Case 401). Akin recovered costs of $3.81, Blunt countersued and lost (Case 402), then sued Akin for slander and libelous statements which, he claimed, had prejudiced booksellers as far away as Philadelphia and Baltimore against him and had cost him $1500 in lost revenues. He also asserted that Akin had failed to live up to his part of the bargain and had ceased working for Blunt as of October 27, 1804. This altercation produced one of Akin's most famous engravings, "Infuriated Despondency," a caricature of Blunt in a rage about to throw a heavy metal frying pan at the head of an invisible artist (Akin himself) who had requested payment for services rendered. The event took place in Josiah Foster's hardware store in Newburyport in the fall of 1804 (Sanborn 227) and led to litigation and counterlitigation that dragged on until July 7, 1806, when it was resolved in Akin's favor by court-appointed referees (Case 257). On October 30, 1807, Akin announced in punning metaphors and allusions that he had had enough of the hospitality of Newburyport and was returning to Phila-delphia, where, out of the reach of the civil authorities of Massachusetts, he planned to publish satirical illustrations of his protracted battle with Blunt "*traced* and *bitten* with *acid*" for the amusement of those who "benevolently encouraged my *Little* labors to prevent the *blunt* wearing of my *points* in *Legal executions*" (*Newburyport Herald*). No such work is known to have been published.

Akin did, however, exercise his satirical talents after returning to Philadelphia in 1808 and establishing himself "just above the Upper Ferry over Schuylkill." As late as 1833, his *A Down[w]right Gabbler,* aimed at the reformer Fanny Wright (Weitenkampf 215), showed that he had not lost the taste for caricature about which Timothy Pickering had warned him in 1805.[26] In 1811, Akin moved to 39 Mulberry Street, then to 39 N. Sixth Street (1813), 32 High Street (1816–1817), and, finally, to 166 Locust Street above Eleventh (1818–1820; Brown and Brown 53: 220). Identi-fied with various professions until his death on July 18, 1846, Akin's name continued to appear in Philadelphia directories. His will was probated August 14 of that year (Stauffer 1: 4–5).

Henry W. Weston, who made eight plates for the *Encyclopaedia,* all of them for the eighteenth volume, did most of his work for Mathew Carey around 1803–06. A one time partner of James Trenchard, he maintained a shop in Loxleys Alley around 1805–06 (Brown and Brown 54: 140). In addition to the plates in the *Encyclopaedia,* Weston left his signature on the frontispiece of William Woodward's edition of William Enfield's *The Speaker* (1799; Evans 35446). According to David McNeely Stauffer, he executed engravings "in a feeble manner" (1: 288), and his work holds only historical interest.

In contrast to Henry Weston, Alexander Lawson was the most tal-ented of the engravers who worked on Dobson's *Encyclopaedia*. Like Wes-ton, Lawson engraved only eight plates for the first eighteen volumes of Dobson's book, but he was to do many more for the three-volume *Supple-ment*. He created one plate for Volume XVII, number 453 ("Ship Bolts"), and seven plates for the final volume. All of these are of mechanical or technical subjects that call for draftsmanship and perspective rather than artistry and do not allow him to exhibit his abilities.

Lawson was born in Ravenstruthers, Lanarkshire, Scotland, on December 19, 1773, and died in Philadelphia on August 22, 1846. Orphaned at the age of fifteen, he came into the care of an older brother, who placed him as apprentice to a dealer in books and engravings in Manchester, England. Here Lawson's interest in drawing and engraving was kindled. His sympathy for the French Revolution caused him to quarrel with his brother, and in 1793 he left Scotland intending to travel to France via America.

Landing in Baltimore on July 14, 1794, Lawson was so taken with the United States that he decided to stay. Like most immigrants with an interest in books and publishing, he gravitated naturally to Philadelphia and there found employment with Thackara and Vallance. A turning point in his career was his engraving of the plates for William Woodward's edition of Thomson's *Four Seasons* (1797; Evans 32927), which established his reputation and enabled him to set up shop on his own. His most famous engravings were done not for Dobson or the *Encyclopaedia,* however, but for Alexander Wilson's *Ornithology* (1808) and the continuations assembled by Charles Lucien Bonaparte. Lawson's first shop was located between South and Shippen streets (1798), but he soon moved to 19 George Street (1799–1800), then to 21 George (1801) and 45 George (1802–1803), and finally to Seventh Street above Spruce. His last known address was on Pine Street near Tenth (*DAB* 11: 56; Brown and Brown 53: 565).

Joseph Bowes engraved six plates for the *Encyclopaedia,* one for Volume XV and five for the final volume. He also engraved several plates for the *American Universal Magazine* (January 9 and 16, 1797) and one for the *Philadelphia Monthly Magazine or Universal Repository of Knowledge and Entertainment* (February 1798). Although Stauffer places Bowes in Philadelphia no earlier than 1796 (1: 28), an advertisement in *Dunlap's American Daily Advertiser* on October 15, 1794 establishes Bowes's arrival in that city a full two years earlier. Though not a member of the Columbianum, or American Academy of the Fine Arts, Bowes was sufficiently established among the artists of the city to be one of the exhibitors at the first and only exhibition of original art sponsored by that organization on May 22, 1795, identifying himself as both "architect and engraver" on that occasion (Sellers 2: 73); this was about a year before his first contribution to the *Encyclopaedia.* At the time, Bowes kept shop at 13 Cherry Alley, but by 1796 he had moved to 157 Vine Street and then to 25 Cressons Alley (1797–98; Brown and Brown 53: 293). Bowes worked in both line and stipple engraving.

Although Philadelphia directories locate the engraver Joseph Seymour in that city between the years 1803 and 1822, it was evidently not Joseph but Samuel Seymour who contributed five plates to the *Encyclopaedia* (Joseph Seymour's dates of residence are too late for him to have contributed to any except the last volume of the *Supplement,* and that work contains no plates signed "Seymour"). Once again, work on the *Encyclopaedia* helps to establish dates of activity a few years earlier than is customarily assumed, for Stauffer says that Seymour began work in Philadelphia around 1797 (1: 244), whereas his first plate for Thomas Dobson, number 348 in Volume XIII, was executed sometime in 1795 or possibly as early as 1794. Indeed, none of the five plates he created for the *Encyclopaedia,* which are confined to Volumes XIII and XIV, was done any later than 1795. In 1823, Seymour accompanied Major Stephen H. Long on his expedition into Yellowstone territory. Nothing further is known about him.

Like Samuel Seymour, William Ralph and William Barker each engraved five plates for Dobson's *Encyclopaedia.* All of Ralph's engravings for Dobson are to be found in Volume XV; he also engraved one plate for the *New York Magazine,* "Inside View of the New Theatre, Philadelphia," in April 1794 (Lewis 1959, 4). William Barker's work includes three maps, and all five of his plates appear in Volume VII. Other examples of Barker's work may be found in the issue of the *American Universal Magazine* dated January 23, 1797 (Lewis 1959, 2) and on the title page of William Birch's *Views of Philadelphia* (1800).

The last contributor to the *Encyclopaedia* to be considered, Thomas Clarke, was responsible for two engravings. Only William Creed contributed fewer plates. Both of Clarke's engravings, numbers 536 and 537, appear in the warfare sequence in Volume XVIII. Between May 1797 and March 1798, Clarke engraved thirteen plates on various subjects for the *American Universal Magazine* of Philadelphia and, later, illustrated David Longworth's *Telemachus* (Evans 32126) in New York, maintaining addresses in both cities. After 1800, Clarke attempted to establish himself in the South. He eventually went insane, imagining that he was being followed by a large black man without a head, and committed suicide (Dunlap 2: 174).

Some plates originally included in the third edition of the *Encyclopaedia Britannica* do not appear in the copies of Dobson's *Encyclopaedia* which were examined for this study. Plate 238, for example, is inexplicably missing from the British edition, Volume VIII, and from all copies of Dobson's edition that I have seen. Another missing plate, number 85, "The Northern Hemisphere with the Figures of the Constellations," is not included either in the copy of the *Encyclopaedia* at Denison University or in the one at the University of Michigan. Four engravings (numbers 307–10) illustrating the article "Midwifery" are not included in the copy at Denison and might at first appear to have been victims of editorial suppression, as was the case when they were originally printed in the first edition of the *Britannica* in 1771; the publisher was supposedly ordered to destroy the plates but apparently did not do so, since they resurfaced in the third edition (Kruse 51). These illustrations are included in other sets of Dobson's *Encyclopaedia,* however, which indicates that either the bookbinder or the individual subscriber but not the publisher was responsible for any act of censorship aimed at the content of the American edition. Although Dobson provided a list for placing illustrations in each volume and undoubtedly oversaw the binding process for volumes ordered directly from him, so many bookbinders had a hand in finishing the various sets of the *Encyclopaedia* that it would indeed be surprising if all the engravings were included or identically placed from one set to another.

About the final aspect of the *Encyclopaedia* as artifact, the binding of the book, there is little to be said. Often the volumes must have been delivered in the cheapest bindings, leaving the subscriber to arrange with a local bookbinder for a more elegant covering. Only in the case of the most expensive editions, as with George Washington's second set, would Dobson have been responsible for contracting with the bookbinder and delivering a finished product. Most American bookbinding of the late eighteenth century was utilitarian in nature, with little room for decoration or the extra artistic gesture that sets one binding apart from another and elevates it aesthetically. The appearance of the *Encyclopaedia* in boards reflected the evolution of bookbinding, like papermaking and typography during this period, toward a national style and away from personal and regional idiosyncrasies. Characterized by modestly decorated spines of five or six compartments divided from each other by a single or double fillet, this new utilitarian style customarily reserved the second compartment from the top for the book's title, as was done with the *Encyclopaedia*. By 1800 or so, the triumph of uniformity in bookbinding, begun at least partly in response to democratic ideology and the newly achieved status of nationhood, would be completed by the Industrial Revolution (Spawm 35).

Still, as Darrell Hyder observes, the range of bindings in which the *Encyclopaedia* was available suggests simple utility at one end of the scale and opulence at the other,[27] with gilt calf, Morocco, and even Russian leather among the options (73). This, in turn, implies varying attitudes toward the book as artifact on the part of Dobson's purchasers—at least those who could afford to choose a more expensive option than boards. In the space of two centuries, many sets of the *Encyclopaedia* have been rebound at least once to preserve them as resources for research. Some, however, survive in their original bindings, as does the set bound in calf at Denison University. Originally purchased by John McAllister, a wealthy merchant whose advertisements for whips and canes appear frequently in Philadelphia's newspapers in the 1790s and the father of the historian of the same name, the set also bears the names of John McAllister Stevenson, evidently a grandson, and Dr. Louis Stevenson, the son—three generations of owners who continued to prize the book long after it had lost all, or nearly all, its value as a source of information. Undoubtedly, each generation had its own reasons. Moreover, the final gesture ending family ownership, the act of donating the volumes to a library, reaffirms the value of the book beyond its contents. One small and sketchy history will not build a case, but it does help establish the existence of certain features of and feelings about the *Encyclopaedia* that cannot be explained entirely in terms of content and utility.

The *Encyclopaedia* now stood at eighteen volumes, the number that Dobson had been promising subscribers since early in 1793. The frontispiece, the title pages, and the 542 copperplate engravings had likewise been delivered, or at least enough of the latter so that anyone who had not been counting on purpose to trip up the publisher would not have noticed the difference. The earlier volumes had probably gone easier than Dobson anticipated, but several of the last nine had caused him enough trouble that he must have wished at times he had not begun the enterprise. In Edinburgh, however, the Reverend Dr. Gleig had already issued proposals for a supplement, citing persuasive reasons for revising and adding to a book of knowledge already outdated in some subjects by almost a decade. As he looked over his own American edition, moreover, Dobson was conscious of regrettable omissions and items that, had they been properly attended to, might have increased sales and enhanced the status of the *Encyclopaedia* as an American book. These considerations, and others, called for an American *Supplement* to match the Edinburgh edition. To his credit, Dobson almost immediately set about the task.

Notes

1. For the estimate of the amount of paper required for the *Encyclopaedia* and, indeed, for a good deal of other information regarding papermaking and watermarks, I am indebted to Thomas Gravell, who shared his thoughts on Dobson's *Encyclopaedia* with me in a letter written January 17, 1989.

By a useful coincidence, the same year in which Dobson announced his intention to publish the *Encyclopaedia* also saw the publication of Arthur Homer's *Bibliotheca Americana,* which claimed that the price of labor was so high in America that the United States produced only enough paper to print "laws, pamphlets, and newspapers" (Hunter 1971, 43). Like Washington Irving's *Sketch Book* more than thirty years later, Dobson's *Encyclopaedia* conclusively answered and disproved an English critique of the state of American culture in the very year the criticism was articulated.

2. For type manufactured in America before John Baine, see Wroth's *Colonial Printer,* 87–109. In "Philadelphia Fine Printing, 1780–1820," *Printing and Graphic Arts* 9 (1961): 72, Darrell Hyder incorrectly states that Dobson "did not even make the usual claim of new type, locally manufactured paper, or 'neat' bindings, but wisely spent his advertisements listing contents and the $5-per-volume price for the fifteen proposed" (72). Hyder must have based his conclusions only on the earliest version of Dobson's proposals.

Mathew Carey followed Dobson by only a short while in claiming to use type especially cast for the purpose of one edition only. He used type manufactured by Baine & Company to print his Douay version of the Bible (Wroth 1938, 110).

3. Ledger books of N. & D. Sellers, HSP. I thank John Bidwell of the William Andrews Clark Library, University of California at Los Angeles, for pointing out this reference in a letter of October 11, 1989.

4. The "Save Rags" watermark was discovered by Thomas Gravell in the copy of the *Encyclopaedia* at the Winterthur Museum. A reasonable guess as to the identity of "J/W" as a Pennsylvania manufacturer is Isaac ("J") and William ("W") Levis, producing paper jointly in their several mills.

5. John Bidwell undertook these measurements of Isaiah Thomas's copy of the *Encyclopaedia* at the American Antiquarian Society and reported his results in a letter of October 11, 1989.

6. For the duty on paper, see Clement Biddle, "Duties Payable on Goods Imported into the United States, by Act of Congress, of the 4th of July, 1790," *Philadelphia Directory* (Philadelphia: James & Johnson, 1791), 71–75 (Evans 23205).

7. For more about typefaces and typefounding, see Stanley Morison's introductory essay, especially pp. [iii]–xxv, to W. Turner Berry and A. F. Johnson, *Catalogue of Specimens of Printing Types by English and Scottish Printers and Founders, 1665–1830* (London: Oxford University Press [Humphrey Milford], 1935). A brief description of John Baine's *Specimen Book* of 1787 appears on page 57; the *Specimen Book* may be seen at the American Antiquarian Society, Worcester, Massachusetts.

8. Rollo Silver, *Typefounding in America, 1787–1825* (Charlottesville: University Press of Virginia, 1965), 8, reprints the same advertisement from the Boston *Gazette* published on February 18, 1793, a month later than the one in the *Federal Gazette* of Philadelphia.

9. The process by which illustrations were copied in reverse from the third edition of the *Encyclopaedia Britannica* involved rubbing the back of the illustration with a pastel and then placing the illustration over a copperplate that had been covered with a thin veneer of wax. The illustration was lightly traced on the wax, leaving grooves to be followed by the burin or graver to incise lines into the

copperplate. This was the cheapest and fastest way to reproduce engraved illustrations. It was probably mandated by Dobson as a way to keep down the costs of production, which makes Alexander Lawson's criticism of some of his fellow engravers sound unduly harsh.

10. The ruins and castles appear for the first time in the second edition of the *Britannica,* also engraved by Bell.

11. This is one of the several problematical references to the *Pennsylvania Packet* in Alfred Coxe Prime's otherwise very useful *Arts and Crafts in Philadelphia, Maryland, and South Carolina, 1721–1785,* 2 vols. (Topsfield, Mass.: Walpole Society, 1929–1932). The *Pennsylvania Packet* ceased publication under that name in 1790 (Brigham 2: 942). Nor does *Dunlap's American Daily Advertiser,* which, according to Brigham, continued the *Packet* without a change in numbering, contain the announcement Prime quotes here.

In her useful but confusing and confused essay "Dobson's *Encyclopaedia,*" Judy L. Larson incorrectly identifies Allardice as the person who answered Dobson's advertisement in 1792; Allardice was already working for Scot by 1790. Most likely it was Allardice, not Thackara and Vallance as Larson claims (they were already engraving as a partnership in 1790) who answered Scot's advertisement in 1789.

12. Articles of Association, *Columbianum,* Papers of the Pennsylvania Academy of the Fine Arts, HSP, quoted by permission. The text of the "Articles" may also be found in Robert D. Crompton, "James Trenchard of the 'Columbian' and 'Columbianum,'" *Art Quarterly* 23 (1960): 378.

13. Evidence for dating the dissolution of the partnership of Thackara & Vallance in 1794 is that their name appears jointly as the engravers of Dennis Griffith's *Map of Maryland* (Evans 27070) in 1794, but only Vallance's name appears on the same map the following year (Evans 28772); Thackara, too, continued to engrave and publish on his own after 1794 (see Evans 38269 for a representative title). Crompton, however, (1958a, 425) asserts that Thackara and Vallance were partners until around 1796.

14. Information about Vallance's career and his engravings has been gathered from a variety of sources, including Crompton (1958a, 424–28); Lewis; Prime (1: 74); Stauffer (2: 519); and Stokes and Haskell (64).

15. Robert D. Crompton, "James Thackara, American Engraver," *Antiques* 74 (November 1958), 425, says that "the exact location of his [Thackara's] place of birth is open to debate" and claims that he was brought to America as an infant in 1767. However, in a letter of January 9, 1957 to Robert W. Hill, Keeper of the Manuscripts at the New York Public Library, Crompton gave the place as Philadelphia and the date as March 12, 1767 (Crompton to Hill, Thackara Collection, Archives of American Art, Smithsonian Institution). Under the theory that Crompton, who married Thackara's great-great-great granddaughter, wrote and submitted his article to *Antiques* some time before it was published and that he was not afforded the opportunity to make changes reflecting any subsequent discoveries he had made about Thackara, I have accepted the more precise date as the correct one.

16. In addition to the standard sources such as Fielding, Lewis, and Stauffer,

I have relied for biographical information about James Thackara on Crompton's "James Thackara, American Engraver" (see note 15 above) and his "James Thackara, Engraver, Friend of the Arts, Legislator and Prison Builder," *Journal of the Lancaster County Historical Society* 62 (April 1958): 74–76. The date of Thackara's death is also given in Prime 1: 267.

17. In addition to Lewis and Stauffer (1: 276), this biographical sketch is based upon Robert D. Crompton's "James Trenchard of the 'Columbian' and 'Columbianum,'" *Art Quarterly* 23 (1960): 378–97. For the *Columbian Magazine*, see Lyon N. Richardson, *A History of Early American Magazines, 1741–1789* (New York: Thomas Nelson and Sons, 1931), 276 ff.

18. For the influence of the limning tradition in American art, see Barbara Novak, *American Painting of the Nineteenth Century: Realism, Idealism, and the American Experience* (New York: Praeger, 1969), 15 ff.

19. The year of Smither's birth may be calculated by simple subtraction from the date of his death, January 10, 1829, when he was described as eighty-nine years of age. Smither's age is discussed in a letter from the Philadelphia historian Joseph Jackson to Frank Weitenkampf, Curator of Prints, New York Public Library, May 13, 1928, Archives of American Art, Smithsonian Institution. See also J. Thomas Scharf and Thompson Westcott, *History of Philadelphia, 1609–1884,* 3 vols. (Philadelphia, 1884) 2: 1005, who record Smither's death "at an advanced age" in 1829.

For Smither's probable place of birth, see Francis Allen to James Smither, February 25, 1806, Society Collection, HSP, cited by permission. The letter discusses particulars of the will of "Diana Brown, of Farnham in the County of Surrey, Widow, deceased," who left to her brother James Smither £127.10.4, which he was having difficulty collecting. This correspondence also has considerable bearing on the question of the identity of "James Smither, engraver," who died in Philadelphia in 1829, since the date of the letter is later than either of the dates usually assigned for Smither's death, 1793 and 1797, and since it is not likely that Smither's son, James Smither, Jr., whom some historians have assumed outlived his father and is the man who died in 1829, would have a widowed sister in England.

20. Jackson to Weitenkampf. Jackson cites "church records here" as the source of his information about the marriage.

21. Citing "church records" again, Jackson gives the date of the younger Smither's death as "September, 1793." So far as the evidence of the *Encyclopaedia* is concerned, this could be correct, for the younger Smither's only contribution to Dobson's publication was engraved early in 1793. Complicating matters, however, is the discovery that one James Smither, Jr., is listed among the members of the Columbianum Association in late 1794 (Sellers 2: 74). Jackson goes on to say that he believes it was the elder Smither who died in 1793. "James Smither came here in the 1760s," he writes to Weitenkampf, "and if he lived until 1829, he must have been engraving as a babe! Therefore, I believe we shall have to conclude that the Senior succumbed in 1793 and the Junior in 1829." But that, of course, would make it impossible for James Smither, Jr., to have been eighty-nine at the time of his death and merely means that Jackson has not performed a simple calculation. Most

engravers and apprentices for whom Dobson and Scot advertised began their careers quite young (Samuel Allardice was only fourteen; Francis Shallus was not much older). Smither would have been twenty-seven or twenty-eight before his first advertisement in Philadelphia, not a "babe" at all, as Jackson supposed.

This story of the two (or, possibly, three) Smithers becomes still more complicated with the appearance of an item in the *Gazette of the United States* announcing the death of "Mr. Smither, Engraver" (September 12, 1797). Who, then, died in 1793? Who is this other "Mr. Smither"? Who lived on until 1829? As indicated in note 19, on the evidence of Diana Brown's will, I believe that the elder Smither is indeed the engraver who died in 1829 and that his son died much earlier. Who the intermediate "Mr. Smither" who died in 1797 may have been remains a mystery.

22. That Smither continued to engrave and to consider himself an artist until the end of his life is evident from his signature on a "Memorial of the Artists of Philadelphia to the Pennsylvania Academy of [the] Fine Arts" in 1828. See Pennsylvania Academy of the Fine Arts, Archives.

23. There is a brief biographical sketch of Akin in John J. Currier's *History of Newburyport, Massachusetts,* 2 vols. (Newburyport, Mass.: Printed for the author, 1906, 1909), 2: 371–77. Pickering's letter to Parsons, cited in the text, is the source of the information about Akin's relationship with "Bishop Smith" and his connection with John Rutledge, said by Pickering to have been the Bishop's son-in-law. This does not accord, however, with the account in the *DAB,* which has Rutledge marrying no one with the last name of Smith. Perhaps Pickering misremembered some of the details about the clerkship of Akin, whom he had not seen for some years until, by chance, he met him again at the session of the Supreme Judicial Court in Salem on October 19, 1805. On that occasion, Akin sketched Pickering's portrait, which he later engraved for broader sale. See Akin to Pickering, October 31, 1804, *Papers* 43: 68, and the account of "Aken [sic] Vs. Blunt," Case 257, in the records of the Supreme Judicial Court of Massachusetts, Essex County (1807). These records are now in the Massachusetts Historical Society in Boston but were copied for me before their removal by Brian Burns of the staff at the Essex County Courthouse. I wish to thank Mr. Burns for his assistance in helping me to shed light on this one part of Akin's career.

24. Supreme Judicial Court Records, December Term 1805, Case 955, "Blunt Vs. Akin and [Ebenezer] Steadman." Steadman was a bookseller in Newburyport who befriended Akin.

25. In this same advertisement, Akin states again that it was the yellow fever which drove him from Philadelphia.

26. In a letter written November 5, 1805, Pickering warned Akin that he had been told by mutual acquaintances that the artist had acquired a reputation for contentiousness among some of the leading citizens of Newburyport. "I cannot . . . forbear to hint, that most persons are afraid of *satyrists,*" Pickering wrote; "lest, in a moment of resentment or ill-humour, they themselves become subjects of his tongue, his pencil or his pen. And I think you considered your *forte* to lie in satyrical drawings" (Pickering, *Papers* 14: 135A). In a letter dated "November 1805," Akin replied, defending himself against what he thought were unfair charges. "Does it

follow that a man otherwise respectable should fear my satyrical talent?" he asked. "Tom Paine, [James Thomson] Callender, and others, I consider *fair game;* but my ideas are not to be prostituted in revenge against every man who shall see & think different from me; & *he* must lower himself very much indeed, who would be rated with such outcasts to society," Pickering, *Papers* 14: 136. Martin P. Snyder, "Liveliness: A Quality in Prints of Philadelphia," in *Philadelphia Printmaking: American Prints before 1860,* ed. Robert F. Looney (West Chester, Pa.: Tinicum Press, 1977), 119, briefly discusses a satiric lithograph by Akin, *Philadelphia Taste Displayed, Or, Bon-Ton Below Stairs,* done around 1830, as an example of Akin's "wry humor" (119); he reproduces the lithograph on page 121. William Feaver, *Masters of Caricature from Hogarth and Gillray to Scharfe and Levine,* ed. Ann Gould (New York: Alfred A. Knopf, 1981), 61, reprints Akin's caricature of the republican editor Richard Folwell and notes Akin's indebtedness to English caricaturists such as Thomas Rowlandson and George Cruikshank. Although he thinks it doubtful that Akin actually had European training as he claimed in some of his advertisements, Feaver finds the artist's work worthy of some attention. "On the strength of his powers of humorous characterization, a fair degree of draughtmanship and a large measure of social concern," Feaver writes, "he did succeed in producing a vivid record of Republican and Jacksonian times" (61). The fullest account of Akin's career is Maureen O'Brien Quimby. "The Political Art of James Akin," *Winterthur Portfolio* 7 (1972): 59–112, an article I had not seen when this chapter was written.

27. It is worth repeating that even in its cheapest binding, the *Encyclopaedia* was beyond the budget of the ordinary American. The pressmen and compositors who worked on it, for example, could not have afforded it, though many engravers, such as Alexander Anderson, David Edwin, Amos Goodwin, and James Rowlandson could and did possess copies. See Donald R. Adams, Jr., *Wage Rates in Philadelphia, 1790–1830,* Dissertations in American Economic History (New York: Arno Press, 1975); Billy G. Smith, "The Material Lives of Laboring Philadelphians, 1750–1800," *William and Mary Quarterly* 3d ser., 90 (1981): 163–202; and United States Department of Labor, *History of Wages in the United States from Colonial Times to 1928,* Bulletin of the United States Bureau of Labor Statistics No. 499 (Washington, D.C.: U.S. Government Printing Office, 1929). In the last-named publication, see especially chapter 11, "Printing and Publishing," 118–23.

7. The *Supplement* to the *Encyclopaedia*: Volumes XIX–XXI

Exactly when Thomas Dobson realized that additional volumes beyond the projected eighteen would be required to "complete" the *Encyclopaedia* and bring it as up-to-date as possible cannot be determined. In his earliest proposals he indicated his awareness that the eventual length of the publication would depend not only on the amount of information available when printing was begun but also, and more importantly, on new information that might be discovered or created before the volume that ought to contain it alphabetically had gone to press. Compounding this problem was a version of Tristram Shandy's dilemma, the realization that publishing and printing can never keep up with available information, if only because words in print inevitably contribute to the world's store of knowledge. An encyclopedia becomes part of the information it seeks to circumscribe, comprehend, and preserve; it both "summarizes the factual knowledge of any generation and mirrors the effect of this knowledge upon the mind and outlook of this same generation" (Steinberg 3).[1] In the case of Dobson's *Encyclopaedia,* moreover, its publication in the United States was an event of cultural and historical importance irrespective of the value of any summary of knowledge it might contain, which could not, of course, include the event of publication.

For any encyclopedist, the requirement of finding an order of arrangement exacerbates the problem of content by dictating that some new material, however important, will have to be ignored until the encyclopedia has been completed and the cycle of categorizing and cataloging can begin all over again with a new edition. There is also the natural tendency of a publisher, evident in both the American and British editions of the third *Britannica,* to begin comprehensive coverage at a leisurely pace for the first letters of the alphabet before fully considering the optimum size of an encyclopedia in terms of cost, shelf space, duration of publication, and other issues. Nearly all encyclopedic compilations tend to rush through the final letters of the alphabet, omitting entries important enough to have found their way in if they had come earlier in the alphabetical series. For these reasons, and others, it was apparent that the *Encyclopaedia* would require a supplement of substantial proportions.

The *Encyclopaedia* contains several indications that Dobson was occasionally dissatisfied with the information certain entries provided and that he hoped to find a way of dealing with the problem. As early as Volume IV, following the entry "Carolina," he directed the reader's attention to fuller entries on "North Carolina" and "South Carolina," which he said would appear in an "(A[ppendix].)." He made a similar reference in Volume VII, where the entry under "Franklin (Dr. Benjamin)" directed the reader to "See Appendix." Later in the same volume, the same directions were given following the article on "Georgia." These references show that Dobson knew something of significance was missing and that he intended to correct the oversight as expeditiously as possible without departing from established pagination and greatly complicating the task of reprinting from a preset text. Following the copy as it arrived from Scotland seems nearly always to have been his primary consideration as a printer and publisher during the preparation of the first eighteen volumes.

There is no appendix in the first eighteen volumes of the *Encyclopaedia* except the four-page "Vindication of the Character of George Fox" at the end of Volume XV. Entries on Franklin, Georgia, and North and South Carolina do appear in the *Supplement*, however, and are among the items that differentiate Dobson's text from the British edition and show that he eventually made good on his promise to provide additional material. Still, since he certainly knew the difference between an appendix and a supplement, it seems reasonable to conclude that, at least when he was preparing Volume VII, Dobson probably imagined that a less complex and comprehensive apparatus than a multivolume supplement could resolve his problems.

Dobson did not directly address the need for a supplement until after the entire *Encyclopaedia* had been published. The earliest dated proposals for the *Supplement* appeared on December 15, 1798, more than six months after the completion of the *Encyclopaedia* itself. Two newspapers carried the announcement simultaneously, the *Gazette of the United States, and Philadelphia Daily Advertiser* and *Porcupine's Gazette.* The advertisement in the *Gazette* was brief, tagged onto a notice of the eighteen-volume set for sale. It informed readers that "T. Dobson has just opened a Subscription for publishing a Supplement" to the *Encyclopaedia,* the aim of which was "to correct such mis-statements as have been found in the Work, and to give an account of the most important discoveries and improvements which have been made for the last ten years." Dobson accurately predicted that the *Supplement* would run to three volumes of about seven hundred pages each, assured the public that the paper and type would remain the same as in the original eighteen-volume *Encyclopaedia,* and set the price at "Six Dollars per volume, in boards, Six Dollars of which [is] to be paid on subscribing." Evidently, he did not intend to make the same economic mistake he had made ten years earlier.

The advertisement in *Porcupine's Gazette* was far more elaborate and detailed. In it, Dobson admitted that the idea of publishing a *Supplement* was not entirely his own; he had been urged to it, he said, "by many of the most zealous patrons" of the *Encyclopaedia.* The twin purposes of the *Supplement,* he repeated from the first version of the proposals, were to correct errors in the *Encyclopaedia* and to provide new information, but this time he went into some detail. Errors, his silence on that subject seemed to imply, were unavoidable in so large a publication as the *Encyclopaedia* and need not be further explained. New information, however, was another matter.

Dobson reminded his readers that "nearly nine years have elapsed" since the first sheets of the *Encyclopaedia* were printed off and given to the public. "No dictionary of arts, sciences, and literature," he added, "has hitherto been published to which a supplement was not necessary," for which he offered several reasons. First, "every dictionary must be arranged in the order of the alphabet," and if only a few years elapse during "its progress through the press," new and important discoveries must be left out unless the editor decides to deviate from the original plan of the work. Such a deviation, presumably, would involve a lengthy and elaborate appendix, possibly at the end of every volume, an alternative that Dobson might once have been considering but finally rejected, perhaps because such a procedure would diminish the sense of the *Encyclopaedia* as product and detract from the material and aesthetic value of the book.[2]

Dobson felt particularly obligated to publish the *Supplement* because, in his words, the nine years between 1789 and 1798 had been "the most eventful period in history!" During that time, new countries had been explored, new scientific principles had been introduced, and previously unknown powers of nature had been revealed, an explosion of knowledge that generated an explosion of language and underscored the urgency of containing the new information within a coherent system. "The progress of publication" had prevented Dobson from including these things in the *Encyclopaedia* because they "could not find a place in the series of the alphabet." On at least one occasion, the same difficulty arose in the *Supplement,* but this time Dobson solved it by redefining categories and deferring discussion until later in the alphabetical series.[3]

Dobson was so caught up in his vision of new scientific discoveries that he did not mention or even obliquely allude to the events and aftermath of the French Revolution, developments that challenged the presumption of rationality and order upon which the *Encyclopaedia* rested. He chose instead to emphasize the theme of human progress and to offer the *Supplement* under that triumphant banner. Nonetheless, the French Revolution was inescapably a part of modern consciousness that would determine a number of entries and illustrations in the supplemental volumes, especially in articles penned by Jedidiah Morse.

The conquest and settlement of the American frontier figured heavily in the story of human progress that Dobson intended to tell in the *Supplement.* Included in his proposals was a call for information about the changed and changing physical environment of the United States, facts and figures to fill in the sketchy and eccentric treatment of some aspects of American geography in the first eighteen volumes. Towns and villages unthought of ten years earlier had sprung up in profusion at the edge of the wilderness, and Dobson was determined to include these new settlements, together with the ones he failed to mention in the first part of the *Encyclopaedia.* "Thomas Dobson will receive with thankfulness," his advertisement declared in the final and most interesting paragraph of the rationale, "communications respecting the different parts of the United States,"

the situation, boundaries, extent and history of the particular states, where these may have been improperly stated in the preceding volumes, descriptions of the different counties, the mountains, plains, waters, soil and productions, the townes [sic], manufactures and commerce of all parts of the states, the scientific or popular discoveries and improvements, natural history of animals and vegetables, the state of agriculture and its improvements, population of the states and districts, seminaries of learning, religious denominations and benevolent institutions, lives of eminent and valuable persons, and in general whatever is interesting to the United States. (*Porcupine's Gazette,* December 15, 1798)

This is not Walt Whitman, to be sure. Nonetheless, in its conglomeration of all the facts and figures about America, the faiths, the factories, the farms, the manufactures, and the people, Dobson's list expresses the same underlying themes of improvement, individual identity within diversity, and unity within multiplicity and obeys the same cataloging impulse that energizes Whitman's complex lines. Nothing like this call for information had accompanied proposals for the *Encyclopaedia,* suggesting that Dobson's sense of the American edition had been radically altered by the experience of publishing the first eighteen volumes. The most striking feature of the *Supplement* is the polyglot poetry of American place names that this advertisement was intended to elicit. The first entry in the first volume, for example, is "Aaronsburg," a posttown in Pennsylvania; the final volume concludes with "Zoneshio, the chief town of the Seneca Indians." In between, in a roll call offered without the least self-consciousness or concession to eighteenth-century decorum save the ubiquitous alphabetizing, the languages of America, and sometimes nothing else for page after page, resound throughout the *Supplement:* Absecon Beach and Abington, Albany, Alexandria, Kaatskill, Peekskill, Hackinsack, Point-au-Fer, Freidenshuetten, Gnadenhuetten, Powhaton, Pocahontas, and the wonderful Quibble Town, New Jersey. Brief and disparate, independent entities yet part of the larger whole now known as the United States, these names arranged by alphabetical accident chant the sometimes mellifluous, often cacophonous song of the open American road. Geography stands as both metaphor and symbol of a bustling, expansive United States.

Apparently oblivious to the poetical potential of his brief catalogue, Dobson concluded his proposal with the prosaic reminder that "considerable time" would be required to organize the materials he expected to receive. "As soon as the work is ready to go to the press," he said, "it will be announced to the public." Dobson also informed prospective clients of the price of each volume and the fact that he alone, rather than the array of booksellers and printers he had employed to market the *Encyclopaedia,* would receive subscriptions at his store "until the first day of July, 1799." He urged all interested parties to "bring forward their subscriptions as soon as possible" so that he could determine how many copies he would need to print and added, almost as an afterthought, that he still had a few sets of the *Encyclopaedia* to sell at "135 dollars per sett, or at various prices in different bindings." All the details in this proposal indicate a clearer sense of size and content and firmer control of the project than had been the case with earlier volumes of the *Encyclopaedia.*

A few days after these proposals appeared in *Porcupine's Gazette* and the *Gazette of the United States,* news of the projected *Supplement* made the papers in a noncommercial way. On December 20, 1798, the *Philadelphia Gazette* carried the brief story that "Thomas Dobson, of this city, has proposed publishing a Supplement to the Encyclopaedia; in which the mistakes of former volumes might be corrected, and some account given of the recent discoveries of the greatest importance." The words suggest that the editor of the newspaper had lifted his story from Dobson's first proposals or even from a copy Dobson had especially provided. The notice remains, nonetheless, one of only a handful of such contemporary comments on Dobson's work as a printer outside of his own advertisements.[4]

In addition to the proposals published in various newspapers, Dobson advertised the forthcoming *Supplement* through broadsheets designed, like those that announced the *Encyclopaedia,* to provide as much information as possible about the project. The surviving broadsheet, dated 1800 by the National Union Catalogue (ND 0302502) but probably printed the year before, offers some of the same information as in the newspapers, but it adds paragraphs from George Gleig's proposals for the British *Supplement* explaining in detail the nature of the "information gap" that had developed in the *Encyclopaedia* and that the *Supplement* was intended to correct. Problem areas included chemistry, which had been entirely rethought since the article in the *Encyclopaedia,* together with new information about the engines, machines, and mills that would soon carry the Industrial Revolution into a new phase, and about clocks and clockmaking. There would be a new article on "Dynamics," concerned with the physics and mechanics of moving forces, and new information about "Electricity" (including new articles on "Lightning" and "Thunder"), "Magnetism," and "Astronomy." In "Architecture" and "Carpentry," readers were to look for new pieces on "Arches" and "Centres," while those philosophically inclined could anticipate a full explanation of "Kantean Philosophy." To this impressive list of new material, Dobson added his plea for information about America and Americans. He closed by reiterating the conditions of subscription he had already publicized in newspaper proposals.

The new volumes of the *Encyclopaedia* were to be printed by Archibald Bartram and Henry Bud, who had printed other works for Dobson from time to time. Perhaps the fire reported by George and David Bruce had helped Dobson make this decision, or perhaps he saw subcontracting as an opportunity to minimize his own financial risk in the event of a significant cost overrun. Whatever the reason, he returned exclusively to the role of publisher for the *Supplement*. For their part, Budd and Bartram handled the printing of the *Supplement* with competence if not aesthetic flair. As Dobson had promised in his proposals, the type was the same, Long Primer oldstyle, and was undoubtedly purchased from the same source, Binny &

Ronaldson, who had supplied type for the first eighteen volumes of the *Encyclopaedia*. The paper, as before, was of superfine quality manufactured in Pennsylvania.

There is, however, one major textual error in the *Supplement*, suggesting either that Budd and Bartram took less trouble with the text than Dobson had—there were no major typographical errors in the eighteen volumes of the *Encyclopaedia*—or that Dobson supervised the work less closely. A gathering of pages from the article on "Machinery" (377–84) in the third supplemental volume (XXI) appears in the midst of the article "Chemistry" in the second (XX) volume. As a result, one of Dr. Gleig's (and, therefore, one of Thomas Dobson's) advertised improvements in the *Supplement* lacks important information. Most of the entries under "Oxy-muriatic Acid" and "Of Acetous Acid," sections VI and XI of the subdivision "Acids," as well as the entire text of sections VII, VIII, IX, and X: "Of Phosphoric Acid," "Boracic Acid," "Flouric Acid," and "Of Carbonic Acid" are missing. The intruding pages from "Machinery" appear again in their proper place in Volume XXI without an acknowledgment of the earlier problem or an appendix to provide material dropped from the subsection "Acids."[5]

Dobson was right that "considerable time" would be required to assemble new materials and integrate them into the text arriving from Edinburgh. The first half volume was completed in May 1800 (Shipton 12: 162), but Dobson did not announce the first full volume (XIX) until August 14 (*Philadelphia Gazette*). Moreover, the content of this announcement was virtually identical to that of the proposals, explaining once again the rationale for publishing a *Supplement*, predicting three volumes of approximately seven hundred pages each, setting the price at six dollars per volume, and calling for American contributions.

No new information about the *Supplement* was provided to potential subscribers until Dobson placed an advertisement for Volume II, Part 1, in the *Philadelphia Gazette* on May 16, 1801. He made a point of highlighting the "Seven Copperplates" that illustrated the recently completed half volume, something he had not mentioned about the first volume, and he repeated many of the details he had stressed in previous proposals and advertisements, particularly the requirement of payment on delivery of each volume. Then, in a paragraph set entirely in italics, he introduced a change in the conditions of subscription. *"The public are respectfully informed,"* he said, *that Subscriptions continue to be received at the above price by T. Dobson, but that as soon as the Second part of this volume is finished the price will be raised to Seven Dollars per volume for such copies of the work as shall not have been subscribed for at that time.*

As matters turned out, subscribers would have a long wait before the second part of the second volume was finished. Dobson was unable to announce Part 2 of Volume XX until November 25, 1802 (*Philadelphia Gazette*)—nearly a full eighteen months after the first part had appeared. This easily sets the record for any volume or partial volume in the entire *Encyclopaedia*. Dobson's announcement, however, made no mention of the long delay. It merely confirmed his promise of a price increase, stating that the cost of the complete *Supplement* was now "21 dollars per set in boards payable on delivering the two volumes now ready." When the third volume was completed "in the ensuing spring," the price per volume would again be raised, both for new purchasers and for those who had not yet "taken up and paid" for the volumes for which they had previously subscribed; despite his attempts to prevent it, Dobson had encountered a familiar problem again. He closed this notice of the twentieth volume with a brief advertisement for the initial eighteen-volume set of the *Encyclopaedia*, still offered at the price quoted in his final advertisement for the *Encyclopaedia* in May of 1798.

Dobson's predictions for the remaining volume of the *Supplement* proved accurate. He announced the completion of Volume XXI, Part I of the *Supplement* in *Poulson's American Daily Advertiser* on March 26, 1803 (over a date of March 23), promising to finish the last part of the third volume "with all convenient speed." He warned that subscriptions would be closed "on the first day of June, 1803" and, as usual, offered for sale to the general public an apparently inexhaustible "few setts of the Encyclopaedia, 18 volumes in boards," at $7.50 per volume.

On June 2, 1803, after nearly fifteen years from planning to production to actual publication, Thomas Dobson announced an end to the *Encyclopaedia*. His final advertisement appeared in the *Gazette of the United States:*

Encyclopaedia, For Sale By Thomas Dobson, *At the Stone House, No. 41 south Second street,* a few copies of the *Encyclopaedia* . . . to which is now added, The Supplement To the Encyclopaedia, in three volumes, making in the whole twenty-one large quarto volumes, illustrated with nearly *six hundred copper-plates.*

The entire twenty-one volumes could be purchased for $156 in boards or various prices up to $240 in Russia. Those who owned sets of the first eighteen volumes could buy the *Supplement* separately, including its fifty-three copperplates, for prices ranging from $21 in boards to $33 in Russia. "Orders from any part of the United States, with the money, and directions how to forward the books, shall be punctually attended to." Thus, with little fanfare, the most ambitious publication project that the United States had witnessed until that time came to a close.

Surviving correspondence between Dobson and Jedidiah Morse makes it possible to reconstruct the reasons why the second part of Volume XX was so many months in coming. On May 10, 1799, Dobson wrote to Morse informing him that work was about to begin on the *Supplement*. He requested Morse to turn his attention "to the History of New England in general, and the particular States and Districts, with whatever is most important there, adapted to the scale of the work."[6] Evidently there had been some previous communication, now lost, on the subject, and Morse must have previously agreed to participate in the project. Dobson reminded Morse that the article had been "wholly omitted" from the first eighteen volumes "from want of proper materials," a claim that was not entirely true, and assured his correspondent that he would be willing to pay "any reasonable compensation" for the essay. "I apply to you with confidence for this account," Dobson went on,

because I wish it to be the best which has been given, and know your fitness for the work. I suppose the article, as it is of importance[,] may occupy from 30 to 50 pages of the Supplement, that however your own judgment may best determine.

There was no pressing need for the essay, Dobson concluded. "It will be in time nine or twelve months hence for the work."

On July 27, 1799, Dobson again wrote to Morse, saying that he was now receiving George Gleig's *Supplement* and that the text was, predictably, "deficient in American Topography."[7] He asked Morse's permission to use information about America from "your Gazetteer," which he preferred over Joseph Scott's *New and Universal Gazetteer* (1799; Evans 36282) for unspecified reasons. He also reminded Morse that they had previously "spoke & wrote" about an article on New England. This new request, Dobson stressed, would not mean any extra work for Morse; he would assume all editorial responsibility for inserting extracts from the *American Gazetteer* at the proper places in the *Supplement*. Thus these three volumes, although heavily indebted to Morse, are Dobson's own texts to a far greater degree than the first eighteen appear to have been.

Dobson's letter of July 27, 1799 also informed Morse that the publisher had only recently received the first part of the first volume of Gleig's *Supplement* "which will comprise as far as the article on *Chemistry,* and am getting the plates engraved & the paper made." Since the initial entry in the *Supplement* is a short paragraph on "Aaronsburg" attributed, like a dozen other entries on the first page, to Jedidiah Morse, Dobson could not yet have begun to print the *Supplement* and would not be able to do so until he received Morse's written permission. Very probably, Volume XIX went to press in August 1799, about a year before it was officially announced as completed.

On April 10, 1800, Dobson sent another brief message to Morse, this one primarily concerned with matters unrelated to the *Supplement* and the article on "New England." Apparently one of Morse's conditions for agreeing to write that article had been to receive a copy of the *Encyclopaedia,* and Dobson wrote to say that he had shipped those eighteen volumes in a tea chest aboard the sloop *Prudence.* In his final paragraph, he also mentioned that "the Supplement is going on, and when you shall have the article *New England* ready I will be glad to receive it."[8] There is no recorded reply.

On June 3, 1801, Dobson again wrote to Morse that he had "now made such progress in the Supplement to the Encyclopaedia that the article *New England* will soon be needed."[9] The article on "Magnetism" was now being printed, and in a "few weeks" at most work would have to be halted to wait "for N. E." if the essay did not arrive by then. Dobson fervently hoped that Morse had the article "in such forwardness as will occasion no delay."

Morse was unable to comply. He sent only the first part of the essay, which was of little use to Dobson. Thus on September 28, 1801, the publisher wrote again to Morse, explaining that "the first part of the History of New-England," which commences on page 608 of Volume XX, had been "printed off" and that he was in daily expectation of "receiving the remainder." But, he added, for want of the manuscript, printing had been completely halted for the last "three or four weeks." He was anxious to know exactly when he might expect the remainder of the article.

The delay has been of considerable disadvantage to me, and I beg that as soon as your health and avocation will permit, that [sic] it may be sent on to me. Please let it come by post, for I would rather pay double postage than wait a month. . . .[10]

Despite Dobson's pleas, work in Philadelphia remained at a standstill far longer than a month. On March 13, 1802, Morse apparently wrote to Dobson promising the completed manuscript at any moment, but a desperate Dobson had still not received it on May 20. "The Second Volume of the Supplement has now been many months delayed waiting for it," he wrote to Morse on that date, "and though the Third Volume has been going forward, my Subscribers are becoming very impatient for the Second." In yet another variation on an economic theme he had articulated so often in his announcements of the final volumes of the *Encyclopaedia,* he tried to explain to Morse that the failure to complete Volume XX on time "keeps me out of a good deal of money which I had flattered myself would have been in my possession before last Christmas." In conclusion, he begged once again "that no time may now be lost, but that it may come by post, as the postage is not of importance in comparison with a months delay."[11]

As this letter indicates, Morse's tardiness, which he seems to have blamed upon illness and the press of church affairs, had forced Dobson to make a desperate decision and move on to the third volume of the *Supplement* even though he had no way of knowing how many pages would be required to bring the second volume to completion. In this impossible situation, he could only exercise his best judgment as to where to begin Volume XXI, relying on his estimate (see the letter of May 10, 1799) of thirty to fifty pages. He concluded that the article "Printing" was as good a place as any to commence the third and final volume.

Morse eventually turned in an article that ran to thirty-eight pages, well within Dobson's guidelines, but somehow the printer's calculations went wrong. As Dobson explained in an editorial aside tipped into Volume XXI on page 48, "the completion of the Second Volume of this work . . . [was] suspended on account of an important article which was delayed much longer than was at first expected" (an understatement if ever there was one). Thus he felt compelled to begin the present volume and had made "considerable progress . . . in the printing" when the long awaited-article arrived. Then he found to his dismay that "some of the original articles [intended for Volume XX] extended to a greater length than the room allotted for them." To compensate, he had arbitrarily closed the second supplemental volume with "Philosophist" and belatedly added a forty-eight-page prefix to Volume XXI "in order to bring forward the subjects which preceded the article PRINTING." Thanks to Morse, in other words, Volume XXI has two sets of pages numbered 1–48. Dobson had done his best to avert such a problem by delaying publication as long as possible, but to no avail.

The article that Morse so tardily submitted for the *Supplement* became the basis for his *Compendious History of New England* (1804) the follow-

ing year, written with the editorial collaboration of Elijah Parish.[12] Like
Morse's earlier contributions, this essay reflects his faith in the Federalist
government and in Congregational orthodoxy as the only true political and
theological models for America to follow. In an era when many Americans
deeply feared the supposed plots and machinations of the French, he called
upon New Englanders to remember their history of conflict with Indians
inspired by French treachery. In defiance of historical actuality, he described the early New England as "an asylum to the oppressed among
mankind," yet paradoxically praised the Puritans for scrupulously regulat-
ing "the morals of the inhabitants within the colony" while preventing the
importation of "dissimilar habits, and heretical principles from without"
(618). His ideology is poised between two myths of America, the national
myth that the United States should serve as a refuge for the persecuted
people of Europe and the regional myth that the exclusion of undesirable
aliens follows a precedent established in New England and represents the
only way to maintain the moral purity of the republic.

To make certain he left no doubt of the identity of those undesirable
aliens, Morse castigated the French as "the malignant instigators of the
Indians in their bloody assaults" on New England (626). Despite the
passage of more than a century, neither their character nor their historical
purposes had changed; they were implacable foes of the pace and prosperity
of New England: "Had the French in Canada been subdued a hundred
years sooner, . . . there would have been more than three hundred thousand
souls in New-England . . . than there now is" (629). A tale of Indian
treachery in the war of 1688 inspires a warning about allowing foreign
influence in American affairs (625); few at the time would have missed the
allusion to the spread of dangerous Jacobin attitudes and, perhaps more
particularly, to Jefferson's appointment of the Swiss-born Albert Gallatin as
secretary of the treasury.[13]

Not all events in the past held warnings about the future of the
American republic. Morse extolled the fortitude and piety of the first
settlers of Connecticut, who "prayed and sang psalms and hymns" as they
advanced into the wilderness (620)—a model, obviously, for westward
expansion in the nineteenth century—and he celebrated the adoption of
the federal Constitution (632) as a modern expression of the spirit of unity
under divine guidance that prevailed in those earliest settlements. He
repeated his claim that New England was the nursery of the United States
(636), and he excused the historical persecution of Quakers on the grounds
of contemporary practice. He defended the witchcraft trials at Salem,

possibly subconsciously sensing an analogy to his own witchhunt against the Bavarian Illuminati and Freemason lodges across America. Thus reconstructed and reinterpreted, the history of New England seemed to Morse to inculcate the proper Federalist and Congregational conduct that could save the troubled republic or, failing that, at least extricate New England from the fate of the rest of the nation.

Morse's other major contribution to the *Supplement,* a long article on the "United States" (21: 462–92) taken from his *American Universal Geography* of ten years earlier, appears in both the British and American editions. The text paraphrases the Declaration of Independence, reprints the Constitution and the Bill of Rights, discourses for four pages on the evils of paper currency while reviewing life in the United States under the Articles of Confederation, and defends the Society of the Cincinnati. It reveals virtually all the errors and prejudices that James Freeman had charged against the *American Universal Geography* when it originally appeared.

Several examples illustrate the nature of the problem. Morse admitted when the article was published in 1793 that he did not know how many states had ratified the Bill of Rights (479), but he had apparently made no effort in the intervening years to find out and so left readers wondering (the first ten amendments had been adopted by the thirteen states in 1791 and an eleventh amendment in 1798). He also allowed the article to appear in the *Supplement* with the statistics of the 1790 census (473), although another had been taken in the meantime. These errors suggest that Morse did not bother to look over his original article once he had granted Dobson permission to reprint it; perhaps, indeed, with the recent experience with "New England" on his mind, Dobson did not ask him to revise it, fearing a repeat of that performance. Morse may also have been too busy with "New England" to consider editing and revising another article. Whatever the reason, the republication of a major entry so many years out of date and with so many errors and omissions on a subject of such vital interest to his subscribers represents a lapse in Dobson's editorial judgment which cannot be explained away by his customary practice of reprinting what George Gleig had included in the British edition. His need to rely on Morse as almost the sole source of information about American history and geography underscores the impossibility of domestically generating an American encyclopedia this early in the history of the republic. For at least the next generation, encyclopedias published in the United States would have to rely heavily upon English editions for most of the information they contained.

Even had Morse been able to revise the article on the United States, certain problems would undoubtedly have remained. Morse's credulity, for example, a major issue for James Freeman, is evident in the account of the small "hissing snake" that was said to inhabit the western shore of Lake Erie; when angered, it exhaled noxious vapors "with great force, a subtile wind . . . [that] if drawn in with the breath of the unwary traveller, will infallibly bring on a decline, that in a few months must prove mortal" (465). Morse's religious views lead him to defend the Mosaic theory of Creation against the geological speculations of Lewis Evans, whose *Essays,* published in 1756, certainly did not represent the latest word in the ongoing controversy between theologists and natural scientists,[14] and to rebuke in his general discussion of the religious denominations of America all "those who plead the sufficiency of natural religion and reject revelation as unnecessary and fabulous" (483). He twice castigates Rhode Island, once for exhibiting more than any other state "the licentiousness and anarchy which always follows a relaxation of moral principles" (489) in its abuse of paper money, then for its reluctance to embrace and ratify the Constitution (491). He faults Massachusetts for the unruliness of its citizenry in Daniel Shay's rebellion (487). Finally, his patriotism produces the extravagant claim, based on no evidence whatsoever, that "the United States of America have produced their full proportion of genius" (473) in every laudable endeavor known to mankind, not excepting poetry, painting, and music. With errors and opinions such as these, the essay on the United States cannot be said to set a standard for works of general reference.

The final paragraph in the entry on the "United States" appears to have been written by Dobson rather than Morse. It identifies Morse's *American Universal Geography* as the source of the preceding pages, apologizes for the comparative brevity of the article, decries "the intrigues and collisions of contending parties" that have marked recent political discourse in the United States, and praises the "wisdom and firmness exhibited by the President and Congress . . . in times most critical and trying" (492). This generic praise for the chief executive and legislators of the United States in some measure offsets the pro-Federalist bias of the article, though that is probably not the reason Dobson wrote and included it. His concern appears to have been more narrowly editorial, a wish to assure the public that the article is what it is largely because a full account of the country's recent tribulations "does not fall in with the plan of this work" (492). Thus he acknowledges, indirectly to be sure, his awareness that the article "United States" is badly out-of-date.

As with the first eighteen volumes, Morse was primarily responsible for most of the new geographical information about the United States that distinguishes the American from the British *Supplement* and accounts for the additional volume. Dobson explained in a paragraph appended to Dr. Gleig's original "Advertisement" in the prefatory pages of Volume XIX that he had relied heavily on "the Rev. Dr. Morse's American Gazetteer." As selected and edited by Dobson, the new entries reveal Morse's deep interest in American Indians, whose languages ring loudly but never outlandishly in both the place names and the tribal designations with which the *Supplement* abounds. There is also much information about Mexico, Guatemala, Cuba, Nicaragua, and other Central and South American nations, people, and places, revealing an incipient sense of Manifest Destiny and American hegemony in the Western Hemisphere that may perhaps be blamed on Dobson as editor but that is also a prominent feature of Morse's thought about the future of the United States (Phillips 30). Indeed, the spirit of Manifest Destiny had begun to express itself in American domestic policy under Thomas Jefferson in a way that guaranteed that the entry on Louisiana as "a Spanish province of North-America" would be out-of-date before the *Supplement* was published.

Some of the geographical entries seem specifically intended to correct oversights in the previous eighteen volumes, as, for example, the articles on "North Carolina," "South Carolina," and "Georgia," and Morse's unbelievably overdue essay on "New England." There was also a new entry on "Rhode Island" (complaining that "the Sabbath and all religious institutions, have been more neglected in this, than in any other of the New England states" [21: 92]) and a separate paragraph on "Providence" as a city instead of a plantation. Despite the article on "New England," however, there was still no adequate account of "Massachusetts" to replace the brief entry in the tenth volume of the *Encyclopaedia*. The entry on "New York," by contrast, was greatly revised, expanded, and improved. A new entry on the "Southern States" discussed Maryland, Virginia, North and South Carolina, Kentucky, Tennessee, and Georgia as a regional entity and attacked slavery by pointing out that "*thirteen fourteenths* of the whole number of slaves in the United States" lived in this area. In writing the original entries in the *Gazetteer*, however, Morse seems to have paid at least some attention to his pro-slavery critics (Phillips 184), for he ameliorated his commentary to some degree and closed with the hope that "the benign effects of the revolution, and the progress of liberty and humanity" would help to soften some of the more brutal and tyrannical aspects of that peculiar institution. To counterbalance the South, Dobson included a new entry on the expansive, sprawling "Territory *North-West of the Ohio, or North-western Territory,*" where slavery was not permitted.

Geographical entries in the American *Supplement* taught the lessons of industry and history to an attentive nation. The article "Albany," for instance, praised entrepreneurs and industrialists such as James Caldwell and other men who "deserve well of their country" for their extraordinary "efforts to advance American manufactures." "Tarrytown" preserved history and folklore in the reference to Andre's tree, the sort of story that held a special appeal to the anglophile Morse. Similarly, the paragraph under "Braddock's Field," Pennsylvania, provided an opportunity to express adulation of George Washington, a prologue to the hagiography that Morse would later write for the final volume:

[T]he place where Gen. Braddock, with the first division of his Army, fell into an ambuscade of 400 men, chiefly Indians, by whom he was defeated and mortally wounded, July 9, 1755. The American militia, . . . disdainfully turned in the rear, continued unbroken and served as rearguard, and under Col. Washington, the late President of the U.S.A., prevented the regulars from being entirely cut off. (19: 144)

The lakes, river, and mountains of America formed another of the themes of Dobson's *Supplement,* thanks once again to the *American Gazetteer.* Here again, as by implication in every one of the American entries, the underlying (and overriding) theme of Dobson's book is American progress, as in the description of the Mississippi or the beautiful Ohio, whose waters might, with proper management and foresight, be navigated by brigantines "from Pittsburgh to the sea. . . . If this be so, what agreeable prospects are presented to our brethren and fellow citizens in the western country!" The rapids at Louisville, surely one of America's wonders, could be "opened for constant navigation" should Americans desire to do so.

Not so another wonder of the American waterways, the thunderous Niagara, with its mighty, mist-enshrouded chasm that "no person can approach without terror." The Falls of the Niagara afford "the greatest curiosity which this, or indeed any other country" can boast, a cataract so mighty that the "sound is frequently heard at the distance of 20 miles," and on some days "40 and even 50 miles." The very foundations of the earth itself tremble at the roar. A heavy, hanging cloud of vapor ascends the falls, producing glorious rainbows on a sunny day—God's special promise to this favored land. "This fog or spray, in the winter season, falls upon the neighboring trees, where it congeals, and produces a most beautiful crystalline appearance," a phenomenon that may also be observed at the "Falls of Genesee." The glorification of tumultuous nature, a common trope in American writing of the Federal period, conceals a fascination with the theme of disorder that men like Morse dared acknowledge only obliquely and only to disavow. His set piece on the sublime emotions aroused by Niagara Falls is a striking illustration of what Christopher Looby has described as the "ritual repetition of moments of transformation, turbulence, and sheer motion . . . which place the conceptual scheme (and the social order) at risk, but which provide the opportunity for its reassertion" (263). Morse's description of the raw natural power of the falls invokes a picturesque sense of the sublime that is as much a part of the meaning of America as are the towns and cities and settlements that encroach upon such splendors.

In the descriptions of towns and villages and settlements, natural spectacles and scenery, Dobson enjoyed his greatest success in transforming the British *Supplement* into an American book. In the area of American biography, however, he did not fare as well. The lives of only three Americans are chronicled in the volumes of the *Supplement,* although Jonathan Edwards, Anthony Wayne, David Rittenhouse, and Joseph Warren spring readily to mind as others who might have been included. Two of these biographies are devoted to eminent Philadelphians, opening the *Supplement* to the same charge of local chauvinism that might with some justice have been made against the first eighteen volumes. This is especially true of the brief sketch of the botanist and philosopher John Bartram, whose life story, like the others added to the *Supplement,* was almost certainly written by Morse. (In his magazine, the *Panoplist,* Morse delighted in presenting biographical pieces about exemplary lives.) Predictably, Bartram earned Morse's praise as "an advocate for liberty, and for the abolition of Negro slavery." His contributions to science are scarcely noted. Like Franklin, he was self-made and self-educated and thus an inspiration to all Americans. His life taught that a love of liberty and a respect for social order were not incompatible but complementary virtues.

The life of Benjamin Franklin is disappointingly brief, especially after the warning in Volume VII that such a biography would eventually be forthcoming. Like all other biographies of Franklin, it relies heavily on the *Memoirs,* and like them, it does not go into detail about Franklin's service during and after the revolutionary war, writing the good doctor off stage after that conflict with one brief paragraph followed by the famous epitaph for "Benjamin Franklin, printer" composed by Franklin for himself.

The final American biography in Dobson's *Supplement*—the British *Supplement* includes no Americans—is, inevitably, a life of George Washington. (Perhaps the rhapsodic account of "Mount Vernon" ought also to be considered as a part of this biography.) Here the hand of Morse is once more evident, particularly in the treatment of Washington's wise action in declining a perpetual presidency, in the defense of Washington as a successful military leader, and in the account of his policies toward the French during the French Revolution and its diplomatic aftermath. Morse had written biographical accounts of Washington in 1790 and 1794. In the *Supplement* he paid tribute to a man who always and unhesitatingly chose duty over feeling, a wise, eminently rational, but also compassionate and generous man fit for canonization as the first and greatest of American saints. "Those whose moral taste is pure," Morse assured his readers, "will always admire in George Washington the nearest approach to uniform propriety, and perfect blamelessness, which has ever been attained by man, or which is perhaps compatible with the condition of humanity." Calvinist orthodoxy blunts this last encomium a bit but not sufficiently to blemish the ideal portrait Morse has painted.

As a native-born Virginian and a slaveholder, Washington won particular praise from Morse for manumitting his slaves in his last will and testament. By providing for gradual rather than immediate emancipation and by ensuring the education of his slaves, Washington offered the nation a model for the abolition of a shameful institution without the risk of social revolution. Every provision of Washington's will in regard to manumission, Morse said, "indicates that union of benevolence and prudence which constitutes the true character of the REFORMER, and which distinguishes him from those restless and fierce disturbers of the world, who usurp the name of . . . Reformers, and bring lasting discredit on the cause of Reformation" (21: 516). As he had done in his article on the history of New England, Morse made one historical event, Washington's last will and testament, serve as symbolic shorthand for commentary on the general social unrest inspired both abroad and in America by the French Revolution and maintained in a constant state of agitation by the irresponsible rhetoric of Jeffersonian democrats.

Exemplary characters and careers like those of Washington, Franklin, and John Bartram provided Americans with much needed models for appropriate conduct. One additional biography included in the American *Supplement,* however, inverted that pattern. It was an account of the rise and fall of Pierre-Gaspard Chaumette, a man who "would hardly have deserved a place in this work, did not his life and the manner of his death hold out an awful warning against those principles that produced the overthrow of social order in France" (19: 256). This biography lends special meaning to plate 29, John Draper's engraving of the guillotine—a gruesome illustration with severed human heads scattered along a cobbled street and streams of blood gushing from headless trunks—and, like the life of Washington, "Federalizes" rather than Americanizes the *Supplement*. As a revolutionary leader who was "among the first who put the tri-coloured cockade on his hat just before the taking of the Bastille" (19: 256), Chaumette provides a stark contrast to Washington. He used his talents, such as they were, to defame the character of Marie Antoinette and stimulate the Parisian mobs to bloodthirsty frenzy. "The revolution intoxicated his brain" (19: 257), writes Morse, and in the end, he was followed only by men and women intoxicated like himself, "the very scum of the revolution; and such recrementitious matter will always be thrown off in national ebullitions of this kind" (19: 256). Proscribed at last by Robespierre, he met his fate as a victim of the same delirious and mindless rage for revenge to which he himself had helped to deliver so many others. In seeking to present Chaumette's career as emblematic of uncontrolled radicalism and as an object lesson on the dangers inherent in mindless party factionalism, Morse pulled out all the rhetorical stops and produced a denunciation remarkably out of keeping with the ideal objectivity of encyclopedic writing.

These four biographies—three positive and one sharply negative—helped to differentiate Dobson's *Supplement* from the British version and to embed Morse's Federalist and conservative Congregationalist values within the text. Each contributed a degree of autonomy to volumes that remained heavily indebted to the original sources. Toward the same end, Dobson deleted the life of James Burnett (Lord Monboddo), whose unfortunate belief that children were born with tails they eventually lost as they matured (*DNB* 3: 412–14) probably helped discredit his work in the eyes of the medical faculty of the University of Pennsylvania and the College of Physicians. More puzzling is the omission of the life of Hugh Blair, like Dobson a Scotsman and the author of a rhetorical treatise, *Lectures on Rhetoric and Belles Lettres* (1782), widely used in American colleges and universities. Notwithstanding his popularity as a rhetorician, Blair was probably omitted because of his outspoken opposition to the American Revolution (*DNB* 2: 622–23). His and Lord Monboddo's disappearance, however, scarcely made a difference in a text that preserved so many lengthy biographical accounts of Scots and English clergymen, many of whom have fallen into obscurity since the eighteenth century and, in the strictest sense appropriate to such limited biographical offerings as an encyclopedia may hope to offer, probably should not have been included in the first place.

Even though Dobson had invited contributions about American geography to the *Supplement,* neither geography nor biography appears to have been his main emphasis of Volumes XIX–XXI. In the paragraph he appended to Gleig's "Advertisement" in the preface, he expressed great satisfaction with the advancements his American edition had made over its British counterpart in the areas of technology and science. He singled out Morse's contributions for special mention but devoted most of his attention to the Reverend John Prince's new full-page essay on the Lucernal microscope, originally published in the *Gentleman's Magazine* in November 1796 and included in the *Supplement* under "Optics," and the same inventor's account of "the *American Air Pump*" in the article on "Pneumatics."[15]

The second contribution is especially interesting because the original article on "Pneumatics," published by Dobson without a close reading in Volume XV, ended by criticizing Prince's pump. Undoubtedly, Dobson had heard from Prince in the intervening years, and now he turned over the pages of the *Supplement* to him for a rebuttal. Prince initiated his additions by observing that for an American edition of the *Encyclopaedia,* to allow any "objections stated . . . against the American air pump to pass unnoticed, would look like a tacit acknowledgment of their truth." He continued:

To some persons, who are acquainted with the operation of the American air-pump, the partial and unjust account of it in the [British] Encyclopaedia appeared at first surprising. But their surprise abated, and the prejudice against it was fully accounted for, on reading the compiler's remark at the end of his account of air pumps. For he seems to have condemned it that he might be able to say [of air pumps generally] "that although this noble instrument originated in Germany, all its improvements were made in Britain!"

There follow two full columns describing the new, improved air pump, concerning which Dobson had previously informed his readers in the preface that "the corrections of the account of this Pump which was published in the *Encyclopaedia* are original" ("Advertisement").

Another matter of contention between European editors and American readers, this time a controversy about which Dobson's brief prefatory remarks did not forewarn his audience, may be found in the pages of the long article on "Chemistry," authored in the British edition, Dr. Gleig informed his readers, by Dr. Thomas Thomason of Edinburgh. Most of this article, as was his custom with scientific writing generally, Dobson simply reprinted verbatim. On page 265, however, Thomason referred skeptically to the conclusions drawn by Count Rumford from experiments to determine whether water is "a conductor of caloric." At the same point in the essay in Dobson's *Supplement,* however, page 311, someone changed this skepticism to full support for Rumford, stating unequivocally that Rumford had "completely proved, that water is a non-conductor" (313). Such close oversight in the first eighteen volumes would have prevented reprinting Gleig's intellectually embarrassing attack on the Newtonian law of gravity in the article under "Motion."

The most likely candidate for the authorship of these revisions under "Chemistry" (311–13) is once again John Prince, who had worked closely with Count Rumford in a number of experiments. If so, Prince was probably also responsible for an earlier emendation in the same article, the deletion of subsections VII ("Of Jargonia"), VIII ("Of Glucina"), and IX ("Of Yttria and Agustina") under the larger heading "Of Earths." He replaced these with a single subsection VII, "Of Adamanta," and referred to only one of the four earth substances Thomason had mentioned, Glucina. Apologizing for not having yet been able to procure an account of the properties of this substance and unwilling, apparently, to accept Dr. Thomason's word for the truth, Prince promised that he would return to "Glucina" at the proper alphabetical place, a promise he fulfilled.

One additional "improvement" in the *Supplement* is the inclusion under "Vision" of a paper written by Dr. David Hosack of New York. Hosack graduated from the College of New Jersey (later Princeton) in 1789, studied medicine under Dr. Benjamin Rush, and established his own medical practice in Alexandria, Virginia, in 1791. In 1792, he traveled to Edinburgh to study and, while visiting in England, presented before the Royal Society the paper Dobson added to his *Encyclopaedia.* It appeared initially in the *Philosophical Transactions* of the Royal Society in 1794. When the essay was republished in the *Supplement,* Hosack was professor of materia medica and botany at Columbia College (*DAB* 9: 239–40). Despite the slightly European flavor of the article, it is the most extensive and significant scientific contribution by an American in the entire *Encyclopaedia.*

The formal text of Dobson's *Supplement* concludes with a brief entry under "Zoneshio," the chief town of the Seneca Indians. Then Dobson added an appendix of four separately numbered pages describing two inventions patented by Chester Gould, a Philadelphia inventor. The new log, a device "for ascertaining a ship's distance at sea" (21: 11), and the artificial horizon, an invention designed "to obtain a level for the purpose of taking the altitude of celestial and other subjects . . . without the assistance of the natural horizon" (21: [i]), may not have been truly deserving of a place in the *Supplement* or even in an appendix, but they did at least fulfill the criterion of utility and so would have appealed to Dobson. He might have seen them and other inventions by Gould—the "Patent Nautical Perambulator," for example—advertised in the *Philadelphia Gazette* (on May 27, 1801, and November 11, 1802, for instance) where his own advertisements for the *Supplement* were also appearing, or Gould might have communicated with him on his own initiative. In any case, this implied biography of an ingenious but unsung ancestor of Thomas Alva Edison, a true spiritual descendant of Benjamin Franklin and hundreds of anonymous Yankee mechanics brought the *Encyclopaedia* to a fitting conclusion by stressing to the very end the themes of progress, improvement, and utility.[16]

The *Supplement* contains fifty-three engravings, fifty illustrating items and articles in the main text and three entirely new ones by Alexander Lawson illustrating Chester Gould's inventions; the second of these, a picture of Dr. Prince's new "Air Pump," is etched, only the second plate in the entire *Encyclopaedia* to be so identified. Several are unsigned, but all may be attributed with reasonable certainty (see Appendix C). One previous commentator has claimed that all of the plates were engraved by Lawson (Kruse 94), but this is not the case. Although Lawson indeed engraved the bulk of them—thirty-three in all (numbers 3, 4, 7, 18, 19, 26–28, and 30–53)—he had help from Robert Scot (four plates, numbers, 14–17), Henry W. Weston (numbers 11–13), Joseph Bowes (numbers 1, 2, 5, 6, 8, and 9), and Benjamin Jones (numbers 20–23). John Draper engraved plates 24, 25 and 29, the illustration of the "Guillotine."

It is not known how many copies of the *Supplement* Dobson printed or eventually sold. Such evidence as exists seems to indicate that sales lagged considerably behind the *Encyclopaedia*. He made one sale to Aaron Burr, who bought all twenty-one volumes on June 20, 1803.[17] Less than a year later, on April 19, 1804, he shipped three sets of the *Supplement* to the firm of Webster and Skinner in Albany.[18] Still hoping to move the book as late as May 7, 1812, he sent the same firm two complete sets of twenty-one volumes, one in sheep and one in boards, priced at $136 and $105, respectively. "As the price of the Encyclopaedia is reduced about fifty

Dollars on the set," he wrote, "they will likely sell with you; if not they can be returned next fall."[19] On August 13, 1813, he shipped a *Supplement* and Volumes XIII through XVIII, which indicates that Webster and Skinner might have disposed of the sets previously dispatched and perhaps done somewhat better than that; this particular set was earmarked for "General Schuyler."[20] "I used to charge Interest on the volumes not taken up from the times of their publication," he informed his Albany connection, "but as that would have amounted to much more, I have charged in the present instance only Six Dollars per volume."[21]

Slightly less than a year elapsed between this letter and Dobson's next communication with Webster and Skinner regarding the *Encyclopaedia*. On June 3, 1814, he wrote to the Albany firm offering the twenty-one volume set at a retail price of $105. Dobson's letter also indicated new terms for the bookseller's discount, which by now had increased from one-seventh of the price (the terms for Mathew Carey in the early 1790s) to 25 percent (33 1/3 percent if six or more copies were sold).[22] That is about the same commission earned by Parson Weems as a travelling salesman of Mathew Carey's books at least a decade earlier.[23]

The Account Books of Mathew Carey tell a similar story of lagging sales in Philadelphia. Apparently, Carey did not order even a single copy of the *Supplement* until May 14, 1805 (at the same 25 percent discount given to Webster and Skinner; 19: item 8465); the price had been reduced from $7.00 to $6.00 per volume, probably as an incentive inspired by Dobson's newspaper "war" with the printer Samuel F. Bradford. Carey received two additional copies of the three-volume set on September 16, 1808 (23: item 1601), then, almost a full year later, another copy (September 6, 1809; 23: item 1442). An additional year passed before the arrival of a fifth set (November 12, 1810; 24: item 1966), now priced again as originally in 1803 at $21 the set. A sixth and final copy of the *Supplement,* once again priced at $18, was delivered and paid for on May 2, 1812 (26: item 3016). These figures contrast sharply with Carey's multiple orders for seventeen or eighteen sets of the *Encyclopaedia* between 1790 and 1795.[24]

With the *Encyclopaedia* now completed, the way was clear for other publishers to cash in on opportunities that Dobson had created. Competitors began to appear in Philadelphia almost as soon as the last page of the last impression had been struck from Dobson's presses. As early as 1796, two of Dobson's engravers, Thackara and Vallance, announced their intention to publish a folio edition of the *New Encyclopaedia,* a work that never materialized. Then in 1805, John Low began his *New and Complete Ameri-*

can Universal Encyclopaedia (Shaw and Shoemaker 8971), the only American encyclopedia of the period to be published in New York, with a prefatory critique of Dobson's *Encyclopaedia* as "too voluminous and too expensive . . . to answer the beneficial purposes of a general circulation" ([ii]). Completed in 1811, it ran to seven volumes and cost only about a quarter of the price of the *Encyclopaedia*, $40 to $60, but the difference was dramatically visible in the quality of workmanship and production (Larson 37).[25]

By far the sharpest challenge to Dobson's dominance of the market was issued by the rival Philadelphia printer Samuel F. Bradford just two years after the *Supplement* appeared. That challenge inspired an energetic and aggressive sales campaign that resulted in some of Dobson's most interesting advertisements. On March 14, 1805 (*United States Gazette*), Bradford announced plans for an American reprint of Abraham Rees's *New Cyclopaedia*, which had begun to appear in London in January 1803; reaching at last to 44 volumes, the English edition would not be completed until 1820 (Walsh 116). The American edition, with new material added, eventually grew to 47 volumes, including a final five volumes of engravings, and drove into bankruptcy both Bradford and the firm of Murray, Draper, Fairman and Company, which took over the project in 1815, before it was finished in 1822 (Larson 44; Shaw and Shoemaker 19907).

Although he did not explicitly mention Dobson's publication in his announcement, Bradford aimed his preprospectus advertising at the most vulnerable areas of the *Encyclopaedia* and *Supplement*, the absence of a full account of American "*Biography, Geography, and History*" and the quality of the engraving. The *New Cyclopaedia*, he assured his readers, would not only contain much new geographical information but also many new maps, "engraved for the work by some of the most distinguished artists." It would also be generally "improved and adapted to this country by gentlemen of known abilities," making it by far "the most complete work of the kind that has yet appeared." Bradford promised full proposals within the next few days.

It would be, in fact, eleven days (*United States Gazette*, March 25, 1805) before those proposals appeared. The advertisement was long, taking up two full columns. Most of the text was taken from the European proposals and did not specifically address the American market. Bradford had enough to say on his own account, however, to alarm Dobson, who had by now invested countless hours and a great deal of money in his own publication. For one thing, Bradford made more explicit his implied criticism of Dobson by pointing out that "*American Biography* . . . has been very greatly, not to say entirely, neglected in all preceding works of this kind." If the heroes and benefactors of mankind were remembered by other nations, Bradford went on to ask, "why should those of the United States be suffered to sink into oblivion, or to survive only in the obscure and neglected column of a newspaper?" Among many others, the names of Washington, Franklin, Hamilton, Hancock, Henry, Rittenhouse, Witherspoon, Penn, Savery, and Emlem deserved to be remembered. "It is the determination of the editor to make such arrangements, that, in this regard, the American edition of Rees's Cyclopaedia will have a claim to some degree of originality."

A second area in which Bradford believed that Dobson was open to unfavorable review lay in the quality of his engraving. "No one who has observed the great progress that has been made in the arts of printing and engraving, within a few years, can doubt of the superiour style of elegance in which this work will be executed, when he is assured that . . . the best printers, and most eminent engravers, will be engaged, every way, worthy the patronage of the friends of literature and science." In all, the *New Cyclopaedia* would contain "between five and six hundred plates engraved in a superior style of elegance . . . by far, a greater number than is to be found in any other Scientifick Dictionary." As appropriate to this increased quality of engraving, the paper on which the new work would be printed was to be woven rather than laid, allowing for sharper, clearer impressions.

Every subscriber to Rees's *New Cyclopaedia* meant one potential purchaser fewer for Dobson's *Encyclopaedia*. Thus on April 5, 1805, Dobson responded with an advertisement of his own in the *Philadelphia Gazette*. Like Bradford, he avoided directly naming his competition, but there was no doubt what collection of "unconnected miscellanies, and detached essays . . . level to the meanest capacities" he intended to attack. As Dobson saw it, the chief virtue of the *Encyclopaedia* lay in its system of major articles, under which were included all subheadings relevant to the main subject. In Rees's *New Cyclopaedia*, by contrast, "topicks, far from being digested into a system, or disposed in their natural order, are, without regard to their proper positions, huddled together as the order of letters which constitute their technical names determine." He did not deny that individual articles might possess merit, but the result of approaching knowledge in this fragmentary fashion could only be confusion, not enlightenment.

Since encyclopedias are, among other things, metaphors of the universe as seen by those who compile and edit them, the theme of chaos and disorder revealed in Dobson's description of Rees's *New Cyclopaedia* is of particular importance to an understanding of his own ideology, the political (as opposed to the economic) rationale for reprinting the *Encyclopaedia* in the first place. From the outset of the enterprise, Dobson had consistently addressed his proposals to "patrons" and "gentlemen," favoring an implicitly aristocratic and entirely male audience as distinguished, for example, from the female readers to whom most novels of the period were addressed. The presentation copies he gave to various government bodies and scientific societies, whatever their considerable value as promotional donations, also reveal the intimate association in his mind between knowledge and social order. Men of "cultivated minds" approved the synthesis of thought, whereas minds of the "meanest capacities" were satisfied with decentralized facts "disposed . . . without any regard to their proper positions, huddled together" in arbitrary or merely alphabetical order rather than as the inherent natural order and unity of the universe dictated.

Dobson had good reason, he must have felt, to be wary of such disconnected information. The explosion of knowledge about the physical universe in the eighteenth century, uncontained by any orderly philosophy adequate to absorb and comprehend it, had already proved to have truly revolutionary implications in the hands of propagandists with a special case to plead. Diderot's and d'Alembert's *Encyclopédie,* for example, was understood by many Americans, Dobson undoubtedly among them, to have provided the egalitarian rationale of the French Revolution, if not, indeed, to have been the underlying cause. A little learning was indeed a dangerous thing. For Dobson, however, as for the editors of the third edition of the *Britannica* whom he followed, an encyclopedia was or ought to be modeled on the taxonomy of nature, quantifying knowledge as a body of objective information for quiet, detached contemplation and eventual mastery. Subdividing knowledge into atomistic, individualized, and fragmented particles according to other and manifestly man-made systems made mastery more difficult if not impossible, deprived the sensory world of any underlying unity or organizing principle, and implicitly subjectivized the empirical world, promoting disorder in human affairs and tacitly acknowledging the possibility of chaos on a cosmic scale.

Dobson, of course, did not admit to any such implications lurking in his language. He presented the matter more simply and commercially, seeing in the *Encyclopaedia* a plan of organization "so decidedly superiour to that of any other work of the kind hitherto published in the English language, or yet proposed for publication, that none of them will bear the comparison" except, of course, the *Encyclopaedia Britannica* from which his own text was derived. He stressed again, however, that the American edition had improved upon the *Britannica* and contained "no inconsiderable number" of original essays, most of them about the United States. Moreover, the recent publication of the *Supplement* meant that the information in the *Encyclopaedia* was up-to-date even in the area of biography, despite Bradford's allegations to the contrary. Besides, Dobson reminded his readers, his book was finished; a subscriber to Rees's *New Cyclopaedia* would have to wait years to read about "*the place and changes of the moon,* of so much importance to navigation" and even longer to come at last to "Zodiac" in Rees's scattered treatment of astronomy, whereas the entire science was covered in the second volume of the *Encyclopaedia*. That the *Encyclopaedia* was completed thus enhanced its general utility.

Dobson's lengthy rejoinder to Bradford's proposals also provides additional insight into his bookselling techniques. After listing the prices of the entire set, which now ranged from $156 in boards to $250 in "Russia elegantly gilt," he offered special terms of payment to those who were "very desirous to possess this truly valuable and important work" and who could "easily pay small sums towards it at different times" but could not afford to pay for it all at once. One volume in boards would be furnished every two months (or more frequently if the subscriber desired) at $7.50 per volume; subscribers could, of course, purchase more than one volume at a time. Upon receiving the first volume, every subscriber was also to pay for the last volume, "this being the only security required that he will take the set regularly." In this way, all who wished could be assured of owning their own copy of a work that had already enjoyed an "extensive circulation" in America and won general approval for its plan of organization as well as for the quality of the workmanship.

Dobson's strategy of not directly naming the competition failed to fool Samuel Bradford or, apparently, any other reader. On April 8, 1805, a writer from Princeton who identified himself only by the initials "H. S." wrote a brief piece in the *United States Gazette* in praise of Rees's *New Cyclopaedia,* alleging that "it exceeds the old *Encyclopaedia* by much in elegance, and being of more modern date, it furnishes contemporary information, which is always most interesting, and generally most useful." The writer, who may have been on the faculty at Presbyterian Princeton and thus may have had more than one motive for criticizing the Universalist Dobson, also sided with Bradford in attacking the virtual absence of American biography from the *Encyclopaedia,* which had "grossly neglected" the subject.

Bradford was even more outspoken. His "Reply, to the Attack on Dr. Rees's *Cyclopaedia*" (April 19, 1805) filled more than three columns in the *United States Gazette*. "Mr. Dobson's Encyclopaedia," he asserted, "in its day, possessed considerable merit, received a due proportion of public patronage, and is an honourable testimony to the industry of its publisher; but the present improved state of science loudly called for a more perfect and complete Dictionary." Viewing Dobson's advertisement as an attempt to undermine his own efforts, which is true only in part—Dobson, after all, had his own *Encyclopaedia* to sell—Bradford struck again at his competitor's weaknesses. He proclaimed Dobson's volumes "almost entirely defective" in American biography, outdated in scientific information, and technologically inferior to his own proposed edition. "Since the time . . . of Mr. Dobson's Encyclopaedia, a degree of improvement, perhaps without a parallel, has been made in . . . paper-making, type-founding, engraving, and every other branch of business connected with the art of printing." All of these innovations, he promised, would be employed in the publication of the new edition. "The Encyclopaedia of Mr. Dobson will not bear a comparison."

Bradford also scoffed at Dobson's claim that the complete systemization of knowledge made his *Encyclopaedia* more immediately useful than Rees's. He made perhaps the first attempt in America to distinguish between democratic and genteel audiences, foreshadowing the arrival of Francis Lieber's *Encyclopaedia Americana* in 1829 through 1833. True men of science or other professionals, he said, do not consult encyclopedias for information; they are much beyond the general level of information that even the best such publications have to offer. The readers he had uppermost in his mind—"merchants, artists, manufacturers, and private gentlemen"—did not want to be burdened with the task of making their way through an entire article of two or three hundred pages to find the information they required. "Possessed of active and well cultivated minds, and still grasping after further improvements in knowledge" but disinterested in or too busy to explore an entire system of thought, they were exactly the kind of reader for whom the *New Cyclopaedia* was meant. Even more than the promised additions in American biography, history, and geography, this implicitly democratic readership, Bradford seemed to feel, would guarantee the authenticity of his edition as a truly American text.

Dobson made one more effort to respond. On April 25 (over a date of April 23), he published in the *United States Gazette* the same full-length advertisement that had provoked Bradford's "Reply," this time prefaced by a brief "CARD Respecting the Encyclopaedia." He had, he professed in that brief introduction, no intention of entering into a "newspaper quarrel" about the virtues of one encyclopedia over another. Still, he felt obliged to point out that the motive behind his original advertisement "was a very natural, and proper desire to dispose, to his own satisfaction, of the work on which he had bestowed so much labour and expense."

The sale appeared to be in danger of being in some measure checked, by the very pompous advertisement of *another work,* which, from its total want of any methodical arrangement . . . he believed to be of far inferior utility. Many improper things in that prospectus were passed over without particular notice; for instance—the declaration in the 5th article of the conditions, that between five and six hundred plates *is by far a greater number than is to be found in any other scientific dictionary.*— Could this arise from ignorance of the fact, that *five hundred and ninety five plates were actually published in the Encyclopaedia?*

Both this "CARD" and the full advertisement that Bradford had found so offensive ran for months not only in the *Philadelphia Gazette,* where it had initially appeared, but also in the *United States Gazette,* where it was sometimes published next to Bradford's own prospectus. But Dobson gradually refined and improved upon the content of his advertisement, eventually dropping the "CARD" as he had time to assess the impact of Bradford's competing edition and gained increased confidence in the quality of his own product. On May 21, 1806, and subsequent dates he placed the revised advertisement in *Poulson's American Daily Advertiser,* offering for sale both the first eighteen volumes and the *Supplement* either separately or together and touting the virtues of the complete *Encyclopaedia* over any and all other encyclopedias. While continuing the comparison with an unnamed competitor, however, the advertisement was less negative than those of April 5 and 25, 1805. The price for the full twenty-one volumes remained what it had been one year earlier, $156 in boards, $250 "in Russia, elegantly gilt," but Dobson declared that it was well worth the money. With *"Five Hundred and Ninety-Five* COPPER-PLATES," the *Encyclopaedia* "greatly exceeded" any similar publication and bore "honourable testimony to the state of the Arts in the United States during the progress of the work." The book was, Dobson continued, "well known in the United States, where an extensive circulation has tested its excellence, and established its character." He invited readers to compare it with any other edition, "the Encyclopaedia of Edinburgh excepted," and confidently promised that "the superiority of method" would become "manifest . . . on a moments reflection." In this advertisement, Dobson spoke with the accents of an entrepreneur who seemed fully to believe in the value of the product he was promoting, taking once again the high patriotic ground and leaving the unseemly wrangling to Bradford.

Despite these brave words, however, Bradford was right about the limitations of the *Encyclopaedia*. Even Dobson had acknowledged in his proposals for the *Supplement* that no encyclopedia could hope to remain timely without constant updating, and the deficiencies of his Americanization of the British text were readily apparent to any reader who took the trouble to compare the two editions. Bradford's promise to provide more American material proved difficult to fulfill, however, despite the opportunity to learn from Dobson's errors. Even as the *New Cyclopaedia* was emerging from the press, reviewers were complaining that Bradford's revisions distorted and misrepresented rather than Americanized the content of articles. They voiced grave doubts about the competence of the anonymous American "literati" to make the improvements that Bradford had advertised; some subscribers apparently also joined in this chorus of disapproval (*Monthly Anthology, and Boston Review* 3 [August 1806]: 423–28; 5 [April 1808]: 213–23). When the edition had finally been completed, moreover, a writer in the December 1829 issue of the *American Quarterly Review* (who may have been George Bancroft)[26] praised "the late Mr. Dobson" for his "successful" edition of the *Encyclopaedia Britannica* (6: 347) but faulted "the publisher of the American edition of Dr. Rees's Cyclopaedia" for leaving out, in spite of all his promises, such men as Ethan Allen, John Adams, Benedict Arnold, Joel Barlow, Joshua Barney, and John Barry, and other American notables (6: 349). Reviews like these almost certainly contributed to the financial disasters that dogged the American edition of Rees from start to finish.[27]

Several encyclopedias followed Bradford's into the market that Dobson had established. On November 2, 1811, the printer Benjamin Johnson announced his plan to publish a prospectus for an American edition of William Nicholson's *British Encyclopaedia*, but that prospectus seems never to have appeared. Perhaps Johnson learned in the meantime of Samuel Augustus Mitchell and Horace Ames's plans to print the same encyclopedia, which appeared in seven volumes in 1815 (Shaw and Shoemaker 38471). Mitchell, Ames, and White (White's first name is unknown) also published two twelve-volume editions in 1818 and three additional editions of the same size between 1819 and 1821 (Walsh 16; Shaw and Shoemaker 48936–38). The *British Encyclopaedia*, despite its title, was more popular in America than it was in the British Isles and, as the only other completed encyclopedia of comparable size and scope in more than a decade since the *Supplement,* was undoubtedly the edition that displaced Dobson's *Encyclopaedia* in the American market.

In April 1811, the Philadelphia firm of Edward Parker and Joseph Delaplaine issued a prospectus in *Poulson's American Daily Advertiser* for an American edition of the twelve-volume *Edinburgh Encyclopaedia.* Parker and Delaplaine had learned from Dobson the value of stressing the American content of their volumes and, perhaps, from the reviews of Bradford's *New Cyclopaedia* the importance of identifying their American contributors. Thus they listed in their prospectus such distinguished names as John Redman Coxe, Benjamin Rush, James Mease, Benjamin Latrobe, and Charles J. Ingersoll, among others (many of these men did not live to contribute, of course). They also cleverly led into their proposal by first publishing in the same newspaper (April 16, 1811) a highly favorable notice of the *Edinburgh Encyclopaedia* reprinted from London's *Monthly Magazine,* and on April 23 they followed the proposals with another puff for the same encyclopedia over the name of "LUCAN." The work eventually grew to eighteen volumes that were very slow to appear in England (1808–1830) and were not completed in America until 1831–32 (Bruntjen and Bruntjen 6932). As individual volumes became available, this edition may also have taken some sales from Thomas Dobson, but by the time it was fully completed, he had been dead for almost a decade.[28]

Although its information was now hopelessly out-of-date, Dobson continued his attempts to sell the aging *Encyclopaedia* until the very end. In 1814, for example, he ran an advertisement in his own *Eclectic Repertory and Analytical Review* (vol. 4, no. 16, no page) offering the whole set of twenty-one volumes for $105. This was about the time he was sending sets to Webster and Skinner in Albany as well. Four years later, in 1818, he was still trying to sell at least a few additional sets of the *Supplement,* if not the entire *Encyclopaedia,* this time by engaging Archibald Bartram to print off new title pages bearing the date 1818 (Shaw and Shoemaker 43065) and reissuing the fifteen-year-old volumes with a new name, the *American Edition of the Encyclopaedia . . . In Three Volumes.* But even that strategy failed to relieve him of all remaining copies, and when the firm of Thomas Dobson and Son at last went out of business sometime in 1822, both the *Encyclopaedia* and the *Supplement* were advertised for sale "to the trade on the most liberal terms" (T. and J. Dobson, *Catalogue* 1822, 8). After Dobson's death on March 9, 1823, his son tried once more to dispose of the surplus volumes, noting in perhaps the last imprint to bear the name of the late firm of Thomas Dobson and Son that the *Supplement* might still "be had in sheets" as well as in boards. The *Encyclopaedia* was also still available in calf, sheep, and boards. Judah Dobson explained in a footnote that titles designated with an asterisk were available in sheets as well as bound volumes:

Encyclopaedia, 21 vols. 4to calf			170
do		sheep	136
do		boards	105
* do	supplement, 3 vols 4to many		
		plates	21.75
do	do	boards	18

This is necessary to complete sets of the Encyclopaedia, and brings the different subjects to a much later period. (J. Dobson, *Catalogue* 1823, 15)

The *Catalogue* makes it clear that "many" copies of the *Supplement* were left but gives no indication of the number of sets of the *Encyclopaedia* still remaining. The supply, however, was more than enough to meet any remaining demand. Except as a used book—see, for example, Moses Thomas' advertisement for a set of "21 vols. 4to complete" in William Fry's *National Gazette and Literary Register,* April 1, 1823—this is the last published advertisement for Dobson's *Encyclopaedia*.

Notes
1. S. H. Steinberg, "Encyclopaedias," *Signature,* n.s., no. 12 (1951): 3, also observes that "the history of encyclopaedias is an informative guide to the evolution of philosophy and education, as well as to the development of political ideas and social conditions." In the spirit of these remarks the present study was undertaken.
2. In contrast to Thomas Dobson, Francis Lieber included a lengthy appendix at the end of each of the thirteen volumes of the *Encyclopaedia Americana* (1829–33), trying to keep pace with such international developments as the liberation of South American nations from Spanish dominion and new scientific and technological discoveries. He viewed the function of an encyclopedia as akin to that of a newspaper, an almanac, or a manual of instruction.
3. This occurs in the article "Chemistry," in which the American editor, probably Dr. John Prince, deferred discussion of "Glucina," a rare earth, and prepared a separately alphabetized entry.
4. Another reference to Dobson's plans to publish a *Supplement* that is not part of an advertisement appears in [Charles Brockden Brown], "Encyclopaedia," *Monthly Magazine, and American Review* 1 (1799): 135, a review of the first eighteen volumes of the *Encyclopaedia*.
5. It is possible, of course, that this error is unique to the copy of the *Supplement* with which I worked most closely, the one in the Rare Books Room of the Margaret I. King Library, University of Kentucky, Lexington, and is a bookbinder's rather than a printer's error.

6. Thomas Dobson to Jedidiah Morse, May 10, 1799, Morse Family Papers, Mss 358, Yale University Library.

7. Thomas Dobson to Jedidiah Morse, July 27, 1799, Gratz Collection, Case 8, Box 8, HSP.

8. Thomas Dobson to Jedidiah Morse, April 10, 1800, Morse Family Papers, Mss 358, Yale University Library.

9. Thomas Dobson to Jedidiah Morse, June 3, 1801, Gratz Collection, Alphabetical Series, HSP.

10. Thomas Dobson to Jedidiah Morse, September 28, 1801, ibid.

11. Thomas Dobson to Jedidiah Morse, May 20, 1802, American Prose, Case 6, Box 2, HSP.

12. A good discussion of Morse's *Compendious History* in terms of contemporary politics is William Gribbin's "A Mirror to New England: The *Compendious History* of Jedidiah Morse and Elijah Parish," *New England Quarterly* 45 (1972): 340–54. See also Conrad Wright, "The Controversial Career of Jedidiah Morse," *Harvard Library Bulletin* 31 (1983): 64–87.

13. Gribbin, "Mirror to New England," 353, makes this point about Albert Gallatin.

14. For Lewis Evans, see Douglas Wilmes, "Lewis Evans," *American Writers before 1800: A Biographical and Critical Dictionary,* ed. James A. Lavernier and Douglas Wilmes, 3 vols. (Westport, Conn.: Greenwood Press, 1983) 1: 541–43.

15. The Reverend Dr. John Prince (Boston, July 11, 1751–Salem, June 7, 1836) was, among other things, a friend of Count Rumford's who joined him in several experiments. A brief biography may be found in Appleton's *Cyclopaedia* 5: 124.

16. Chester Gould's patents in Great Britain, including patents for both of the items included in the *Supplement,* may be found in Bennett Woodcraft's *Alphabetical Index of Patentees of Inventions* (London: Evelyn, Adams & McKay, 1854). Gould held patents number 2405, 2458, 2559, 2706, 2734, 2945, 3002, 3045, and 3133. Many of these patented items are advertised in the *Philadelphia Gazette* during the early years of the nineteenth century.

Gould's patents in England include a machine for mangling paper to be used in papermaking (1807), a machine for washing clothing (1808), a machine for weighing items heavier than ten tons (1807), a hydrometer (1803), and nearly a dozen others. His patents for the new log and the artificial horizon are registered in England on May 26, 1800, December 17, 1800, and November 17, 1801, respectively.

18. Thomas Dobson, receipt to Aaron Burr, June 20, 1803, Gratz Collection, Alphabetical Series, HSP.

18. Thomas Dobson to Ch[arle]s. R. & G[eorge]. Webster, April 19, 1804, Dreer Collection, American Prose Writers, HSP.

19. Thomas Dobson to Messrs. Webster & Skinner, May 7, 1812, Gratz Collection, Alphabetical Series, HSP.

20. Since Philip Schuyler had died in 1804 (*DAB* 16: 477–80), this order must have been for one of his sons, Philip Jeremiah or Rensselaer Schuyler.

21. Thomas Dobson to Messrs. Webster & Skinner, August 13, 1813, Gratz Collection, Alphabetical Series, HSP. The notation that this set of the *Encyclopaedia* had been ordered for General Schuyler appears next to the address on the outside sheet of the letter.

22. Thomas Dobson to Messrs. Webster & Skinner, June 8, 1814, Gratz Collection, Alphabetical Series, HSP.

23. For a brief account of the percentages requested and, most often, allowed to Mason Locke Weems, Mathew Carey's famous itinerant bookseller, see Henry Walcott Boynton, *Annals of American Bookselling, 1638–1850* (New York: Wiley, 1932), 134–35.

24. Mathew Carey, Account Books, Folio volumes "C," NUC No. 62-4846, American Antiquarian Society, Worcester, Massachusetts.

25. Because John Low desired to publish his *New and Complete American Universal Encyclopaedia* as inexpensively as possible, he made no claims about the quality of the paper, the excellence or newness of his type, or the skill of his engravers, nor did he offer a variety of bindings. The price was "about one quarter" ([ii]) of the cost of Dobson's *Encyclopaedia,* probably $40 or $45, for which the subscriber received seven volumes of seven hundred or so pages and about one hundred and seventy illustrations. It was not uncommon for Low to place ten or more figures on one page, illustrating the like number of articles widely scattered throughout the text. The illustrations were commonly reduced and reproduced from the *Encyclopaedia* or, occasionally, from the third edition of the *Encyclopaedia Britannica* (Trenchard's eagle, for example, returns to its contorted dive in Low's publication) and illustrations from books and magazines; plates are numbered redundantly, creating an impossible situation for the reader who is referred to (for example) Plate X; there are three or four plates with that number in Volume I. Aesthetically considered, even at $40 or $45, Low's encyclopedia was not worth the price.

26. For the possibility that Bancroft wrote this review, see Jean Hoornstra and Trudy Heath, eds., *Index to American Periodicals, 1741–1900* (Ann Arbor: University Microfilms, 1979), 26. George Bancroft was primarily responsible for reviews of politics, history, and general literary subjects for Mathew Carey's short-lived *American Quarterly Review.* The review essay "Encyclopedias" appears in vol. 6, no. 12 (September & December, 1829), 331–60. Unfortunately, records of payment which could establish Bancroft's authorship apparently no longer exist. See David Kaser, ed., *The Cost Book of Carey & Lea,* 1825–1838 (Philadelphia: University of Pennsylvania Press, 1963), Appendix B, 291.

27. By 1830, however, the author of the article "Encyclopaedia" in Francis Lieber's *Encyclopaedia Americana* (1829–33) would describe Bradford's edition of Rees's *Cyclopaedia* as "the most complete work of the kind which we have" (4: 500), especially in the technical department, while failing to mention Dobson's *Encyclopaedia* as one of its own American progenitors.

28. Several other, much smaller encyclopedias also appeared during this period, including Anthony Florian Modinger Willich's *Domestic Encyclopaedia,* edited by James Mease and printed in Philadelphia by Robert Carr for William Young

Birch and Abraham Small in 1804 (Shaw and Shoemaker 7772), and Isaac Pierce's edition of George Gregory's *New and Complete Dictionary of Arts and Sciences* (published in Charleston and Philadelphia) in 1815 (Shaw and Shoemaker 34812–13). In size and scope, neither of these seriously competed with Dobson's comprehensive *Encyclopaedia*.

8. Thomas Dobson in the Nineteenth Century: The Hebrew Bible and Other Publications

With the completion of the *Encyclopaedia* and *Supplement,* Thomas Dobson brought to a close the major project of his career. He was still at work on the *Supplement* when the nineteenth century dawned, but other notable projects lay ahead of him, including the first American edition of the Hebrew Bible. During the years that remained, his interest in Unitarian and Universalist tenets deepened, leading him to write several books expanding on ideas he had first expressed in *Letters on the Existence and Character of Deity* in 1799. His name figures less and less prominently, however, in the advertising columns of Philadelphia's newspapers, replaced by the names of Mathew Carey, Moses Thomas, and even, for a time, Samuel F. Bradford. Undoubtedly the technological innovations in printing and publishing of which Bradford had spoken in his criticisms of the *Encyclopaedia* played a part in Dobson's diminishing presence among the city's publishers and booksellers, for there is no evidence in his advertisements that he accommodated his printing office to such new developments as woven paper or stereotyping. Perhaps he could not afford to do so, for the fact that he worked until he was seventy-one suggests straitened circumstances. The years between 1801 and 1823 conclude not only his personal story but also, in a measure, the story of American printing and publishing in its final premodern phases.

Not only print technology but also readership and publishing were changing. In a nation of expanding literacy with an increasing taste for entertainment, Dobson reprinted only occasional editions of popular poets like Robert Burns (1801; Shaw and Shoemaker 260) and popular pieces such as Isaac Pocock's musical adaptation of Sir Walter Scott's *Rob Roy* (1818; Shaw and Shoemaker 45363). He sold other publishers' editions of best-selling authors such as Sir Walter Scott, Lord Byron, and Thomas

Campbell (J. Dobson *Catalogue*, 4, 11, 12, and 38) but printed none himself and included few novels by any authors in his inventory.[1] He seems never to have adapted his bookselling procedures to acknowledge the growing class of professional rather than amateur authors. While the firm of Carey & Son was expanding, modernizing its printing facilities, and taking on new partners en route to becoming one of the great American publishing houses,[2] Dobson & Son, perhaps lacking capital and family connections, seems barely to have held its own in the final years of its founder's life and did not survive his funeral.

The list of books Dobson published as the century advanced suggests that he continued to think of his principal audience as the professional men of the city: churchmen, physicians, educators, and statesmen. He maintained his ties with the American Philosophical Society, the College of Physicians, and, informally, the University of Pennsylvania. Philadelphians such as John Redman Coxe, John Andrews, and Benjamin Smith Barton, along with distinguished international visitors such as Francois Andre Michaux and Constantine Rafinesque, bought books at his shop and wrote new ones for him to sell, providing a core clientele. So did men like the aging Benjamin Rush and Caspar Wistar until their deaths in the second decade of the nineteenth century. But Philadelphia's intellectual life was declining in vigor during this period. Many of the new medical and scientific writers made their homes in New York or, if they stayed in the city, formed new professional societies and found new publishers for their transactions (Bell 45–49; Greene 4). Perhaps, too, Dobson's trade was adversely affected by the removal of the capital to Washington, D.C., which must have cost him clients in the diplomatic class. Strategies that worked well in the eighteenth century became less effective in the nineteenth as the audience he had long cultivated diminished.

Symbolically if not chronologically, the eighteenth century ended with the election of 1800, which pitted Thomas Jefferson and Aaron Burr against the Federalists John Adams, John Jay, and Charles C. Pinckney. The election looked forward to an unbroken string of presidential victories for democrat-republicans until the Whig Zachary Taylor carried the White House in 1848. Here, too, was a change that could not fail to have repercussions for a publisher leaning toward Federalism. The spirit of compromise and accommodation that had marked the earliest years of the republic dissolved into acrimonious debate, a continuation of the political campaigns of the previous century, and fear of the other party found expression in countless polemical pamphlets and controversial tracts. One of these, apparently a diatribe against Jefferson or perhaps an attack on masonic societies written by the Reverend James Kemp, rector of the Great Choptank Parish in Maryland, came Dobson's way while the campaign of 1800 was still in progress, but he did not decide what he should do with it until John Adams was defeated and the lingering Federalist majority in Congress had persuaded itself that Jefferson was a lesser evil than Aaron Burr. Though a conservative in politics, Dobson probably felt that there was no more to say on the subject on which Kemp had written or no point in saying it and declined the manuscript.

On February 22, 1801, he wrote to Kemp explaining his reasons. He was evidently responding to an angry letter in which Kemp seems to have charged him with rejecting his manuscript because he disagreed with Kemp's politics. Dobson admitted his "blameable" neglect in keeping the manuscript too long, but nothing more. "As to suppressing a piece, how-ever contrary to my own opinions, I would never attempt [it]," he assured Reverend Kemp. (Since he printed Benjamin Rush's and William Currie's opposing views of the yellow fever epidemic of 1793, he is probably to be believed on this point.) Indeed, he said, he had read the piece with great pleasure because Kemp's sentiments coincided so nearly with his own. He thought it "by far the best [essay] I have seen on the subject," and several gentlemen to whom he had shown it had also agreed. The problem was, he pointed out, that "it was too late to be of Service to the cause which was expressed." Perhaps remembering his consternation when the article "Quaker" was ascribed to him by the Society of Friends, he added that he would not publish anything, especially anything that censured a man or a "Society," unless the piece bore the author's name. In a hasty aside, he assured Kemp that he had not revealed Kemp's identity to those whose opinion of the manuscript he had solicited.[3]

Dobson was deeply troubled by developments in American politics and distressed by the drift he detected in America toward the abyss of infidelity. In 1802, he voiced his concerns about the future of America in a continuation of his *Letters on the Existence and Character of the Deity, and on the Moral State of Man* (Shaw and Shoemaker 2149), by far the most political piece he ever wrote. The ostensible purpose of this part of the *Letters* was religious and not political, but religious speculations soon led to other matters. The new part began with an examination of the civil and domestic obligations of Christians to each other, discussing philanthropy and other "moral advantages of useful labor" (167) and "the *domestic state*" as the origin and model of all larger social associations and, eventually, of civil governments. "Among the social duties in the domestic state," Dobson wrote, "sympathizing tenderness to one another in distress as well as mutual assistance and economy, are particularly important," as are also "the moral and religious education of children, bringing them up in the nurture and admonition of the Lord" (186–87). In these words, Dobson provides a distant glimpse of the domestic situation within his own family.

Dobson's reflections on domestic order and harmony provide an occasion to discuss the educational and religious responsibilities "Of Civil Government," which he does in Letters X–XII, comprising seventy pages of his continuation. "As mankind in every age stand in need of direction, restraint, or chastisement," he asserts, "every form and every degree of energy in government seem to be parts of that general plan of moral discipline which God is superintending for the ultimate benefit of man" (225). This is so not only in "free states" (225) but in despotic nations as well; "the kinds of government, and the degrees of energy therein, are adapted to the moral and intellectual state of the people" (263). "For instance," he continues, "the government of the United States of America would not answer in Russia or Turkey," for "the people could not understand its excellence nor enjoy its privileges" (230–31). From this follows naturally a divine prohibition against vast social upheavals and revolutions in general, as if God Himself preordains each form of government to be exactly what it is at a particular moment in history:

> In that state of society which renders kingly government necessary, a republican form of government would be one of the greatest evils which could befall a people. . . . This was the case with the Jewish nation before their destruction . . . and . . . it has been the case with some of the nations of Europe in a most exemplary degree [surely he had in mind Napoleon's rise from the turmoil of the Revolution to be Emperor of France, a nation not intended by God to be a democracy], and ought to be a solemn warning to the nations who are under kingly government that they might not wantonly bring such tremendous sufferings on themselves. (252–53)

"Much has been said against KINGLY GOVERNMENT," Dobson goes on, undoubtedly with Joel Barlow's *Advice to the Privileged Orders* (1792, 1794) and *Conspiracy of Kings* (1794) and Thomas Paine's *Rights of Man* (1791, 1792) in mind, "but the fault lies in the *depravity* of the PEOPLE, which renders such discipline necessary. The original institution of *kingly* government is just as much from God himself as the origin and institution of *republican* government" (250). This is a truth that those who preach revolution to the masses would do well to consider.

Dobson reminds his readers that all empires are destined to disappear in the fullness of time or to experience an early demise as a result of internal discord. It had been so with the kingdom of Israel and with the empires of Greece and Rome (228–29), and it might prove to be so in America. "We shall find the observation generally applicable, and even in this same country, though the people are certainly not *righteous overmuch,* yet let them beware of the progress of corruption, for should they become depraved like the nations already mentioned, they will become incapable of maintaining their *liberties* . . . which they now so justly prize" (229–30). If the political consequences of national transgressions are decidedly local and contemporary, the voice of the prophet Dobson adopts is as ancient as the books of Jeremiah and Isaiah.

In light of recent political turmoil and the virulence of party faction in America, a grim admonition seemed to Dobson the only sensible order of the day. "The REIGN OF THE LAW . . . is indispensibly requisite in every republic," Dobson insists, which "ought to be a government, not of *men* nor of *parties,* but of the LAWS. When the moral state of any people is such as to admit of republican government, the people ought to watch with unremitting attention over the administration of the laws" (244–45):

Modern times furnish ample evidences of the encroachments of anarchy by a licentious opposition to the operation of the laws, which have been at least equally destructive of liberty, and tend as strongly to the subversion of every valuable privilege, as official usurpations: of this the history of Europe for the last ten or twelve years presents an awful warning to the people of the United States of America, and they need to be particularly on their guard against *licentiousness* when it assumes the specious name of liberty. (246–67)

After this disquisition, Dobson takes up in "Letter XII" the related subject of "how far Christians ought to interfere in local politics" (265), apparently in tacit recognition that the outcomes of elections can also be rationalized as expressions of the will of God and as part of His design for disciplining a wayward people. Although he does not straightforwardly confront that objection, he makes it clear that if the voters in a Christian republic, the most favored of all political arrangements, attended properly to their duty, only godly, God-fearing candidates will be elected. Without explicitly naming names or candidates, he feels secure in prophesying that honest Christians will always "give their suffrages . . . to raise or maintain . . . *men fearing God and hating covetousness,* as such will be most likely . . . to protect the liberties of the people, which the atheist or deist, having no principles . . . may be more ready to infringe or betray" (265–66). The popular idea that "deists make the best legislators" (266), presumably because they do not support the establishment of any religion, Dobson holds to be false: "What dependence ought to be placed on men who have no permanent or well grounded moral principles, and who do not believe in a future state" (266)? Given Jefferson's popular reputation as an atheist and an enemy of religion, these sentiments clearly establish Dobson's sympathy for Federalist positions and Federalist politicians, making it easier to understand his apparently cordial working relationship with Jedidiah Morse despite his adherence to liberal Universalist tenets.

Contemporary politics and history viewed through the glass of scriptural prophecy occupy Dobson throughout most of Part II of the *Letters*. His thoughts lead him in the sixth letter on an excursion into millennarianism in which he comes close to asserting that America may already be under the reign of the Antichrist (278–79). Only in the seventh letter does he return to theological matters, arguing for the universal salvation of all mankind in Letter VII. The seven letters of Part II thus balance the seven of Part I and give the book an appearance of formal structure which the content contradicts.

Like the first part of *Letters*, the second part was reviewed by Charles Brockden Brown (*American Review* 2 [1802]: 215–20). By far the larger part of Brown's review consists of extensive quotation (three and a quarter pages out of four and a quarter), and most of what remains is only a brief description of the contents. Since Dobson believes in the salvation of all men but does not try to argue the case, Brown says, "it would be unseasonable to enter into a discussion of the subject" (220). He commends Dobson for having "carried his theological reading and inquiries to an extent not very common with laymen" (216) and approves of the "plain and unaffected" (216) style of the writing. "The reader of taste will, indeed, sometimes be disposed to find fault with long and heavy sentences, and inelegant expressions," he admits, "but he will find, on the whole, more to commend than to censure" (216). Brown says nothing about Dobson's political views and reviews his work respectfully rather than enthusiastically.

In 1803, the Reverend Samuel Miller, who had contributed a revised and expanded article on Delaware to the *Encyclopaedia*, published his best-known work, *A Brief Retrospect of the Eighteenth Century*. Dobson must have been pleased by Miller's account of the "zeal and enterprise" (2: 267) with which he had pursued the publication of the *Encyclopaedia* and to find his work described as "decidedly superiour to that from which the greater part of it was copied" (2: 268). "Besides other matter," Miller wrote with the air of one who knew whereof he spoke, "Mr. DOBSON'S edition contains much important information respecting the United States, not contained in the work as it came from the British press" (2: 268n.). Nor does Miller neglect to mention that Dobson's *Encyclopaedia* had been "executed in a manner equally honourable to himself and his patrons" and was at the time "altogether unrivalled in the United States" (2: 267). It was the most favorable notice that the *Encyclopaedia* would receive until Joseph Hopkinson's *Annual Discourse* in 1810.

On February 17, 1804, Dobson copyrighted Volume II of his *Letters* (Shaw and Shoemaker 6171). In it, he continued the topic with which Part II of *Letters* had closed, examining and rejecting the Calvinist doctrine of election and eternal damnation (Letter XIV) and offering instead the Universalist doctrine that punishment for sin will not be eternal. One feature of his argument consists of ten pages (5–15) of corrected translations from the Greek of key scriptural texts which "prove" this theory over the mistaken view of eternity embraced by the Calvinists and establish the sonship rather than the co-divinity of Jesus. Later in the book (235–50), he attempts to rectify similar errors of translation regarding the Hebrew word *Alehim,* borrowing both content and rhetorical technique from James Purves's *Humble Attempt to Investigate and Defend the Scripture Doctrine Concerning the Father, the Son, and the Holy Spirit,* which he had published in 1788 (Evans 21413). This is undoubtedly one of the books that earned him a reputation for knowing classical Greek and Hebrew. As he had done in previous discourses on religion, he showed himself adept at typological exegesis, explicating and defending the symbolism of baptism by water and arguing in favor of the practice as the best means "to impress spiritual things more strongly on the minds of young Christians, through the medium of . . . earthly things, which are adapted to their . . . comparatively infantile state" (180). These arguments Dobson urges with high earnestness, but there is nothing in them to challenge his own claim, made in the prefaces of all three versions of *Letters,* that his ideas are not original and manage to convince, if they convince at all, by familiarity and frequency of repetition.

The final version of Dobson's *Letters* was not reviewed by any of the literary journals of Philadelphia. The book was not favorably regarded, however, by at least one reader. Sometime early in 1805, Dobson's sister, one Mrs. Charleton (who is otherwise, alas, unknown to history) wrote to her brother to take him to task for his heretical views of Christ (she called it Sabellianism) and his use of anti-republican allegories. Dobson replied to the first charge that it simply was not true and sent her some pages on the subject of Sabellianism he had just written and printed off though not yet published. These pages would not appear until three years later, in *Thoughts on the Scripture Account of Faith in Jesus* (1807).

Dobson was right, he maintained, to employ historical allegory to comment on contemporary events. "The intention with which ancient historical facts were recorded and transmitted to us," he insisted,

was not that we were more interested in the revelation of Edom, Moab, or Israel merely as nations, than we are in those of France, Italy, and Holland; but that they were written for our learning, our example, to the intent that we should avoid similar misconduct, or follow the pattern as recorded for our imitation. (Thomas Dobson to Mrs. Charleton, July 25, 1805, Society Collection, HSP)[4]

Dobson then launched into a lengthy defense of his use of the title "Lord of Hosts" as equally applicable to Jesus Christ and God and as one clue to understanding Christ's divine yet subordinate nature. This reasoning largely recapitulates the etymological excursion of *Letters* 2: 235–50. "I am of the opinion," he concluded, anticipating a point on which he would elaborate in his last books, *Scripture Account of Faith in Jesus* and *Thoughts on Mankind*, "that Jesus Christ before he came into the world was cloathed with the fulness of Divine Power" (July 25, 1805).

His sister, however, was not convinced and apparently responded with renewed criticism. Thus on August 17, 1805, a patient Dobson wrote to her again, characterizing himself as her "sincere friend for the truth's sake." His use of the word friend may have been intended as an allusion to his sister's religion, for in this letter he employs the formal locution of "thee" and "thy" as he had done much earlier when writing to James Pemberton (and does not do in any other surviving correspondence). Dobson's adaptation of his style suggests that his sister had converted to Quakerism, perhaps after her marriage. This implication seems borne out by Dobson's comment that she is the last person from whom he would expect "censure, ridicule, or contempt, for exercising the same right of Judging for which thou hast suffered persecution, and thereby knowest how inconsistent with the Christian spirit persecution in any form must be" (August 17, 1805).

The heart of Dobson's letter appears in the first paragraph, some twenty lines of which constitute a two-hundred-plus word prospectus of another book he was to write, *Thoughts on Mankind*, and a succinct summary of most of his major religious beliefs. It contains ideas from all three versions of *Letters* and anticipates not only *Thoughts on Mankind* but also *Scripture Account of Faith in Jesus.* "My own thought," he explained to his sister,

is that not only Jesus Christ existed before the Six days creation recorded by Moses, but also that every individual of Mankind before that period in their individual capacities, created in Christ Jesus, abiding in Him in a spiritual state; from which state they could only fall by their individual transgressions, which I think to be the true source of their evil propensities in the present state, and the different degrees of their falling from Him occasion the various degrees of depravity observable among mankind, with the various disciplines under which they are placed, from Infancy to old age; So that however much the individuals may appear to suffer through the misconduct of others, no suffering can possibly befal [sic] them but what comes as a chastisement perfectly adapted to their own personal condition; and that they will all be made to *return* to the Shepherd and Bishop of their Souls, and be restored by him to their former estate.

Further discussion of his religious convictions, Dobson had concluded simultaneously with his sister, could not prove fruitful. "I agree with thee to give up . . . the correspondence," he declared. However foolish or absurd his opinions might appear in her view, he wanted her to know that "I believe these things and deem them matters of great importance." There would be no use in trying to dissuade him from beliefs of such long standing, for, he reminded her, "Thou art sufficiently acquainted with human nature to know that it is no easy matter to get over long established habits of thinking." He signed himself "thy sincere friend for the truth's sake" and must have imagined that he had found a way out of a correspondence which, reading only his side of the exchange, had begun somewhat testily and degenerated from there.

But his sister was not finished. Since writing her last letter, she had, apparently, read the proof sheets he had sent her with his letter of July 25, and she was disturbed anew by his sentiments. On August 22, therefore, obviously in response to another letter from her, Dobson again picked up his pen, hoping to restore family harmony. He must have despaired of ever explaining himself to his sister or of gaining her toleration of, much less acquiescence in, his views. His comments were directed toward his sister's critique of some ideas in *Thoughts on the Scripture Account of Faith in Jesus* (1807, Shaw and Shoemaker 12442, ND 0302504; 1808, ND 0302502), which it is therefore necessary to summarize.

Thoughts on the Scripture Account of Faith in Jesus was written, as

Dobson says, "to induce others to think and examine the scriptures for themselves" (vii) and so to be no longer fooled by "human inventions" (vi) concerning matters of the highest spiritual importance. The book consists of fifteen chapters and 288 pages, the most important of which attack the doctrine of the Trinity. Dobson first attempts to establish that the designation of Jesus Christ as the "Son of God" refers to an autonomous and independent existence rather than to a mystical union of Father, Son, and Holy Ghost identical in being and essence. As he had previously done with *Letters,* Dobson divided *Thoughts* into letters rather than chapters, devoting Letter I to an examination of Psalm 90, verse 15, "Touch not mine anointed, do my prophets no harm," to demonstrate that Christ, considered typologically as the antitype of all the anointed prophets, was anointed as a separate and individual entity (see esp. pp. 14–15). He also criticized "the doctrine taught by Sabellius" (the sheets sent to his sister), which, as he defined it, held "that there is only one Supreme God, who is at once Father, Son, and Holy Ghost" and that "these names are not expressive of personal distinctions; there being no plurality of persons in the Deity" (29–31).

In a separate chapter of the book, Chapter V, Dobson discussed and dismissed "The Socinian Scheme" of "considering our Lord Jesus Christ simply as a man, the Son of Joseph and Mary . . . without any thing extraordinary respecting his origin"; he denied the notion that Christ had "no existence" before his birth in Bethlehem (77). He held that the doctrine of the Trinity originally arose "from a misdirected zeal to exalt the character of our Lord Jesus Christ, beyond what he himself claims" (76), and that the Socinian mistake arose in an equally honorable wish to keep as great a theological distance as possible from the "inconsistencies" of the doctrine of the Trinity (77). There were excellent Christians in both camps, he readily conceded, and he wrote not to "cast reflections" on them but to invite them "to leave the dogmas and traditions of men, and attend to the teachings of God himself in the Scriptures of Truth" (90).

Dobson also cited as a grievous error which had laid Christianity open to scoffing and derision "the doctrines of annihilation, or of the eternal misery of part of mankind" (50). "A principal source of mistake," he said, "has consisted in supposing that the *Almighty, and All-Perfect God* must act as men do, who are often weak and wicked" (163). But "the Doctrine of Divine Truth . . . is harmonious in all its parts; unincumbered [sic] with those difficulties, which press, with insurmountable force upon the schemes devised by human wisdom."

It needs no defense against the weakness of the Arminian Scheme, which represents a great proportion of mankind as irrecoverably lost, through the perverseness of their own wills; notwithstanding the Gracious designs of God, and the Wisdom and Energy with which he employs those means which will make his Grace abound over sin. Nor has it to encounter the horrors of the gloomy system of John Calvin; which represents, or rather misrepresents, that a great proportion of mankind, by an irreversible decree, without regard to their own conduct, are predestinated to Eternal Misery. (215–16)

Dobson's response to his sister indicates that she challenged virtually everything he had to say in *Thoughts,* but especially his interpretation of the identity of the "Lord's anointed" and his argument concerning the purity of priests. Dobson attempted to refute these criticisms by pointing out that he had not meant that priests were pure, only that, as types of Christ the antitype, their purity was symbolic. Much of the letter centered on other disagreements regarding Aaron's culpability in casting the golden calf and about the signification of the Ten Lost Tribes of Israel. Dobson suggested that if she had witnessed the casting of metal, as he must have done in visiting typefoundries, she would have known that her reading of the biblical passage could not possibly be correct. The argument became as esoteric in this piece of family correspondence as it was in the passages in Dobson's text out of which it arose. Sensibly, Dobson tried to extricate himself from a debate that was leading nowhere, pointing out that neither he nor his sister could be certain his or her argument was not in error. He acknowledged that the quest for truth was important by signing himself "thy brother enquirer," but he wanted to have done with the exchange. This time, it seems, the truce was honored all around, for no further correspondence between Dobson and his sister can be found.

While engaged in controversy with his sister, Dobson was also oc-cupied with business matters, publishing, among other titles, his *Index to the Bible* (1804; Shaw and Shoemaker 6171) and several other religious texts, many for local Unitarians and Universalists. In late 1807, Ralph Eddowes of Philadelphia sent one of these Unitarian publications, Edward Rigg's *The Right, Duty, and Importance of Free Inquiry into Matters of Religion* (1807; Shaw and Shoemaker 13503), to Thomas Jefferson. Inter-ested as always in open inquiry into religion and especially interested in Unitarianism, Jefferson wrote to Dobson on November 18, 1807, request-ing that additional copies in the series be sent to him "as they appear," together with a "translation of the New Testament, announced on page 22" of Dobson's publication. On January 20, 1809, Dobson complied with

Jefferson's request, "forwarding . . . one of the best copies of the New Testament published in London last year, and the four successive numbers of the Unitarian pieces."[5] He may have been surprised to discover in this straightforward and unequivocal way that Jefferson was not the atheist of popular report, but the formal nature of the transaction gave him no opportunity to show it.

Although involved in both personal and professional ways with matters of religion, Dobson had not neglected scientific publications. His close association with the College of Physicians produced some of his most successful publishing ventures in the nineteenth century. In 1805, with John Redman Coxe serving as editor, he began the publication of the *Philadelphia Medical Museum,* printed by Archibald Bartram (Hoornstra and Heath 178). This journal lasted until 1810, when Dobson transferred his attention to the *Eclectic Repertory and Analytical Review,* edited by "a Society of Physicians," for which Dobson and, later (with Volume VII in 1817), Dobson & Son, remained the publisher and William Fry the printer until replaced by Eliakim Littel in 1820 (Volumes II–X). The name was then changed to the *Journal of Foreign Medical Science and Literature.* The prospectus for this publication, later reprinted at the head of Volume VIII (1818), set the price at three dollars per year, the money to be paid on delivery of the second number, and promised that the work would be printed on "good paper, with distinct type." The impending change of publisher was not announced in the final issue Dobson printed, Volume X in 1820, but perhaps a satisfactory reason may be that he was now sixty-eight or sixty-nine years old and was no longer able to comply with a rigorous publication schedule.

In 1811, just a year after he became the publisher of the *Eclectic Repertory,* Thomas Dobson took his son Judah into partnership. Individual titles still continued to appear as published by or for him only, but increasingly "Thomas Dobson & Son" was the logo printers impressed on new title pages. The last mention of Dobson & Son before their *Catalogue* described them as the "late firm" in 1822 appears in an advertisement for the Reverend George Paxton's *Illustrations of the Holy Scriptures* in William Fry's *National Gazette and Literary Register* on July 31, 1822. Paxton's book, along with "Carpenter's Introduction to the Geography of the New Testament," was available, according to the advertisement, at D. Hogan's bookstore, "No. 223 Market Street" and at "T. Dobson & Son's, No. 41, South Second Street." Nearly every other bookseller in Philadelphia was advertising Scott's *The Fortunes of Nigel* in the same issue of the newspaper.

After his father's death, Judah Dobson published another *Catalogue of Books* (1823) and would later attempt to establish himself as a printer in his own right with *The North American Medical and Surgical Journal* (1826–31) and *The Philadelphia Monthly Magazine* (1827–30; Hoornstra and Heath 66–67, 178), but the name of Dobson would not again be dominant among Philadelphia's publishers and booksellers as it had been in the late eighteenth and early nineteenth centuries.

Dobson's final contribution to the literature of religious controversy in America, *Thoughts on Mankind, Considered as Individuals, Originally Created Upright; Their State Under Discipline, Rendered Needful by Their Disobedience; and Their Recovery by Jesus Christ* (ND 0302502), was also written in 1811. Essentially, it recapitulates arguments that he had advanced in his previous writings. Like them it begins with his standard disclaimer that the reader need not look for originality or brilliant flashes of wit and style in the writing; its purposes, like theirs, are to "free the evidences of Christianity from much of the obscurity" that has surrounded scriptural texts and so to "silence the triumph of infidelity" (5–6). The first part of the title, however, accurately reflects a change in Dobson's emphasis, if not absolutely in his content. Whereas *Letters on the Existence and Character of Deity,* at least in its earliest version of 1799, had been primarily concerned with the Unity of God, and *Thoughts on the Scripture Account of Faith in Jesus* was principally occupied with the sonship of Jesus and the errors of Trinitarianism, Sabellianism, and Socinianism, *Thoughts on Mankind* attempted to confront the vexing question of why an all-wise and benevolent Deity condemned mankind to suffering and sorrow. What was there about the nature of the human race that justified the undeniable experience of misery and woe, often suffered most by those whose lives appeared most blameless or, indeed, too short for any culpability?

Dobson explained at several points throughout his treatise that there were two generally accepted answers to that question. The first, the Calvinistic doctrine of innate depravity, supposed that the human race was born into an inheritance of sin and pain as a result of the original transgression of Adam, whose guilt all subsequent generations had inherited. But this doctrine, Dobson argued, is inimical to the nature and essence of God. "That *God himself* should make mankind guilty, corrupt, and prone to wickedness . . . and then punish them without any view to their benefit by the punishment . . . appear[s] so monstrous, so utterly repugnant to all our ideas of the perfection of the *divine character,* that he must be a sturdy believer indeed, who can for a moment admit the possibility of it" (12–13).

The doctrine of original sin could not be true because it failed to harmonize with the premises of God's goodness and benevolence.

The second explanation of man's liability to death had been put forward by Lockean rationalists (in *Thoughts on the Scripture Account of Faith in Jesus,* Dobson had identified them with the Arminian position). Theirs was the notion "that the human mind, when it comes into the world, has no stain or evil propensity; but, like a clean sheet of paper, is capable of receiving whatever impression may be made upon it, and generally becomes in a measure corrupted by evil example" (20). But why should the examples of humanity so frequently be evil, and why should the otherwise innocent mind gravitate so readily toward evil instead of good? The rationalists, Dobson contended, could offer no plausible explanation. Indeed, he continued, they found themselves involved in a logical contradiction every time they tried to account for the human preference for evil, for although they denied the concept of original sin, they nonetheless viewed "the corruptions produced by it in mankind, as the necessary means whereby the cause operates in producing labour, sorrow, and death" (22). Moreover, they failed to take into account the evidence of experience and common sense, including the observable fact that different people display a variety of tempers and dispositions from infancy. No single explanation, therefore, would seem adequate to cover all the varieties of character or inclination among the human race.

How, then, may one account for the realities of sin and punishment and death? Dobson proposed that mankind had existed before the Fall, that the Fall took place long before the events narrated in the Bible, and that creation as described in Genesis did not refer to creation ex nihilo but to God's "arranging existing materials into particular order and form" where all had previously been desolation and destruction for "many thousands or millions of years" (57) as a consequence of man's true first disobedience. He had sketched this position in *Thoughts on the Scripture Account of Faith in Jesus,* arguing that "God first created mankind . . . by and in Jesus Christ, pure, holy, spiritual, like himself" but that "they fell by transgression from their original purity" (102); their new state of sin was symbolized by the natural state of darkness.

In *Thoughts on Mankind,* Dobson developed this argument at some length. "That all had sinned in a former state of existence appears to have been the sentiment of the writers of both the old and new Testaments" (52), he asserted. At the same time he argued that "the changes which are described [in Genesis] as having been made in six days, seem more like gradual renovation than original creation" (57). Recognizing that this theory might expose him "to ridicule and contempt" (39), a painful recollection of his correspondence with his sister, he nevertheless felt that the only way to explain the punishment of mankind in terms consistent with the character of the Deity was to extend the doctrine of the preexistent soul of Christ to all mankind in general and to assume an ancient and individual transgression of every single, separate soul in that time before the beginning of time. Such an explanation, Dobson pointed out, had the additional virtue of bringing Mosaic history into alignment with new geological discoveries, which clearly indicated a history of the earth far older than the six thousand years traditionally thought to have passed since the Creation described in Genesis. One need not, in this formulation, choose between science and religion, for there was no contradiction between them.

Dobson's books on religion are of value to the history of American Universalism, which so far has not acknowledged his contributions. He conducted his side of the debate with tolerance toward other beliefs and a sense of human fallibility. The spirit of Philadelphia, with its tradition of open inquiry and toleration of all religions, played a part in his writings as in all other significant works of his life. Although his ideas may have been conventional, the common coin of Unitarian and Universalist thought in the formative years of the movement, there can be no doubt that they arose from his deepest beliefs and convictions. In Francis Drake's *Dictionary of American Biography* (1879), he is remembered not as an important early American printer or as the publisher of the *Encyclopaedia* but as the author of *Thoughts on Mankind*. He might have agreed that it was his most important achievement.

Among the major titles Dobson undertook in the nineteenth century was Hugh Williamson's *History of North Carolina* (1812; Shaw and Shoemaker 27566). To be sure, the work is more notable because Williamson wrote it than as a history, for Williamson was not a good historian. Born in West Nottingham, Pennsylvania, he was a member of the first class to graduate from the College of Philadelphia (1751) and a prominent member of the American Philosophical Society, as well as a statesman and occasional associate of Benjamin Franklin. In 1776, he settled in Edenton, North Carolina and resided there more or less permanently (between stints as a delegate to the Constitutional Convention and as a member of the Continental Congress) until 1793, when he moved to New York. There he founded the Literary and Philosophical Society of New York and the New-York Historical Society. His interest in historical matters was not confined to New York, however, for it was while he was living there that he wrote his *History of North Carolina* (*DAB* 20: 298–300).

Dobson issued proposals for subscribers in North Carolina only (*Proposals, History of North Carolina,* [1]). Apparently, he had experienced some success in that state with an earlier title, the first and second volumes of Ebenezer Hazard's *Historical Collections* (Evans 24388 and 27105); the first volume was advertised in the *North-Carolina Gazette* on July 16, 1791 and published in 1792 and 1794 (Powell 428). The sole surviving copy of the proposals for Williamson's book bears the signature of the North Carolinian John Haygood of Wake County, who subscribed for two sets at five dollars each, and a general description of the contents of the *History*. Volume I (Books I and II) includes the natural history of North Carolina, an account of Sir Walter Raleigh's Lost Colony, other early attempts at colonization, and early successful settlements; Volume II narrates the role of North Carolina in the revolutionary war. Dobson's Conditions of Subscription announced that the book would be printed "on a new type and fine paper, carefully stitched in boards" and would be available in Newbern, Edenton, Wilmington, Fayetteville, Halifax, and Raleigh. The price was $4.00 or, "neatly bound in leather and lettered," $4.50 (one wonders what Haygood's subscription price of $5.00 bought). Included in the edition was "a correct Map of the State."[6]

Williamson was dissatisfied with the printing of the *History*. On March 28, 1812, he wrote to Dobson from New York complaining that the paper on which the map was printed was too spongy and spread out the ink in his corrections (Fry and Kammerer printed the *History* for Dobson). "There should be a small river near James Town to the East," he informed Dobson, and instructed him to make an appropriate mark for the town on the west side of that river. "The small lake that joins Collins' canal is called lake Phelps, not Phillip." Williamson allowed that Fry and Kammerer's typeface was acceptable, but the scabbard was too broad. "The lines at present seem to my eye to be too far asunder. A thin scabbard adds greatly to the beauty of the page." Williamson closed by telling Dobson he had recently received "some very remarkable accounts of some Indian antiquities. . . . If the proofs come in time they may be very properly placed among the Proofs and explanations, or at the end of them."[7] These and other difficulties with the *History* were eventually ironed out, and on August 11, 1812 (*Poulson's American Daily Advertiser,* September 20, 1812), Dobson filed for copyright of the initial volume. Subscriptions must have been scant, however, for the second volume of Williamson's *History of*

North Carolina advertised in the proposals was never published (Powell 428).

On May 21, 1813, Dobson began seeking subscribers for *A New Harmony of the Gospels* prepared by Charles Thomson, former secretary to the Continental Congress (*DAB* 18: 481–82). The book would be printed, Dobson's proposals promised, "with a good type on fine paper" and would make "a handsome volume octavo." He had not firmly set the price, but he was certain it would not exceed "two dollars per copy in boards." Printing would begin "as soon as subscriptions sufficient to defray the expense shall be received" (*Poulson's American Daily Advertiser,* May 21, 1813).

That date never arrived, however. Although he published proposals off and on for several months in various Philadelphia newspapers and retained possession of Thomson's manuscript for well more than a year, Dobson could not enroll a sufficient number of subscribers. Eventually, he attributed this lack of interest to the excellence and availability of competing editions. Finally on August 10, 1814, he wrote a brief letter to Thomson, informing him that the slow trickle of subscriptions raised serious doubts about the salability of the book. "The knowledge that both [John] McKnight & [Philip] Doddridge had made arrangements of the Gospels somewhat similar in their respective harmonies," he wrote, "induced me to relinquish the idea of printing the *Synopsis* because I do not expect a sale for it which would pay for the expence [sic] of publication, in many years." Sounding a bit disillusioned after long experience with the American bookbuying public, Dobson reminded Thomson that "it is not the intrinsic merit of a work which will ensure an extensive circulation." He cited the lagging sales of Thomson's own translation of the Bible, printed by Jane Aitken in 1808, as an illustration.[8] "I would not wish to circulate a bad book" only for the sake of profit, Dobson concluded, but "I am obliged to consider even a good one as an article of trade." Convinced that the book would be "unsaleable," he reluctantly returned it to its author.[9] Another printer, William McCulloch, did not agree with Dobson's analysis of the market and, early in 1815, brought out the work under the new title of *A Synopsis of the Four Evangelists* (McCulloch 218; Shaw and Shoemaker 36085).

By the time he returned Thomson's manuscript, Dobson had completed his most important publishing project of the nineteenth century, the first American edition of the Hebrew Bible (1814; Shaw and Shoemaker 30857). The story of this edition of the Hebrew Scriptures antedates by several years Dobson's commitment to the project. It begins with the publication in New Haven of Mills Day's proposals for the printing of Edvardo Van der Hooght's Hebrew Bible on March 20, 1810, a work intended, as Day declared, to mitigate a rising anti-Jewish sentiment in America and to provide American clergymen with "immediate access to the fountain of truth" in the original language of the Bible's composition. "A Hebrew Bible will be a new thing in the history of American typography," Day stressed, adding that his edition would appear "without the points" because the points "originally formed no part of the language, and were not employed by the inspired penmen." Of Day himself (September 30, 1783–June 20, 1812), a Yale graduate, little is known (Wegelin 224–26). In this attempt to become the sponsor and godfather of the earliest American edition of the Hebrew Bible, however, he failed to secure a sufficient number of subscribers "to enable the publisher to prosecute this expensive undertaking and at the same time afford the book at a moderate price." Perhaps his major problem was only that he allowed too little time for subscribers to come forward, for he concluded his prospectus by directing interested persons to sign up in time for subscription papers to be sent to "[Joel] Walter, [William] Austin & Co., Booksellers, New-Haven, by the 1st of July."[10] From late March to the first of July does not seem a sufficient interval to interest the bookbuying public in a title for which divinity students and clergymen were the only natural audience.

Day's untimely death at the age of twenty-eight might have doomed his project for the immediate future had it not been for a Jewish scholar named Jonathan Horwitz, a well known and respected teacher of "some of the oriental languages, particularly the Hebrew" (as he was described in his prospectus). Horwitz arrived in America from Amsterdam in 1812, bringing with him a font of Hebrew type and the nearly completed manuscript of a Hebrew grammar. He may, indeed, have emigrated to the United States with the sole purpose of publishing an American edition of the Hebrew Bible, certain that America would prove a receptive market (Simonhoff 160). At any rate, he experienced some notable successes in his endeavor, obtaining orders from both Harvard College and Andover Theological Institution for forty copies each. But then he learned that Samuel Whiting and Ebenezer Watson in New York were also planning to bring out an edition of the Hebrew Scripture, supervised and directed by the American scholars S. M. Mathews and J. M. Mason. Two other editions were also in the planning stages, one under the sponsorship of a missionary society and another by a printer named Benjamin Boothroyd. This knowledge induced Horwitz to sell his Hebrew type to William Fry[11] and to turn over his list of subscriptions to Thomas Dobson. He then helped to plan the format of the edition, proofread and assisted in correcting the galleys, and may even have worked in the print shop, all the while earning a degree in medicine at the University of Pennsylvania (Simonhoff 160–61).

The surviving copy of Horwitz's proposal bears brief notes dated early May 1812 that testify to his character and ability as a scholar. This, then, must have been the date of the original proposals. Yet the text of the proposals already identifies William Fry and directs subscriptions to be returned to Thomas Dobson the publisher by the first of August. It also advertises that the work had already been "Put to Press." Since this did not happen until March of 1813, the claim that printing had already begun establishes that month and year as the probable date of this version of Horwitz's proposals. Though originally drafted by Horwitz, in other words, the proposals were later modified by Thomas Dobson.

Some of Horwitz's reasons for proposing an American edition of the Hebrew Bible echo those of Mills Day. It was obviously desirable that American clergymen have direct access to the word of God in the original language. But the hand of Thomas Dobson is also evident in the proposals, especially in the appeal to national pride and American honor. The proposals lament "the great scarcity of Hebrew scriptures in this country," asserting that Horwitz had been able to discover from his own inquiries "not a dozen copies for sale in the whole United States." This included four in New York, two in Philadelphia, and none in Boston, despite that city's reputation as a center of theological study. In addition, few college libraries owned editions—an alarming situation that Americans should attempt to rectify with all deliberate speed.

The conditions of subscription were not complicated. According to the prospectus, the work was to be printed in two octavo volumes on superfine paper "with a new pica Hebrew type, cast for the purpose at the foundry of Binny and Ronaldson." The cost was $15.00 per set, "neatly bound in calf lettered," with payment on delivery and a reduction of $1.00 to subscribers. Anyone who subscribed for nine copies received one copy free (this was a modification of Mills Day's proposal that anyone who obtained twelve subscriptions would receive a thirteenth copy gratis). Any college or other institution that purchased sixty copies would receive thirty copies free "to be given away to necessitous students" as the controlling corporation or the governing board directed. Smaller institutions could buy forty and receive a complimentary twenty copies.

It is doubtful whether Dobson was aware of Mills Day's earlier efforts to publish a Hebrew Bible. In a flyleaf advertisement inserted into Volume I in February 1814, he described Jonathan Horwitz's prospectus as "the first proposals of the kind ever offered in the United States." He was keenly aware, however, of a competing edition under preparation by the firm of Whiting and Watson in New York, and this may explain why he did not follow his customary pattern of advertising in newspapers for subscribers to augment the list that Horwitz had gathered. He may have wished to keep his edition secret, and in any case he could not afford to waste the time. Even so, he appears to have won only a Pyrrhic victory, for the Whiting and Watson edition, published in 1815 (Shaw and Shoemaker 34058), was "stereotyped by D. & G. Bruce." This meant that errors could be easily corrected and that the Whiting and Watson Hebrew Bible could be released in a relatively small edition and reprinted whenever the market seemed to warrant. By contrast, errors in Dobson's text would have to be painstakingly reset by hand and the type would be redistributed once the impression was deemed adequate for the market. Sales could continue only until the edition was exhausted, without the possibility of inexpensive reprints.[12]

The progress of Dobson's edition of the Hebrew Bible may be followed through a combination of letters and advertisements. On March 15, 1813, Dobson wrote to the firm of Hezekiah Howe and DeLauzin DeForest in Mills Day's home town of New Haven, Connecticut, that he had just "put to press the edition of Van der Hooghts [sic] Hebrew Bible, proposed by Mr. Horwitz." The proofs, he continued, would be read by both Horwitz and the Reverend Mr. James Patriot Wilson, pastor of the First Presbyterian Church in Philadelphia and author of *An Easy Introduction to the Knowledge of the Hebrew Language Without the Points* (1811; Shaw and Shoemaker 22465; and 1812, Shaw and Shoemaker 27574),[13] information that raises questions about Dobson's supposed proficiency in Hebrew. Dobson enclosed a copy of his proposals with this letter and expressed the hope that Howe and DeForest would be able to secure additional subscribers. Presumably, they would have been able to enlist at least Joab Bruce of Wethersfield and John Hyde of Hamden, both of whom had signed Mills Day's earlier proposals (Wegelin 223).

A little less than a year later, Dobson announced the completion of the first volume of the Hebrew Bible (*Poulson's American Daily Advertiser,* March 5, 1814). The advertisement he inserted in the endpapers of this volume is dated February, just slightly earlier than the newspaper announcement. "Too new to be properly bound," the book would be delivered to subscribers "in boards at seven dollars" per copy. "This is the first edition of the Hebrew Scripture which has ever been attempted in the United States," Dobson said, sounding once more like the publisher and promoter of the *Encyclopaedia,* "and the encouragement to the undertaking does great honor to the learned gentlemen who have patronized it." A great part of the second volume had already been printed off, and Dobson predicted that the complete edition would be available soon.

Dobson announced that completed edition on May 21, 1814 (*Poulson's American Daily Advertiser*), priced to the general public at $15.00 for both volumes in boards. "Elegantly printed by William Fry," this "First American Edition of the Hebrew Bible," Dobson said, had already won acclaim as one of the "finest specimens of *Hebrew Printing* ever executed," although just who had bestowed that high praise he did not deem it necessary to say. Another "arduous undertaking . . . happily accomplished," he concluded his announcement, this edition of the Hebrew Bible was well deserving of the patronage of "the Reverend Clergy of different denominations" and "other lovers of the Sacred Scripture in the Hebrew Language."

Just a few weeks later, on June 8, he sent one copy of his latest publication to Webster and Skinner in Albany, a firm with which he maintained an active business correspondence in the nineteenth century. "I have just completed my edition of the Hebrew Bible," he wrote, "and think it likely you may be able to dispose of a number of copies when it comes to be seen; more especially as the edition proposed by [Samuel] Whiting & [Ebenezer] Watson New York is stopped for present." Then, probably again referring to Jonathan Horwitz's list of subscribers, Dobson promised to send copies for William Neil, John Bradford, and John Keys of Albany at the subscription price of $14.00. "I have put in the parcel some proposals for publishing the Septuagint," he added, "which I have just issued with considerable prospect of Success, and expect you will be able to obtain a good many Subscriptions for the work."[14] Dobson's optimism was unfounded, however, for his edition of the Septuagint failed for lack of subscribers.[15]

Although bookselling and publishing were Dobson's avocation and his major source of income, he sought other sources of revenue as the nineteenth century advanced, perhaps compelled by the uncertain American economy during the War of 1812, when copper was in short supply and prices for many items rose dramatically. Indeed, it is possible that in 1814 he attempted at least once to get out of the bookselling business but either experienced a quick change of heart or else could not find a buyer at a satisfactory price. On February 15, 1814, *Poulson's American Daily Adver-*

tiser carried an advertisement for a "Book-Store Establishment" directly under Dobson's notice of an edition of John Murray's *Letters and Sketches of Sermons* "just received and now available." The value of the bookstore is considerable, and the stock seems extensive. According to the advertisement, "The Stock in store can be made to fit purchasers at from 5 to 10,000 dollars, and Books in sheets can be given if wished, to an amount of 3 to 4,000 dollars." The owner promises to train any novice wishing to come into the business as a condition of sale and notes that the shop comes with an established clientele. Clearly, this is a large concern for sale, probably beyond the price range of most people not already engaged in the business in some way or other. The advertisement, which never reappeared in Poulson's paper, may not describe Dobson's establishment, but it does describe one of similar size—perhaps the establishment of Samuel F. Bradford, now on the verge of bankruptcy because of expenses incurred by his edition of Rees's *New Cyclopaedia*.

That Dobson was pursuing other economic interests during this period is established by a notice that appeared in *Poulson's American Daily Advertiser* on November 12, 1813. The advertisement announced that an installment of $5.00 was due by November 15 from stockholders of the Mutual Assistance Coal Company, "Thomas Dobson, President." Stockholders who had not yet paid their initial installment of $15 were reminded that this amount was also due and payable. Possibly a response to the wartime economy, the Mutual Assistance Coal Company was probably an organization through which merchants and businessmen pooled their resources and bought in volume at the lowest available prices. Whether they also speculated in coal prices for a profit is not apparent from the advertisement.

Another advertisement in the same newspaper a few months later (January 22, 1814 and other dates) shows that Dobson had begun to diversify the stock in his bookstore. Along with his books he also offered "Platina Points for Lightning Rods," guaranteed not to "melt down by lightning, nor run. Roofs . . . once provided with them, require afterwards no further attention and may be relied on for efficacy." Unlike earlier notices that included boots, shoes, and "fine old porter" as an afterthought in advertisements meant to sell books and stationery, these advertisements use the bookstore only as an address and are intended to sell lightning rods only. Platina, the old name for platinum, was a relatively recent discovery, and Dobson seems to have been speculating on the novelty.

It was not platinum but copper, one of the staple commodities of the publishing business, that took Dobson farthest afield from printing, publishing, and bookselling in the nineteenth century. Once again, as in the case of the *Encyclopaedia,* Dobson's interest in promoting American manufactures combined with the opportunity to realize substantial personal profit. A little more than a month after completing the Hebrew Bible, he wrote to the firm of Paul Revere and Son (Joseph Warren Revere) confiding his plans for "getting a rolling Mill erected for the purpose of making . . . Copper into sheets, & c. for sheathing and other purposes."[16] Because such a venture would have required considerable capital—Revere himself spoke of conscripting "every farthing I can rake and scrape" in order to establish his mill on the Neponset River in 1801[17]—Dobson's printing business must still have been supplying him with ready cash. With the war against Great Britain in full swing and imported supplies cut off just as demand for copper sheathing for ships was exploding, copper prices had escalated from a low of twenty cents to a high of eighty cents per pound,[18] and Dobson, like many another American, was trying to cash in on the boom market as a copper speculator.

Dobson's will appears to have been lost,[19] so it is impossible to know where his rolling mill was to be located. Tax records of Germantown and Chestnut Hill, however, which include frontage on the Wissahickon Creek and its many mills (the famous Rittenhouse paper mill was located on this creek, for example), may provide a clue. These records indicate that Dobson paid taxes on property in one of these two neighborhoods under the designation of "Est." (T. Shoemaker 43), which, in the ambiguous language of the records, means that he did not own the property but rented it—rented it out or rented it from someone else? This property in the vicinity of a stream known for its ability to power mills of all types is a likely location for Dobson to have attempted to establish a rolling mill for copper.

Wherever Dobson's mill might have been and however advanced his plans, his reasons for writing to Revere are practical and obvious enough. For years, Revere and others had been trying to no avail to persuade Congress to impose a tariff on copper imported from Great Britain. The American copper industry, truly in its infancy during this period, was hampered by a combination of circumstances: a scarcity of known deposits of the rich oxide copper ore, a lack of technological expertise and experience for refining the plentiful but poor-grade sulfide ores, and the distance of seacoast smelting plants from copper and coal deposits in the inland. Welsh coal, smelters along the seacoast, and skilled workmen who received less per hour than their American counterparts gave Britain a decided edge in copper production that meant she could dump her goods in American markets at a fraction of the cost to American producers. Even with the tariff Revere had been requesting, the cost of British copper would still have been much lower than that of American copper. Congress felt far greater pressure from American shipbuilders to keep the cost of imported copper for sheathing low than from the handful of American copper manufacturers who requested a tariff. During the War of 1812, when supplies from England were cut off, the American copper industry was reduced to rolling used copper sheathing salvaged from old ships. Revere's mill had been closed in 1810, but the new need for copper induced him to reopen it, and he soon became the chief supplier to the American navy. Now the industry boomed, in large part because of the inflated prices, and Dobson must have seen a chance to cash in on the demand.[20]

Thus Dobson's letter to Paul Revere and Son. He had, it seems, laid the groundwork with copper producers in the Baltimore and Philadelphia areas: Levi Hollingsworth, the former Philadelphia merchant now the owner of a rolling mill on Gunpowder Creek near Baltimore; Harmon Hendricks and his foreman and partner Solomon Isaacs of the Soho Works in New Jersey; and Raborg and Son in Baltimore, whose involvement in the copper industry has not been determined. Anticipating that Congress would draw up new tariff legislation at its upcoming session, Dobson proposed to Revere that all "the different gentlemen who are engaged in the business, should inform the Secretary of the Treasury the actual or probable extent of their manufactures." This, Dobson reasoned, would provide the secretary with the detail he would need "to report to Congress the duty which would be proper, Suppose 10 Cents per lb. or thereabout which might answer the purpose." Then he reminded Revere of something that the aging patriot probably had no need to hear again, having tried unsuccessfully to make a similar argument for years. "The interest of the United States," he said, "is connected with the encouragement of domestic Manufactures." The argument had served him well in selling the *Encyclopaedia* at a time when printing was a struggling industry. That it remained true for the copper industry in 1814 suggests how far copper manufacturing had lagged behind printing in receiving government and public encouragement in the United States.

Although Dobson seems to have had the support of Hendricks, Hollingsworth, and Raborg, the firm of Revere and Son, which by this time had been in the business of fabricating copper far longer than anyone else in the United States, may have regarded him as an interloper pure and simple. At any rate, he was a possible competitor, and Revere did not reply to Dobson's inquiry. Undaunted, Dobson wrote again on November 14, 1814, this time with the information that a change in the secretary of the treasury—George Campbell was out and Alexander Dallas was in[21]— made it highly unlikely there would be any action on tariff bills this year. Adam Seybert, the representative from the Philadelphia district and an author whom Dobson had published, had advised him that a memorial on the subject might be the best way to proceed, and Dobson had drafted such a document. "If it meets your approbation," he wrote to Revere,

you may give it your signature at Boston; or if you think it would be better to draw up another form, you can draw it up more to your mind, and after Signing, transmit to Mr. Hendricks N York, for his Signature, and desire him to . . . send it on to me, I will sign it & send it on to Baltimore for the Signatures of Mr Hollingsworth & of Messrs Raborg & Sons, and get them to send it on to Congress.

Dobson closed his letter by advising Revere to write to his own congress-men in Washington and by informing him that, if necessary, he would be willing to make the trip to Washington with him, although he was in ill health and could not travel at present.[22]

A month and a half went by without an answer from Revere. Dobson wrote a third and final time, requesting Revere on December 31, 1814, to "have the goodness to advise me of your decision in this matter in which we are all interested." Congress now seemed to be in the mood to impose duties on "all articles hitherto imported free of duty," and Dobson felt that a jointly endorsed memorial might help the tariff-makers to discriminate appropriately, "so that if the Pigs should pay, the foreign Refined Copper should be taxed heavier in proportion." He reminded Revere that he could revise and rewrite anything in the memorial with which he did not agree and urged him to take action soon. "The present embarrassed state of the public Treasury, now openly acknowledged," he concluded, "seems to mark out this as the proper time to get such duties laid, as will meet the first great importation."[23] "Peace must come," he concluded, and when it did the unrestrained importation of English copper would "bid fair to crush our infant manufactures."[24]

Although Revere failed to reply or take any action at the time, Dobson was right, without question. When the War of 1812 was over, British manufacturers dumped surplus copper on the American market, and prices plummeted to twenty-seven cents per pound (Whiteman 117). Established manufacturers like Hendricks and Revere withstood this drop in market value, but speculators were wiped out. The year after Dobson wrote these letters, Hendricks, Hollingsworth, and Revere presented their petition for tariff protection to Congress, only to be turned down once again. That Dobson did not accompany them may mean that, lacking encouragement from Revere and the prospect of government protection, he had lost interest in his rolling mill for copper. Whether the petition they presented was derived from his memorial is an unanswerable question. Not until the tariff of 1816 did Hendricks, Hollingsworth, and Revere achieve the shelter they wanted. How this new tariff may have affected Dobson's economic prospects as a copper manufacturer (if, indeed, he ever really became one) is not known.

Dobson's efforts to influence the course of events in the fledgling American copper industry did not keep him from new publishing projects. In 1815, he brought out one of his most successful technical and scientific books, Thomas Cooper's *Practical Treatise on Dyeing, and Callicoe Printing* (Shaw and Shoemaker 34442), regarded as the best treatise on the subject by most American readers. Cooper may have turned to Dobson because of Dobson's friendship with Joseph Priestley and because of his Universalist views, which Cooper shared. The next year, Dobson began making plans to publish a semi-annual magazine, the *American Register, or Summary Review of History, Politics, and Literature,* to be edited by Robert Walsh, Jr.[25] In a letter to Webster and Skinner on February 15, 1816, he enclosed a prospectus for the new magazine and promised to send additional copies "when our Navigation & yours opens." Dobson thought it likely that Webster and Skinner would be able to obtain "numerous Subscriptions" for this publication, which his prospectus described as "a Sketch of the political history foreign and domestic, of the six months immediately preceding the appearance of each volume," accompanied by "an Exposition of domestic and foreign Literature for the same interval," a "free Synopsis of the debates in Congress" and of the most important legislation passed in the individual states, and "a Record of occurrences which tend to mark the progress of the arts and sciences, or to illustrate the peculiar genius and manners of the American people." Each volume, the prospectus specified, would contain four hundred or more pages and cost three dollars on delivery. Anyone paying for nine copies would get the tenth copy free. "The first volume of the work will probably be published in July or early August 1816," the publisher and editor stated, "and the second volume in the autumn." After that, the public was assured, "the times of publication will be more regular."

Unfortunately for Dobson, matters did not work out that way. "Circumstances, above the control either of the Editor or Publisher of this Work, have deferred the appearance of the first volume for some months beyond the period originally intended," wrote Robert Walsh in the "General Introduction by the Editor" (ix) when the *American Register* at last appeared in 1817 (Shaw and Shoemaker 39985; the copyright date was February 4). "The materials of the second [volume] are for the most part collected," Walsh assured any anxious readers, "and it may be put to the press without delay, should the public be disposed to extend to the undertaking the degree of patronage required by the interests of the Bookseller" (ix). Apparently the public was, though just barely, and Volume II (copyrighted August 6, 1817) was issued later in the year. This was Walsh's third attempt at editing a magazine. His other efforts, the final two volumes of Charles Brockden Brown's *American Register; or, General Repository of History, Politics, and Science* and his own *American Review of History and Politics,* the first quarterly in the United States, lasted a total of about three years (1810–13). Destined for greater success with both the *National Gazette* (1819–36) and a resurrected version of the *American Review* in 1827, Walsh could not make the *American Register* pay, and the magazine ceased publication after two volumes (Appleton's 6: 340–41; Hoornstra and Heath 26). Like Mathew Carey's equally ill-fated *American Quarterly Review* ten years later, also edited by Walsh, it may have demanded too much of readers whose tastes in periodical literature had come to favor fiction and sentimental verses.

Walsh was disappointed by what he considered Dobson's premature decision to terminate the *American Register*. On January 27, 1818, he wrote to Thomas Jefferson from Washington, D.C., where he had gone to gather material for the third volume, expressing his fears that the *American Register* was about to be discontinued. "I fear . . . that the undertaking is about to be abandoned by the Bookseller, Mr. Dobson of Philadelphia, in consequence of a more limited subscription, than is compatible with his views of profit. . . . He hesitates about putting a third volume to press, & is to communicate to me 'ere long, his determination." Then he added, in evident chagrin, that Dobson was "in no ways qualified for the business of superintending the distribution of such a work," although he immediately added that results would probably have been the same with any bookseller.[26] More moderate in his response, Jefferson agreed that perhaps Dobson "has not allowed time for the work to become known to the public" but reminded Walsh that "the number of abortive periodical publications which we have seen, have made the public slow in subscribing to them generally."[27] Within a month, Walsh learned that his worst fears had come true; the *American Register* was abandoned, and the third volume never appeared (Lochemes 88). Its quick demise may have been the result of many factors, including a worsening economic situation in Philadelphia and the nation, but one of them must have been Dobson's financial condition. Where once he had underwritten the massive *Encyclopaedia* almost on his own for many years, now he was unwilling or unable to support for several months a magazine whose importance to American letters and national prestige he could hardly have disputed.

Short-lived though it was, the *American Register* provides an important piece of information about Dobson's plans as publisher and printer that cannot be discovered anywhere else. This was his proposal, printed in the spare leaves of the first gathering of the first volume of the *American Register*, for publishing by subscription "A Supplement to the Encyclopaedia." Although Dobson spoke in generic terms of the *Encyclopaedia Britannica* "from which the American edition was printed, with large additions," this statement was misleading, for what he proposed to reprint on this occasion was not a continuation of the third edition but the five-volume Supplement to the fifth edition—Archibald Constable's famous *Supplement*, edited by Macvey Napier with general introductions to the first two volumes by Dugald Stewart and John Playfair, respectively. Dobson's reasons for disguising this fact seem obvious enough: if subscribers believed that these new volumes represented a continuation of the third edition, it might reinvigorate sales of both the *Encyclopaedia* and the *Supplement*.

Dobson assured subscribers that the proposed five-volume *Supplement* would be printed on "excellent paper, with numerous engravings, to be executed by the best artists." It was to be published in half volumes, each priced at "four dollars and fifty cents," and would go to press "as soon as the progress of the engravings will authorise the printing of the letter press." That, however, seems never to have happened, most likely because Dobson could not gather the required number of subscribers. If he had actually invested in engravings, their expense was a dead loss. When he printed his proposals, he evidently did not know that Archibald Constable had already contracted with the Philadelphia bookseller Thomas Wardle to handle American sales. His belated discovery of this fact may explain why only this one set of proposals ever appeared in print (at any rate, no others have been located). It was probably just as well that his proposals were withdrawn, for Constable's *Supplement* would eventually extend through seven volumes and not be completed until 1824, the year after Dobson's death (Kogan 30–43).

Few titles can be attributed to Thomas Dobson after 1818. In 1819, he published the second edition of William Potts Dewees' *Essay on the Means of Lessening Pain, and Facilitating Certain Cases of Difficult Parturition* (Shaw and Shoemaker 47824), maintaining faith with the local medical community and the College of Physicians almost to the last. In *The Critic,* he attempted a publication with a distinctly literary flavor. A twice-weekly magazine that appeared most Wednesdays and Saturdays between January 29 and May 10, 1820, the journal featured topical and political satire aimed at local politicians, together with the literary opinions of "Geoffey Juvenal, Esq," who gleefully lambasted William Wirt's biography of Patrick Henry, satirized James Kirke Paulding's *The Backwoodsman* and other writings by so-called Knickerbockers, mocked the poetry of Lord Byron and Samuel Taylor Coleridge's "Rhime of the Ancient Mariner," and disparaged American literary taste in general. Advertisements for *The Critic* appeared in *Poulson's American Daily Advertiser* on March 3 (no. 13) and April 26 (no. 19),[28] in which Dobson was identified as the publisher. His name appears also in an advertisement at the end of no. 14 (118). The subject matter, the literary, political, and critical attitudes expressed, and the general tone of the essays suggests that Robert Walsh, Jr. had been at least temporarily reconciled with Dobson and had returned as "Geoffrey Juvenal, Esq.," possibly with help from other hands.[29]

Except for the *Catalogue* of 1822, the final publications to emerge from Dobson's press date from 1821. Several are reprints of medical works, including James Johnson's *Diseases of Tropical and Tropicoid Climates* (R. Shoemaker 5724) and *Practical researches on the Nature, Cure, and Prevention of the Gout* (R. Shoemaker 5725). These were projected in an advertisement in the *Journal of Foreign Medical Science and Literature* (11: 36) as a part of a series entitled "Modern Medical Classics," but no other titles in that advertisement have been assigned to Dobson by American bibliographers. The advertisement suggests, however, that several ought to be, including one last attempt at an encyclopedia, *Willich's Domestic Encyclopaedia* improved by Thomas Cooper.[30]

In the fall or early winter of 1822, Thomas Dobson retired from the bookselling business. Dobson & Son became "the late firm" of booksellers and stationers, as it is designated on the title page of the catalog of books offered "to the trade on the most liberal terms."[31] It is possible that Dobson was already ill at this time, for the official cause of his death is given in the cemetery records of Philadelphia as "Lethargy"—a catchall phrase describing symptoms that could be associated with a dozen different wasting illnesses. He died on Sunday morning, March 9, 1823, at the age of seventy-two, remembered in the single obituary to take note of his passing as "an eminent printer and book-seller, of the city of Philadelphia; a man of the purest morals and most devout piety . . . who enjoyed the respect and reverence of all who knew him" (Little 89). The notice of his death in the *United States Gazette* said only that he had been "for many years an eminent Printer and Bookseller in this city." Friends were invited to attend his funeral at three o'clock on Tuesday afternoon, March 12, at his late place of residence, "No. 41, south Second street." He was interred, writes Joseph Jackson, "in the burial ground of First Baptist Church, then on Second Street, west side, south of Arch" (86).[32] In 1855, this graveyard was removed to Mt. Moriah Cemetery, 62nd Street and Kingsessing Avenue, where, as far as anyone knows, Dobson reposes today.

Dobson's story thus comes to a close. As the checklist in Appendix C establishes, he had a hand in many important publications of the period, either as printer or publisher or both, and can claim a number of "first American" editions of significant British books. Despite some difficulties selling the *Encyclopaedia* and what may have been an ill-fated excursion into copper speculation, his longevity in the business in an age when many printers failed and few truly prospered, fewer still without publishing a newspaper or holding a sinecure as government printer, testifies to his ability as a printer and publisher and to his good sense as a man of business. After his early partnership with Thomas Lang, he kept business affairs entirely within the family, and the lack of outside energy and investment, rather than any errors of judgment on his part, may be the reason that his firm did not continue past his death.

His lasting and most impressive monument is the *Encyclopaedia*, which, along with the Hebrew Bible, and, perhaps, the first American edition of Adam Smith's *Wealth of Nations*, must be counted as his chief contributions to the history of American printing. His career appears to have been inspired as much by the political independence of America and the nationalistic wish to establish a separate, viable tradition of bookmaking in the United States as by any mere motives of profit. In that domain, perhaps no other printer of his era except Isaiah Thomas left a larger or more lasting legacy.

Dobson's practicality and his patriotic idealism speak from the pages of the *Encyclopaedia*. The gratitude "To the Patrons of the Arts and Sciences" and "the promoters of useful and ornamental Literature in the United States of America" that he inscribed in the dedication of the *Encyclopaedia* has a ring of sincerity that even our own ears, taught by sad experience to distrust public displays of patriotism as masquerades for other, more dubious or downright ignoble enterprises, can still detect and respond to. In Dobson's words may be heard the accents of an age that regarded the judgment of posterity as highly as contemporary opinion and that acted in its finest moments not in the interests of the self alone but in the interests of the society it was shaping. Though not one of the legendary giants who walked the earth in those much mythologized days, Thomas Dobson was an important and successful early American printer whose patriotic pragmatism and shrewd sense of the possible led him to achievements more than worthy of whatever modest immortality a study such as this one may bestow.

Notes

1. For the popularity of Byron, Campbell, Moore, and Scott among American audiences, see James D. Hart, *The Popular Book in America: A History of America's Literary Taste* (Berkeley and Los Angeles: University of California Press, 1963), 67–77.

2. Mathew Carey's figurative progeny are discussed in Lea & Febiger, *One Hundred and Fifty Years of Publishing, 1785–1935* (Philadelphia: Lea & Febiger, 1935).

3. Thomas Dobson to James Kemp, February 28, 1801, Gratz Collection, Alphabetical Series, HSP.

4. All three letters to Mrs. Charleton are part of the Society Collection, HSP, and are quoted here by permission. The letters are dated July 25, August 17, and August 22, 1805.

5. Thomas Jefferson to Thomas Dobson, November 18, 1807, Jefferson Papers, No. 23581.1, Library of Congress; Dobson to Jefferson, January 20, 1809, ibid. I am grateful to Professor John Catanzariti, editor of the *Papers of Thomas Jefferson,* for providing me with a polygraph copy and unverified transcript of the letter from Jefferson to Dobson. Despite Herman Kogan's claim that Jefferson once "wrote to Dobson to tell him of his delight with the articles on architecture" in the *Encyclopaedia* (25), this is the only known correspondence between the two men.

6. The broadside proposal for Williamson's *History* is in the John Haygood Papers, No. 1901, Southern Historical Collection of the University of North Carolina, to which I am grateful for permission to quote these passages. It is also reproduced in Powell, 429.

7. Hugh Williamson to Thomas Dobson, March 28, 1812, Dreer Collection 212, Federal Convention, HSP, quoted by permission.

8. Dobson's name is listed in advertisements in *Poulson's American Daily Advertiser* (for example, on April 16, 1814) as one of several booksellers stocking

Aitken's edition of Thomson's translation, so he would have known about the sales record of the volume, at least in his own shop.

9. Thomas Dobson to Charles Thomson, August 10, [1814]; Thomson Correspondence, Case 14, Box 31, HSP.

10. The text of Mills Day's proposal, along with the text of Jonathan Horwitz's later proposal and Oscar Wegelin's autographed copy of his essay on Mills Day's proposals, are now in the Klau Library, Hebrew Union College, Cincinnati, Ohio, Book D. I have quoted Horwitz's Conditions of Subscription from this text and wish to thank the Klau Library for the use of its resources.

11. Simonhoff's account here conflicts with Dobson's claim in the proposals that Binny & Ronaldson cast the type for his edition of the Hebrew Bible.

12. Dobson seems to have been fully aware of the limitations of his edition from the standpoint of its commercial competitiveness. In an advertisement bound into the first volume, he made a special plea to "Gentlemen of learning, into whose hands this volume may come" to transmit to him lists of any mistakes they might find. "Several typographical errors," he added, had already been discovered.

13. Thomas Dobson to Howe and DeForest, March 15, 1813, Mellon Chamberlain Collection (Ch.A.12.80), Boston Public Library. For James Patriot Wilson, see Allibone 3: 2776.

14. Thomas Dobson to Webster & Skinner, June 8, 1814; Gratz Collection, Alphabetical Series, HSP.

15. Neither Shaw and Shoemaker nor O'Callaghan records an edition of the Septuagint from Dobson's press.

16. Thomas Dobson to Paul Revere and Son, July 27, 1814, Revere Papers, MHS, quoted by permission.

17. Revere is quoted in Isaac F. Marcosson's *Copper Heritage: The Story of Revere Copper and Brass, Incorporated* (New York: Dodd, Mead, 1955), 39.

18. The effect of the War of 1812 on the price of copper in America and the widespread speculation in copper during those years are treated in Maxwell Whiteman, *Copper for America: The Hendricks Family and a National Industry, 1755–1939* (New Brunswick, N.J.: Rutgers University Press, 1971), 102–34. Whiteman also treats the rivalry between Hendricks and Revere, which could have been a contributing factor in Revere's silence. Dobson's name has not previously been connected with the American copper industry in any way.

19. Steven Saninni of the Registry of Wills in Philadelphia reported to me in a telephone conversation that records indicate the will had been lent to some unspecified historical group twenty years ago and was not returned.

20. In addition to Whiteman's and Marcosson's books, I have found Otis E. Young, Jr., "Origins of the American Copper Industry," *Journal of the Early Republic* 3 (1983): 117–37, very useful. See also J. Leander Bishop's *History of American Manufacturing from 1608 to 1860 . . .,* 3 vols. (Philadelphia: 1864–66) 2: 126, 155, and 190. Bishop is also an important source of information about American paper manufacturing.

21. For George Campbell and Alexander Dallas, see Mary Beth Norton, *A*

People and a Nation: A History of the United States (Boston: Houghton Mifflin, 1982), A-22.

22. Thomas Dobson to Paul Revere and Son, November 14, 1814, Revere Papers, MHS, quoted by permission.

23. Dobson is probably referring to recent revelations from the Treasury Department about how expensive the War of 1812 had been and continued to be. *Poulson's American Daily Advertiser* carried a story entitled "A Peep into the Treasury!" on February 2, 1814.

24. Thomas Dobson to Paul Revere and Son, December 3, 1814, Revere Papers, MHS, quoted by permission.

25. Dobson's prospectus for the *American Register* accompanied his letter of February 15, 1816 to Webster & Skinner, Gratz Collection, Alphabetical Series, HSP. I have quoted Dobson's prepublication publicity from this prospectus. It is more conveniently available in Woodall, 327.

26. Robert Walsh, Jr., to Thomas Jefferson, January 27, 1818, Miscellaneous Manuscripts, MHS; quoted in Lochemes, 87.

27. Thomas Jefferson to Robert Walsh, Jr., February 18, 1818, Jefferson Papers; quoted in Lochemes, 88.

28. The thirteenth number is not microfilmed with the rest of *The Critic* by the American Periodical Series, University Microfilms, Ann Arbor, Michigan, II, reel 100. By the time no. 13 appeared, *The Critic* had begun to appear irregularly, so this advertisement in *Poulson's American Daily Advertiser* is the only indication that a no. 13 was actually published.

29. For literary opinions characteristic of Walsh and not many other essayists in the early republic, see Lochemes, 151–63. Guy R. Woodall, "Robert Walsh," *Dictionary of Literary Biography,* 99 vols., volume 59, *American Literary Critics and Scholars,* ed. John W. Rathbone and Monica Greene (Detroit: Gale, 1987), 324–31, offers an overview of some of Walsh's literary and political opinions, as well as a selected bibliography of articles, most of them by Woodall, which cover Walsh's ideas in greater detail.

30. Some of the titles contained in this "List of Late American Republications" in the *Journal of Foreign Medical Science and Literature* 11 (1821): 136, such as "Baillies' Morbid Anatomy," have been attributed by Shaw and Shoemaker (185) to other publishers (Hickman & Hazard, 1820). Yet since the "List" differentiates between "Proposed American Republications" and those already finished and since it unequivocally attributes those titles to Thomas Dobson & Son as part of their "Modern Medical Classics" series, I am inclined to believe he did print them. Rather than err entirely on the side of conservatism, I shall by way of compromise reproduce the pertinent part of the advertisement:

> Thomas Dobson and Son, have commenced the publication of the Modern Medical Classics; selected and revised by Drs. Physick and Chapman.—The first work of the series is Johnson's celebrated work on the Diseases of Tropical and Tropicoid Climates—which is just finished in two volumes, 12mo. price in boards $2 or neatly bound $2.50, each of the works composing the series, will be for sale separate.

[Usher] Parson's Sailor's Physician, bds. 8vo. $1.75
Frost on the Yellow Fever of Havanna, stitched, 8vo. 50.
New York Hospital Reports, pt. 2. bd. 8vo. 1 50.
Facts and Observations on Liver Complaints and Bilious
    Disorders in General—by John Faithhorn, M.D.
    8vo. 1 dollar 50 cents.
Baillies' Morbid Anatomy, 8vo $2.50.
London Dissector—First American from the fifth London Edition.
Willich's Domestic Encyclopaedia, improved. By Thomas Cooper, M.
    D. 3 vols. 8vo. $10 50 in boards. $12 00 bound.

31. The full title of Dobson's final catalog of 1822 is *A Catalogue of Books, in the Various Departments of Ancient and Modern Literature, Being Some of the Most Numerous of the Stock of the Late Firm of Thomas Dobson & Son, Now Offered to the Trade on the Most Liberal Terms by T. Dobson & J. Dobson, Agents.* The catalogue Judah Dobson issued the next year contains a far larger list of books. Judah Dobson retained the title from the previous year but dropped his father's name from the title page.

32. Cemetery records confirm Jackson's identification of the cemetery in which Dobson was buried. The graves were removed to Mt. Moriah Cemetery, 62nd & Kingsessing Streets, Philadelphia, but I have been unable to locate Dobson's gravesite.

Appendix A. Dobson's Encyclopaedia: A Chronology

WEEKLY NUMBERS (FEDERAL GAZETTE)

[No. I—Jan. 2, 1790]
[No. II—Jan. 9]
No. III—Jan. 16, 20
No. IV—Jan. 23
No. V—Jan. 30
No. VI—Feb. 6, 10
No. VII—Feb. 13, 17
No. VIII—Feb. 20, 24
No. IX—Feb. 27, Mar. 3
No. X—Mar. 6, 10 [this is the only advertisement for No. X as such rather than as Part 1, Volume I]
No. XI—Mar. 13, 17
No. XII—Mar. 20
No. XIII—Mar. 27; Apr. 3, 5
No. XIV—Apr. 6, 7, 8, 11
No. XV—Apr. 19
No. XVI—Apr. 12, 14
No. XVII—Apr. 17
No. XVIII—Apr. 24
No. XIX—Apr. 28
No. XX—May 11

Other dates of weekly numbers are, in the *Pennsylvania Mercury*, Jan. 16, 23, 30; Feb. 6, 9, 13, 20, 27; Mar. 4. No advertisements for I or II, which must have been published on January 2 and 9, respectively, appear in any newspaper I have examined. The advertisements in the *Pennsylvania Packet* appear on the following dates: Jan. 20, 28, 30; Feb. 6, 13, 20; Mar. 3. In both papers, the advertisements for No. X are headed "Volume I,

Part 1," and, unlike the *Federal Gazette,* do not identify the publication as weekly No. X.

There are no further advertisements for weekly numbers, yet Dobson's intentions seem clear enough, since the final advertisement for No. XX, like all other advertisements for weekly numbers that had preceded it, contains the phrase *"To be Continued Weekly."* Up to and after May 11, 1790, Dobson issued no public notice that he planned to discontinue or had discontinued weekly numbers but stopped seeking new subscribers to that particular plan.

VOLUMES AND HALF VOLUMES (VARIOUS NEWSPAPERS)

Volume I, Part 1 (A–Alb)—Mar. 3, 1790 (*Pennsylvania Packet*)
Volume I, Part 2 (Alg–Ang)—June 18, 1790 (*Pennsylvania Mercury*)
Volume II, Part 1 (Ang–Asp)—Oct. 9, 1790 (*Pennsylvania Mercury*)
Volume II, Part 2 (Bar–Bor)—Feb. 19, 1791 (*Pennsylvania Mercury*)
Volume III (Bor–Bzo)—May 3, 1791 (*Pennsylvania Packet*)
Volume IV (Caa–Cic)—Sept. 17, 1791 (*Pennsylvania Mercury*)
Volume V (Cic–Dia)—Mar. 10, 1792 (*American Daily Advertiser*)
Volume VI (Dia–Eth)—July 21, 1792 (*Gazette of the United States*)
Volume VII (Etm–Goa)—Jan. 17, 1793 (*Federal Gazette*)
Volume VIII (Gob–Hyd)—Apr. 5, 1793 (*Federal Gazette*)
Volume IX (Hyd–Les)—June 15, 1793 (*Pennsylvania Gazette*)
Volume X (Les–Mec)—Dec. 11, 1793 (*Gazette of the United States*)
Volume XI (Med–Mid)—Apr. 26, 1794 (*Gazette of the United States*)
Volume XII (Mie–Neh)—Nov. 5, 1794 (*Federal Gazette*)
Volume XIII (Nig–Pas)—Apr. 10, 1795 (*Gazette of the United States*)
Volume XIV (Pas–Pla)—Aug. 8, 1795 (*Gazette of the United States*)
Volume XV (Pla–Ron)—Apr. 30, 1796 (*American Daily Advertiser*)
Volume XVI (Ron–Sco)—Nov. 24, 1796 (*Philadelphia Gazette*)
Volume XVII (Sco–Str)—June 1, 1797 (*Porcupine's Gazette*)
Volume XVIII, Part 1 (Str–xxx)—Jan. 9, 1798 (*Porcupine's Gazette*)
Volume XVIII, Part 2 (xxx–Zym)—May 19, 1798 (*Porcupine's Gazette*)[1]

THE SUPPLEMENT

Volume XIX, Part 1—May, 1800 [Shipton]
Volume XIX, Part 2—Aug. 14, 1800 (*Philadelphia Gazette*)
Volume XX, Part 1—May 16, 1801 (*Philadelphia Gazette*)

Volume XX, Part 2—Nov. 25, 1802 (*Philadelphia Gazette*)
Volume XXI, Part 1—Mar. 26, 1803 (*Poulson's American Daily Advertiser*)
Volume XXI, Part 2—June 2, 1803 (*Gazette of the United States*)

Signature Collation of Volumes XIX–XXI[2]

XIX: A–H^4, I^2–L^2, M–Z^4, Aa–Zz^4, $_3$A–$_3$Z^4, $_4$A–$_4$X^2; 352 leaves, pp. [2]–704.

XX: A–Z^4, Aa–Zz^4, $_3$A–$_3$Z^4, $_4$A–$_4$Z^4, $^*_4$Z; 378 leaves, pp. [2]–734.

XXI: [A]–[F^4], pp. 1–48; A–Z^4, Aa–Zz^4, $_3$A–$_3$Z^4, $_4$A–$_4$C^2; 285 leaves, pp. [1]–566, i–iv Appendix.

Notes

1. None of the sets I examined was published in half volumes. Alphabetical coverage of the first four half volumes but not the final two is given in Dobson's advertisements. I indicate my inability to ascertain where the final half volumes were divided with "xxx."

2. For collation of Volumes I–XVIII, see G. Thomas Tanselle, "Press Figures in America: Some Preliminary Observations," *Studies in Bibliography* 19 (1966): 123–60.

Appendix B. Engravers and Engravings in the Encyclopaedia

The following list identifies by plate number and short title engravings done by each of the engravers who contributed to Dobson's *Encyclopaedia*. Unsigned plates have been attributed mainly on the basis of context: unless there is strong reason to think otherwise, signed plates in a series are taken to mean that unsigned plates in the same series were executed by the same artist. Attributions are enclosed in brackets; doubtful attributions are enclosed in brackets with a question mark. Also bracketed are the names of engravers whose initials or other form of signature supersedes the official signature on a given plate. Only Robert Scot's apprentices and journeymen signed plates in this manner: SA or A for Samuel Allardice; JD or D for John Draper; BJ for Benjamin Jones; and FS, S, or Shallus for Francis Shallus.

In some cases the style of the artist provides a basis for attribution. James Trenchard's engravings are uniformly more lightly shaded and the crosshatching is more widely spaced than in the work of any other engraver. John Draper leaves white spaces with no crosshatching around labeling initials in his figures; no other engravers do. Occasionally, too, the subject matter of a plate offers a clue. Robert Scot favored engraving geometrical shapes and designs, for example. Only six plates in the *Encyclopaedia* have not been assigned on some basis: numbers 220, 380, 500, 509, and 541–42.

VOLUME I (1790)

PLATE NUMBER AND SHORT TITLE	ENGRAVER
Frontispiece	Vallance
1—Accoustics, aerostation	Scot
2—Aerostation	Scot
3—Aerostation	Scot
4—Africa [map]	Scot
5—[Agriculture]	Scot

6—Agriculture: Harrow	Scot
7—Agriculture: Plow	[Scot]
8—Agriculture	Scot
9—Agriculture	Scot
10—Aerology	Scot
11—*Alphabeta antiqissma*	[Scot]
12—*Alphabeta antiqua*	[Scot]
13—Altars	Scot
14—North America [map]	Scot
15—South America [map]	Scot
16—Amphitheatre	[Scot]
17—*Amyris demifera*	Scot
18—*Anacardium occidentalis*	Scot
19–25—Anatomy	Scot
26—Anatomy, lymphatic vessels	[Scot]
27–30—Anatomy	Scot
31—*Anquis ventralis*	Scot

VOLUME II (1791)

PLATE NUMBER AND SHORT TITLE	ENGRAVER
32—Animal flowers	Scot [SA]
33–34—Animalcules	Scot
35—Architecture	[Scot]
36—Architecture: Huts	Thackara & Vallance
37—Tuscan order	Scot
38—Doric order	Scot
39—Ionic order	Scot
40—Volute	Scot
41—Corinthian	Scot
42—Composite	Scot
43—Pilaster capitals	Scot
44—Piers and doorways	Scot
45—Gateways and piers	Scot [SA]
46—Windows	Scot
47—Ceilings	Thackara & Vallance
48–49—Stairs and staircases	Scot
50—Twistrails	Scot
51—Trusses	Scot
52—Country house	Thackara & Vallance

53—Country seat	Scot
54—House, Earl of Weynriss	Thackara & Vallance
55—*Ardea pavonia*	Scot
56—*Ardea herodia*	Thackara & Vallance
57—Noah's Ark	Thackara & Vallance
58—*Artocarpus*	Scot
59—Asia [map]	[Thackara & Vallance]
60–66—Astronomy	Scot
67—Astronomy	Thackara & Vallance
68—Astronomy	[Scot]
69—Astronomy	Scot
70—Astronomy	Thackara & Vallance
71—Astronomy	Scot
72—Astronomy	[Scot]
73–75—Astronomy	Scot
76—Astronomy	[Scot]
77—Astronomy	Thackara & Vallance
78—Astronomy	[Scot]
79–84—Astronomy	Scot
85—Astronomy: Northern Hemi- sphere	Missing
86—Astronomy: Southern Hemi- sphere	[Scot]
87—Astronomy	Scot
88—Astronomy	Scot [SA]
89—Mechanical paradox	Thackara & Vallance
90—Portable quadrant	Thackara & Vallance
91—*Atryra mandragora*	Thackara & Vallance

VOLUME III (1791)

PLATE NUMBER AND SHORT TITLE	ENGRAVER
92—Barometer	Scot
93—Basaltes	Scot
94—Basaltes	Thackara & Vallance
95—Battering ram	Thackara & Vallance
96—Beehives	Scot
97—Beehives	Thackara & Vallance
98—Blind	[Thackara & Vallance]
99—Blow pipe	Scot [SA]

101—*Bos* (Cape ox)	Scot
102–7—Botany	Scot
108—*Balaena mystecetus;* Flying bridge	Scot
109—Burrough's mockbird	Scot
110—Burning lens	Scot [SA]
111—*Buceros* (Pied hornbill)	Scot [SA]

VOLUME IV (1791)

PLATE NUMBER AND SHORT TITLE	ENGRAVER
112—Caliber	Thackara & Vallance
113—*Camelus*	Scot
114—Canal with locks	Thackara & Vallance
115—*Caesalpinia brasilienssis*	Scot [SA]
116—*Camelia alba*	Thackara & Vallance
117—*Canis*	Scot
118—*Canis*	Thackara & Vallance
119—*Canis*	Scot [SA]
120—*Canis*	Scot
121—*Capra*	Scot [SA]
122—*Capra*	Scot
123—*Capra*	Thackara & Vallance
124—*Capra*	Scot
125—*Carica* (Pawpaw tree, male)	Scot [SA]
126—*Carica* (Papwpaw tree, female)	Scot [SA]
127—Castle	Thackara & Vallance
128—Catoptrics	[Samuel Allardice]
129—*Cervus camelopardalis*	Scot
130—*Cervus* (Roebuck)	Scot
131—*Cervus* (Moose deer)	[Scot]
132—Chemical characters and symbols	Scot
133—Chemical characters and symbols	Thackara & Vallance
134—Chemistry (apparatus)	Scot [SA]
135—Chromatic	Scot [SA]
136—Centrifugal machine	[Samuel Allardice]
137—Chimes	[Samuel Allardice]

VOLUME V (1792)

PLATE NUMBER AND SHORT TITLE	ENGRAVER
138—Citrus, Forbidden fruit	[Samuel Allardice]
139—Clock	[Scot]
140—Clock	Scot]
141—Clock	Scot
142—Coal mines	[Scot]
143—*Cocos nucifera*	Thackara & Vallance
144—Coining	[Scot]
145—Compass	[Scot]
146—Conic sections	Scot
147—Corallines	[Scot]
148—Corallines and Coralloides	[Scot]
149—*Cicadae*	Scot [A]
150—Corona	Scot
151—Shining cuckow	Scot [SA]
152—Chrystals of salts	Thackara & Vallance
153—Chrystallization	Scot
154—Cuculus indicator	[Thackara & Vallance]
155—Cyder press	[Thackara & Vallance]
156—Deck; Table of descents	[Scot]
157—Scandanavian peninsula [map]	Smither, Sr.
158–59—Dialing [clock faces]	Scot
160–61—Dialing	Thackara & Vallance

VOLUME VI (1793)

PLATE NUMBER AND SHORT TITLE	ENGRAVER
162—Dioptrics	Scot
163—Haly's diving bell	Scot
164—*Dermestes;* Dodo	Thackara & Vallance
165—Dendrometer; Drawbridge	Scot
166–70—Drawing	Scot
171–72—Drawing	Scot [SA]
173–74—Electricity	Thackara & Vallance
175—Electricity	Scot [SA]
176—Electricity	Thackara & Vallance
177–79—Electricity	Scot
180—Elephant	Scot

181—England [map]	Scot
182—*Emberiza,* or Bunting	[Scot]
183—*Equus*	Scot

VOLUME VII (1793)

PLATE NUMBER AND SHORT TITLE	ENGRAVER
184—Etna	Trenchard
185—Etna; *Erinacus,* or Hedgehog	Trenchard
186—Endiometer	[Trenchard]
187—*Euphurbia*	Trenchard
188—Europe [map]	Creed
189—Evaporation	[Trenchard]
190—*Falco*	Trenchard
191–92—*Felis*	Trenchard
193—Fire-ship	[Scot]
194—Flags	Scot
195—Fluxions; Foundry	[Scot]
196—*Fluyus;* Formica	Trenchard
197–98—Fortification	Thackara & Vallance
199—Fortification	[Thackara & Vallance]
200–01—Fossils	[Scot?]
202—France [map]	[Scot?]
203—*Frangilia*	Smither, Jr.
204—Furnace	Scot [A]
205—Gages	Thackara & Vallance
206—*Garcinia*	Allardice
207–08—Gas	[Scot]
209—Geography	[Barker]
210—Geography	Barker
211—Geography	Smither, Sr.
212—Geography; *Analemma*	Barker
213—North and South Pole to Tropics	Barker
214—Map of the world	Barker
215–17—Geometry	[Barker]
218—Geometry	Barker
219—Germany [map]	[Barker]
220—Glass; Gems	unattributed
221—Globe; *Gryllus*	Smither, Sr.

VOLUME VIII (1793)

PLATE NUMBER AND SHORT TITLE	ENGRAVER
222—Geosfroal	Thackara & Vallance
223—Grasses	Thackara & Vallance
224–25—Gunnery	Thackara & Vallance
226—Harmonic	Thackara & Vallance
227–29—Heraldry	Thackara & Vallance
230—Heraldry	Allardice
232–33—Heraldry	Thackara & Vallance
234—Hippomane	Thackara & Vallance
235—*Holcus surghum*	Thackara & Vallance
236—Huer, or Boiling fountain	Thackara & Vallance
237—Historical chart	Thackara & Vallance

VOLUME IX (1793)

PLATE NUMBER AND SHORT TITLE	ENGRAVER
238—	Missing
239—Hydrostatics	Scot
240—Hydrostatics	Scot [A]
241–42—Hydrostatics	Scot
243—Hydrostatics	Scot [A]
244—Hydrostatics	Smither, Sr.
245—Hydrostatics	Scot [SA]
246–47—Hygrometer	Trenchard
248—*Jatropha manichot*	Scot
249—*Jatropha elishia*	Scot [Allardice]
250—Ice boat	Scot [Allardice]
251—Iceberg	Thackara & Vallance
252–53—Jesuits bark (chincona)	Scot [FS]
254—East Indies [map]	Allardice
255—West Indies [map]	Allardice
256—Ireland [map]	Allardice
257—Italy [map]	Allardice
258—Knighthood	Scot [FS]
259—Labyrinth	Thackara & Vallance
260—*Lacerta* (crocodile)	Scot [SA]
261—*Lacerta*	Trenchard
262—*Lanius*	Smither, Sr.
263—*Laurus sassafras*	Scot [A]
264—*Laurus cinnamonum*	Scot [FS]

265—*Laurus camphora*	Scot [Allardice]
266–67—Legerdemain	Thackara & Vallance
268—Lemur	Allardice
269—*Lepus*	Thackara & Vallance

VOLUME X (1793)

PLATE NUMBER AND SHORT TITLE	ENGRAVER
270—Levels	Trenchard
271—Levelling	Trenchard
272—Lock	Allardice
273—Log	Allardice
274—*Loxia*	Smither, Sr.
275—Bellows for inflating lungs	Allardice
276—Magnetism	Allardice
277–78—Magnetism	Thackara & Vallance
279—*Manis;* Mantis	Thackara & Vallance
280—Distilling apparatus	Scot [FS]
281—Mast	Scot [FS]
282—Malt bruiser	Thackara & Vallance
283—Mechanics	Thackara & Vallance
284–85—Mechanics	Scot [FS]
286—Mechanics	Allardice
287–88—Mechanics	Scot [FS]
289—Mechanics	Allardice
290—Mechanics	[Allardice]
291—Mechanics	Thackara & Vallance

VOLUME XI (1794)

PLATE NUMBER AND SHORT TITLE	ENGRAVER
292–93—Medals	Thackara & Vallance
294—Magic circle of circles	Thackara & Vallance
295—Micrometer	Trenchard
296—Micrometer	Allardice
297—Microscope	Scot [FS]
298—Microscope	Smither, Sr.
299—Microscope	Allardice
300—Microscope	Scot [FS]
301—Microscope	Trenchard
302—Microscopic objects	Allardice
303—Microscopic objects	Smither, Sr.

304–5—Microscopic objects	Allardice
306—Midwifery	Scot [FS]
307–8—Midwifery	Thackara & Vallance
309—Midwifery	Allardice
310—Midwifery	Smither

VOLUME XII (1794)

PLATE NUMBER AND SHORT TITLE	ENGRAVER
311—MIMOSA	SCOT & ALLARDICE [S]
312—Mimosa (nondescript)	Scot & Allardice
313—Mineralogy	Scot & Allardice [S]
314—Midship frame	Scot & Allardice [FS]
315—*Mordella*	Akin
316—Moss or bog	Scot & Allardice
317–19—*Mus*	Scot & Allardice
320—*Muscicapa*	Thackara & Vallance
321–22—*Musci* mosses	Thackara & Vallance
323—Music	Thackara & Vallance
324–32—Music	[Thackara & Vallance]
333—*Mustellae* ["Aqua forti Fecit"]	Akin
334–35—*Myristica*	Thackara & Vallance
336—*Myrtus pimenta*	Trenchard
337–38—Navigation	Akin
339–40—Navigation	Thackara & Vallance
341—Navigation	Trenchard
342—Navigation	Scot & Allardice
343—Navigation	Akin
344—Inland navigation	Scot & Allardice
345—Dipping needle	Akin

VOLUME XIII (1795)

PLATE NUMBER AND SHORT TITLE	ENGRAVER
346—Nodes; Nocturnal	Scot & Allardice
347—Bramin's Observatory	Scot & Allardice
348—Nut cracker	Seymour
349—Sharptailed oriole	Smither, Sr.
350—*Orchis mascula*	Scot & Allardice
351—*Opapona*	Scot & Allardice
352—Optics	Vallance

353—Optics	Thackara
354—Optics	Trenchard
355—Optics	Thackara
356–57—Optics	Scot & Allardice
358—Optics	Trenchard
359—Optics	Vallance
360—Optics	Thackara
361—Optics	[Thackara]
362—Optics	Scot & Allardice
363–65—Optics	Thackara
366—Boring of ordnance	Thackara
367—Organ	Thackara
368—Ornithology	Seymour
369—Orrery	Scot & Allardice
	[Francis Shallus]
370—*Ovis*	Vallance
371—*Ovis*	Seymour
372—Ruins, Temple of Palmyra	Smither, Sr.
373—*Panis quinquefolium*	Trenchard
374—Bird of Paradise	Trenchard
375—Papyrus	Thackara
376—Paper mill	Vallance
377—Parhelion	Trenchard

VOLUME XIV (1795)

PLATE NUMBER AND SHORT TITLE	ENGRAVER
378–79—Passions	Seymour
380—Pendulum	unattributed
381—*Pavo cristatus*	Scot & Allardice
382—*Patellae*	Ralph
383—Perspective	Vallance
384—Perspective	[Scot & Allardice]
385—Perspective	Scot & Allardice
386—Perspective	Vallance
387—Perspective	Trenchard
388—Peppermint tree	Ralph
389—Persepolis	Smither, Sr.
390—Philology	Ralph
391—Physiology	Ralph

392—*Phaens copterus ruber*	Scot & Allardice [JD]
393—Machine for boring wooden pins	Scot & Allardice [BJ]

VOLUME XV (1796)

PLATE NUMBER AND SHORT TITLE	ENGRAVER
394–96—Anatomy of plants	Vallance
397—Vegetable cabinet	Thackara
398—Plough	Thackara
399—Pneumatics	Thackara
400—Pneumatics	Scot & Allardice
401—Pneumatics	Scot & Allardice [BJ]
402—Pneumatics	Scot & Allardice
403—Pneumatics	Trenchard
404—Pneumatics	Shallus
405—Pneumatics	Thackara
406–7—Pneumatics	[Thackara]
408—Pneumatics	Smither, Sr.
409—Pneumatics	Trenchard
410—Poland, Lithuania, Prussia [map]	Vallance
411—Polytheism	Vallance
412—Island of Ponza	Thackara
413—Machine for draining ponds	Trenchard
414—Piano forte; Printing press	Trenchard
415—Printing press	Shallus
416—*Pristic*	Smither, Sr.
417—Projectiles	Trenchard
418—Projectiles	Thackara
419—Projections of the sphere	Vallance
420–21—Projections of the sphere	Thackara
422–23—Projections of the sphere	[Thackara]
424–25—Pump	Vallance
426—Pump	Trenchard
427—Quadrant	Vallance
428–29—Pyrotechny	Thackara
430—Pyrotechny	Smither, Sr.

431—Pyrotechny	Vallance
432—Pyrotechny	Bowes
433—Ramsden's machine	Scot & Allardice
434—Ramsden's engine	Vallance

VOLUME XVI (1796)

PLATE NUMBER AND SHORT TITLE	ENGRAVER
435—*Recuvinastra americana*	Thackara
436—Resistance to fluids	Smither, Sr.
437—*Ramphastos* (tucan)	Smither, Sr.
438—Rhinoceros	Thackara
439—Theory of the motion of rivers	Vallance
440—Roofs	Vallance
441—Rope making	Smither, Sr.
442—Rotation	Scot & Allardice
443—Russia or Muscovy [map]	Scot & Allardice
444—*Scarobus carnifex*	Thackara
445—Scorpion	Thackara
446—Scotland [map]	Scot & Allardice

VOLUME XVII (1797)

PLATE NUMBER AND SHORT TITLE	ENGRAVER
447—Seamanship	Vallance
448—Screw; Sea water	Vallance
449—*Sepia,* or cuttlefish	Vallance
450—Ship	Allardice
451—Ship	[Allardice]
452—Ship	Allardice
453—Ship bolts	Lawson
454–55—Shipbuilding	Smither, Sr.
456–58—Shipbuilding	Thackara
459–61—Shipbuilding	Smither, Sr.
462–65—Shipbuilding	[Smither, Sr.]
466—Naval signals	Thackara
467–70—*Simae*	Smither, Sr.
471—Smoke; Smoke jack	Thackara
472—Specific gravity	Vallance
473—Spain and Portugal [map]	Vallance

474—Spinning wheel	Vallance
475—Sponges	Smither, Sr.
476—Squid	[Thackara?]
477—Steam engine	[Vallance?]
478—Beighton's steam engine	Vallance
479—Watt's steam engine	Scot
480—Steam engine	Vallance
481—Steelyard	Vallance
482–83—Stenography	Vallance

VOLUME XVIII (1798)

PLATE NUMBER AND SHORT TITLE	ENGRAVER
484–85—Strength of materials	[Vallance]
486—*Struthio* (ostrich)	Akin
487—Surgery	Scot
488—Surgery	Scot [D]
489—Surgery	Bowes
490—Surgery	Akin
491—Surgery	Jones
492—Surgery	Akin
493–95—Naval tactics	Jones
496–99—Naval tactics	Bowes
500—Teat tree	unattributed
501—*Taenia*	Jones
502—Telegraph	Vallance
503–4—Telescope	Vallance
505—Herschel's grand telescope	Vallance
506—Thermometers	Lawson
507—Thermometers	[Lawson]
508—Thrashing machine	Jones
509—Tide	unattributed
510—White bear	Allardice
511—Trigonometry	Allardice
512—Articulate trumpet	Jones
513—Variations; Ventilator	Weston
514—War (plan of march)	Allardice
515–17—War (march in mountains and forests; camped)	Weston

518—War (entrenched camp)	Lawson
519—War (passage of a river)	Jones
520—War (order of battle)	Allardice
521—War (order of battle)	Allardice
522—War (order of battle)	Weston
523—War (order of battle)	Allardice
524—War (order of battle)	Weston
525—War (order of battle)	Lawson
526—War (order of battle)	Weston
527—War (order of battle)	Lawson
528—War (attack on fortifica- tions)	Lawson
529—War (Philipsburg, 1734)	Lawson
530–32—War (trenches)	Weston
533—War (lodgments and bat- teries)	Vallance
534–35—War (cavalier of trenches)	Vallance
536—War (attack on fortified grounds)	Clarke
537—War; Watch works	Clarke
538—Weighing	Scot
539—Weaving	Lawson
540—*Winera aromatica*	Jones
541–42—Waterworks	unattributed

SUPPLEMENT VOLS. XIX, XX, XXI (1800–1803)

PLATE NUMBER AND SHORT TITLE	ENGRAVER
1–2—[Geometric figures]	Bowes
3—Male anhinga	Lawson
4—Iron bridge	Lawson
5—Gothic arch	Bowes
6—[Geometric figures]	Bowes
7—Large snouted boar	Lawson
8–9—Carpentry	Bowes
10—Carpentry	Lawson
11–13—Carpentry	Weston
14—Centres	[Scot]
15–17—Centres	Scot

18–19—Chemistry	Lawson
20—Chimney	Jones
21—Dendrometer	[Jones]
22—Dynamics	[Jones]
23—Dynamics; Collier's apparatus	Jones
24—Electricity	[Draper]
25—Electricity	Draper
26—Electricity	[Lawson]
27—Electricity	Lawson
28—Euphorbia	Lawson
29—Guillotine	Draper
30—*Jonesia;* Indian spikenard	Lawson
31—Involution	Lawson
32—Lens grinding	Lawson
33—Laboratory plate	Lawson
34–35—Magnetism	Lawson
36—Meridian line	Lawson
37—Mineralogy	Lawson
38–39—Oil well	Lawson
40—Position; Printing press	Lawson
41—Photometer	Lawson
42—Reaping scythes	Lawson
43—Spinning	Lawson
44—Temperament of music	[Lawson]
45—Temperament; Trumpet marine	[Lawson]
46—Rochon's engraving machine	Lawson
47—*Urceola elastica*	Lawson
48–49—Watch work	Lawson
50—Weaving loom	Lawson

APPENDIX

1—[Air pump]	Lawson
2—Air pump	"Etch'd by Lawson"
3—[Artificial horizon; log at sea]	Lawson

Appendix C. A Checklist of Titles Printed by and for Thomas Dobson

This checklist has been prepared using Charles Evans's *American Bibliography;* Clifford K. Shipton's continuation of Evans's work through 1800; Roger Bristol's *Supplement* to Evans; Ralph Shaw and Richard Shoemaker's checklist of *American Imprints* (to 1819); Shoemaker's continuation of the same bibliographical guide (to the year of Dobson's death, 1823); the *National Union Catalog, Pre-1956 Imprints*; Edmund O'Callaghan's *List of Editions of the Holy Scriptures and Parts Thereof, Printed in America Previous to 1860*; and other sources as noted in the bibliography. Corrections to these sources, when necessary, have been inserted in brackets.

The checklist has been augmented by advertisements in early American newspapers and magazines, especially those that Dobson published or with which he was closely associated. Some titles, particularly broadside proposals, have been identified from Dobson's letters. The card catalog at the American Antiquarian Society, Worcester, Massachusetts, includes a number of titles not recorded elsewhere, indicated by "[AAS]." These supplementary resources significantly expand the number of imprints attributed to Dobson in the standard bibliographical sources and help present a more complete picture of his role in the history of American publishing and printing.

1785

The Constitutions of the Thirteen United States of North America—The Declaration of Independence—The Articles of Confederation—also, Treaties of Alliance and Commerce Between His Most Christian Majesty and Said States. "Just published . . . and sold by W. Young . . . and T. Dobson." *Pennsylvania Mercury*, August 26, 1785.

Goethe, Johann Wolfgang von. *The Sorrows of Werter*. [Advertised with *Constitutions*, above].

Original Tales, Histories, Essays, and Translations. By Different Hands. Edinburgh: Printed for Charles Eliot; and Thomas Dobson, Philadelphia. [AAS].

1786

Armstrong, John. *The Art of Pursuing Health*. Printed for Thomas Dobson. [AAS].

Burgh, James. *The Art of Speaking. Containing I. An Essay; in Which Are Given Rules for Expressing Properly the Passions and Humours, Which Occur in Reading or Public Speaking; and II. Lessons Taken from the Ancients and Moderns (with Additions and Alterations Where Thought Useful) Exhibiting a Variety of Matter for Practice; the Emphatical Words Being Printed in Italics; with Notes of Direction Referring to the Essay; to Which Are Added, a Table of the Lessons, and an Index of the Various Passions and Humours in the Essay and Lessons.* Printed [by Charles Cist] for Thomas Dobson, Bookseller, Second-Street, two doors above Chesnut-Street. Evans 19535.

Churchman, John. *Map of the Peninsula Between Delaware and Chesapeake Bays. Pennsylvania Gazette*, July 26, 1786.

Cowper, William. *Tirocinium: or, a Review of Schools . . . A New Edition*. Printed for Thomas Dobson. Evans 19590.

du Four, Phillipe Sylvestre. *Moral Instructions of a Father to His Son, Ready to Undertake a Long Voyage; or an Easy Manner of Forming a Young Man to All Kinds of Virtue: Translated from the French of Sylvestre du Four: To Which Is Added, a Collection of Moral Instructions in Prose and Verse, from the Best Authors.* Printed for Thomas Dobson. Evans 19613.

Edwards, Jonathan. *A History of the Work of Redemption.* [Printed for Thomas Dobson?]. *Pennsylvania Mercury*, October 3, 1786: an "AMERICAN EDITION . . . correctly printed with good type and paper, and neatly bound, at a very easy price."

Goldsmith, Oliver. *The Deserted Village. A Poem.* Printed for Thomas Dobson. Evans 19689.

A New Set of Geographical Cards, for the Agreeable Improvement of Gentlemen. [Printed for] T. Dobson. Bristol 6332; Evans 44933.

The New Testament of Our Lord and Saviour Jesus Christ: Translated out of the Original Greek; and with the Former Translations Diligently Compared and Revised. Printed for J. Crukshank, F. Bailey, Young, Stewart, and M'Culloch, and T. Dobson. Evans 19511.

[Pain, William.] "This Day is Published and Sold by Thomas Dobson . . . Pain's builders golden rule with 106 copperplates, 30s." *Pennsylvania Gazette*, July 26, 1786; Prime 2: 74.

Rush, Benjamin. *A Plan for the Establishment of Public Schools and the Diffusion of Knowledge in Pennsylvania; to Which Are Added Thoughts upon the Mode of Education, Proper in a Republic. Addressed to the Legislature and Citizens of the State.* Printed for Thomas Dobson. Evans 19974.

Scott, William. *Scott's Lessons in Elocution, or a Selection of Pieces in Prose and Verse, for the Improvement of Youth in Reading and Speaking, as Well as for the Perusal of Persons of Taste; with an Appendix, Containing the Principles of English Grammar; Being One of the Best Books of the Kind Ever Offered to the Public.* Printed for Thomas Dobson. Evans 19980.

Stanhope, Philip Dormer, 4th Earl of Chesterfield. *Lord Chesterfield's Advice to His Son, on Men and Manners: or, a New System of Education. In Which the Principles of Politeness, the Art of Acquiring a Knowledge of the World, Are Laid Down in a Plain, Easy, and Familiar Manner. To Which Are Annexed the Polite Philosopher: or an Essay on the Art Which Makes a Man Happy in Himself, and Agreeable to Others.* [By James Forrester.] *Also, Lord Burghley's Ten Precepts to His Second Son, Robert Cecil, Afterward the Earl of Salisbury.* Printed for Thomas Dobson. Evans 20002.

Young, Edward. *The Last Day. A Poem. In Three Books.* . . . Printed for Thomas Dobson. Evans 20173.

1787

The Adventures of Alphonso, After the Destruction of Lisbon. Related by Himself, in a Letter to His Brother. Printed for Thomas Dobson. Evans 20183.

Aitken, John. *A Compilation of the Litanies and Vespers. Hymns and Anthems, as They Are Sung in the Catholic Church; Adapted to the Voice or Organ.* . . . *To Which Is Prefixed, a New Introduction to the Grounds of Music.* Printed for Thomas Dobson. Evans 20186.

Armstrong, John. *The Art of Preserving Health. A Poem.* Printed for Thomas Dobson. Evans 20204.

Beattie, James. *Evidences of the Christian Religion; Briefly and Plainly Stated.* Printed for Thomas Dobson. Evans 20223.

———. *Poems on Several Occasions.* . . . Printed for Thomas Dobson. Evans 20224.

Blair, Robert. *The Grave. A Poem* . . . *To Which Is Added, An Elegy, Written in a Country Churchyard. By Mr. Gray.* Printed for Thomas Dobson. Bristol 6455; Evans 45401.

[Butterworth, Edmund.] "This Day is Published by Thomas Dobson, 4 Butterworth's new copperplate copy books." *Pennsylvania Gazette,* March 14, 1787; Prime 2: 74.

Chatterton, Augustus [pseudonym]. *The Buds of Beauty; or, Parnassian Sprig. Being a Collection of Original Poems, upon Various Subjects.* . . . Printed for Thomas Dobson. Evans 20270.

Cowper, William. *The Task. A Poem.* . . . *A New Edition.* Printed for Thomas Dobson. Bristol 6474; Evans 45056.

———. *The Task. A Poem. In Six Books. To Which Is Added, Tirocinium: or, a Review of Schools.* . . . *A New Edition.* Printed for Thomas Dobson. Evans 20304.

———. *Tirocinium: or, A Review of Schools* . . . *A New Edition.* Printed for Thomas Dobson. Evans 20304.

Crawford, Adair. *Experiments and Observations on Animal Heat, and the Inflammation of Combustible Bodies. Being an Attempt to Resolve These Phenomena into a General Law of Nature.* . . . Printed for T. Dobson. Evans 20308.

Cumberland, Richard. *The Carmelite. A Tragedy.* Printed for Thomas Dobson. Evans 20310.

Dibdin, Charles. *The Deserter, a Comic Opera: As Performed by the Old American Company, at New-York, with Great Applause.* Printed for Thomas Dobson. Evans 20332.

Dodd, William. *The Beauties of History, or Pictures of Virtue and Vice Drawn from Real Life; Designed, and Admirably Calculated for the Instruction and Entertainment of Youth.* Printed for Thomas Dobson. Evans 20336.

Fordyce, James. *Sermons to Young Women . . . A New Edition.* Printed for Thomas Dobson. Evans 20362.

Fragments of the Confederation of the American States. Printed for Thomas Dobson. Evans 20367.

Genlis, Stephanie Felicite Ducrest de St. Aubin, comtesse de. *Alphonso and Dalinda: Or, The Magic of Art and Nature. A Moral Tale. Written in French by Madame La Comtesse de Genlis. Translated into English by Thomas Holcroft.* Printed for Thomas Dobson. Evans 20385.

Geographical Cards, for the Exercise and Entertainment of Youth in the Knowledge of Geography. Printed for Thomas Dobson. Evans 20386.

Gray, Thomas. *Elegy in a Country Churchyard.* Printed for Thomas Dobson. Evans 20395.

Macklin, Charles. *The True Born Irishman, or The Irish Fine Lady. A Comedy.* Printed for Thomas Dobson. Evans 22475.

Magaw, Samuel. *An Address, Delivered in the Young Ladies Academy, at Philadelphia, on February 18, 1787. . . .* Printed for Thomas Dobson. Bristol 6514; Evans 45089.

Moore, Edward. *Fables for the Ladies. . . . To Which Are Added, Fables of Flora. By Dr. Langhorne.* Printed for Thomas Dobson. Evans 20530.

———. *A Prayer, Delivered at the Close of the Quarterly Examinations, and After Mr. Swanwick's Address . . . October 31, 1787. . . .* Printed for Thomas Dobson. Bristol 6515; Evans 45090.

Moore, James. *A Letter to Mr. John Stancliff, Containing Some Remarks on His Vindication of His Account of the Murrinitish Plague, & c. in a Letter to the Author.* [Evans's note: "Advertised, and probably published by Thomas Dobson, in 1787." (7: 238).]

More, Hannah. *Sacred Dramas; Chiefly Intended for Young Persons: The Subjects Taken from the Bible. To Which Are Added: Reflections of King Hezekiah, and Sensibility, a Poem. . . .* Printed for Thomas Dobson. Evans 20534.

Newton, Thomas. *Dissertation on the Prophecies Which Have Been Remarkably Fulfilled, and Are at This Time Fulfilling in the World. Pennsylvania Mercury,* June 2; Advertised at half the price of the London edition under the general rubric of "Just Published, and Sold by Thomas Dobson."

Pope, Alexander. *An Essay on Man. . . .* Printed for Thomas Dobson. Bristol 6565; Evans 45142.

Reinagle, Alexander. *A Select Collection of the Most Favourite Scots Tunes. With Variations for the Piano Forte or Harpsichord. Composed by A. Reinagle.* Printed for the Author; and Sold by T. Dobson & W. Young, at Their Respective Book Stores. Evans 20674.

The Returned Captive; A Poem, Founded on a Late Incontestable Fact. Printed for Thomas Dobson. Evans 20677.

Rush, Benjamin. *An Inquiry into the Effects of Spirituous Liquors upon the Human Body, and Their Influence upon the Happiness of Society. . . .* Printed for Thomas Dobson. Evans 20690.

Scott, William. *An Introduction to the Reading and Spelling of the English Tongue. A New Edition, Very Much Improved.* Printed for Thomas Dobson. Evans 20697.

Selectae ae Profanis Scriptoribus Historiae. Quibus Admissa Sunt Variae Honeste Vivendi

Praecepts ex Iisdem Scriptoribus Deprompta. Nova Editio; Prioribus Longe Emendatior. Printed for Thomas Dobson. Evans 20227.

Shakespeare, William. *The Twins: Or Which Is Which? A Farce, in Three Acts, Altered from Shakespeare's Comedy of Errors. by William Woods.* Printed for Thomas Dobson. Evans 20700.

Sheridan, Richard Brinsley Butler. *The Critic: A Tragedy.* Printed for Thomas Dobson. Evans 20703.

Smith, Charlotte Turner. *Elegaic Sonnets. . . . A New Edition.* Printed for Thomas Dobson. Evans 20711.

Swanwick, John. *Thoughts on Education, Addressed to the Visitors of the Young Ladies' Academy in Philadelphia, October 31, 1787. At the Close of the Quarterly Examination. By John Swanwick, Esquire, One of the Visitors of the Said Academy. To Which Are Added; A Prayer, Delivered on the Same Occasion, by Samuel Magaw, D.D. and a Poem, on the Prospect of Seeing the Fine Arts Flourish in America.* Printed for Thomas Dobson. Evans 20736.

The Theatre of Education, Consisting of Entertaining Moral Instructions, in the Form of Short Comedies. Printed for Thomas Dobson. Evans 20744.

Wraxall, Sir Nathaniel William. *A Short Review of the Political State of Great Britain at the Commencement of the Year One Thousand Seven Hundred and Eighty-Seven.* Printed for Thomas Dobson. Evans 20899.

The Young Misses Magazine. Containing Dialogues Between a Governess and Several Young Ladies Her Scholars. Printed for Thomas Dobson. Evans 20907.

1788

Barnard, Sir John. *A Present for an Apprentice: Or, A Sure Guide to Gain Esteem and Estate. With Rules for His Conduct to His Master, and in the World. More Especially, While an Apprentice, His Behaviour After He Is Free, Care in Setting up, Company with the Ladies, Choice of a Wife, Behaviour in Courtship, and Wedding-Day, Complaisance After Marriage, Education of Children, & c. By a Late Lord-Mayor of London.* Printed [by Henry Taylor] for Thomas Dobson. Evans 20953.

Booth, Abraham. *An Apology for the Baptists. In Which They Are Vindicated from the Imputation of Laying Unwarrantable Stress on the Ordnance of Baptism; and Against the Charge of Bigotry in Refusing Communion at the Lord's Table to Paedobaptists. . . .* Printed [by Henry Taylor] for Thomas Dobson. Evans 20976.

Booth's Paedobaptism Examined and Refuted, upon the Principles and Concessions of Pseudo-Baptist Writers. Printed for Thomas Dobson. Evans 20977.

Collins, William. *The Poetical Works of William Collins. Containing His Miscellanies, Oriental Epilogues, Odes Descriptive and Allegorical, & c. & c. & c. Also His Ode on the Popular Superstitions of the Highlands of Scotland. With the Author's Life, and Observations, by Dr. Langhorne.* Printed for Thomas Dobson. Evans 21004.

Dobson, Thomas. *Thomas Dobson, Bookseller and Stationer, at the New Stone House, in Second Street . . . has for Sale, Wholesale and Retail. . . .* T. Dobson. Bristol 6696; Evans 45252.

Edwards, Morgan. *Two Academical Exercises on Subjects Bearing the Following Titles: Millennium, Last-Novelties. Published by Morgan Edwards, A. M.* Printed by Dobson and Lang. Evans 21070.

Falconer, William. *The Shipwreck. A Poem. . . .* [Two lines from] *Virgil. The Eighth Edition, Corrected* Printed for Thomas Dobson. Evans 21080.

Hopkinson, Francis. *A Set of Eight Songs. The Words and Music Composed by the Honorable Francis Hopkinson. These Songs Are Composed in an Easy, Familiar Style, Intended for Young Practitioners on the Harpsichord or Forte Piano, and Is the First Work of This Kind Attempted in the United States. J. Aitken, Sculp.* Printed for Thomas Dobson. Evans 21152.

————. *Seven Songs for the Harpsichord or Forte Piano. . . .* Publish'd & Sold by Thomas Dobson. Bristol 6718.

[Hutchins, Joseph.] *An Abstract of the First Principles of English Grammar. . . .* Printed for the Editor, by T. Dobson and T. Lang. [AAS].

Lavater, Johann Caspar. *Aphorisms on Man: Translated from the Original Manuscript by the Rev. John Casper Lavater, Citizen of Zuric.* [By Johann Heinrich Fuessli.] *(Embellished with an Elegant Frontispiece).* Printed for Thomas Dobson. Evans 21194.

The Messiah, a Sacred Poem, from the German of Klopstock, a New Edition. [Printed by Thomas Dobson?; *Pennsylvania Mercury,* June 6].

More, Hannah. *Thoughts on the Importance of the Manners of the Great to General Society.—"You Are the Makers of Manners." Shakespeare. The Fourth Edition.* Printed [by Henry Taylor] for Thomas Dobson. Evans 21271.

New and Old Principles of Trade Compared, or a Treatise on the Principles of Commerce Between Nations, with an Appendix. Printed for Thomas Dobson. Evans 21281.

Nicholson, William. *An Introduction to Natural Philosophy. Illustrated with Copperplates. . . .* [Three lines from] *Seneca. The Third Edition, with Improvements. In Two Volumes.* Printed for Thomas Dobson. Evans 21333.

Paley, William. *The Principles of Moral and Political Philosophy. . . . The Seventh Edition, Corrected.* Printed for Thomas Dobson. Evans 21356.

Percival, Thomas. *A Father's Instructions: Consisting of, Moral Tales, Fables, and Reflections; Designed to Promote the Love of Virtue, a Taste for Knowledge, and an Early Acquaintance with the Works of Nature. . . .* Printed for Thomas Dobson. Evans 21382.

Price, Richard. *Sermons. On the Security and Happiness of a Virtuous Course, On the Goodness of God, and the Resurrection of Lazarus. To Which Are Added, Sermons on the Christian Doctrine, as Received by the Different Denominations of Christians. . . .* Printed for Thomas Dobson. Evans 21404.

Purves, James. *Humble Attempt to Investigate and Defend the Scripture Doctrine Concerning the Father, the Son, and Holy Spirit; to Which Is Added Observations Concerning the Mediation of Jesus Christ in the Various Dispensations of God the Father, and the Final Issue of the Administration; with an Appendix, in Which the Objections Commonly Urged from the Hebrew Names, 'Alehim' and 'Jehovah,' & c. Are Considered, and the Significance of the Names Pointed Out.* Printed for Thomas Dobson. Evans 21413.

Reinagle, Alexander. *A Collection of Favorite Songs; Divided into Two Books. Each Containing Most of the Airs in the Poor Soldier, Rosina, &c. and the Principal Songs Sung at Vauxhall. The Basses Rendered Easy and Natural for the Piano Forte or Harpsichord.* . . . Printed for, and Sold by Messrs. Rice, Poyntell, Dobson, and Young. Evans 21420.

Rural Eoconomy, or Essays on the Practical Parts of Husbandry. [Printed for Thomas Dobson?; *Pennsylvania Mercury,* June 6].

Sarjeant, Thomas. *Elementary Principles of Arithmetic; with Their Application to the Trade and Commerce of the United States of America. In Eight Sections.* . . . *For the Use of Schools and Private Education. Parvum Parva Decent. Hor. Ep.* [Vignette.] Printed by Dobson and Lang for the Editor. Evans 21445.

————. *A Paradigm of Inflections of Words in the English Language.* Printed by Dobson and Lang. Evans 21446.

————. *Select Arithmetrical Tables.* Printed by Dobson and Lang. Evans 21447.

————. *A Synopsis of Logarithmical Arithmetic in Which the Nature of Logarithms, and Their Application Are Made Easy to Those Who Have Not Studied Higher Branches of Mathematics.* . . . Printed by Dobson and Lang. Evans 21448.

Sherlock, Thomas. *The Trial of the Witnesses of the Resurrection of Jesus. N.B. Not Only Mr. Woolston's Objections in His Sixth Discourse on Our Saviour's Miracles, But Those Also Which He and Others Have Published in Other Books Are Here Considered. First Published About the Year 1729.* Printed for Thomas Dobson. Evans 21461.

Smith, Charles. *An Oration, Delivered at the Town of Sunbury, in the County of Northumberland, on the Anniversary of St. John the Evangelist, December 27, 1787. At the Request of the Members of the Antient and Honorable Society of Free and Accepted Masons—Lodge No. 22, and Published at the Earnest Desire of the Said Lodge.* . . . Printed for Thomas Dobson. Evans 21463.

1789

Aesopus. *Fabulae Aesopi Selectae, Or, Select Fables of Aesop; with an English Translation, more Literal than Any yet Extant. Designed for the Reader Instruction of Beginners in the Latin Tongue. By H. Clarke, Teacher of the Latin Language. The Ninth Edition, Corrected and Amended.* Printed [by Dobson and Lang] for T. Dobson. Evans 21631.

Alleine, Joseph. *The Believer's Triumph in God's Promises; and the Various Conflicts and Glorious Conquests of Faith over Unbelief: Being an Appendix to The Voice of God in His Promises.* . . . *The Third Edition.* Printed by Dobson & Lang, for Thomas Ustick. Evans 21638.

A Comprehensive Grammar; in Which the Principles of the English Language Are Methodically Digested into Plain and Easy Rules. Illustrated by Exercises of True and False Syntax. With Notes and Observations, Explaining the Terms of Grammar, and Improving Its Use. The Third Edition. [Two lines from] *Pope.* Printed [by Dobson and Lang,] for Thomas Dobson. Evans 21746.

Dobson, Thomas. *Proposals, by Thomas Dobson, Bookseller . . . for Printing by Subscription, Encyclopaedia Britannica; or, A Dictionary of Arts, Sciences.* . . . Thomas Dobson. Bristol 6937; Evans 45466.

Gurney, Thomas. *An Easy and Compendious System of Short-Hand; Adapted to the Arts and Sciences, and to the Learned Professions. By Thomas Sarjeant.* Printed by Dobson & Lang for the Editor. Evans 21869.

Hopkinson, Francis. *An Oration, Which Might Have Been Delivered to the Students in Anatomy, on the Late Rupture Between the Two Schools in This City.* Printed by T. Dobson and T. Lang. Evans 21892.

Pennsylvania. State. *Judgements in the Admiralty of Pennsylvania in Four Suits, Brought as for Maritime Hypothecations. Also, the Case of Silas Talbot, Against the Brigs Achilles, Patty, and Hibernia, and of the Owners of the Hibernia Against Their Captain, John Angus. With an Appendix, Containing the Testimony Exhibited in the Admiralty in Those Cases. The Hon. Francis Hopkinson Judge.* Printed by T. Dobson and T. Lang. Evans 22053.

Reinagle, Alexander. *My Soul Is Thine, Sweet Nora. Song, Arranged for the Pianoforte or Harpsichord by Alexander Reinagle.* Published and Sold by Thomas Dobson. Evans 22096.

———. *Tantive Back Forward. Song Arranged for the Pianoforte by Alexander Reinagle.* Published and Sold by Thomas Dobson. Evans 22097.

———. *'Tis Not the Bloom on Damon's Cheek. Song. Arranged for the Pianoforte, by Alexander Reinagle.* Published and Sold by Thomas Dobson. Evans 22098.

Rogers, William. *An Oration, Delivered July 4th, 1789, at the Presbyterian Church, in Arch-Street, Philadelphia. . . . To Which Is Added, a Prayer Delivered on the Same Occasion, by the Rev. Ashbel Green. . . .* Printed for Thomas Dobson. Evans 22120.

Sarjeant, Thomas. *An Introduction to the Counting House; or, A Short Specimen of Mercantile Precedents, Adapted to the Present Situation of the Trade and Commerce of the United States of America. For the Use of Schools and Private Education. . . . Intended as a Supplement to the Elementary Principles of Arithmetic.* Printed by Dobson and Lang for the Editor. Evans 22127.

———. *Select Arithmetrical Tables.* [Printed by Dobson and Lang.] Evans 22128.

Shield, William. *Overture to the New Opera Marian. Arranged for the Pianoforte by Alexander Reinagle.* Published and Sold by Thomas Dobson. Evans 22142.

Smith, Adam. *An Inquiry into the Nature and Causes of the Wealth of Nations. . . . In Three Volumes. Vol. I. [–III] A New Edition.* Printed for Thomas Dobson. Evans 22148.

Smith, William. *Two Sermons, Delivered in Christ-Church, Philadelphia, Before the General Convention of the Protestant Episcopal Church of the States of New-York, New Jersey, Pennsylvania, Delaware, Maryland, Virginia, and South Carolina;— viz. Serm. I. On Wednesday, July 29, 1789, at the Opening of the Said Convention. Serm. II. On Tuesday, August 4, 1789, at the Funeral of the Rev. David Griffith, D.D. Late Bishop-Elect of the Said Church, in the State of Virginia. . . .* Printed by Dobson & Lang. Evans 22149.

Spangenberg, Augustus Gottlieb. *An Account of the Manner in Which the Protestant Church of the Unitas Fratrum, or United Brethren, Preach the Gospel, and Carry on Their Missions Among the Heathens. Translated from the German of the Rev'd Augustus Gottlieb Spangenberg.* [Two lines from] *Mark xvi. 15.* Printed for Thomas Dobson. Evans 22155.

Stanhope, Philip Dormer, fourth Earl of Chesterfield. *Lord Chesterfield's Advice to His Son, on Men and Manners: or, A New System of Education; in Which the Principles of Politeness, and the Art of Acquiring a Knowledge of the World Are Laid Down in a Plain, Easy, and Familiar Manner. To Which Are Annexed, The Polite Philosopher: or, An Essay on the Art Which Makes a Man Happy in Himself, and Agreeable to Others.* [By James Forrester.] *Also, Lord Burghley's Ten Precepts to His Second Son, Robert Cecil, Afterwards the Earl of Salisbury.* Printed for T. Dobson. Evans 22158.

Two Discourses. . . . Printed by T. Dobson and T. Lang. [AAS].

Watts, Isaac. *Logick; or, The Right Use of Reason in the Enquiry After Truth. With a Variety of Rules to Guard Against Error, in the Affairs of Religion and Human Life, as Well as in the Sciences.* . . . *The Sixteenth Edition.* Printed for Thomas Dobson. Evans 22246.

1790

Brown, or Bruno, John. *The Elements of Medicine; or, A Translation of the Elementa Medicinae Brunonis. With Large Notes, Illustrations, and Comments. By the Author of the Original Work. A New Edition.* Printed by T. Dobson. Evans 22372.

Campbell, George. *A Dissertation of Miracles: Containing an Examination of Principles Advanced by David Hume, Esq.; in an Essay on Miracles.* . . . [Two lines from] *John x. 25. The Third Edition, with Additions and Corrections.* Printed by Thomas Dobson. Evans 22387.

de Rosset, Armand John. *De Febribus Intermittentibus.* Typis T. Dobson. Evans 22460.

Dobson, Thomas. *A New Edition, Corrected, Improved, and Greatly Enlarged. Proposals, by Thomas Dobson . . . for Printing by Subscription, Encyclopaedia Britannica.* . . . Thomas Dobson. Bristol 7363; Evans 45866.

Encyclopaedia; or, a Dictionary of Arts, Sciences, and Miscellaneous Literature. . . . [Vols. I and II, Pt. 1]. Printed by Thomas Dobson. Evans 22486 [amended].

[Fyfe, Andrew.] *A Compendious System of Anatomy.* Printed by Thomas Dobson. [AAS].

Hamilton, Alexander. *Outlines of the Theory and Practice of Midwifery. A New Edition.* Printed by T. Dobson. Evans 22551.

Jenyns, Soame. *Disquisitions on Several Subjects . . . A New Edition.* Printed by Thomas Dobson. Bristol 7396; Evans 45895.

Morse, Jedidiah. *The History of America. In Two Books. Containing, I. A General History of America, II. A Concise History of the Late Revolution. Extracted from the American Edition of the Encyclopaedia; Now Publishing.* Printed by Thomas Dobson. Evans 22682.

Rush, Benjamin. *An Eulogium in Honor of the Late Dr. William Cullen, Professor of the Practice of Physic in the University of Edinburgh; Delivered Before the College of Physicians of Philadelphia, on the 9th of July; Agreeably to Their Vote on the 4th of May, 1790.* . . . Printed by Thomas Dobson. Evans 22862.

Smith, William. *A Sermon, on Temporal and Spiritual Salvation: Delivered in Christ-Church, Philadelphia, Before the Pennsylvania Society of the Cincinnati.* . . . From the Press of T. Dobson. Evans 22891.

Universalist Church. *Articles of Faith, and Plan of Church Government. Composed and Adopted by the Churches Believing in the Salvation of All Men.* . . . Printed by Thomas Dobson. Evans 23009.

1791

Bell, Benjamin. *A System of Surgery. Extracted from the Works of Benjamin Bell of Edinburgh; by Nicholas B. Waters.* . . . *Illustrated with Notes* [by John Jones, M.D.] *and Copper Plates.* Printed by Thomas Dobson. Evans 23170.

Bissett, John. *A Sermon Delivered in St. Paul's Church, Baltimore, on the 19th of June (Trinity Sunday) 1791. With an Appendix.* Printed by T. Dobson. Evans 23208.

Blundell, James. *An Inaugural Dissertation, on the Dysentery.* Printed by T. Dobson. Evans 23212.

Cozens, William R. *An Inaugural Dissertation on the Chemical Properties of Atmospheric Air.* Printed by Thomas Dobson. Evans 23296.

Dobson, Thomas. *A New Edition, Corrected, Improved, and Greatly Enlarged . . . Just Published, by Thomas Dobson . . . Volume III. of Encyclopaedia . . . Philadelphia. April 1791.* Thomas Dobson. Bristol 7690; Evans 56160.

Encyclopaedia; or, A Dictionary of Arts, Sciences, and Miscellaneous Literature. . . . [Vols. II, Pt. 2; III; IV.] Printed by Thomas Dobson. Evans 23351 [amended].

Evans, Davis. *A Letter to the Rev'd Doctor [Samuel] Jones; Containing, Some Remarks on the Circular Letter by the Baptist Association, 1791 [sic: 1790.] Wrote by Himself.* . . . Printed by Thomas Dobson. Evans 23357.

Fielding, Sarah. *The Governess: or, Little Female Academy, Being the History of Mrs. Teachum, and Her Nine Girls. With Their Nine Days Amusement. Calculated for the Instruction and Entertainment of Young Ladies in Their Education. By the Author of David Simple.* Printed by Thomas Dobson. Evans 23372.

Hart, Oliver. *America's Remembrancer, with Respect to Her Blessedness and Duty. A Sermon Delivered in Hopewell, New Jersey, on Thanksgiving Day, November 26, 1789.* . . . Printed by T. Dobson. Evans 23428.

Imlay, William Eugene. *Observations on the Minutes and Circulation Letter of the Baptist Association: Held at New-York, October 5th, 6th, and 7th, 1790.* . . . Printed by Thomas Dobson. Evans 23463.

Lewis, William. *The Edinburgh New Dispensatory: Containing I. The Elements of Pharmaceutical Chemistry. II. The Materia Medica; or, an Account of the Natural History, Qualities, Operations and Uses, of the Different Substances Employed in Medicine. III. The Pharmaceutical Preparations and Medicinal Compositions of the New Editions in London (1788) and Edinburgh (1783) Pharmacopoeias; with Explanatory, Critical, and Practical Observations on Each: Together with the Addition of Those Formulae, from the Best Foreign Pharmacopoeias, Which Are Held in Highest Esteem in Other Parts of Europe. The Whole Interspersed with Practical Cautions and Observations, and Enriched by the Latest Discoveries in Natural History, Chemistry, and Medicine; with New Tables of Elective Attractions, of Antimony, of Mercury, &c. And Copperplates of the Most Convenient Furnaces, and Principal Pharmaceutical Instruments. Being an Improvement upon the New Dispensatory of Dr. Lewis. A New Edition; with Many Alterations, Corrections, and Additions.* [By Andrew Duncan, Jr.] Printed by T. Dobson. Evans 23503.

MacGowan, John. *The Life of Joseph, the Son of Israel. Chiefly Designed to Allure Young Minds to the Love of the Sacred Scriptures.* . . . Printed by Thomas Dobson. Evans 23525.

Pfeiffer, George. *An Inaugural Dissertation on the Gout.* Printed by T. Dobson. Evans 23693.

Porter, Robert. *An Oration, to Commemorate the Independence of the United States of North-America; Delivered at Zion Church, in Fourth-Street, Philadelphia, July 4, 1791; and Published at the Request of the Society of the Cincinnati.* . . . Printed by T. Dobson. Evans 23709.

Rowe, Elizabeth Singer. *Devout Exercises of the Heart, in Meditation, Soliloquy, Prayer, and Praise. By the Late Pious and Ingenious Mrs. Rowe. Revised and Published, at Her Request. By I. Watts, D.D.* Printed by T. Dobson. Evans 23744.

A System of Chemistry; Comprehending the History, Theory and Practice of the Science, According to the Latest Discoveries and Improvements. Extracted from the American Edition of the Encyclopaedia. Printed by Thomas Dobson. Evans 23817.

United States. *The Excise Law, or, "An Act Repealing After the Last Day of June Next, the Duties Heretofore Laid upon Distilled Spirits Imported from Abroad, and Laying Others in Their Stead; and also upon Spirits Distilled in the United States, and for Appropriating the Same.* Printed by Thomas Dobson. Evans 23896.

Wilson, James. *An Introductory Lecture to a Course of Law Lectures . . . to Which Is Added, a Plan of the Lectures.* From the Press of T. Dobson. Evans 24007.

1792

Burke, Edmund. *Reflections on the Revolution in France.* Printed by D. Humphreys, for Young, Dobson, Carey, and Rice. Evans 24757.

Currie, William. *An Historical Account of the Climates and Disease of the United States of America; and of the Remedies and Methods of Treatment, Which Have Been Found Most Useful and Efficacious, Particularly in Those Diseases Which Depend upon Climate and Situation. Collected Principally from Personal Observation, and the Communications of Physicians of Talents and Experience, Residing in the Several States.* . . . Printed by T. Dobson. Evans 24239.

Edwards, Morgan. *Materials towards a History of the Baptists in Jersey; Distinguished into Firstday Baptists, Seventhday Baptists, Tuncker Baptists, Rogerene Baptists. Vol. II.* . . . Printed by Thomas Dobson. Evans 24292.

Encyclopaedia; or, A Dictionary of Arts, Sciences, and Miscellaneous Literature. . . . [Vols. V & VI.] Printed by Thomas Dobson. Evans 24300.

[Fyfe, Andrew.] *A Compendious System of Anatomy. In Six Parts. Part I. Osteology. II. Of the Muscles. III. Of the Abdomen. IV. Of the Thorax. V. Of the Brain and Nerves. VI. Of the Senses. Extracted from the American Edition of the Encyclopaedia, now Publishing, by Thomas Dobson, Philadelphia.* Printed by Thomas Dobson. Evans 24206.

Hazard, Ebenezer. *Historical Collections; Consisting of State Papers, and Other Authentic Documents; Intended as Materials for an History of the United States of America.* . . . *Volume I.* Printed by T. Dobson. Evans 24388.

Hopkinson, Francis. *The Miscellaneous Essays and Occasional Writings of Frangis [sic] Hopkinson, Esq. Volume I. [–III.]* Printed by T. Dobson. Evans 24407.

Mease, James. *An Inaugural Dissertation on the Disease Produced by the Bite of a Mad Dog, or Other Rabid Animal; Submitted to the Examination of the Rev. John Ewing, S.T.P. Provost; the Trustees and Medical Faculty of the University of Pennsylvania, on the Eleventh Day of May, 1792, for the Degree of Doctor of Medicine.* . . . Printed by Thomas Dobson. Evans 24534.

Observations on Novel-Reading: In an Essay Written by a Member of the Belles-Lettres Society of Dickinson College, at Carlisle, in the Year 1789. Printed by Thomas Dobson. Evans 24639.

Pope, Alexander. *An Essay on Man: In Four Epistles, to Henry St. John, L. Bolingbroke.* . . . Printed for Thomas Dobson. Evans 24702.

Psalms, Hymns, and Spiritual Songs. . . . Printed by Thomas Dobson. Bristol 8119; Evans 46555.

Roulle, John. *A Complete Treatise on the Mineral Waters of Virginia.* Printed for the Author by Charles Cist, and to be Sold by Thomas Dobson. [AAS].

Universalist Church. *Evangelical Psalms, Hymns and Spiritual Songs; Selected from Various Authors . . . and Published by a Committee of the Convention of the Churches Believing in the Restitution of All Men, Met in Philadelphia May 25, 1791.* Printed by Thomas Dobson. Evans 24951.

1793

Bache, William. *An Inaugural Experimental Dissertation, Being an Endeavour to Ascertain the Morbid Affects of Carbonic Acid Gas, or Fixed Air, on Healthy Animals.* Printed by Thomas Dobson. Evans 26598.

Bradford, William. *An Enquiry How Far the Punishment of Death Is Necessary in Pennsylvania. With Notes and Illustrations. . . . To Which Is Added, An Account of the Gaol and Penitentiary House of Philadelphia, and of the Interior Management Thereof. By Caleb Lownes, of Philadelphia.* [Three lines from] *Montesq.* Printed by T. Dobson. Evans 25225.

[Second Title.] *An Account of the Alteration and Present State of the Penal Laws of Pennsylvania, Containing Also an Account of the Goal [sic] and Penitentiary House of Philadelphia and the Interior Management Thereof. By Caleb Lownes.* Printed by T. Dobson.

Brown, or Bruno, John. *The Elements of Medicine; or, A Translation of the Elementa Medicinae Brunonis. With Large Notes, Illustrations and Comments. By the Author of the Original Work.* Printed by T. Dobson. Evans 25232.

Currie, William. *A Description of the Malignant, Infectious Fever Prevailing at Present in Philadelphia; with an Account of the Means to Prevent Infection, and the Remedies and Method of Treatment, Which Have Been Found Most Successful.* . . . Printed by T. Dobson. Evans 25366.

Dallas, Alexander James. *A Case Decided in the Supreme Court of the United States, in February, 1793. In Which Is Discussed the Question—"Whether a State be Liable to Be Sued by a Citizen of Another State?"* Printed by T. Dobson. Evans 25370.

Dunn, Thomas. *Equality of Rich and Poor: A Sermon, Preached in the Prison of Philadelphia, on Thursday, December 12th, 1793. Being the Day Appointed for Humiliation and Thanksgiving, on the Ceasing of the Late Epidemic Fever.* . . . Printed by Thomas Dobson. Evans 25424.

Ecclesiastical Establishments Detrimental to a State. Written in English. Printed by Thomas Dobson. Evans 25429.

Encyclopaedia; or, A Dictionary of Arts, Science, and Miscellaneous Literature. . . . [Vols. VII, VIII, IX, and X] Printed by Thomas Dobson. Evans 25450 [amended].

Hardie, James. *The Philadelphia Directory and Register: Containing the Names, Occupations and Places of Abode of the Citizens, Arranged in Alphabetical Order: A Register of the Executive, Legislative, and Judicial Magistrates of the United States and the State of Pennsylvania, with Their Salaries; the Governors of the Different States; the Magistrates of the City: Also, an Account of the Different Societies, Charitable and Literary Institutions, with the Names of Their Present Officers. To Which Is Added, an Accurate Table of the Duties on Goods, Wares, and Merchandise; and Extracts from Sundry Acts of Congress, for the Regulation of Trade, & c. With a Chronological Table of Remarkable Events, Which Have Happened from the First Discovery of America to the Present Period.* Printed for the Author, by T. Dobson. Evans 25585.

Medical and Philosophical Commentaries. By a Society of Physicians in Edinburgh. [Two lines of Latin from] *Ovid. Volume First.* [—Volume Third.] *A New Edition.* Printed by T. Dobson. Evans 25798.

Philadelphia. Pennsylvania. College of Physicians. *Transactions of the College of Physicians of Philadelphia. Volume I.—Part 1. Non Sibi sed Toti.* Printed by T. Dobson. Evans 25992.

Ravara, Joseph. *A Statement of Facts, Concerning Joseph Ravara, Written by Himself.* Printed by Thomas Dobson. Evans 26053.

Rush, Benjamin. *Medical Inquiries and Observations* . . . *Volume I.* Printed by Thomas Dobson. Evans 26111.

Sarjeant, Thomas. *The Federal Arithmetician, or, the Science of Numbers, Improved.* . . . Printed and Published by Thomas Dobson. Evans 26137.

————. *Select Arithmetrical Exercises; or the Application of the Elementary Principles of Arithmetic to the Mathematical Sciences, and to Various Branches of Natural Philosophy.* Printed by Thomas Dobson. Evans 26138.

Sawyer, Matthias E. *An Inaugural Dissertation: Containing an Enquiry into the Existence of the Living Principle and Causes of Animal Life. Submitted to the Examination of the Rev. John Ewing, S.T.P. Provost; the Medical Professors and Trustees of the University of Pennsylvania, for the Degree of Doctor of Medicine.* . . . [Two lines from] *Pope.* Printed by T. Dobson. Evans 26140.

Seybert, Adam. *An Inaugural Dissertation: Being an Attempt to Disprove the Doctrine of the Putrefaction of the Blood of Living Animals. Submitted to the Examination of the Rev. John Ewing, S.T.P. Provost; the Trustees, and Medical Professors of the University of Pennsylvania, for the Degree of Doctor of Medicine; on the 8th Day of May, A.D. 1793.* . . . [One line from] *Leviticus.* Printed by T. Dobson. Evans 26153.

Underwood, Michael. *A Treatise on the Dieases [sic] of Children, with General Directions for the Management of Infants from Birth.* . . . *Two Volumes in One. A New Edition, Revised and Enlarged.* [One line of Latin from] *Manill.* Printed by T. Dobson. Evans 26291.

Wallace, James Westwood. *An Inaugural Physiological Dissertation on the Catemenia.* Printed by Thomas Dobson. Evans 26414.

Zimmermann, Johann Georg, ritter von. *Solitude Considered with Respect to Its*

Influence upon the Mind and Heart. Written Originally in German by M. Zimmermann, Aulic Counselor and Physician to His Britannic Majesty at Hanover. Translated from the French of J. B. Mercier. [Six lines of French from] *La Fontaine. Le Songe d'un Habitant du Mogol, L. XI. Fable IV.* Printed for J. Crukshank, W. Young, T. Dobson, M. Carey, H. & P. Rice, B. Johnson, and P. Hall. Evans 26528.

1794

Asplund, John. *The Annual Register of the Baptist Denomination, in North-America, to the First of November, 1790. Containing an Account of the Churches and Their Constitutions, Ministers, Members, Associations, Their Plan and Settlements, Rule and Order, Proceedings and Correspondence. Also Remarks upon Practical Religion. Humbly Offered to the Public, by John Asplund.* Printed by Thomas Dobson. Evans 26583.

Cathrall, Isaac. *A Medical Sketch of the Synochus Maligna, or Malignant Contagious Fever; as It Lately Appeared in the City of Philadelphia: To Which Is Added, Some Account of the Morbid Appearances Observed After Death, on Dissection. . . .* Printed by T. Dobson. Evans 26747.

Chemin-Dupontes, Jean Baptiste. *Morality of the Sans-Culottes of Every Age, Sex, Country and Condition or, the Republican Gospel. By Chemin, Jun. Author of the Republican Alphabet and Catechism.* [One line of quotation.] *Translated by a Citizen of Philadelphia.* Printed by Thomas Dobson. Evans 26764.

Currie, William. *An Impartial Review of That Part of Dr. Rush's . . . Publication Entitled "An Account of the Bilious Remitting Yellow Fever, as It Appeared in the City of Philadelphia, in the Year 1793 . . . in Which His Opinion Is Shown to Be Erroneous; the Importation of the Disease Established; and the Wholesomeness of the City Vindicated.* Printed by Thomas Dobson. Evans 26836.

———. *A Treatise on the Synochus Icteroides, or Yellow Fever; as It Lately Appeared in the City of Philadelphia. Exhibiting a Concise View of Its Rise, Progress and Symptoms, Together with the Method of Treatment Found Most Successful; also Remarks on the Nature of the Contagion, and Directions for Preventing the Introduction of the Same Malady, in Future. . . .* Printed by Thomas Dobson. Evans 26837.

Drysdale, Thomas. *Tentamen Medicum Inaugurale Varia de Hepate Proferens.* Impensis T. Dobson. Evans 26914.

Encyclopaedia; or, A Dictionary of Arts, Sciences, and Miscellaneous Literature. . . . [Vols. XI and XII] Printed by Thomas Dobson. Evans 26943.

Extract of a Letter from a Gentleman in America to a Friend in England, on the Subject of Emigration. Printed by Thomas Dobson. Evans 26956.

Findley, William. *A Review of the Revenue System Adopted by the First Congress under the Federal Constitution; Wherein the Principles and Tendency of the Funding System and the Measures Connected with It to the End of the Second Congress Are Examined. In Thirteen Letters to a Friend. By a Citizen.* Printed by T. Dobson. Evans 26973.

Fuller, Andrew. *The Calvinistic and Socinian System. Philadelphia Gazette,* November 3, 1794. ["Just Published and for Sale by Thomas Dobson"].

Hazard, Ebenezer. *Historical Collections; Consisting of State Papers, and Other Au-*

thentic Documents; Intended as Materials for an History of the United States of America. . . . Volume II. Printed by T. Dobson. Evans 27105.

Lempriere, William. *A Tour from Gibraltar to Tangier, Sallee, Mogodore, Santa Cruz, and Tarudant; and Thence over Mount Atlas to Morocco. Including a Particular Account of the Royal Harem, & c. . . . The Third Edition, with Additions and Corrections.* Printed by T. Dobson. Evans 27216.

Medical and Philosophical Commentaries. [1788, 1789.] *By a Society of Physicians in Edinburgh.* [Two lines of Latin from] *Ovid. Volume Seventh. A New Edition.* Printed by T. Dobson. Evans 27305.

Paine, Thomas. *The Writings of Thomas Paine.* T. Dobson, W. Young, M. Carey, J. Jackson & Co., W. Woodhouse, J. Rice & Co., and W. Gibbons. [AAS].

Perrin, Jean Baptiste. *A Grammar of the French Tongue.* Printed for William Young, Mathew Carey, Henry & Patrick Rice, Thomas Dobson, and Joseph Crukshank. Evans 27493.

Philadelphia—Citizens, 1793. *Minutes of the Proceedings of the Committee Appointed on the 14th of September, 1793, by the Citizens of Philadelphia.* Printed by R. Aitken & Son, and Sold by J. Crukshank, W. Young, T. Dobson, and Other Booksellers. Evans 27501.

Priestley, Joseph. *An Appeal to the Serious and Candid Professors of Christianity on the Following Subjects, viz. I. The Use of Reason in Matters of Religion. II. The Power of Man to Do the Will of God. III. Original Sin. IV. Election and Reprobation. V. The Divinity of Christ. and VI. Atonement for Sin by the Death of Christ. . . . To Which Are Added, A Concise History of the Rise of Those Doctrines; and An Account of the Trial of Mr. Elwall, for Heresy and Blasphemy at Stafford Assizes.* [Two lines from] *I Cor. VIII, 6.—I Tim. II, 5.* Printed by Thomas Dobson. Evans 27552.

―――. *A Familiar Illustration of Certain Passages of Scripture Relating to the Power of Man to Do the Will of God, Original Sin, Election and Reprobation, the Divinity of Christ; and, Atonement for Sin by the Death of Christ. . . . "Search the Scriptures." John v. 39.* Printed by Thomas Dobson. Evans 27553.

―――. *A General View of the Arguments for the Unity of God; and Against the Divinity and Pre-existence of Christ, from Reason;—from the Scriptures;—and from History. . . .* Printed by Thomas Dobson. Evans 27554.

―――. *Letters Addressed to the Philosophers and Politicians of France, on the Subject of Religion. To Which Are Prefixed, Observations Relating to the Causes of the General Prevalence of Infidelity. . . .* [One line of Latin from] *Terence.* Printed by Thomas Dobson. Evans 27557.

―――. *Two Sermons, viz. I. The Present State of Europe Compared with Ancient Prophesies; Preached on the Fast-Day in 1794; with a Preface, Containing the Reason for the Author's Leaving England. II. The Use of Christianity; Especially in Difficult Times; Being the Author's Farewell Discourse to His Congregation at Hackney. . . .* Printed by Thomas Dobson. Evans 27559.

Rush, Benjamin. *An Account of the Bilious Remitting Yellow Fever, as It Appeared in the City of Philadelphia, in the Year 1793. . . .* Printed by Thomas Dobson. Evans 27658.

―――. *An Account of the Bilious Remitting Yellow Fever, as It Appeared in the City of Philadelphia, in the Year 1793. . . . Second Edition.* Printed by Thomas Dobson. Evans 27659.

————. *Medical Inquiries and Observations. . . . Volume I. Second American Edition.* Printed by Thomas Dobson. Evans 27660.

Smith, William Loughton. *The Speeches of Mr. Smith, of South-Carolina, Delivered in the House of Representatives of the United States, in January, 1794, on the Subject of Certain Commercial Regulations, Proposed by Mr. Madison, in the Committee of the Whole, on the Report of the Secretary of State.* Printed by Thomas Dobson. Evans 27714.

Taplin, William. *The Gentleman's Stable Directory; or, Modern System of Farriery. Comprehending All the Most Valuable Prescriptions and Approved Remedies, Accurately Proportioned and Properly Adapted to Every Known Disease to Which the Horse Is Incident; Interspersed with Occasional References to the Dangerous and Almost Obsolete Practice of Gibson, Bracken, Bartlet, Osmer, and Others; also Particular Directions for Buying, Selling, Feeding, Bleeding, Purging, and Getting into Condition for the Chase; with Experimental Remarks upon the Management of Draft Horses, Their Blemishes and Defects. To Which Is Added, a Supplement, Containing Practical Observations upon Thorn Wounds, Punctured Tendons, and Ligamentary Lameness. With Ample Instructions for Their Treatment and Cure; Illustrated by a Recital of Cases, Including a Variety of Useful Remarks. With a Successful Method of Treating the Canine Species, in That Destructive Disease Called the Distemper. . . .* Printed by T. Dobson. Evans 27771.

[Second Title.] *The Gentleman's Stable Directory; or, Modern System of Farriery. Volume the Second. Containing Experimental Remarks upon Breeding, Breaking, Shoeing, Stabling, Exercise, and Rowelling. To Which Are Added, Particular Instructions for the General Management of Hunters and Road Horses; with Concluding Observations upon the Present State of the Turf. . . .* Printed by T. Dobson. Evans 27771.

Tappan, David. *An Enquiry into the Principles and Tendency of Certain Public Measures.* Printed by Thomas Dobson. Evans 27783.

[Taylor, John.] *An Enquiry into the Principles and Tendencies of Certain Publick Measures.* Printed by Thomas Dobson. Evans 27782.

Truxton, Thomas. *Remarks, Instructions, and Examples Relating to the Latitude & Longitude; also, the Variation of the Compass, &c. &c. &c. To Which Is Annexed, a General Chart of the Globe, Where the Route Made by the Author, in Different Ships Under His Command, to the Cape of Good Hope, Batavia, Canton in China, the Different Parts of India, Europe, and the Cape de Verde Islands Are Marked, for the Purpose of Shewing the Best Tract of Sea To Meet the Most Favourable Winds, and to Avoid Those Perplexing Calms Which Too Often Attend Asiatic Voyages: Together with a Short, but General Account of Variable Winds, Trade-Winds, Monsoons, Hurricanes, Tornadoes, Tuffoons, Calms, Currents, and Particular Weather Met in Those Voyages, & c. &c. . . .* Printed by Thomas Dobson. Evans 27823.

1795

Anderson, Aeneas. *A Narrative of the British Embassy to China, in the Years 1792, 1793, and 1794; Containing the Various Circumstances of the Embassy, with Accounts of the Customs and Manners of the Chinese; and a Description of the Country, Towns, Cities, & c. & c. . . .* Printed by T. Dobson. Evans 28190.

Blumenbach, Johann Friedrich. *Elements of Physiology. . . . Translated from the Original Latin, and Interspersed with Occasional Notes. By Charles Caldwell. To Which Is Subjoined, by the Translator, an Appendix, Exhibiting a Brief and Compendious View of the Existing Discoveries Relative to the Subject of Animal Electricity. Volume I. [–II.]* Printed by Thomas Dobson. Evans 28310.

Brown, or Bruno, John. *The Elements of Medicine; or, a Translation of the Elementa Medicinae Brunonis. With Large Notes, Illustrations, and Comments. By the Author of the Original Work. Two Volumes in One. Vol. I [–II.]* Printed by Thomas Dobson. Evans 28364.

Buchan, William. *Domestic Medicine: or, A Treatise on the Prevention and Cure of Diseases, by Regimen and Simple Medicines. With an Appendix, Containing a Dispensatory for the Use of Private Practitioners . . . Revised and Adapted to the Diseases and Climate of the United States of America. By Samuel Powell Griffitts. . . .* Printed by Thomas Dobson. Evans 28366.

Callender, James Thomson. *The Political Register; or, Proceedings in the Session of Congress, Commencing November 3d, 1794, and Ending March 3d. [sic] 1795. With an Appendix, Containing a Selection of Papers Laid before Congress During That Period. . . . Vol. I [Part I–II.]* Printed by Thomas Dobson. Evans 28382.

[Cobbett, William.] *A Rub from Snub; or, A Cursory Analytical Epistle. Evening Herald,* May 2. ["Just Published and Sold by Thomas Dobson."]

Cowper, William. *The Task. A Poem. . . . The Sixth Edition.* Printed by Thomas Dobson. Evans 28497.

Encyclopaedia; or, A Dictionary of Arts, Sciences, and Miscellaneous Literature. . . . [Vols. XIII and XIV.] Printed by Thomas Dobson. Evans 28628.

Fielding, Henry. *The History of Tom Jones.* 3 Volumes. Printed at the Columbian Press, by and for Robertson and Gowan. Volumes 2 & 3 have imprint: Printed at the Columbian Press, by and for Robertson and Gowan . . . S. Campbell . . . T. Dobson and R. Campbell, Philadelphia. [AAS].

Godwin, Mrs. Mary (Wollstonecraft). *An Historical and Moral View of the . . . French Revolution.* Printed by Thomas Dobson. Evans 29916.

Hardie, James. *The American Remembrancer, and Universal Tablet of Memory: Containing a List of the Most Eminent Men, Whether in Ancient or Modern Times, with the Atchievements for Which They Have Been Particularly Distinguished: as also the Most Memorable Events in History, from the Earliest Period till the Year 1795, Classed under Distinct Heads, with Their Respective Dates. To Which Is Added, a Table, Comprehending the Periods at Which the Most Remarkable Cities and Towns Were Founded, Their Present Population, Latitude, and Longitude. The Whole Being Intended to Form a Comprehensive Abridgement of History and Chronology, Particularly of That Part Which Relates to America. . . .* Printed for the Author by Thomas Dobson. Evans 28800.

[————.] *Selectae e Veteri Testamento, Historiae; or, Select Passages from the Old Testament. To Which Is Added, An Alphabetical Vocabulary, or Dictionary of the Words Contained in This Book; Wherein the Primitives of Compound and Derivative Words Are Minutely Traced, and the Irregularities of Anomolous Nouns and Verbs Are Particularly Mentioned. For the Use of Those Who Are Entering the Study of the Latin Language. Quo Citius, Quo Facilus, Eo Melius. . . .* Printed by Thomas Dobson. Evans 28272.

[Herezet, Jean.] *Selectae et Veteri Testamento, Historiae*. Printed by Thomas Dobson. Evans 28272.

Homerus. *The Iliad of Homer*. Printed for J. Crukshank, W. Young, M. Carey, H. & P. Rice, T. Dobson, J. Ormrod, J. McCulloch, P. Stuart. Evans 28852.

Macgowan, John. *The Life of Joseph, the Son of Israel. In Eight Books. Chiefly Designed to Allure Young Minds to a Love of the Sacred Scriptures. . . . A New Edition*. Printed by Thomas Dobson. Evans 29008.

Medical Commentaries, for the Years 1780, 1781, 1782. Exhibiting a Concise View of the Latest and Most Important Discoveries in Medicine and Medical Philosophy. Collected and Published by Andrew Duncan. . . . [Two lines of Latin from] *Baglivius. Volume Forth*. Printed by Thomas Dobson. Evans 29057.

Medical Commentaries for the Years 1783–84–85. . . . Volume Fifth. Printed by Thomas Dobson. Evans 29058.

Medical Commentaries for the Years 1786, 1787. . . . Volume Sixth. Printed by Thomas Dobson. Evans 29059.

Medical Commentaries for the Years 1790, 1791. . . . Volume Eighth. Printed by Thomas Dobson. Evans 29060.

Medical Commentaries for the Years 1792, 1793. . . . Volume Ninth. Printed by Thomas Dobson. Evans 29061.

Medical Commentaries for the Year 1794. . . . Volume Tenth. Printed by Thomas Dobson. Evans 29062.

Mercier, Louis Sebastien. *Memoirs of the Year Two Thousand Five Hundred. Le Tems Present Est Gros de L'Avenir. Leibnitz. Translated from the French, by W. Hooper, M.A.* Printed by Thomas Dobson. Evans 29068.

Morse, Jedidiah. *The History of America, in Two Books. Containing, I. A General History of America. II. A Concise History of the Late Revolution. Extracted from the American Edition of the Encyclopaedia. The Second Edition*. Printed by Thomas Dobson. Evans 29111.

Paley, William. *A View of the Evidences of Christianity. In Three Parts. Part I. Of the Direct Historical Evidence of Christianity, and Wherein It Is Distinguished from the Evidence Alleged for Other Miracles. Part II. Of the Auxiliary Evidence of Christianity. Part III. A Brief Consideration of Some Popular Objections. . . .* Printed by Thomas Dobson. Evans 29274.

Priestley, Joseph. *Letters to a Philosophical Unbeliever. Part III. Containing an Answer to Mr. Paine's Age of Reason. . . . The Second Edition*. Printed by Thomas Dobson. Evans 29354.

Shultz, Benjamin. *An Inaugural Botanico-Medical Dissertation, on the Phytolaca Decandra of Linnaeus. . . .* Printed by Thomas Dobson. Evans 29510.

————. *An Oration Delivered before the Mosheimian Society, on July 23d, 1795; Being the Day Appointed for Their Yearly Meeting. . . .* Printed by T. Dobson. Evans 29511.

————. *Oration Delivered before the Mosheimian Society, on July 23d, 1795. . . .* Thomas Dobson. Bristol 9288; Evans 47593.

Sierra Leone Company. *Substance of the Report Delivered by the Court of Directors of the Sierra Leone Company, to General Court of Proprietors, on Thursday, March 27th, 1794*. Printed by Thomas Dobson. Evans 29513.

————. *Substance of the Report of the Court of Directors of the Sierra Leone Company,*

Delivered to the General Court of Proprietors, on Thursday, the 26th of February, 1795. Published by Order of the Directors. Printed by Thomas Dobson. Evans 29514.

A System of Mineralogy and Metallurgy. Extracted from the American Edition of the Encyclopaedia. Printed by Thomas Dobson. Evans 29601.

Wollstonecraft, Mary. *An Historical and Moral View of the French Revolution, and the Effect It Has Produced in Europe.* Volume I. Printed by Thomas Dobson. Evans 29916.

1796

Barrington, George. *A Voyage to New South Wales; with a Description of the Country; the Manners, Customs, Religion, & c. of the Natives, in the Vicinity of Botany Bay. . . .* Printed by Thomas Dobson. Evans 30032.

Barton, Benjamin Smith. *Papers Relative to Certain American Antiquities. By Winthrop Sargent, Esq. Secretary to the Territory of the United-States, North-West of the River-Ohio: and by Benjamin Smith Barton. . . .* Printed by Thomas Dobson. Evans 30038.

Caldwell, Charles. *An Attempt to Establish the Sameness of Three Phenomena of Fever (Principally Confined to Infants and Children), Described by Medical Writers Under the Several Names of Hydrocephalus Internus, Cynanche Trachealis, and Diarrhoea Infantum. . . .* Printed by Thomas Dobson. Evans 30148.

[Campbell, George.] *The Four Gospels, Translated from the Greek. With Preliminary Dissertations, and Notes Critical and Explanatory. . . .* Printed by Thomas Dobson. Evans 30086; O'Callaghan 52.

Chaptal de Chantiloup, Jean Antoine Claude. *Elements of Chemistry.* Printed by Lang & Ustick, for Selve, M. Carey, J. Crukshank, H. & P. Rice, T. Dobson, R. Campbell, & J. Ormrod. Evans 30183.

[Dickinson, John.] *A Fragment.* Printed by Thomas Dobson. Evans 30438.

Ellicott, Andrew. *Several Methods by Which Meridianal Lines May Be Found with Ease and Accuracy: Recommended to the Attention of the Surveyors in the United States. . . .* Printed by Thomas Dobson. Evans 30385.

Encyclopaedia; or, A Dictionary of Arts, Sciences, and Miscellaneous Literature. . . . [Vols. XV and XVI.] Printed by Thomas Dobson. Evans 30390.

Friends, Society of. *The Following Vindication of the Character of George Fox, from the Account Given of Him in the Encyclopaedia, Vol. XV. Page 734, Was Drawn up by the Society Called Quakers. . . .* [Printed by Thomas Dobson.] Bristol 9552.

[Hardie, James.] *Selectae et Veteri Testamento Historiae, or Select Passages from the Old Testament. To Which Is Added, An Alphabetical Vocabulary or Dictionary of the Words Contained in This Book Wherein the Primitives of Compound and Derivative Words Are Minutely Traced and the Irregularities of Anomalous Nouns and Verbs Are Particularly Mentioned. For the Use of Those Who Are Entering the Study of the Latin Language. . . .* Printed and Sold by Thomas Dobson. Evans 30069.

Houdet, Rene. *A Treatise on Morality: Chiefly Designed for the Instruction of Youth. . . .* Printed for the Author by Thomas Dobson. Evans 30594.

Hurdis, James. *Poems. . . . Viz.—The Village Curate, Adriano; or. The First of June, and Tears of Affection. To Which Is Added, The Bouquet, a Collection of Scattered Pieces, by the Same Author.* Printed by T. Dobson. Evans 30613.

[Second Title.] *The Village Curate, a Poem. . . . The Second Edition Corrected.* Printed by T. Dobson.

[Third Title.] *Adriano; or, The First of June, a Poem. By the Author of the Village Curate. . . .* Printed by T. Dobson.

[Fourth Title.] *Tears of Affection, a Poem, Occasioned by the Death of a Sister Tenderly Beloved. By the Author of the Village Curate.* Printed by T. Dobson.

[Fifth Title.] *The Bouquet, a Collection of Scattered Pieces. By the Author of the Village Curate.* Printed by T. Dobson.

Lewis, William. *The Edinburgh New Dispensatory: Containing, I. The Elements of Pharmaceutical Chemistry. II. The Materia Medica; or, an Account of the Different Substances Employed in Medicine. III. The Pharmaceutical Preparations and Medicinal Compositions of the Latest Editions of London and Edinburgh Pharmacopoeias. The Whole Interspersed with Practical Cautions and Observations; and Enriched with the Latest Discoveries in Natural History, Chemistry, and Medicine; with New Tables of Elective Attractions of Antinomial and Mercurial Preparations. & c, and Several Copperplates of the Most venient Furnaces, and Principal Pharmaceutical Instruments. Being an Improvement of the New Dispensatory by Dr. Lewis.* [By John Rotheram.] *The Fourth Edition; with Many Alterations, Corrections, and Additions: and a Full and Clear Account of the New Chemical Doctrines Published by Mr. Lavoisier.* Printed by Thomas Dobson. Evans 30693.

Macgowan, John. *The Shaver's New Sermon for the Fast Day. Respectfully Inscribed to the Rev. and Laborious Clergy of the Church of England, by Their Humble Servant, Pasquin Shavelock, Esq. Shaver Extraordinary.* [Two lines from] *Peter Pinder. Sixth Edition. To Which Is Added Reflections on French Atheism and on English Christianity.* Printed by Thomas Dobson, for Griffiths and Rhees. Evans 30724.

[Second Title.] *Reflections on French Atheism and on English Christianity. By William Richards. . . . Third Edition with Additions.* Printed by Thomas Dobson, for Morgan J. Rhees. Evans 30724[a].

Priestley, Joseph. *Considerations on the Doctrine of Phlogiston and the Decomposition of Water. . . .* [One line of Latin from] *Horace.* Printed by Thomas Dobson. Evans 31049.

———. *Discourses Relating to the Evidence of Revealed Religion, Delivered in the Church of the Universalists at Philadelphia 1796. . . .* [Four lines from] *I. Peter III. 15. Vol. I.* Printed by Thomas Dobson. Evans 31050.

———. *Unitarianism Explained and Defended in a Discourse Delivered in the Church of the Universalists, at Philadelphia, 1796.* [Six Lines of Scripture Text]. Philadelphia: Printed by John Thompson [for Thomas Dobson, as Proprietor]. Evans 31055.

Richards, William. *Reflections on French Atheism.* Printed by Thomas Dobson. Evans 30724.

Rush, Benjamin. *Medical Inquiries and Observations: Containing an Account of the Bilious Remitting and Intermitting Yellow Fever, as It Appeared in Philadelphia in the Year 1794. Together with an Inquiry into the Proximate Cause of Fever: and a Defence of Blood-Letting as a Remedy for Certain Diseases. . . . Volume IV.* Printed by Thomas Dobson. Evans 31144.

Sargent, Winthrop. *Papers Relative to Certain American Antiquities.* Printed by Thomas Dobson. Evans 30038.

Smith, Adam. *An Inquiry into the Nature and Causes of the Wealth of Nations. . . . In Three Volumes. Vol. I [–III.] A New Edition.* Printed by Thomas Dobson. Evans 31196.

Stewart, John, "Walking." *Prospectus of a Series of Lectures, or a New Practical System of Human Reason, Calculated to Discharge the Mind from a Great Mass of, Error, and to Facilitate Its Labour in the Approximation of Moral Truth, Divested of All Metaphysical Perplexities and Nullities; Accomodated [sic] to the Most Ordinary Capacities, in a Simple Method, Which Dispenses Equally with the Study of the College, or the Lecture of Musty Libraries. . . .* Printed by Thomas Dobson. Evans 31237.

Williams, Helen Maria. *Letters Containing a Sketch of the Politics of France.* Printed for Mathew Carey, William Young, Thomas Dobson, Henry & Patrick Rice, and John Ormrod. Evans 31634.

1797

Addison, Alexander. *Causes and Error of Complaints and Jealousy of the Administration of the Government. Being a Charge to Grand Juries of the Counties of the Fifth Circuit, of the State of Pennsylvania, at March Session, 1797. . . .* Printed by T. Dobson. Evans 31694.

Aikin, John, and Barbauld, Anna Letitia (Aikin). *Evenings at Home; or, The Juvenile Budget Opened. Consisting of a Variety of Miscellaneous Pieces, for the Instruction and Amusement of Young Persons. Vol. I. [–VI.] Second Edition.* Printed by Thomas Dobson. Evans 31698; Welch 31698.

Beddoes, Thomas. *Observations on the Nature and Cure of Calculus, Sea Scurvey, Consumption, Catarrh, and Fever: Together with Conjectures upon Several Other Subjects of Physiology and Pathology. . . .* Printed by T. Dobson. Evans 31782.

Buchan, William. *Domestic Medicine: or, A Treatise on the Prevention and Cure of Diseases, by Regimen and Simple Medicines. With an Appendix, Containing a Dispensatory for the Use of Private Practitioners. . . . Revised and Adapted to the Diseases and Climate of the United States of America, by Samuel Powell Grifitts. . . . Second Edition.* Printed by Thomas Dobson. Evans 31886.

Campbell, Donald. *A Journey over Land to India, Partly by a Route Never Gone before by Any European, by Donald Campbell. . . . In a Series of Letters to His Son. Comprehending His Shipwreck and Imprisonment with Hyder Ali and His Subsequent Negociations [sic] and Transactions in the East.* Printed by T. Dobson. Evans 31911.

A Compendious History of Rome, with an Appendix, Containing Sketches of the History of Carthage, Macedon, Spain, Pontus, Cimbri, Gaul, Numantia, England, Germany, Parthia, Munda, Philippi, Rhodes, Sicily, and Syracuse. As Connected with Roman History. Printed by Thomas Dobson. Evans 31965.

Darwin, Erasmus. *Zoonomia; or, The Laws of Organic Life. . . . A New Edition; with an Introductory Address, and a Short Appendix, by Charles Caldwell. . . . Vol. I. [–II.]* Printed by T. Dobson. Evans 32017.

Decambon, Maria Gertruida van de Werken. *Letters and Conversations between Several Young Ladies.* Printed by Thomas Dobson. Evans 32027.

Dobson, Thomas. *First Lessons for Children.* [Volume First—Second.] Printed by Thomas Dobson. Evans 32054.

————. *The Holiday, or Children's Social Amusement*. Printed by Thomas Dobson. Evans 32055.

————. *Pleasing Instructions for Young Minds*. Printed by Thomas Dobson. Evans 32056.

————. *Proposal of Thomas Dobson, for Printing by Subscription on a Very Large and Beautiful New Type, and Superfine Paper: An Elegant Edition of the Sacred Scriptures....* Thomas Dobson. ND 0302497.

Encyclopaedia; or, A Dictionary of Arts, Sciences, and Miscellaneous Literature.... [Vol. XVII.] Printed by Thomas Dobson. Evans 32088.

Gilpin, William. *An Account of a New Poor-House, Erected in the Parish of Boldre, in New Forest, near Lymington*. Printed by Thomas Dobson. Evans 32194.

Hamilton, Alexander. *Outlines of the Theory and Practice of Midwifery. . . . A New Edition*. Printed by Thomas Dobson. Evans 32221.

 [Second Title.] *A Set of Anatomical Tables, with Explanations, and an Abridgement of the Practice of Midwifery; with a View to Illustrate a Treatise on That Subject, and a Collection of Cases. By William Smellie....* Printed by Thomas Dobson. Evans 32221.

Hosack, Alexander, Jr. *History of the Yellow Fever, as It Appeared in the City of New-York, in 1795....* Printed by Thomas Dobson. Evans 32282.

Maclean, John. *Two Lectures on Combustion: Supplementary to a Course of Lectures on Chemistry, Read at Nassau-Hall. Containing an Examination of Dr. Priestley's Consideration of the Doctrine of Phlogiston, and the Decomposition of Water....* Printed by T. Dobson. Evans 32412.

Medical Commentaries, for the Year 1795. Exhibiting a Concise View of the Latest and Most Important Discoveries in Medicine and Medical Philosophy. Collected and Published by Andrew Duncan.... [Two lines of Latin from] *Baglivius. Volume Tenth.* [sic: Eleventh.] Printed by Thomas Dobson. Evans 32459.

Pain, William. *The Practical House Carpenter; or, Youth's Instructor.... The Whole Illustrated, and Made Perfectly Easy, by One-Hundred and Forty-Eight Copper-Plates, with Explanations to Each.... The Sixth Edition, with Additions*. Printed by Thomas Dobson. Evans 32628.

Percival, Thomas. *A Father's Instructions; Consisting of Moral Tales, Fables, and Reflections; Designed to Promote the Love of Virtue, a Taste for Knowledge, and an Early Acquaintance with the Works of Nature.... The Ninth Edition*. Printed by T. Dobson. Evans 32666.

Priestley, Joseph. *Discourses Relating to the Evidences of Revealed Religion, Delivered in Philadelphia....* [Two lines from] *1 Pet. III. 15*. Printed by Thomas Dobson. Evans 32715.

————. *Dr. Priestley Having Continued His History of the Christian Church from the Fall of the Western Roman Empire to the Reformation by Luther, Is Desirous of Publishing It*. Printed by Thomas Dobson. Evans 32716.

————. *Letters to Mr. Volney, Occasioned by a Work of His Entitled Ruins, and by His Letter to the Author....* [One line of Latin from] *Ovid*. Printed by Thomas Dobson. Evans 32718.

————. *Observations on the Doctrine of Phlogiston and the Decomposition of Water. Part the Second...* Printed by Thomas Dobson. Evans 32719.

————. *Observations on the Increase of Infidelity ... The Third Edition. To Which Are*

Added, Animadversions on the Writings of Several Modern Unbelievers, and Especially the Ruins of Mr. Volney. [Three Lines of French from] *Bonnet.* Philadelphia: Printed [by John Thompson] for Thomas Dobson. Evans 32721.

———. *An Outline of the Evidences of Revealed Religion.* . . . [Three lines of French from] *Bonnet.* Printed by T. Dobson. Evans 32722.

———. *Observations on the Increase of Infidelity.* . . . *The Third Edition. To Which Are Added, Animadversions on the Writings of Several Modern Unbelievers, and Especially the Ruins of Mr. Volney.* Printed [by John Thompson] for Thomas Dobson. Evans 32721.

Purves, James. *Observations on Doctor Priestley's Doctrines of Philosophical Necessity and Materialism.* . . . Printed by Thomas Dobson. Evans 32732.

Rush, Benjamin. *Medical Inquiries and Observations.* . . . *Volume II. A New [second American] Edition.* Printed by Thomas Dobson. Evans 32784.

United States Congress. *Acts Passed at the First [–Second] Session of the Fourth Congress.* . . . Printed by Thomas Dobson. Bristol 10151; Evans 48291.

1798

Campbell, John. *The Complete Soldier's Pocket Companion; or, A Plain and Easy Method of Military Discipline. Containing: The New System of Manual and Platoon Exercise, Now Practiced in the Army of Great-Britain: Together with Filing, Grounding, Advancing, Handling, Easing and Reversing of Arms, with Field Manoeuvres, Camp and Garrison Duty. To Which Are Added, Forms of Morning Reports, Monthly Returns, Muster Rolls, Returns of Arms, Accoutrements, Cloathing, & c. with a Roll of Country, Age, Size and Servitude. Also, the Field Piece and Great Gun Exercise, with Some Extracts and Observations from Baron Steuben's Publication.* . . . Printed by Thomas Dobson. Evans 33489.

Collin, Nicholas. *Philological View of Some Very Ancient Words in Several Languages.* Printed by Thomas Dobson. Evans 33534.

Encyclopaedia; or, A Dictionary of Arts, Sciences, and Miscellaneous Literature. . . . [Vol. XVIII.] Printed by Thomas Dobson. Evans 33676.

Fenn, Lady Eleanor Frere. *Fables in Monosyllables by Mrs. Teachwell. To Which Are Added Morals in Dialogues Between a Mother and Children.* [Six lines of French from] *Rousseau.* Printed by Thomas Dobson. Evans 33728.

[Second Title.] *Morals to a Set of Fables, by Mrs. Teachwell. The Morals in Dialogues between a Mother and Children. In Two Sets.* Printed by Thomas Dobson. Evans 33728.

Goldsmith, Oliver. *Dr. Goldsmith's Roman History, Abridged by Himself. For the Use of Schools.* Printed by Thomas Dobson. Evans 33805.

Morse, Jedidiah. *The History of America, in Two Books. Containing, I. A General History of America. II. A Concise History of the Late Revolution. Extracted from the American Edition of the Encyclopaedia. The Third Edition.* Printed by Thomas Dobson. Evans 34147.

Percival, Thomas. *Moral and Literary Dissertations; Chiefly Intended as the Sequel to A Father's Instructions. The Second Edition, Revised and Much Enlarged.* . . . Printed by Thomas Dobson. Evans 34342.

Philadelphia College of Physicians. *Facts and Observations Relative to the Nature and*

Origin of the Pestilential Fever Which Prevailed in This City, in 1793, 1797, and 1798. . . . Printed by Thomas Dobson. Evans 34355.

———. *Proceedings of the College of Physicians of Philadelphia, Relative to the Prevention of the Introduction and Spreading of Contagious Diseases.* Printed by Thomas Dobson. Evans 34356.

Robison, John. *Proof of a Conspiracy Against All the Religions and Governments of Europe, Carried on in the Secret Meetings of Free Masons, Illuminati, and Reading Societies. Collected from Good Authorities, by John Robison. . . . The Third Edition. To Which Is Added a Postscript.* Printed for T. Dobson. Evans 34477.

Rush, Benjamin. *Medical Inquiries and Observations: Containing an Account of the Yellow Fever, as It Appeared in Philadelphia in 1797, and Observations upon the Nature and Cure of the Gout and Hydrophobia. . . . Volume V.* Printed by Budd and Bartram, for Thomas Dobson. Evans 34496.

Thrum, Tam [pseudonym]. *Look Before Ye Loup; or, A Healin' Sa' for the Crackit Crowns of Country Politicians. Tam Thrum, an Auld Weaver.* Printed by Thomas Dobson. Evans 34661.

United States. *Abstract of the Stamp Law. Treasury Department, March 1, 1798. Public Notice Is Hereby Given. . . . Thomas Dobson, at the Stone House, No. 41 South Second-Street, Philadelphia, Has for Sale an Assortment of the Above Stamps, also a Large and Very General Assortment of Stationery.* Printed by Thomas Dobson. Evans 34874.

United States, President, 1797–1801 (John Adams). *Message . . . April 3d, 1798.* Printed by T. Dobson and J. Ormrod. Evans 34814.

1799

American Philosophical Society. *Transactions of the American Philosophical Society, Held at Philadelphia, for Promoting Useful Knowledge. Volume IV.* Printed by Thomas Dobson. Evans 35106.

Brown, Charles Brockden. *Arthur Mervyn; or, Memoirs of the Year 1793. By the Author of Wieland and Ormond, or The Secret Witness.* Printed and Published by H. Maxwell . . . and Sold by Messrs. T. Dobson, R. Campbell, H. and P. Rice, A. Dickins, and the Principal Booksellers in the Neighboring States. [AAS].

———. *Edgar Huntly; or, A Memoir of a Sleep-Walker. By the Author of Arthur Mervyn, Wieland, Ormond, & c. Vol. I [–III].* Printed by H. Maxwell . . . and Sold by Thomas Dobson, Asbury Dickins, and the Principal Booksellers. [AAS].

Chisholm, Colin. *An Essay on the Malignant Pestilential Fever Introduced into the West Indian Islands from Boullam, on the Coast of Guinea, as It Appeared in 1793 and 1794. . . . To Which Is Annexed, A Description of the American Yellow Fever, Which Prevailed at Charleston in 1748. In a Letter from Dr. John Lining.* Printed for Thomas Dobson. Evans 35302.

[Clerk, John.] *A System of Seamanship, and Naval Tactics. Extracted from the Encyclopaedia, Published by Thomas Dobson. . . .* Printed by Thomas Dobson. Evans 36393; ND 0302500.

Dobson, Thomas. *Letters on the Existence and Character of the Deity, and on the Moral State of Man.* Printed for Thomas Dobson. Evans 35413.

Helme, Elizabeth. *Instructive Rambles in London, and the Adjacent Villages. Designed to Amuse the Mind, and Improve the Understanding of Youth.* . . . Printed by Budd and Bartram, for Thomas Dobson. Evans 35610.

The Holy Bible, Containing the Old and New Testaments: Translated out of the Original Tongues: and with Three Former Translations Diligently Compared and Revised. With Marginal References. Printed for Thomas Dobson. Evans 35188.

Lining, John. *A Description of the American Yellow Fever, Which Prevailed at Charleston, in South Carolina, in the Year 1748.* . . . Printed for Thomas Dobson. Evans 35733.

The New-England Primer; Much Improved. Containing, a Variety of Easy Lessons, for Attaining the True Reading of English. Printed by T. Dobson. Evans 35876.

Rush, Benjamin. *Observations upon the Origin of the Malignant Bilious, or Yellow Fever in Philadelphia.* . . . Printed by Budd and Bartram, for Thomas Dobson. Evans 36253.

———. *A Second Address to the Citizens of Philadelphia, Containing Additional Proofs of the Domestic Origin of the Malignant Bilious, or Yellow Fever.* . . . Printed by Budd and Bartram, for Thomas Dobson. Evans 36254.

———. *Three Lectures upon Animal Life, Delivered in the University of Pennsylvania.* . . . Printed by Budd and Bartram, for Thomas Dobson. Evans 36255.

Sierra Leone Company. *Substance of the Reports Delivered by the Court of Directors of the Sierra Leone Company.* . . . *To Which Is Prefixed Memoirs of Naimbanna, an African Prince.* Printed for Thomas Dobson. Evans 36310.

1800

Dobson, Thomas. *Proposals for Publishing by Subscription an Elegant Edition of the New Testament.* Thomas Dobson. ND 0302496.

———. *Thomas Dobson . . . Having Happily Completed the American Edition of the Encyclopaedia . . . Have [sic] Been Urged to Offer a Proposal for Publishing a Supplement.* . . . Thomas Dobson. ND 0302502.

Hall, Robert. *Modern Infidelity.* "This day is Published by Thomas Dobson." *Poulson's American Daily Advertiser,* Nov. 10.

More, Hannah. *Strictures on the Modern System of Female Education. With a View of the Principles and Conduct Prevalent Among Women of Rank and Fortune.* . . . Printed by Budd and Bartram, for Thomas Dobson. Evans 37996.

A New System of Chemistry, Comprehending the Latest Discoveries and Improvements of the Science, Illustrated with Copper-Plates. Printed for Thomas Dobson. Evans 38072.

Supplement to the Encyclopaedia; or, A Dictionary of Arts, Sciences, and Miscellaneous Literature. In Three Volumes. Illustrated with Copperplates. [Vol. I, Pt. 1, Evans 38592 (amended); Vol. I, Pt. 2, Bristol 162] Printed by Budd and Bartram, for Thomas Dobson.

1801

Andrews, John. *A Compend of Logick; for Use of the University of Pennsylvania.* Printed by T. Dobson. Shaw and Shoemaker 68.

Bordley, John Beale. *Essays and Notes on Husbandry and Rural Affairs . . . The Second*

Edition. Printed by Budd and Bartram, for Thomas Dobson. Shaw and Shoemaker 210.

Burns, Robert. *The Works of Robert Burns.* . . . Printed by Budd and Bartram, for Thomas Dobson. Shaw and Shoemaker 260.

Dobson, Thomas. *A Catalogue of Books, Consisting of a Selection of Valuable Works in Various Branches of Literature.* Printed by Thomas Dobson. *Philadelphia Gazette,* October 7, 1801. ["This Day is Published."]

New Testament. Published by Thomas Dobson. O'Callaghan; *Portfolio* 1: 51 (February 14, 1801). ["Mr. Dobson's elegant edition of the New Testament is in the press, and in a state of great forwardness"; see also *Poulson's American Daily Advertiser* (December 6), "an Elegant Edition of the NEW TESTAMENT."]

Raffald, Mrs. Elizabeth (Whitaker). *The Experienced English Housekeeper, for the Use and Ease of Ladies.* . . . *Twelfth Edition.* Printed for Thomas Dobson, by John Bioren.

Supplement to the Encyclopaedia; or, A Dictionary of Arts, Sciences, and Miscellaneous Literature. . . . [Vol. II, Pt. 1.] Printed by Budd and Bartram, for Thomas Dobson. *Philadelphia Gazette,* May 16, 1801.

1802

American Philosophical Society. *Transactions of the American Philosophical Society, Held at Philadelphia, for Promoting Useful Knowledge. Volume V.* Printed by Budd and Bartram, for Thomas Dobson. Shaw and Shoemaker 1755.

Bell, Benjamin. *A System of Surgery.* . . . *Second Edition.* Printed by Budd and Bartram, for Thomas Dobson. Shaw and Shoemaker 1859.

Dobson, Thomas. *Letters on the Existence and Character of the Deity, and on the Moral State of Man. Part II.* Printed by Thomas Dobson. Shaw and Shoemaker 2149.

Kerr, Patrick. *An Investigation into the Properties of the Liriodendron Tulipifera or Poplar Tree, Philadelphia Gazette,* November 24, 1802. ["This Day is Published."]

Mace, John. *The Proximate Cause of Disease.* Printed by Budd and Bartram, for Thomas Dobson. Shaw and Shoemaker 2562.

Supplement to the Encyclopaedia; or, A Dictionary of Arts, Sciences, and Miscellaneous Literature. . . . [Vol. II. Pt. 2.] Printed by Budd and Bartram, for Thomas Dobson. *Philadelphia Gazette,* November 25, 1802.

A Treatise of the Construction of Logarithms; to Which Are Added, Tables of Logarithms, Sines and Tangents. From the Encyclopaedia. Printed by Thomas Dobson. Shaw and Shoemaker 3177.

Underwood, Michael. *A Treatise on the Diseases of Children.* . . . *A New Edition, Revised and Enlarged.* Printed by Thomas Dobson. Shaw and Shoemaker 3188.

1803

Ellicott, Andrew. *The Journal of Andrew Ellicott.* . . . Printed by Budd and Bartram, for Thomas Dobson. Shaw and Shoemaker 4147.

[Hardie, James.] *Selectae e Veteri Testamenti, Historiae; or, Select Passages from the Old Testament.* . . . Printed by Thomas Dobson. Shaw and Shoemaker 3816.

[Heuzet, Jean.] *Selectae et Veteri Testemento Historiae*. Printed by Thomas Dobson. [AAS].

Krafft, Michael. *The American Distiller*. Printed for Thomas Dobson, Archibald Bartram, Printer. [AAS].

Supplement to the Encyclopaedia; or, A Dictionary of Arts, Sciences, and Miscellaneous Literature.... [Vol. III.] Printed by Budd and Bartram, for Thomas Dobson. Shaw and Shoemaker 4162. [Item 4161 incorrectly notes 1803 as the date of publication for the first eighteen volumes as well.]

Thomson, Thomas. *A New System of Chemistry*.... Printed by T. Dobson. Shaw and Shoemaker 5164.

1804

B., S. *The Rich Man and Lazarus. To Which Is Added, The Wolf and Hireling. The Straight Gate & Narrow Way. The Wedding Guests*.... Printed by Thomas Dobson. Shaw and Shoemaker 5747.

Clavigero, Abbe D. Francesco Saverio. *The History of Mexico, Collected from Spanish and Mexican Historians, from Manuscripts, and Ancient Paintings of the Indians*.... *Translated from the Original Italian, by Charles Cullen, Esq*. Printed by Budd and Bartram, for Thomas Dobson. Shaw and Shoemaker 6034.

Dobson, Thomas. *Index to the Bible, in Which the Various Subjects Which Occur in the Scriptures Are Alphabetically Arranged*.... Printed by Archibald Bartram, for Thomas Dobson. Shaw and Shoemaker 6171.

———. *Letters on the Existence and Character of the Deity*.... Printed by Thomas Dobson. Shaw and Shoemaker 6172.

Krafft, Michael. *The American Distiller*.... Printed by Archibald Bartram, for Thomas Dobson. Shaw and Shoemaker 6606.

1805

Bible. *Psalms, Carefully Suited to the Christian Worship in the United States of America*. Printed by Archibald Bartram, for Thomas Dobson. Shaw and Shoemaker 8006.

Buchan, William. *Domestic Medicine: or a Treatise on the Prevention and Cure of Diseases*.... *A New Edition*. Printed by A. Bartram, for Thomas Dobson. Shaw and Shoemaker 8097.

Coxe, John Redman, ed. *The Philadelphia Medical Museum*. Volume I. T. Dobson. American Periodical Series II, Reel 38.

Eddowes, Ralph. *Account of the Wheat Moth or Virginia Fly*.... Printed by Dobson. Shaw and Shoemaker 8370.

[Fyfe, Andrew.] *A Compendious System of Anatomy*.... Printed by Archibald Bartram, for Thomas Dobson. [AAS].

[Sansom, Joseph.] *Letters from Europe*.... Printed by A. Bartram, for T. Dobson. Shaw and Shoemaker 9311.

Savin, Richard. *An Inaugural Essay on the Effects of External Cold, in the Cure of Fevers*.... Printed by Archibald Bartram, for Thomas Dobson. Shaw and Shoemaker 9318.

1806

Beddoes, Thomas. *Observations on . . . Writings of John Brown.* Printed by T. Dobson. Shaw and Shoemaker 9944.

Bell, Benjamin. *A System of Surgery . . . Edition Third.* Printed by Archibald Bartram, for Thomas Dobson. Shaw and Shoemaker 9954.

[Brown, or Bruno, John.] *The Elements of Medicine. . . . With Observations on the Character and Writings of the Author, by Thomas Beddoes. . . . New Edition.* Printed by A. Bartram, for Thomas Dobson. Shaw and Shoemaker 10004.

Buchan, William. *Domestic Medicine. . . . A New Edition.* Printed by A. Bartram, for T. Dobson. Shaw and Shoemaker 10049.

College of Physicians. *Additional Facts and Observations Relative to the Nature and Origin of the Pestilential Fever. . . .* Printed by A. Bartram, for Thomas Dobson. Shaw and Shoemaker 10176.

Coxe, John Redman. *The American Dispensatory, Containing the Operations of Pharmacy; Together with the Natural, Chemical, Pharmaceutical and Medical History of the Different Substances Employed in Medicine. . . .* Printed by A. Bartram, for Thomas Dobson. Shaw and Shoemaker 10222.

———, ed. *The Philadelphia Medical Museum.* Volume II. T. Dobson. American Periodical Series II, Reel 38.

Hamilton, Alexander. *Management of Female Complaints, and of Children in Early Infancy. Revised and Enlarged by His Son, Dr. James Hamilton. . . .* Reprinted by Archibald Bartram, for Thomas Dobson. Shaw and Shoemaker 10514.

———. *Outlines of the Theory and Practice of Midwifery. . . . A New Edition.* Printed by A. Bartram, for Thomas Dobson. Shaw and Shoemaker 10515.

Huber, Marie. *The World Unmask'd; or, The Philosopher the Greatest Cheat. In Thirty-Four Dialogues. A New Edition. Translated from the French.* Printed by Archibald Bartram, for Thomas Dobson. Shaw and Shoemaker 10598; 11901.

Smellie, William. *A Set of Anatomical Tables. . . .* Printed by A. Bartram, for Thomas Dobson. [Bound with Alexander Hamilton's *Theory and Practice of Midwifery.*] Shaw and Shoemaker 11371.

The Sonship of Jesus Defended in Two Letters. Printed by T. Dobson. Shaw and Shoemaker 11398.

Truxton, Thomas. *A Few Extracts, from the Best Authors, on Naval Tactics, to Be Found Also in Dobson's Encyclopaedia. . . .* Printed by A. Bartram, for Thomas Dobson. Shaw and Shoemaker 11477.

Vyse, Charles. *The Key to the Tutor's Guide. Ninth Edition.* Printed by Joseph Crukshank, and Sold by P. Byrne, M. Carey, T. & W. Bradford, James Crukshank, T. Dobson, Kimber, Conrad, & Co. and John McCulloch. [AAS].

———. *The Tutor's Guide . . . The Thirteenth Edition.* Printed by Joseph Crukshank, and Sold by P. Byrne, M. Carey, T. & W. Bradford, James Crukshank, T. Dobson, Kimber, Conrad, & Co. and John McCulloch. [AAS].

1807

Baudelocque, Jean Louis. *An Abridgment of Mr. Heath's Translation of Baudelocque's Midwifery. . . .* Printed by Bartram and Reynolds, for Thomas Dobson. Shaw and Shoemaker 12092.

Bible. *The Psalms of David Imitated in the Language of the New Testament and Applied to the Christian State and Worship.* . . . Printed by Bartram and Reynolds, for Thomas Dobson. Shaw and Shoemaker 12137.

Chaptal de Chanteloup, Jean Antoine Claude. *Elements of Chemistry.* Published by Benjamin & Thomas Kite. Sold also by Thomas Dobson, and B. B. Hopkins & Co Philadelphia. . . . [AAS].

Coxe, John Redman, ed. *The Philadelphia Medical Museum.* Volume III. T. Dobson. American Periodical Series II, Reel 38.

Dobson, Thomas. *Thoughts on the Scripture Account of Faith in Jesus, and Life through His Name.* . . . Printed by the Author. Shaw and Shoemaker 12442; ND 0302503.

[Feldborg, Andreas Andersen.] *A Tour in Zealand, in the Year 1802; with an Historical Sketch of the Battle of Copenhagen.* . . . Printed by Bartram and Reynolds, for Thomas Dobson. Shaw and Shoemaker 12555.

Jones, Samuel. *A Century Sermon; Delivered in Philadelphia, at the Opening of the Philadelphia Baptist Association, October 6th, 1807.* . . . Printed by Bartram and Reynolds, for Thomas Dobson. Shaw and Shoemaker 12845.

Medford, Macall. *Oil without Vinegar, and Dignity without Pride; or British, American, and West-India Interests Considered. Second Edition.* Printed by Thomas Dobson. Shaw and Shoemaker 13049.

Rigg, Edward. *The Right, Duty, and Importance of Free Inquiry into Matters of Religion.* Printed by Bartram & Reynolds, for Thomas Dobson. Shaw and Shoemaker 13503.

1808

Coxe, John Redman. *Philadelphia Medical Dictionary.* . . . Printed by Thomas and George Palmer, for Thomas Dobson. Shaw and Shoemaker 14791.

———, ed. *The Philadelphia Medical Museum.* Volume IV. T. Dobson. American Periodical Series II, Reel 38.

Cutbush, Edward. *Observations on the Means of Preserving the Health of Soldiers and Sailors; and on the Duties of the Medical Department of the Army and Navy: with Remarks on Hospitals and Their Internal Arrangement.* . . . Printed by Fry and Kammerer, for Thomas Dobson. Shaw and Shoemaker 14816.

Dobson, Thomas. *Thoughts on the Scripture Account of Faith in Jesus.* Thomas Dobson. ND 0302504.

Law, Edmund. *Reflections on the Life and Character of Christ.* Printed for Thomas Dobson, Reynolds and Palmer, Printers. [AAS].

[Morse, Jedidiah.] *The History of America, in Two Books; Containing, 1st. A General History of America. 2nd. A Concise History of the Late Revolution.* . . . Printed by Bartram and Reynolds, for Thomas Dobson. Shaw and Shoemaker 15240.

Rush, Benjamin. *Directions for Preserving the Health of Soldiers. Addressed to the Officers of the Army of the United States.* . . . Printed by Fry and Kammerer, for Thomas Dobson. Shaw and Shoemaker 16113.

1809

Buchan, William. *Domestic Medicine.* . . . *Revised* . . . *by Samuel Powell Griffiths [sic].* . . . Printed by Fry and Kammerer, for Thomas Dobson. Shaw and Shoemaker 17101.

Coxe, John Redman, ed. *The Philadelphia Medical Museum.* Volume V. T. Dobson. American Periodical Series II, Reel 38.

[Eddowes, Ralph.] *On the Early Treatment of Children; a Discourse Delivered at the Place of Worship of the First Unitarian Society in Philadelphia, April 9th, 1809. . . .* Printed by T. and G. Palmer, for Thomas Dobson. Shaw and Shoemaker 17423.

[Marcet, Mrs. Jane (Haldimand).] *Conversations on Chymistry. 2 volumes in 1. The Second American Edition.* Printed for and Sold by James Humphreys; Hopkins & Earle, Kimber & Conrad, B. & T. Kite; and Thomas Dobson; also White, Burditt & Co. Boston. J. Humphreys, Printer. [AAS].

Unitarian Pieces and Tracts. No. viii. Containing 1. The Importance of Adhering to First Principles in Religion (Concluded.) 2. A Search after Truth, Being a Dialogue Between Criton and Philo. 3. Trinity Twin-Sister to Transubstantiation. 4. Thoughts on the Unity of God. 5. On the Existence of the Devil. Printed by Thomas and George Palmer, for Thomas Dobson. Shaw and Shoemaker 18803.

1810

Coxe, John Redman. *The American Dispensatory. . . . Second Edition.* Printed by Fry and Kammerer, for Thomas Dobson. Shaw and Shoemaker 19883.

————, ed. *The Philadelphia Medical Museum.* New Series. Volume V. T. Dobson. American Periodical Series II, Reel 186.

Eclectic Repository and Analytical Review, Medical and Philosophical. Edited by a Society of Physicians. 10 vols. Published by Thomas Dobson; Fry and Kammerer, Printers. [Dobson continued as publisher until 1820.] American Periodical Series II, Reels 116–18.

[Eddowes, Ralph.] *Unity of God, and the Salvation of Sinners by His Free Grace.* Printed by Thomas Dobson. Shaw and Shoemaker 21874.

Murray, Adolphus. *A Description of the Arteries of the Human Body. . . .* Printed by Fry and Kammerer, for Thomas Dobson. Shaw and Shoemaker 20796.

O'Conway, Matthias James. *Hispano-Anglo Grammar. . . .* Printed by Fry and Kammerer, for Thomas Dobson. Shaw and Shoemaker 20943.

Philadelphia. Pennsylvania. First Unitarian Church. *A Collection of Pieces and Tracts. . . .* Printed by T. and G. Palmer, for Thomas Dobson. Shaw and Shoemaker 21064.

Rigg, Edward. *The Right, Duty and Importance, of Free Inquiry in Matters of Religion. A Discourse Delivered at the Evening Lecture, Instituted by the First Society of Unitarian Christians, in the City of Philadelphia; November 1st, 1807. . . .* Printed by Bartram and Reynolds, for Thomas Dobson. Shaw and Shoemaker 13503.

Rush, Benjamin. *An Inquiry into the Effects of Ardent Spirits. . . . Fourth Edition.* Printed by T. Dobson. Shaw and Shoemaker 21246.

[Wright, Richard.] *A Collection of Pieces and Tracts, Chiefly Intended to Establish the Doctrines of the Unity of God, and the Salvation of Sinners. . . .* Printed by Thomas and George Palmer, for Thomas Dobson. Shaw and Shoemaker 22113.

————. *The Salvation of Sinners by the Free Grace of God. . . .* Printed by Thomas and George Palmer, for Thomas Dobson. Shaw and Shoemaker 22114.

1811

Abernethy, John. *Surgical Observations on Injuries of the Head. . . .* Printed by Fry and Kammerer, for Thomas Dobson. Shaw and Shoemaker 22137.

————. *Surgical Observations, on the Constitutional Origin and Treatment of Local Disease and on Aneurisms. On Diseases Resembling Syphillis, and on Diseases of the Urethra.* Printed by Fry and Kammerer, for Thomas Dobson. Shaw and Shoemaker 22138.

Baudelocque, Jean Louis. *An Abridgment of Mr. Heath's Translation of Baudelocque's Midwifery. With Notes, by William P. Dewees.* . . . Printed by Thomas Dobson. Shaw and Shoemaker 22305.

Bristed, John. *The Resources of the British Empire.* Published by Ezra Sergeant . . . And for Sale by Bradford & Inskeep and T. Dobson, Philadelphia. [AAS].

Cox, Joseph Mason. *Practical Observations on Insanity.* . . . Printed by Fry and Kammerer, for Thomas Dobson. Shaw and Shoemaker 22632.

Dobson, Thomas. *Thoughts on Mankind, Considered as Individuals, Originally Created Upright; Their State Under Discipline, Rendered Needful by Their Disobedience; and Their Recovery by Jesus Christ.* . . . Published by the Author, Fry and Kammerer, Printers. ND 0302502.

Evans, John. *A Narrative of the Proceedings of the Religious Society of the People Called Quakers, in Philadelphia, Against John Evans.* . . . Printed for Thomas Dobson by John Adams & Co., Printers. Shaw and Shoemaker 22786.

Jones, John Frederick Drake. *A Treatise on the Process Employed by Nature in Suppressing the Hemorrhage from Divided and Punctured Arteries, and on the Use of the Ligature.* . . . Printed by Fry and Kammerer, for Thomas Dobson. Shaw and Shoemaker 23130.

Wistar, Caspar. *A System of Anatomy for the Use of Students of Medicine.* . . . Printed by Fry and Kammerer, for Thomas Dobson. Shaw and Shoemaker 24475.

1812

Dobson, Thomas. *In a Short Time Will Be Published, The History of North Carolina, from Its Discovery to the End of the Revolution War. In Two Volumes. By Hugh Williamson.* Dobson. ND 0302494.

Hallam, Henry. *A View of the State of Europe during the Middle Ages.* Thomas Dobson and Son. Shaw and Shoemaker 25587.

Selection of Sacred Poetry. . . . *Psalms and Hymns from Watts, Doddridge, Merrick, Scott, Cowper, Barbauld, Steele and Others.* Dobson. Shaw and Shoemaker 26716.

Williamson, Hugh. *The History of North Carolina.* . . . Printed by Fry and Kammerer, for Thomas Dobson. Shaw and Shoemaker 27566.

1813

Cavallo, Tiberius. *The Elements of Natural or Experimental Philosophy. First American Edition.* Thomas Dobson. Shaw and Shoemaker 28093.

Eddowes, Ralph. *The Unity of God, and the Worship That Is Due Him Alone. A Discourse.* . . . Printed by William Fry, for Thomas Dobson. Shaw and Shoemaker 28400.

[Horowitz, Jonathan.] *Just Put to Press, and Will Be Published with All Convenient Speed, the First American Edition of van der Hoogt's Hebrew Bible, Without the Points.* [Printed by William Fry, for Thomas Dobson; AAS].

Richerand, Anthelme. *Elements of Physiology.* . . . Printed by William Fry, for Thomas Dobson. Shaw and Shoemaker 29663.

Staughton, William. *A Greek and English Lexicon for the Sacred Scriptures. Poulson's*

American Daily Advertiser, June 11 and often thereafter, 1813. ["In the Press and Will be Published."]

Svinin, Pavel Petrovich. *Sketches of Moscow and St. Petersburg.* . . . Printed by William Fry, for Thomas Dobson. Shaw and Shoemaker 29903.

1814

Bancroft, Edward. *Experimental Researches Concerning the Philosophy of Permanent Colours.* . . . T. Dobson. Shaw and Shoemaker 30738.

Bible. *Biblia Hebraica, Secundum ultimam Editonem Jos. Athiae, a Johanne Leusden Denuo recognitam, Recensita variisque notis Latinis illustrata ab Everardo Van Der Hooght, V. D. M. Editio Prima Americana, sine punctis Masorethicis. Tom. I. Philadelphae: Cura et Impemsis Thomae Dobson edita ex AEdibus Lapideis. Typis Gulielmi Fry.* Shaw and Shoemaker 30857; O'Callaghan, 120.

Coxe, John Redman. *The American Dispensatory, Containing the Operations of Pharmacy.* . . . *Third Edition.* Printed by William Fry, for Thomas Dobson. Shaw and Shoemaker 31255.

Desault, Pierre Joseph. *The Surgical Works, or Statement of the Doctrine and Practice of P. J. Desault.* . . . *by Xavier Bichat.* . . . *Translated from the Original by Edward Darrell Smith.* . . . T. Dobson. Shaw and Shoemaker 31327.

Dobson, Thomas. *Proposals for Publishing the Septuagint.* [Letter to Webster & Skinner (June 8, 1814): "I have put in the parcel some proposals for publishing the Septuagint, which I have just issued with considerable prospect of Success."]

Henry, William. *The Elements of Experimental Chemistry "by Stillman."* "Medical Books for Sale by Thomas Dobson." *Poulson's American Daily Advertiser,* October 13, 1814, "In the press"; November 9, "This Day Is Published."

1815

Cooper, Thomas. *A Practical Treatise on Dyeing, and Callicoe Printing; Exhibiting the Processes in the French, German, English, and American Practices of Fixing Colours on Woolen, Cotton, Silk, and Linen.* . . . Printed by William Fry, for Thomas Dobson. Shaw and Shoemaker 34442.

Dyckman, Jacob. *A Dissertation on the Pathology of the Human Fluids. Poulson's American Daily Advertiser,* February 13. ["This Day Is Published by Thomas Dobson . . ."; also announces Swediaur, below.]

Gregory, James. *A Dissertation on the Influence of a Change of Climate in Curing Diseases.* . . . T. Dobson. Shaw and Shoemaker 34814.

Murray, John. *A System of Materia Medica and Pharmacy.* . . . Printed by William Fry, for Thomas Dobson. Shaw and Shoemaker 35240.

Swediaur, Francois Xavier. *A Complete Treatise on the Symptoms, Effects, Nature and Treatment of Syphillis.* . . . *Translated from the Fourth French Edition, by Thomas T. Hewson.* . . . T. Dobson. Shaw and Shoemaker 36040.

1816

Cullen, William. *First Lines of the Practice of Physic.* . . . *with Notes and Observations, Practical and Explanatory.* . . . *by Charles Caldwell. With Notes and Selections, from Various Writers since the Time of Cullen.* . . . T. Dobson. Shaw and Shoemaker 37369.

[Priestley, Joseph.] *Catalogue of the Library of the Late Dr. Joseph Priestley, Containing*

Many Very Scarce and Valuable Books, for Sale by Thomas Dobson. Published by Thomas Dobson. NP 0578638; [AAS].

Feldborg, Andreas Andersen. *Poems, from the Danish. Selected and Illustrated with Historical Notes. . . .* Printed by William Fry, for Thomas Dobson. Shaw and Shoemaker 37575.

Ferriar, John. *Medical Histories and Reflections. . . . First American Edition.* Printed by William Fry, for Thomas Dobson. Shaw and Shoemaker 37590.

Izard, George. *Official Correspondence with the Department of War, Relative to the Military Operations of the American Army under the Command of Major General Izard, on the Northern Frontier of the United States in the Years 1814 and 1815.* T. Dobson. Shaw and Shoemaker 37938.

Mann, James. *Medical Sketches of the Campaigns of 1812, 13, and 14—To Which are Added, Surgical Cases; Observations on Military Hospitals and Flying Hospitals. Also, an Appendix on Dysentery and Peripneumonia Notha.* T. Dobson?; attributed to Samuel Wood & Sons, Shaw and Shoemaker 38137; but see "Recent American Publications. By Thomas Dobson," *Eclectic Repertory* 6 (1816): 554.

Merriman, Samuel. *A Synopsis of the Various Kinds of Difficult Parturition, with Practical Remarks on the Management of Labours. . . . First American Edition, from the Second London Edition.* Printed by William Fry, for Thomas Dobson. Shaw and Shoemaker 38238.

Pinkerton, John. *A Modern Atlas, from the Latest and Best Authorities, Exhibiting the Various Divisions of the World . . . and States. . . .* [Thomas Dobson to Webster & Skinner, February 15, 1816: "I mean to send you . . . Pinkertons elegant Atlas, which I am now publishing." Gratz Collection, Alphabetical Series, HSP.]

Stevens, Alexander, trans. *A Treatise on Surgical Diseases, by the Celebrated Baron Boyer.* T. Dobson? Edition not previously known; attributed to T. & J. Swords in Shaw and Shoemaker 37066. But see "Recent American Publications. By Thomas Dobson," *Eclectic Repertory* 6 (1816): 554.

1817

Carmichael, Richard. *An Essay on the Venereal Diseases Which Have Been Confounded with Syphillis and the Symptoms Which Exclusively Arise from That Poison. First American Edition.* Printed by William Fry, for Thomas Dobson. Shaw and Shoemaker 40405.

Clavijero, Francisco Javier. *The History of Mexico. Collected from Spanish and Mexican Historians, from Manuscripts, and Ancient Paintings of the Indians. . . .* T. Dobson. Shaw and Shoemaker 40488.

Coxe, John Redman. *The Philadelphia Medical Dictionary. . . . Second Edition.* Printed by William Fry, for Thomas Dobson. Shaw and Shoemaker 40583.

Edgeworth, Maria. *Comick Dramas, in Three Acts. . . .* London Printing; Reprinted, T. Dobson and Son. Shaw and Shoemaker 40727.

Merriman, Samuel. *A Dissertation on Retroversion of the Womb. . . .* Printed by William Fry, for Thomas Dobson and Son. Shaw and Shoemaker 41415.

Michaux, François André. *The North American Sylva; or, A Description of the Forest Trees of the United States, Canada, etc., Added, the European Forest Trees;*

Translated by A. L. Hillhouse. Three Volumes. Thomas Dobson. Shaw and Shoemaker 41426.

Smith, John Augustine. *A Syllabus of the Lectures Delivered to the Senior Students in the College of William and Mary, on Government.* . . . T. Dobson and Son. Shaw and Shoemaker 42140.

Thomas, Robert. *The Modern Practice of Physic, Exhibiting the Character, Causes, Symptoms, Prognostics, Morbid Appearances, and Improved Method of Treating the Diseases of All Climates. Abridged from the Fifth and Last London Edition.* T. Dobson and Son. Shaw and Shoemaker 42274.

Walsh, Robert, Jr., ed. *The American Register; or, Summary Review of History, Politics, and Literature.* . . . Printed by William Fry, for Thomas Dobson and Son. Shaw and Shoemaker 39985. American Periodical Series II, Reel 59.

Wistar, Caspar. *A System of Anatomy for the Use of Students of Medicine.* . . . T. Dobson and Son. Shaw and Shoemaker 42938.

1818

Abernethy's Surgical Works Complete. Thomas Dobson & Son. Edition not seen; reported in "Thomas Dobson & Son . . . Have Recently Published . . .," *Eclectic Review* 8 (1818): [583].

American Edition of the Encyclopaedia, or Dictionary of Arts, Sciences, and Miscellaneous Literature in Three Volumes. Printed by Budd and Bartram, for Thomas Dobson. Shaw and Shoemaker 43065. [New title pages only for 1803 *Supplement.*]

Caldwell, Charles. *An Eulogium on Caspar Wistar, M. D., Professor of Anatomy . . . Delivered by Appointment, before the Members of the Philadelphia Medical Society.* . . . T. Dobson and Son. Shaw and Shoemaker 43520.

Cavallo, Tiberius. *The Elements of Natural and Experimental Philosophy. First American Edition.* T. Dobson. Shaw and Shoemaker 43558.

Clarke, John. *An Answer to the Question, Why Are You a Christian? Seventh Edition.* Printed by William Fry, for Thomas Dobson and Son. Shaw and Shoemaker 43634.

Coxe, John Redman. *The American Dispensatory.* . . . *Fourth Edition.* Printed by William Fry, for Thomas Dobson and Son. Shaw and Shoemaker 43760.

Darby, William. *The Emigrant's Guide.* Published by Kirk and Mercein . . . and for Sale by Thomas Dobson, M. Carey and Son, M. Thomas, and E. Earle, Philadelphia . . . [AAS].

Dobson, Thomas and Son. [Printed Circular Offering for Sale Adam Seybert's Statistical Annals.] Dobson. Shaw and Shoemaker 43866.

Eddowes, Ralph. *A Selection of Sacred Poetry, Consisting of Psalms and Hymns.* . . . *Second Edition.* Thomas Dobson and Son. Shaw and Shoemaker 43910.

Fenwick, Athanasius. *An Essay on Volition and Pleasure.* Printed for the Author, and Sold by Thomas Dobson and Son. [AAS].

Hazlitt, William. *Lectures on the English Poets.* . . . *First American Edition.* Printed by William Fry, for Thomas Dobson and Son. Shaw and Shoemaker 44292.

Kneeland, Abner. *A Series of Lectures on the Doctrine of Universal Benevolence.* . . . Printed by Clark and Raser, for the Author [and T. Dobson and Son, M. Carey and Son, . . .]. Shaw and Shoemaker 44526.

Orfila, Matieu Joseph Bonaventure. *Practical Chemistry.* . . . Printed by William Fry, for Thomas Dobson and Son. Shaw and Shoemaker 45184.

Pinkerton, John. *A Modern Atlas, from the Latest and Best Authorities.* . . . Printed by William Fry, for Thomas Dobson and Son. Shaw and Shoemaker 45342.

Pocock, Isaac. *Rob Roy Macgregor; or, Auld Lang Syne! A Musical Drama, in Three Acts. Founded on the Popular Novel of Rob Roy.* . . . Printed by William Fry, for Thomas Dobson and Son. Shaw and Shoemaker 45363.

Richerand, Anthelme Balthasar. *Elements of Physiology.* . . . *From the Fifth London Edition.* Printed by William Fry, for Thomas Dobson and Son. Shaw and Shoemaker 45540.

Schlegel, Karl Wilhelm Freidrich von. *Lecture on the History of Literature, Ancient and Modern.* . . . Printed by William Fry, for Thomas Dobson and Son. Shaw and Shoemaker 45646.

Seybert, Adam. *Statistical Annals: Embracing Views of the Population, Commerce, Navigation, Fisheries, Public Lands, Post-Office Establishment, Revenues, Mint, Military and Naval Establishments, Expenditures, Public Debt and Sinking Fund, of the United States of America.* . . . Printed by William Fry, for Thomas Dobson and Son. Shaw and Shoemaker 45692.

"Thomas Dobson and Son Have in Press, and Will Publish in the Course of a Few Weeks, Sir William Adams on the Eye. Scudamore on Gout [attributed to William Brown, for Edward Earle, Shaw and Shoemaker 49388]. Blackall on Dropsy." Items 1 and 3 are not recorded elsewhere. [*Eclectic Repertory* 8 (1818): 584.]

Wilson, James. *Pharmacopoeia Chirurgica.* . . . *First American Edition.* Printed by William Fry, for Thomas Dobson Son. Shaw and Shoemaker 46825.

Wistar, Caspar. *Eulogium on Doctor William Shippen.* . . . Printed by William Fry, for Thomas Dobson and Son. Shaw and Shoemaker 46841.

1819–1823

Cavallo, Tiberius. *Elements of Natural and Experimental Philosophy.* . . . *with Additional Notes, Selected from Various Authors by F. X. Brosius. Second American Edition.* Thomas Dobson, 1819. Shaw and Shoemaker 47529.

DeRocca, M. *Memoirs of the War of the French in Spain.* Printed by William Fry, for Thomas Dobson & Son, 1820. R. Shoemaker 3036.

Dewees, William Potts. *An Essay on the Means of Lessening Pain, and Facilitating Certain Cases of Difficult Parturition.* . . . *Second Edition.* Printed by William Fry, for Thomas Dobson, 1819. Shaw and Shoemaker 47824.

Dobson, Firm, Booksellers. *A Catalogue of Books, in the Various Departments of Ancient and Modern Literature, Being Some of the Most Numerous of the Stock of the Late Firm of Thomas Dobson & Son; Now Offered to the Trade on the Most Liberal Terms by T. Dobson & J[udah]. Dobson.* T. and J. Dobson. 1822. R. Shoemaker 8554.

Dobson, J. *A Catalogue of Books.* . . . J. Dobson, 1823. R. Shoemaker 12383.

Hallam, Henry. *A View of the State of Europe during the Middle Ages, from A.D. 450 to A.D. 1500.* [Advertised in *Poulson's American Daily Advertiser* October 10, 1820.]

Johnson, James. *Diseases of Tropical and Tropicoid Climates*. Printed by J. Harding, for Thomas Dobson & Son, 1821. R. Shoemaker 5724.

――――. *Practical Researches on the Nature, Cure, and Prevention of the Gout*. T. Dobson. 1821. R. Shoemaker 5725.

Juvenal, Geoffrey [pseudonym]. *The Critic*. [*Poulson's American Daily Advertiser*, March 3, 1820 (no. 13); April 26 (no. 19).

["The *Critic* was a weekly serial publication conducted by Geoffrey Juvenal; each number contained one or two essays and occasionally the satire was in the form of a letter or poem." (Hoornstra and Heath 70).] The essays, signed "R. A." and, less frequently, "O.," attack, among other targets, William Wirt's life of Patrick Henry, James Kirk Paulding's *The Backwoodsman*, and Coleridge's "Rhime of the Ancient Mariner." Dobson is identified as the publisher on page 118 at the end of no. 14, a "Syllabus of a Course of Lectures on Lalematology." There were twenty numbers in all published between January 29 and May 10, 1820. The probable author is Robert Walsh, Jr., with assistance from other hands.

"*Proposed American Republications*." "*Armstrong on Scarlatina*, &c. &c. to match Johnson on Tropical Diseases, in 12mo. By Thomas Dobson and Son." Advertisement in *Journal of Foreign Medical Science and Literature* 11 (1821): 136.

Bibliography

MANUSCRIPT COLLECTIONS

Permission to quote from the following manuscript collections is gratefully acknowledged (HSP = Historical Society of Pennsylvania, Philadelphia; MHS = Massachusetts Historical Society, Boston, Massachusetts).

American Prose Collection, HSP
Clifford-Pemberton Papers, HSP
Dreer Collection, HSP
John Haygood Papers, Southern Historical Collection, University of North Carolina
Hobart Papers, Archives of the Episcopal Church, Austin, Texas
Ledger Books of N[athan]. and D[avid]. Sellers, HSP
Levi Hollingsworth Papers, HSP
Logan Papers, HSP
McAllister Papers, Library Company of Philadelphia, HSP
Mathew Carey Account Books, American Antiquarian Society, Worcester, Massachusetts
Mellon Chamberlain Collection, Boston Public Library, Boston, Massachusetts
Morse Family Papers, Mss 358, Yale University Library, New Haven, Connecticut
Pennsylvania Academy of the Fine Arts, Archives, Philadelphia
Pemberton Papers, HSP
Pennsylvania Series, Provincial Conference Papers, HSP
Pennsylvania Series, Provincial Conference Papers, HSP
Quaker Collection, Cadbury Papers, Ms 950, Haverford College Library, Haverford, Pennsylvania
Revere Papers, MHS
Simon Gratz Collection, HSP
Society Collection, HSP

Special Collections, Van Pelt Library, University of Pennsylvania, Philadelphia
Stauffer Collection, HSP
Supreme Judicial Court Records, Commonwealth of Massachusetts, Essex County, Essex County Courthouse, Salem, Mass.
Thomas Dobson Miscellaneous Papers, Rare Books and Manuscripts Division, The New York Public Library, Astor, Lenox, and Tilden Foundations
Thomson Correspondence, HSP
Timothy Pickering Papers, MHS
Wallace Papers, HSP

NEWSPAPERS
Aurora (Philadelphia), 1794–1820.
Claypoole's American Daily Advertiser (Philadelphia), 1796–1800.
Connecticut Journal (New Haven), 1767–1820+.
Daily Advertiser (New York), 1785–1806.
Dunlap's American Daily Advertiser (Philadelphia), 1791–1795.
Edinburgh Gazette (Edinburgh, Scotland).
Federal Gazette (Philadelphia), 1788–1793.
Freeman's Journal (Philadelphia), 1781–1792.
Gales's Independent Gazetteer (Philadelphia), 1796–1797.
Gazette of the United States (Philadelphia), 1790–1804.
General Advertiser (Philadelphia), 1790–1794.
Independent Gazetteer (Philadelphia), 1782–1798.
Maryland Journal (Baltimore), 1773–1797.
Newburyport Herald, 1797–1820+.
New-York Journal, 1784–1793.
North-Carolina Gazette (New Bern), 1786–1798.
Pennsylvania Evening Herald (Philadelphia), 1785–1788.
Pennsylvania Gazette (Philadelphia), 1728–1815.
Pennsylvania Mercury, and Universal Advertiser (Philadelphia), 1784–1792.
Pennsylvania Packet (Philadelphia), 1771–1790.
Philadelphia Gazette, 1794–1802.
Porcupine's Gazette (Philadelphia), 1797–1799.
Poulson's American Daily Advertiser (Philadelphia), 1800–1820.
Relf's Philadelphia Gazette, 1803–1820+.

OTHER PRIMARY AND SECONDARY SOURCES
Adams, Donald R., Jr. *Wage Rates in Philadelphia, 1790–1830.* Dissertations in American Economic History. New York: Arno Press, 1975.
Alden, John. "Scotch Type in Eighteenth-Century America." *Studies in Bibliography* 3 (1950–51): 270–74.
Alexander, John K. *Render Them Submissive: Responses to Poverty in Philadelphia, 1760–1800.* Amherst: University of Massachusetts Press, 1980.

Allibone, Samuel Austin. *A Critical Dictionary of English Literature and British and American Authors.* . . . 2 vols. and supplement. Philadelphia: J. B. Lippincott, 1899.

Appleton's Cyclopaedia of American Biography. 6 vols. New York: D. Appleton, 1889.

Ashmead, Henry Graham. *History of Delaware County, Pennsylvania.* Philadelphia: L. H. Everts, 1884.

[Bancroft, George ?] "Encyclopaedias." *American Quarterly Review* 6 (September and December, 1829): 331–60.

Barker, I. N. Phelps Stokes and Daniel C. Haskell. *American Historical Prints: Early Views of American Cities . . . from the Phelps Stokes and Other Collections.* New York: New York Public Library, 1933.

Bartram, William. "Observations on the Creek and Cherokee Indians, 1789." *Transactions of the American Ethnological Society* vol. 3, pt. 1, pp. 11–81. New York: George P. Putnamn, 1853.

Bell, Whitfield, Jr. *The College of Physicians of Philadelphia: A Bicentennial History.* Philadelphia: Science History Publications, 1987.

———. "Scottish Emigration to America: A Letter of Dr. Charles Nisbet to Dr. John Witherspon." *William and Mary Quarterly* 3rd ser., 11 (1954): 275–89.

Berry, W. Turner and A. F. Johnson. *Catalogue of Specimens of Printing Types by English and Scottish Printers and Founders, 1665–1830.* London: Oxford University Press, 1935.

Biddle, Clement. *The Philadelphia Directory.* Philadelphia: James & Johnson, 1791. Evans 23205.

Bidwell, John. "The Size of the Sheet in America: Paper-Moulds Manufactured by N. & D. Sellers of Philadelphia." *Proceeding of the American Antiquarian Society* 87, pt. 2 (1978): 299–342.

Birch, William and Sons. *Views of Philadelphia: The City of Philadelphia as It Appeared in 1800.* Philadelphia: W[illiam]. Birch, 1800. Evans 38259.

Bishop, J. Leander. *A History of American Manufactures from 1608 to 1860: Exhibiting the Origin and Growth of the Principal Mechanic Arts and Manufactures, from the Earliest Colonial Period to the Adoption of the Constitution; and Comprising Annals of the Industry of the United States in Machinery, Manufactures and Useful Arts, with a Notice of the Important Inventions, Tariffs, and the Results of Each Decennial Census.* 3 vols. Philadelphia: Edward Young, 1864–66.

Blumenthal, Joseph. *The Printed Book in America.* Boston: David R. Godine, 1977.

Boynton, Henry Walcott. *Annals of American Bookselling, 1638–1850.* New York: John Wiley, 1932.

Brenni, Vito J. *Book Printing in Britain and America: A Guide to the Literature and a Directory of Printers.* Westport, Conn.: Greenwood Press, 1983.

Brigham, Clarence S. *History and Bibliography of American Newspapers, 1690–1820.* 2 vols. Worcester, Mass.: American Antiquarian Society, 1947.

Brissot (de Warville), Jacques-Pierre. *New Travels in the United States of America Performed in 1788.* New York: T. & J. Swords, 1792. Evans 24166.

Bristol, Roger P. *Supplement to Charles Evans' American Bibliography.* Charlottesville: University Press of Virginia, 1970.

[Brown, Charles Brockden.] "[Review of] *Encyclopaedia.*" *Monthly Magazine and American Review* 2 (1799): 134–35.

[———.] "[Review of] *Letters on the Existence and Character of the Deity.*" *Monthly Magazine and American Review* 3 (1800): 196–200.

[———.] "[Review of] *Letters on the Existence and Character of the Deity . . . Part ii.*" *American Review and Literary Journal* 2 (1802): 215–20.

Brown, H. G., and Maude O. Brown. "A Directory of the Book-Arts and Book Trade in Philadelphia to 1820 Including Printers and Engravers." *Bulletin of the New York Public Library* 53 (1949): 211–26, 290–98, 339–47, 387–401, 447–58, 492–503, 564–73, 615–22; 54 (1950): 25–37, 89–92, 123–45.

———. "Philadelphia Contributions to the Book Arts and Book Trade, 1796–1810." *Papers of the Bibliographical Society of America* 37 (1943): 275–92.

Bruce, David. *The History of Typefounding in the United States.* New York: Privately printed, 1925.

Bruntjen, Carol and Scott Bruntjen. *A Checklist of American Imprints for 1831.* Metuchen, N.J.: Scarecrow Press, 1975.

———. *A Checklist of American Imprints for 1832.* Metuchen, N.J.: Scarecrow Press, 1977.

Bugbee, Bruce W. *Genesis of American Patent and Copyright Law.* Washington, D.C.: Public Affairs Press, 1967.

Cheyney, Edward Potts. *History of the University of Pennsylvania, 1740–1940.* Philadelphia: University of Pennsylvania Press, 1940.

Conkwright, P. J. "Binny & Ronaldson's First Type." *Printing and Graphic Art* 1 (1953): 27–33.

Cook, Frederick. *Journals of the Military Expedition of Major General John Sullivan Against the Six Nations of Indians in 1779, with Records of Centennial Celebrations.* Auburn, N.Y.: Knapp, Peck & Thomson, 1887.

Cook, Lewis D. "George Trenchard of Salem, N.J. and Descendants." *Pennsylvania Genealogical Magazine.* 19, no. 1 (1952): 3–71; no. 2 (1953): 199–207.

Crawford, Richard and D. W. Krummel, "Early American Music Printing and Publishing." In *Printing and Society in Early America.* Ed. William L. Joyce, David D. Hall, Richard D. Brown, and John B. Hench. Worcester, Mass.: American Antiquarian Society, 1983.

Crompton, Robert D. "James Thackara, American Engraver." *Antiques* 74 (November 1958): 424–28.

———. "James Thackara, Friend of the Arts, Legislator and Prison Builder." *Journal of the Lancaster County Historical Society* 62 (April 1958): 64–95.

———. "James Trenchard of the 'Columbian' and 'Columbianum.'" *Art Quarterly* 23 (1960): 378–97.

Currier, John J. *History of Newburyport, Massachusetts.* 2 vols. Newburyport: Printed for the author, 1906, 1909.

Darnton, Robert. *The Great Cat Massacre and Other Episodes in French Cultural History.* New York: Basic Books, 1984.

Davies, Benjamin. *Some Account of the City of Philadelphia.* Philadelphia: Benjamin Davies, 1794. Evans 26853.

de St. Mery, Moreau. *Moreau de St. Mery's American Journey [1793–1798].* Trans. and ed. Anna M. Roberts and Kenneth Roberts. Garden City, N.Y.: Doubleday, 1947.

Dennie, Joseph. *Port Folio.* 5 vols. Philadelphia: Asbury Dickins, 1801; Hugh Maxwell, 1802–05; n. s., 6 vols. Philadelphia: Hugh Maxwell, 1806–08.

Dictionary of American Biography. Edited by Allen Johnson. 20 vols. plus supplement. New York: Scribner's, 1929–.

Dictionary of National Biography. Edited by Sir Sidney Lee and Sir Leslie Stephen. 21 vols. plus supplement. London: Oxford University Press, 1917–.

Dobson, Judah. *A Catalogue of Books, in the Various Departments of Ancient and Modern Literature, Being Some of the Most Numerous of the Stock of the Late Firm of Thomas Dobson & Son, Now Offered to the Trade on the Most Liberal Terms by J. Dobson.* Philadelphia: [Judah Dobson], 1823.

Dobson, Thomas. *A Catalogue of Books, in the Various Departments of Ancient and Modern Literature, Being Some of the Most Numerous of the Stock of the Late Firm of Thomas Dobson & Son, Now Offered to the Trade on the Most Liberal Terms by T. Dobson & J. Dobson.* Philadelphia: [Thomas and Judah Dobson], 1822.

———. *Encyclopaedia; or, a Dictionary of Arts, Sciences, and Miscellaneous Literature. . . .* Philadelphia: Thomas Dobson, 1798. Evans 33676.

———. *First Lessons for Children.* Philadelphia: Thomas Dobson, 1797. Evans 32054. [Extant copy: Thomas Dobson Miscellaneous Papers, Rare Books and Manuscripts Division, The New York Public Library, Astor, Lenox, and Tilden Foundations.]

———. *First Lessons for Children, Volume Second.* Philadelphia: Thomas Dobson, [Deposited March 6] 1797. Evans 32054. [No extant copy].

———. *The Holiday, or Children's Social Amusement.* Philadelphia: Thomas Dobson, 1797. Evans 32055. [No extant copy.]

———. *In a Short Time Will be Published, The History of North Carolina, from Its Discovery to the End of the Revolution War. In Two Volumes. With a Correct Map of the State. By Hugh Williamson.* [Philadelphia: Thomas Dobson], 1812. ND 0302494 [Pre-1956 Imprints].

———. *Letters on the Existence and Character of the Deity, and on the Moral State of Man.* Philadelphia: Printed for Thomas Dobson, 1799. Evans 35413.

———. *Letters on the Existence and Character of the Deity, and on the Moral State of Man . . . Part II.* Philadelphia: Thomas Dobson, 1802. Shaw and Shoemaker 2149.

———. *Letters on the Existence and Character of the Deity, and on the Moral State of Man . . . Volume II.* Philadelphia: Printed by Archibald Bartram for Thomas Dobson, 1804. Shaw and Shoemaker 6171.

———. *Pleasing Instructions for Young Minds.* Philadelphia: Thomas Dobson, 1797. Evans 32056 [No extant copy].

———. *Proposal of Thomas Dobson, for Printing by Subscription on a Very Large and Beautiful New Type, and Superfine Paper: An Elegant Edition of the Sacred Scripture.* [Philadelphia: Thomas Dobson], 1797. ND 0302497 [Pre-1956 Imprints].

———. *Proposals for Printing by Subscription, Encyclopaedia Britannica.* [Philadelphia: Thomas Dobson], 1789. Bristol 6937; Evans 45466.

———. *Proposals for Publishing by Subscription an Elegant Edition of the New Testament.* [Philadelphia: Thomas Dobson], 1800. ND 0302496 [Pre-1956 Imprints].

————. *Thomas Dobson . . . Having Happily Completed the American Edition of the Encyclopaedia . . . Offer[s] a Proposal for Publishing a Supplement*. [Philadelphia: Thomas Dobson, ca. 1800]. ND 0302502 [Pre-1956 Imprints].

————. *Thoughts on Mankind, Considered as Individuals, Originally Created Upright; Their State Under Discipline, Rendered Needful by Their Disobedience; and Their Recovery by Jesus Christ*. Philadelphia: Published by the Author. Fry and Kammerer, Printers, 1811. ND 0302502 [Pre-1956 Imprints].

————. *Thoughts on the Scripture Account of Faith in Jesus, and Life Through His Name*. Philadelphia: Printed by the Author, 1807. Shaw and Shoemaker 12442; ND 0302503 [Pre-1956 Imprints].

————. *Thoughts on the Scripture Account of Faith in Jesus, and Life Through His Name*. Philadelphia: [Thomas Dobson?], 1808. ND 0302504 [Pre-1956 Imprints].

Drake, Francis S. *Dictionary of American Biography . . . and a Supplement*. Boston: Houghton, Osgood, 1879.

Dunlap, William. *Diary of William Dunlap (1766–1839)*. 3 vols. The John Watts DePeyster Publication Fund Series No. 44. New York: New York Historical Society, 1930.

————. *History of the Rise and Progress of the Arts of Design in the United States*. 2 vols. New York: George P. Scott, 1834.

Early Proceedings of the American Philosophical Society for the Promotion of Useful Knowledge Compiled by One of the Secretaries, from the Manuscript Minutes of Its Meetings from 1744 to 1838. Philadelphia: McCalla & Stavely, 1884.

Eberlein, Harold Donaldson and Cortlandt Van Dyke Hubbard. "Music in the Early Federal Era." *Pennsylvania Magazine of History and Biography* 69 (1945): 103–27.

Eclectic Repertory and Analytical Review. 10 vols. Philadelphia: Thomas [& Judah] Dobson, 1810–20 [American Periodical Series II, Reels 116–18].

Emlen, S[amuel], Jr., and William Price, eds. *Journal of Foreign Medical Science and Literature*. n. s., 4 vols. Philadelphia: Eliakim Littel, 1821–24 [American Periodical Series II, Reels 118–19].

Evans, Charles. *American Bibliography*. 12 vols. Chicago: The Blakely (later Columbia) Press, 1903–1934.

Fagerstrom, Dalphy I. "Scottish Opinion and the American Revolution." *William and Mary Quarterly* 3rd ser., 11 (1954): 252–75.

Farren, Donald. "Subscription: A Study of the Eighteenth-Century American Book Trade." PhD dissertation, Columbia University. 1982.

Feaver, William. "James Akin." *Masters of Caricature from Hogarth and Gillray to Scarfe and Levine,* 61. New York: A. A. Knopf, 1981.

Fielding, Mantle. *Dictionary of American Artists, Sculptors and Engravers*. Enlarged ed. Green Farms, Conn.: Modern Books and Crafts, 1974.

Flower, Milton E. *John Dickinson: Conservative Revolutionary*. Charlottesville: University Press of Virginia, 1983.

Forbes, Eric Gray. *Euler-Mayer Correspondence (1751–55): A New Perspective on Eighteenth-Century Advances on Lunar Theory*. New York: Macmillan, 1971.

———. "Tobias Mayer (1732–1762): A Case of Forgotten Genius." *British Journal for the History of Science* 5, no. 77, pt. 1 (June 1970): 1–20.

———. "Who Discovered Longitude at Sea?" *Sky and Telescope* 41 (January 1971): 4–6.

Fowble, E. McSherry. *Two Centuries of Prints in America, 1680–1880*. Charlottesville: University Press of Virginia, 1987.

Franklin, Benjamin. "Letter to Ezra Stiles, March 9, 1790." In *Benjamin Franklin: Writings*. Edited J. A. Leo Lemay, 1178–80. New York: Library of America, 1987.

Franklin, Benjamin V, ed. *Boston Printers, Publishers, and Booksellers; 1640–1800*. Boston: G. K. Hall, 1980.

Freeman, James. *Remarks on the American Universal Geography*. Boston: Belknap & Hall, 1793. Evans 25510.

French, Hannah Dustin. "Scottish-American Bookbindings: Six Examples from Colonial North America." In *Bookbinding in Early America: Seven Essays on Masters and Methods*, 1–19. Worcester, Mass.: American Antiquarian Society, 1986.

Gaine, Hugh. *The Journals of Hugh Gaine, Printer*. Ed. Paul Leicester Ford. 2 vols. New York: Dodd, Mead, 1902.

Gilreath, James. "American Book Distribution." *Proceedings of the American Antiquarian Society* 95, pt. 2 (1985): 501–83.

———. "Mason Weems, Mathew Carey and the Southern Booktrade, 1794–1810." *Publishing History* 10 (1981): 27–49.

Goff, Frederick R., ed. *Essays Honoring Lawrence C. Wroth*. Portland, Me.: Anthoensen, 1951.

———. "The First Decade of the Federal Act for Copyright, 1790–1800." In *Essays Honoring Lawrence C. Wroth*, edited by Frederick R. Goff, 101–28. Portland, Me.: Anthoensen, 1951.

Gravell, Thomas L. and George Miller. *Catalogue of American Watermarks, 1690–1835*. New York: Garland, 1979.

———. *A Catalogue of Foreign Watermarks Found on Paper Used in America, 1700–1835*. New York: Garland, 1983.

Green, James N. "From Printer to Publisher: Mathew Carey and the Origins of Nineteenth-Century Book Publishing." In *Getting the Books Out: Papers of the Chicago Conference on the Book in 19th-Century America*. Ed. Michael Hackenberg. Washington, D.C.: Center for the Book, Library of Congress, 1987. 26–44.

Greene, John C. "Science, Learning, and Utility: Patterns of Organization in the Early American Republic." In *The Pursuit of Knowledge in the Early American Republic: American Scientific and Learned Societies from Colonial Times to the Civil War*, ed. Alexandra Oleson and Oleson and Sanborn Brown, 1–20. Baltimore: Johns Hopkins University Press, 1976.

Gribbin, William. "A Mirror to New England: The *Compendious History* of Jedidiah Morse and Elijah Parish." *New England Quarterly* 45 (1972): 340–54.

Groce, George C. and David H. Wallace. *The New-York Historical Society's Dictionary of Artists in America, 1564–1860*. New Haven and London: Yale University Press, 1957.

Hamilton, Alexander. "Report on the Subject of Manufactures." In *Papers of Alexander Hamilton*, ed. Harold C. Syrett and Jacob E. Cooke. 27 vols. vol. 10: December 1791–January 1792, 230–40. New York: Columbia University Press, 1966. 230–340.

Hamilton, Sinclair. *Early American Book Illustrators and Wood Engravers, 1670–1870: A Catalogue of a Collection of American Books*. Princeton, N.J.: Princeton University Press, 1958.

Hardie, James. *The Philadelphia Directory and Register*. Philadelphia: Thomas Dobson, 1793. Evans 25585.

———. *The Philadelphia Directory and Register*. Philadelphia: Jacob Johnson & Co., 1794. Evans 27089.

Hawkins, Dorothy Lawson. "James Adams, the First Printer of Delaware." *Papers of the Bibliographical Society of America* 28, pt. 1 (1934): 28–63.

Hildeburn, Charles R. *Sketches of Printers and Printing in Colonial New York*. 1875; repr. Detroit: Gale Research Company, 1969.

Hixson, Richard F. *Isaac Collins: A Quaker Printer in Eighteenth-Century America*. New Brunswick, N.J.: Rutgers University Press, 1968.

Hoornstra, Jean, and Trudy Heath, eds. *American Periodicals 1741–1900: An Index to the Microfilm Collections—American Periodicals 18th Century, American Periodicals 1800–1850, American Periodicals 1850–1900, Civil War and Reconstruction*. Ann Arbor, Mich.: University Microfilms, 1979.

Hopkinson, Joseph. *Annual Discourse Delivered before the Pennsylvania Academy of the Fine Arts*. Philadelphia: Bradford and Inskeep; New York: Inskeep and Bradford; Boston: William M'ilhenny, 1810.

Hornung, Clarence P. and Friedholf Johnson. *200 Years of American Graphic Art: A Retrospective Survey of the Printing Arts and Advertising since the Colonial Period*. New York: George Braziller, 1976.

[Horowitz, Jonathan.] *Just Put to Press, and Will Be Published with All Convenient Speed, the First American Edition of van der Hoogt's Hebrew Bible, Without the Points*. Philadelphia: [Printed by William Fry, for Thomas Dobson, 1813; NH 0534148.]

Howe, Daniel Walker. *The Unitarian Conscience: Harvard Moral Philosophy, 1805–1861*. Cambridge, Mass.: Harvard University Press, 1970.

Howell, George Rogers, and Jonathan Tenney. *Bi-Centennial History of the County of Albany, New York, from 1609 to 1866*. New York: Joel Munsell, 1866.

Hudak, Leona M. *Early American Women Printers and Publishers, 1639–1820*. Metuchen, N.J.: Scarecrow Press, 1978.

Hughes, Arthur. "Science in English Encyclopaedias, 1704–1875." *Annals of Science* 7 (1951): 340–70; (1952): 323–67.

Hunter, Dard. *The Literature of Papermaking, 1390–1800*. 1925; repr. New York: Burt Franklin, 1971.

———. *Papermaking by Hand in America*. Chillicothe, Ohio: Mountain House Press, 1950.

———. *Papermaking: The History and Technique of an Ancient Craft*. 2d. ed. New York: Knopf, 1927.

Hyder, Darrell. "Philadelphia Fine Printing 1780–1820." *Printing and Graphic Arts* 9 (1961): 70–99.

Jackson, Joseph. *Literary Landmarks of Philadelphia*. Philadelphia: David McKay, 1939.

Janson, Charles William. *The Stranger in America, 1793–1806*. 1807; repr. New York: Press of the Pioneers, 1935.

Jefferson, Thomas. *The Papers of Thomas Jefferson*. Edited by Julian P. Boyd et al. 24 vols. Princeton, N.J.: Princeton University Press, 1950–.

———. *The Portable Thomas Jefferson*. Edited by Merrill D. Peterson. New York: Viking, 1975.

Kogan, Herman. *The Great EB: The Story of the Encyclopaedia Britannica*. Chicago: University of Chicago Press, 1958.

Kruse, Paul. "The Story of the Encyclopaedia Britannica, 1768–1943." PhD dissertation, University of Chicago, 1958.

Larson, Judy L. "Dobson's *Encyclopaedia*: A Precedent in American Engraving." In *The American Illustrated Book in the Nineteenth Century*, ed. Gerald W. R. Ward, 21–51. Winterthur, Del.: Henry Francis du Pont Winterthur Museum, 1987.

Lehmann-Haupt, Hellmut. *The Book in America: A History of the Making and Selling of Books in the United States*. New York: Bowker, 1951.

Leif, Irving P. *An International Sourcebook of Paper History*. Hamden, Conn.: Archon, 1978.

Lewis, Benjamin M. *A Guide to Engravings in American Magazines 1741–1810*. New York: New York Public Library, 1959.

———. *A Register of Editors, Printers, and Publishers of American Magazines, 1741–1810*. New York: New York Public Library, 1957.

Library of Congress. *A Bibliography of the History of Printing in the Library of Congress*. Springwater, N.Y.: Horace Hart, 1987.

Lippincott, Horace Mather. *Early Philadelphia: Its People, Life and Progress*. Philadelphia: J. B. Lippincott, 1917.

[Little, Robert.] "Obituaries, Remarkable Occurences, &c.: Pennsylvania." *Washington Quarterly Review of Art, Science and Literature* 1 (July 1823): 89. [American Periodical Series II, Reel 246].

Lochemes, Sr. M. Fredericka. *Robert Walsh: His Story*. New York: Irish Historical Society, 1941.

Magee, James F., Jr. "Robert Scot, Engraver of the First Federal United States Revenue Stamps 1798 and Coins of the United States Mint." *Embossed Revenue Stamped Paper News* 8, no. 3 (January 1941): 27–32.

Marcosson, Isaac F. *Copper Heritage: The Story of Revere Copper and Brass, Incorporated*. New York: Dodd, Mead, 1955.

Maxted, Ian. *The British Book Trades, 1710–1777: An Index of Masters and Apprentices Recorded in the Inland Revenue Registers at the Public Record Office, Kew*. Exeter [England]: Published by the author, 1983.

May, Henry F. *The Enlightenment in America*. New York: Oxford University Press, 1976.

McCulloch, William. "William McCulloch's Additions to Thomas's History of Printing." Worcester, Mass.: Published by the Society, 1922.

McKay, George L. "A Register of Artists, Booksellers, Printers and Publishers in New York City, 1781–1820." *Bulletin of the New York Public Library* 43 (1939): 1: 711–24; 2: 849–58.

McMurtrie, Douglas C. *The Book: The Story of Printing & Bookmaking*. New York, London, and Toronto: Oxford University Press, 1943.

———. *Eighteenth-Century North Carolina Imprints, 1749–1800*. Chapel Hill: University of North Carolina Press, 1938.

Mease, James. *The Picture of Philadelphia*. . . . Philadelphia: B. & T. Kite, 1811. Shaw and Shoemaker 23363.

Miller, Samuel. *A Brief Retrospect of the Eighteenth Century*. 2 vols. New York: T. & J. Swords, 1803. Shaw and Shoemaker 4654.

Milligan, Jacob. *The Charleston Directory*. . . . Charleston: T. B. Bowen, 1790. Evans 22670.

Minick, A. Rachel. *A History of Printing in Maryland, 1791–1800*. Baltimore: Enoch Pratt Free Library, 1949.

[Mitchill, Samuel L.] "List of Subscribers." *Medical Repository of Original Essays and Intelligence* 1 (1798): [9]–14.

Morse, Jedidiah. *The American Geography*. . . . Elizabethtown, [N.J.]: Shepard Kollock, 1790. Evans 21978.

———. *The American Universal Geography; or, A View of the Present State of All the Empires, Kingdoms, States, and Republics in the Known World, and of the United States in Particular*. 2 vols. Boston: Isaiah Thomas & Ebenezer T. Andrews, 1793. Evans 25847.

———. *A History of America, in Two Books. Containing I. A General History of America. II. A Concise History of the Late Revolution. Extracted from the American Edition of the Encyclopaedia*. Philadelphia: Thomas Dobson, 1790. Evans 22682.

Mullin, John. *The Baltimore Directory for 1799*. Baltimore: Warner & Hanna, 1799. Evans 35850.

Munsell, Joel. *A Typographical Miscellany*. Albany: Joel Munsell, 1850.

National Union Catalog Pre-1956 Imprints. 754 vols. Chicago: American Library Association; London: Mansell Information, 1968–81.

Nelson, Paul David. *Anthony Wayne: Soldier of the Early Republic*. Bloomington: Indiana University Press, 1985.

Nye, Russell B. *The Cultural Life of the New Nation, 1776–1830*. New York: Harper & Row, 1960.

Oberholtzer, Ellis Paxton. *The Literary History of Philadelphia*. Philadelphia: George W. Jacobs, 1907.

O'Callaghan, Edmund Bailey. *A List of Editions of the Holy Scriptures and Parts Thereof, Printed in America Previous to 1860*. Albany: Joel Munsell, 1861.

One Hundred and Fifty Years of Printing in English America (1640–1790): An Exhibition to Celebrate the 300th Anniversary of the Establishment of the First Press in This Country from the Collection of Dr. A. S. W. Rosenbach. [Philadelphia]: Free Library of Philadelphia, 1940.

Parker, Peter J. "Asbury Dickins, Bookseller, 1798–1801, or, The Brief Career of a Careless Youth." *Pennsylvania Magazine of History and Biography* 94 (1970): 464–83.

Paschal, George W. *A History of Printing in North Carolina, 1749–1946*. Raleigh: Edwards & Broughton, 1946.

Pasko, Wesley Washington. *American Dictionary of Printing and Bookmaking, Con-*

taining a History of These Arts in Europe and America, with Definitions of Technical Terms and Biographical Sketches. 1894; repr. Detroit: Gale Research Company, 1967.

Pessalono-Filos, Francis. *The Venus Numismatics Dictionary of Artists, Designers, Modellers, Engravers and Die Sinkers Whose Works Were Commissioned by or Struck by the United States Mint, 1792–1977.* New York: Eros Press, 1983.

Phillips, Joseph W. *Jedidiah Morse and New England Congregationalism.* New Brunswick, N.J.: Rutgers University Press, 1983.

Plomer, Henry R. *A Dictionary of the Printers and Booksellers Who were at Work in England, Scotland and Ireland from 1726 to 1775.* London: Oxford University Press, 1932 (for 1930).

Preece, Warren E. "The Organization of Knowledge and the Planning of Encyclopaedias: The Case of the Encyclopaedia Britannica." *Cahiers d'histoire mondiale* 9 (1966): 799–819.

Priestley, Joseph. *Original Letters from Doctor Joseph Priestley, F. R. S., to the Reverend Theophilus Lindsey, 1766–1803, and to the Reverend Thomas Belsham, 1789–1803.* 2 vols. Film No. 4988, British Records Relating to America. London: Dr. William's Library, 1965.

Prime, Alfred Coxe. *The Arts and Crafts in Philadelphia, Maryland, and South Carolina, 1721–1785.* 2 vols. Topsfield, Mass.: Walpole Society, 1929, 1932.

Quenzel, Carrol H. *Preliminary Checklist for Fredericksburg, 1778–1876.* Virginia Imprint Series No. 4. Richmond: Virginia State Library, 1947.

Rees, Abraham. *The Cyclopaedia; or, Universal Dictionary of the Arts, Sciences, and Literature.* London, 1802–20.

Richardson, Lyon N. *A History of Early American Magazines, 1741–1789.* New York: Thomas Nelson and Sons, 1931.

Rink, Evold. *Printing in Delaware 1761–1800: A Checklist.* Wilmington, Del.: Eleutherian Mills Historical Library, 1969.

"Robert Scot, First Engraver at the Philadelphia Mint." *The Numismatist* 54, No. 4 (1941): 84–85.

Roberts, Martin A. "Records in the Copyright Office of the Library of Congress Deposited by the United States District Courts, 1790–1870." *Papers of the Bibliographical Society of America* 31 (1937): 81–101.

Roberts, Raymond. *Typographic Design.* London: Ernest Benn, 1966.

Robinson, David. *The Unitarians and the Universalists.* Westport, Conn.: Greenwood Press, 1985.

Rush, Benjamin. *An Eulogium in Honor of the Late Dr. William Cullen. . . .* Philadelphia: Thomas Dobson, 1790. Evans 22862.

———. *Letters of Benjamin Rush.* Ed. Lyman H. Butterfield. 2 vols. Princeton, N.J.: Princeton University Press, 1951.

Sanborn, B. F. "Thomas Leavitt and His Artist Friend, James Akin." *Granite State Monthly* 25 (October 1898): 225–34.

Scharf, J. Thomas and Thompson Westcott. *History of Philadelphia, 1609–1884.* 3 vols. Philadelphia, 1884.

Scott, Joseph. *New and Universal Gazetteer.* Philadelphia, 1798 (Evans 34519); 1799 (Evans 36282); 1800 (Evans 38473).

Sellers, Charles Coleman. *Charles Willson Peale*. 2 vols. Philadelphia: American Philosophical Society, 1947.

Shaw, Ralph R., and Richard H. Shoemaker. *American Bibliography: A Preliminary Checklist for 1801[–1819]*. New York: Scarecrow Press, 1958[–65].

Sher, Richard B. *Church and University in the Scottish Enlightenment: The Moderate Literati of Edinburgh*. Princeton, N.J.: Princeton University Press, 1985.

Shera, Jesse H. "The Beginning of Systematic Bibliography in America, 1642–1799: An Exploratory Essay." *Essays Honoring Lawrence C. Wroth*, edited by Frederick R. Goff, 263–78. Portland, Me.: Anthoensen, 1951.

Shipton, Clifford K. *The American Bibliography of Charles Evans, 1799–1800*. Worcester, Mass.: American Antiquarian Society, 1955.

Shoemaker, Richard H. *A Checklist of American Imprints for 1822, 1823, 1824*. Metuchen, N.J.: Scarecrow Press, 1967–69.

Shoemaker, Thomas H. "List of Inhabitants of Germantown and Chestnut Hill in 1809." *Pennsylvania Magazine of History and Biography* 15 (1891): 449–80; 16 (1892): 42–63.

Shorter, Alfred H. *Paper Mills and Paper Makers in England, 1495–1800*. Vol. 6 in *Monumenta Chartae Papyraceae Historiam Illustratia, or Collection of Works and Documents Illustrating the History of Paper*. Edited by E. J. LaBarre. Hilversum, Holland: Paper Publications Society, 1957.

Silver, Rollo G. *The American Printer, 1787–1825*. Charlottesville: University Press of Virginia, 1967.

———. *The Baltimore Book Trade, 1800–1825*. New York: New York Public Library, 1953.

———. *Typefounding in America, 1787–1825*. Charlottesville: University Press of Virginia, 1965.

———. "Aprons Instead of Uniforms: The Practice of Printing, 1776–1787." *Proceedings of the American Antiquarian Society* 87, pt. 1 (1977): 111–94.

Simonhoff, Harry. *Jewish Notables in America, 1776–1865: Links of an Endless Chain*. New York: Greenberg, 1956.

Simpson, Lewis P. "The Ideology of Revolution." In *The History of Southern Literature,* ed. Louis D. Rubin, Jr. et al., 57–67. Baton Rouge: Louisiana State University Press, 1985.

Smith, Elihu Hubbard. *The Diary of Elihu Hubbard Smith (1771–1798)*. Edited by James E. Amin. *Memoirs of the American Philosophical Society*, vol. 95. Philadelphia: American Philosophical Society, 1973.

Smyth, Albert Henry. *The Philadelphia Magazines and Their Contributors 1741–1850*. Philadelphia: R. M. Lindsay, 1892.

Snyder, Martin P. "Liveliness: A Quality in Prints of Philadelphia." In *Philadelphia Printmaking: American Prints before 1860,* ed. Robert F. Looney, 111–30. West Chester, Pa.: Tinicum Press, 1977.

Sonneck, Oscar George. *A Bibliography of Early Secular American Music (18th Century)*, rev. and enlarged by William Trent Upton. New York: DaCapo, 1964.

Spawm, Wilman. "The Evolution of American Binding Styles in the Eighteenth Century." In *Bookbinding in America, 1680–1910,* 29–37. Bryn Mawr: Bryn Mawr College Library, 1983.

Stafford, Cornelius William. *The Philadelphia Directory for 1797*. Philadelphia: William Woodward, 1797. Evans 32868.

———. *The Philadelphia Directory for 1798*. Philadelphia: William Woodward, 1798. Evans 34593.

———. *The Philadelphia Directory for 1799*. Philadelphia: William Woodward, 1799. Evans 36353.

———. *The Philadelphia Directory, for 1800*. Philadelphia: William Woodward, 1800. Evans 38549.

Stauffer, David McNeely. *American Engravers upon Copper and Steel*. 2 vols. New York: Grolier Club, 1907.

Stephens, Thomas. *Stephenss's* [sic] *Philadelphia Directory for 1796*. Philadelphia: William Woodward, 1796. Evans 31235.

Stewart, Frank H. *History of the United States Mint*. Boston, 1924; repr. Lawrence, Mass.: Quartermain Publications, 1974.

Tanselle, G. Thomas. *Guide to the Study of United States Imprints*. 2 vols. Cambridge, Mass.: Harvard University Press, 1971.

———. "Press Figures in America: Some Preliminary Observations." *Studies in Bibliography* 19 (1966): 123–60.

Tebbel, John. *A History of Book Publishing in the United States*. 4 vols. Volume 1. *The Creation of an Industry, 1630–1865*. New York: R. R. Bowker, 1972.

Thomas, Isaiah. *The History of Printing in America, with a Biography of Printers and an Account of Newspapers*. 2 vols. Albany: Joel Munsell, 1874.

Toppan, Robert Noxon. *A Hundred Years of Bank Note Engraving in the United States*. New York: [American Bank Note Company], 1896.

United States Department of Labor. *History of Wages in the United States from Colonial Times to 1928*. Bulletin of the United States Bureau of Labor Statistics No. 499. Washington, D.C.: United States Government Printing Office, 1929.

Updike, Daniel Berkeley. *Printing Types: Their History, Forms, and Use. A Study in Survivals*. 2d ed. 2 vols. Cambridge, Mass.: Harvard University Press, 1951.

United States Congress. *The Debates and Proceedings in the Congress of the United States; with an Appendix Containing Important State Papers and Public Documents, and All the Laws of a Public Nature; with a Copious Index . . . [First to] Eighteenth Congress.—First Session: Comprising the Period from [March 3, 1789] to May 27, 1824, Inclusive. Comp[iled]. from Authentic Materials*. 42 vols. Washington, [D.C.]: [Joseph] Gales and [William Winston] Seaton, 1834–56.

Walsh, Robert, Jr., ed. *American Register; or, Summary Review of History, Politics, and Literature*. 1817 [American Periodical Series II, Reel 59].

[———.] *The Critic; by Geoffrey Juvenal, Esq*. nos. 1–20. January 29–May 22, 1820 [American Periodical Series II, Reel 100].

Walsh, S. Padraig. *Anglo-American General Encyclopedias: A Historical Bibliography, 1703–1967*. New York: R. R. Bowker, 1968.

Washington, George. *The Writings of George Washington, from the Original Manuscript Sources, 1745–1799*. Ed. by John C. Fitzpatrick. Bicentennial Edition. 39 vols. vol. 36: August 4, 1797–October 28, 1798. Washington, D.C. U.S. Government Printing Office, 1941.

Watters, James. *Proposal of 'James Watters', for Publishing by Subscription, a NEW WORK, ENTITLED THE Weekly Magazine.* [Philadelphia: James Watters, 1798.] Evans 33159.

———, ed. *The Weekly Magazine of Original Essays, Fugitive Pieces, and Interesting Intelligence.* February 3, 1798–June 1, 1799 [American Periodical Series I, Reel 31].

Watson, John F. *Annals of Philadelphia, and Pennsylvania, in the Olden Time; Being a Collection of Memoirs, Anecdotes, and Incidents of the City and Its Inhabitants. . . . Enlarged, with Many Revisions and Additions by Willis P. Hazard.* 3 vols. Philadelphia: Edwin S. Stuart, 1897.

Weeks, Lyman Horace. *A History of Paper-Manufacturing in the United States, 1690–1960.* [New York]: Lockwood Trade Journal, 1916.

Weeks, Stephen B. *The Press in North Carolina in the Eighteenth Century, with Biographical Sketches of Printers . . . and a Bibliography of the Issues.* Brooklyn, N.Y.: Historical Printing Club, 1891.

Wegelin, Oscar. "Mills Day's Proposed Hebrew Bible." In *Bibliographical Essays: A Tribute to Wilberforce Eames,* edited by George Parker Winship, 220–36. Cambridge, Mass.: Harvard University Press, 1924.

Weitenkampf, Frank. *American Graphic Art.* 1912. rev. ed. New York: Macmillan, 1924.

Welch, d'Alte A. *A Bibliography of American Children's Books Printed Prior to 1821.* [Worcester, Mass.]: American Antiquarian Society and Barre Publishers, 1972.

Wheeler, Joseph Towne. *The Maryland Press, 1777–1790.* Baltimore: Maryland Historical Society, 1938.

White, Francis. *The Philadelphia Directory.* Philadelphia: Young, Stewart & McCulloch, 1789.

Whiteman, Maxwell. *Copper for America: The Hendricks Family and a National Industry, 1755–1939.* New Brunswick, N.J.: Rutgers University Press, 1971.

Wightman, William P. D. "William Cullen." *Dictionary of Scientific Biography.* New York: Scribner's, 1971. 3: 494–95.

Wilbur, Earl Morse. *A History of Unitarianism in Transylvania, England and America.* Cambridge, Mass.: Harvard University Press, 1952.

Wilkinson, Norman B. *Papermaking in America.* Greenville, Del.: Hagley Museum, 1975.

Winship, George Parker, ed. *Bibliographical Essays: A Tribute to Wilberforce Eames.* Cambridge, Mass.: Harvard University Press, 1924.

Winterich, John T. *Early American Books and Printing.* Boston: Houghton Mifflin, 1935.

Wolf, Edwin, 2d. *The Book Culture of a Colonial American City: Philadelphia Books, Bookmen, and Booksellers.* Oxford: Clarendon Press, 1988.

———. *Philadelphia: Portrait of an American City.* [Harrisburg]: Stackpole Books, 1975.

Wolfe, Richard J. *Early American Music Engraving and Printing: A History of Music Publishing in America from 1787 to 1825 with Commentary on Earlier and Later Practices.* Urbana: University of Illinois Press, 1980.

Woodall, Guy R. "Robert Walsh, Jr." In *Dictionary of Literary Biography*. General editor Matthew Bruccoli. 99 vols. vol. 59. *American Literary Critics and Scholars,* ed. John W. Rathbone and Monica M. Greene, 324–30. Detroit: Gale, 1987.

Woodcraft, Bennett. *Alphabetical Index of Patentees of Inventions*. London: Evelyn, Adams & McKay, 1854.

Wright, Conrad. "The Controversial Career of Jedidiah Morse." *Harvard Library Bulletin* 31 (1983): 64–87.

———. *The Beginnings of Unitarianism in America*. Boston: Starr King, 1955.

Wright, John. *Early Bibles in America*. New York: Thomas Whittaker, 1894.

Wroth, Lawrence C. "Book Production and Distribution from the Beginning to the American Revolution." In Hellmut Lehmann-Haupt, *The Book in America: A History of the Making and Selling of Books in the United States*. 2d ed. New York: R. R. Bowker Company, 1951.

———. *The Colonial Printer*. Portland, Me.: Southworth-Anthoensen, 1938.

Wroth, Lawrence C. and Rollo G. Silver. "Book Production and Distribution from the American Revolution to the War Between the States." In Hellmut Lehmann-Haupt, *The Book in America: A History of the Making and Selling of Books in the United States*. 2d ed. New York: R. R. Bowker Company, 1951.

Young, Otis E., Jr. "Origins of the American Copper Industry." *Journal of the Early Republic* 3 (1983): 117–37.

Young, William. *A Dictionary of American Artists, Sculptors and Engravers. From the Beginnings Through the Turn of the Twentieth Century*. Cambridge, Mass.: William Young, 1968.

Index

This book has been set in Linotron Galliard. Galliard was designed for Mergenthaler in 1978 by Matthew Carter. Galliard retains many of the features of a sixteenth century typeface cut by Robert Granjon but has some modifications that give it a more contemporary look.

Printed on acid-free paper.